FREUD, JUNG, AND HALL THE KING-MAKER

THE HISTORIC EXPEDITION TO AMERICA (1909)

Clark University: Main Building, with Clock Tower

FREUD, JUNG, AND HALL THE KING-MAKER

THE HISTORIC EXPEDITION TO AMERICA (1909)

with G. Stanley Hall as Host and
William James as Guest

By
Saul Rosenzweig

Including the
Complete Correspondence of
Sigmund Freud and G. Stanley Hall

and a
New Translation of
Freud's Lectures at Clark University on
the Origin and Development of Psychoanalysis

Rana House Press, St. Louis

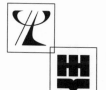

Hogrefe & Huber Publishers
Seattle • Toronto • Bern • Göttingen

1992

Copies may be ordered from:

Hogrefe & Huber Publishers   *OR*   Matthews-McCoy
Box 2487   11559 Rock Island Court
Kirkland, Washington   98083-2487   Maryland Heights, MO   63043
(206) 820-1500   Toll free number: 1-800-633-2665
Toll free number: 1-800-228-3749

Library of Congress Cataloging-in-Publication Data

Rosenzweig, Saul, 1907–
   Freud, Jung, and Hall the King-Maker: The historic expedition to
America (1909), with G. Stanley Hall as host and William James as
guest / by Saul Rosenzweig.
    Including the complete correspondence of Sigmund Freud and
G. Stanley Hall and a new translation of Freud's lectures at Clark
University on the origin and development of psychoanalysis.
    Includes bibliographical references and index.
      p.   cm.
    ISBN 0-88937-110-5 (hard) 3-8017-0347-9
    1. Psychoanalysis—History.   2. Freud, Sigmund, 1856–1939—
Journeys—Massachusetts—Worcester.   3. Jung, C. G. (Carl Gustav),
1875–1961—Journeys—Massachusetts—Worcester.   4. Hall, G. Stanley
(Granville Stanley), 1844–1924.   5. James, William, 1842–1910.
6. Psychoanalysis—United States—History.   7. Clark University
(Worcester, Mass.)—Anniversaries, etc.   I. Title.
BF175.R672   1992
150.19′5′0922   dc20   92-32360
                                                      CIP

Printed in the United States of America

First Edition

10   9   8   7   6   5   4   3   2   1

Designed and set in type by Graphic World, St. Louis.

To the Memory of G. Stanley Hall

Pioneer of Modern Psychology

and Founder of the American Psychological Association

Contents

Part One
THE EXPEDITION TO AMERICA (1909)

Part Two
THE FREUD/HALL LETTERS

Part Three
FREUD'S CLARK LECTURES

Illustrations

PART ONE

The Historic Expedition to America (1909)

In 1909 G. Stanley Hall invited Jung and me to America to go to Clark University, Worcester, Mass., . . . to spend a week giving lectures at the celebration of the twentieth anniversary of its opening. Hall was justly esteemed as a psychologist and educator and had introduced psychoanalysis into his courses . . . ; [but] there was a touch of the "king-maker" about him, a pleasure in setting up authorities and then deposing them. . . . Another event of this time which made a lasting impression on me was a meeting with William James the philosopher.

> Sigmund Freud: *An Autobiographical Study* (1925)

Peace, impudent and shameless Warwick, peace,
Proud setter up and puller down of kings!

> William Shakespeare: *King Henry VI, Part III*

Speaking of "functional" psychology, Clark University, of which Stanley Hall is President, had a little international congress the other day in honor of the twentieth year of its existence. I went there for one day in order to see what Freud was like.

> Letter of William James to Théodore Flournoy (1909)

It was these association studies which later, in 1909, procured me my invitation to Clark University; I was asked to lecture on my work. Simultaneously, and independently of me, Freud was invited.

> C. G. Jung: *Memories, Dreams, Reflections* (1963)

We commemorated the close of our second decennium in the summer of 1909 by a series of conferences. . . . The conferences . . . were attended not only by psychologists but by eminent psychiatrists, and the influence of Freudian views in this country, where they had been little known before, from this date developed rapidly, so that in a sense this unique and significant culture movement owed most of its initial momentum in this country to this meeting.

> G. Stanley Hall: *Life and Confessions of a Psychologist* (1923)

In the Beginning . . .

. . . psychoanalysis, like many other cultural movements, encountered numerous obstacles to its acceptance in the land of its origin. As one of Freud's disciples later stated, there was a "Golden Age" of isolation from which the theory of unconscious psychodynamics only gradually emerged into the light of open controversy. A turning point arrived when G. Stanley Hall, President of Clark University in Worcester, Massachusetts, boldly invited Sigmund Freud and C. G. Jung to come to the New World and participate, with 27 other distinguished scientists, in celebrating the twentieth anniversary of this pioneering university. The expedition served to create a watershed for the spread of psychoanalysis in the continents of North America and Europe. For better or for worse, a new epoch in the history of ideas began.

This volume describes the one and only visit of Sigmund Freud to America and places it in historical perspective. It describes the background of this crucial event and its consequences for psychoanalysis as a theory and a cultural movement. It utilizes, and publishes here for the first time, the newly recovered correspondence between Sigmund Freud and G. Stanley Hall, who extended the invitation. The role of C. G. Jung, who shared the visit with Freud, is explained. The vicissitudes of their relationship, which reached its apogee during this journey, are described. The significance of the expedition in terms of Freud's own psychodynamics is explored. In that vein the relationship of Freud and Hall before and after the event is examined. Similarly, the role of William James, who attended the Clark celebration "to see what Freud was like," is reconstructed. The long friendship of James and Hall, which entered its final phase at the time of this visit, is portrayed with emphasis on their opposing views on psychology as science.

During his visit James heard a lecture by Freud, including the interpretation of dreams, and, some hours later, took a walk with him. The analysis of this interaction brought to light an unknown and poignant, romantic relationship extending over the last 15 years of James's life. In response to Freud's theory, James reexamined some of his own earlier dreams and produced a spiritistic interpretation quite unlike what Freud's would probably have been.

Some new insights have been made possible through the use of several original sources not hitherto available. By their means a detailed chronicle of events germane to the 1909 visit has been prepared. It is presented in a synoptic chapter at the end of Part One and is thus available for summary reading or for ready reference at will.

Part One describes and analyzes the expedition through an idiodynamic study of the principal participants—Freud, Jung, Hall and James. Part Two reproduces in translation from the German the complete letters of Freud to Hall along with the English letters of Hall to Freud. All the letters are historically annotated.

In Part Three the five lectures that Freud delivered at Clark University on the origin and development of psychoanalysis are presented in a new translation made from the original German. This translation aims at both accuracy and audibility; it recognizes that, though not actually written out until later, these *were* lectures.

It is believed that this historic visit is here now portrayed in a reliable chronological account and understood by attempting to view it from within the life and work of the chief participants.

The manner in which the book originated and developed over a period of 40 years will be briefly recounted. My indebtedness to the many individuals who generously cooperated along the way will be acknowledged in that setting.

My undergraduate major at Harvard College was philosophy, with a minor in psychology. The major was capped by the writing of an honor's thesis entitled "Philosophy and Psychoanalysis: the Relationships of Freud and Schopenhauer, Adler and Nietzsche, Jung and Bergson." It was demonstrated that each of the philosophers in question had anticipated the pioneer psychoanalyst paired with him in the title and that, reciprocally, it was the theory of that particular psychoanalyst which most successfully accounted for the life and work of the apposite philosopher. Later I saw that something in the nature of a dialectical process was involved!

Schopenhauer and/or Freud had avowed the *thesis* (the dominance of love or sexuality); Nietzsche and/or Adler asserted the *antithesis* (power or aggression); finally, Bergson, with his evolutionary *élan vital* and Jung in his comprehensive redefinition of the libido concept, offered a combining *synthesis*.

This beginning became an introduction to my graduate work in psychology, in which I sought to define and validate by laboratory methods the clinically derived theories of psychoanalysis, and, in particular, the concept of repression. Most of this research was devoted to the investigation of the selective recall of pleasant and unpleasant experiences that had previously been produced experimentally.

This research bore its first fruit as a paper in 1933 entitled "The experimental situation as a psychological problem," which empirically established the paradigm for studying the complementary interrelations of experimenter and experimentee. This initial article illustrated the categories of the paradigm from my own research and that of others. Thus was established a blueprint for the field of the experimental-social psychology of the human subject in the laboratory encounter which began fully to flourish in the 1950s. Only in retrospect, much later, did I see that my exploration in the field of experimental psychology was what Freud had studied as the transference and countertransference in therapy.

By the end of my graduate studies, chiefly at the newly founded Harvard Psychological Clinic, I was fully launched in an attempt to comprehend empirically the grounds from which had grown both the philosophical theories of the voluntaristic philosophers and the coordinated psychological theories of the psychoanalytic pioneers. This research was continued for two years as research associate at the Harvard Psychological Clinic and as collaborator in Henry Murray's *Explorations in Personality* (published in 1938). In 1934, I joined the research service of the Worcester State Hospital to participate in a comprehensive multidisciplinary program of investigation into the enigma of schizophrenia. In that setting some of the methods I had first used with normal experimentees were applied to the study of schizophrenic patients as compared to normal individuals. Having already intensively explored the projective techniques, in particular the Rorschach method and the Thematic Apperception Test, and having formulated the beginnings of a frustration theory, these two approaches were combined and resulted in the Rosenzweig Picture-Frustration (P-F) Study, a tool for both experimental research and clinical psychodiagnosis. In the course of the ensuing 40 years that instrument has been adapted and restandardized worldwide in the countries of Europe, Asia, the Middle East, South America and Africa.

During the latter half of my association with the research service of the State Hospital, I became affiliated with the teaching faculty of Clark University, also located in Worcester, and thus revived the liaison between the Hospital and the University which, a generation earlier, had been forged and fostered by the pathologist-psychiatrist Adolf Meyer at the Hospital and the psychologist G. Stanley Hall, President and head of the Psychology Department at Clark. Incidentally, many of Hall's published works were acquired by browsing in Worcester's secondhand bookstores, but it was not until much later that I began fully to use them. Moreover, in this fertile soil Freud's one and only visit to America, which had occurred at Clark in 1909, attracted my attention. This interest opened up a new vista in my continuing exploration of the origin and development of psychoanalysis. It took root and grew insistently. Teaching at Clark University and using its well-stocked Library, which had benefited from the efforts and interests of G. Stanley Hall and his close association with its chief librarian, Louis Wilson, led me to become truly intrigued and committed to a study of Freud's visit, about which little was then reliably known. At the Library there were still some brochures published in connection with the 20th anniversary celebration, and some firsthand information about Freud's presence on the scene was culled from a veteran librarian who still remembered the event.

Of greater significance were the discoveries I made, then and later, concerning the correspondence between Freud and Hall that had started with Hall's invitation to Freud to participate in the 1909 celebration. When in 1957, some years after leaving Worcester, I embarked on an active search for these letters by writing to the then president of Clark University, Howard B. Jefferson, he replied that these were not at Clark; he believed they were in the possession of Hall's son Robert, a retired pediatrician living in Portland, Oregon. I contacted Dr. Hall, who soon replied that he had none of the letters in question except one from Freud to his father dated 1923. In 1966 I wrote to Sigmund Freud's literary executor, his son Ernst, then living in England,

and established that Hall's letters to Freud concerning the celebration had survived. I was able to arrange with Ernst Freud to receive copies of these letters and he granted me permission to reproduce them if I could also obtain permission from Hall's heirs. Ernst Freud stated that he did not have his father's letters to G. Stanley Hall but believed that these were in the hands of Hall's heirs or in the Clark University Archives. Hall's son Robert gladly granted me permission to reproduce his father's letters. But Freud's letters to Hall were nowhere to be found—not until the imminent retirement of President Jefferson in 1967. On that occasion he made a search of old files in the lower recesses of the administration building; he intended to sort these materials and decide what was worth saving. In the process he unexpectedly came upon the letters for which I had been persistently asking him. And at the same time he discovered with them other papers concerning the celebration that Hall had assembled for preservation. President Jefferson sent me some of these materials and a year later I was able to obtain photocopies of the entire cache through the kind offices of Tilton Barron, the Clark Librarian.

During the long period over which the work for the present volume was performed, my indebtedness has continued to grow. It has involved help in the necessary research as well as in the preparation of it for publication.

First, there is my indebtedness to the group associated with the role of G. Stanley Hall and of Clark University. Robert G. Hall of Portland, Oregon, the son of G. Stanley Hall, corresponded with me from 1957 to 1970, a year before his death. In these letters he answered numerous questions about his father's relationship to Clark and to Freud and tried to help locate the missing letters. After their recovery, he granted permission to quote them without restriction. He was grateful that the contemplated book would contribute to a revival of interest in his father's work. Howard B. Jefferson, then President of Clark University, was patient and generous in responding to my persistent inquires about the lost Freud/Hall correspondence. My indebtedness to him is warmly acknowledged. The director of the University Library, Tilton M. Barron, who had already answered numerous questions, supervised the transmission of photocopies of the recovered documents. He also sent me copies of photographs related to Hall and the celebration, some of which are reproduced in this book. He was succeeded by William A. Koelsch, the University Archivist, who, with his capable assistant Suzanne Hamel, extended numerous courtesies. The successors of Mr. Koelsch, Stuart W. Campbell and Dorothy E. Mosakowski, have continued to aid me with various favors. Mortimer H. Appley, until recently President of Clark, graciously encouraged my research. I am also grateful to an earlier President of Clark, Frederick H. Jackson. I acknowledge with thanks the supplementary permission of Clark University Archives to publish Hall's letters. The continuous and painstaking cooperation of Nancy E. Gaudette, Librarian of the Worcester Collection, Worcester Public Library, has earned my heartfelt gratitude.

Ernst L. Freud, son of Sigmund Freud and the first director of the Sigmund Freud Copyrights, Ltd., gave formal permission to translate and publish the letters of his father to G. Stanley Hall. He also sent photocopies of Hall's letters to Freud from his collection before copies were discovered in the cache. His role passed to Mark Paterson and his assistant Pat Marsden. Final arrangements for the publication of Freud's letters were made through Mr. Paterson. His kindness in these negotiations is sincerely appreciated.

I am particularly indebted to the late Anna Freud who, for the first time, released to me the diary kept by her father during the 1909 journey to America, then and now on restricted deposit at the Library of Congress. In that connection the favors of Ronald Wilkinson, John Broderick and James Hutson, of the Manuscript Division of the Library of Congress, are remembered with gratitude.

Franz Jung, the son of C. G. Jung, conscientiously answered inquiries and sent abstracts and excerpts of some of his father's unpublished letters from America in 1909. He and the other Jung heirs, Küsnacht, and the C. G. Jung-Institut, Zurich, granted permission to quote these materials. Aniela Jaffé, Jung's personal secretary, generously replied to numerous questions and sent me an inscribed copy of Jung's posthumously published autobiography in the 1962 original German edition which she had compiled and edited. With these benefits belong the courtesies of William McGuire, executive editor of the *Collected Works* of Jung, including the *Freud/Jung Letters.*

Edmund Brill, son of A. A. Brill who was the host of Freud, Jung and Ferenczi on their arrival and stay in New York on August 29, 1909 and the ensuing week, granted permission to use unpublished correspondence of Freud with his father related to the American visit and supplied information about his mother, Rose Owen Brill. Similarly, Grant Allan, son of the Berlin psychoanalyst Karl Abraham, made special efforts to find unpublished letters received by his father from Freud in 1908-1909, and he sent copies of these with permission to quote.

Edward J. Kempf and his widow Dorothy provided firsthand information and documents concerning Kempf's visit to Freud and Hall's aid in arranging for it. I am grateful for their favors and permission to quote.

Houghton Library, Harvard University, generously made available numerous unpublished letters of William James. Permission to quote from these letters was granted by the Library Director, Richard Wendorf, and by Henry J. Vaux and Alexander R. James, descendants of William James. Permission to reproduce the portrait of William James painted by Rand in 1910 was granted by Fogg Museum, Harvard University. Bryn Mawr College Archives found information on the careers of their alumnae Pauline and Susan Goldmark and granted permission to quote. Wellesley College Archives supplied information about their first psychology professor, Mary W. Calkins, and, in particular, her relation to William James at Harvard. The Special Collections Division, Nimitz Library, U. S. Naval Academy, sent me materials from the Albert A. Michelson Papers deposited by Michelson's daughter and biographer, Dorothy Livingston, and gave permission to use them.

Among the historians and biographers who have responded to inquiries are the following: Heinz L. Ansbacher, an outstanding authority on the work of Alfred Adler; Arcangelo D'Amore, historian of the American Psychoanalytic Association; and Dorothy Ross, the biographer of G. Stanley Hall.

The late David Shakow, my friend and former colleague, for years shared and aided my interest in Freud, Hall, and Clark University. Margarethe C. Steinberg gave generously of her time and knowledge in the transcription and translation of thorny passages in Freud's letters written in his notoriously difficult Gothic script. More recently, Renate Vambery extended similar assistance with other Freud documents.

My former assistant Stuart Adelman collected and collated newspaper reports of the 1909 Clark celebration and helped with other aspects of its history. Members of the reference department of the Washington University Medical Library were very helpful. For devoted secretarial assistance I thank Lorraine M. Constantine. I am indebted to Pamela A. Hug whose unfailing cooperation gave Louise and me the freedom to perform our necessary professional work.

Kenneth L. Nabors, senior reference librarian at the John M. Olin Library of Washington University, verified innumerable points. He critically read the final draft. My debt to him is beyond reckoning.

My debt to my wife Louise, whom I first met in Worcester, outweighs what is owed to all others combined. She has participated in the transcription and translation of Freud's letters and has rendered continuous and unstinting help in the completion of this book.

The research for this work and its publication were supported by the Foundation for Idiodynamics and the Creative Process, St. Louis, Missouri.

July 1992   Saul Rosenzweig

A Note to the Reader

The superscript numbers that appear throughout the pages of the following 13 chapters point to the COMMENTARY ON PART ONE printed after Chapter XIII. This series of comments—notes and references—is arranged by chapter. These comments are essential for the serious reader. They are printed unobtrusively at the end of Part One so as not to interrupt the flow of the text.

Chapter I

Cast in Context

When in 1925, a year after the death of G. Stanley Hall and a dozen years after Freud's breach with C. G. Jung, Sigmund Freud published his brief autobiography, he epitomized his visit to America. G. Stanley Hall, President of Clark University, had invited him and Jung to spend a week giving lectures during the celebration of the twentieth anniversary of the University. Hall had introduced psychoanalysis into his courses at Clark several years earlier. Freud continued: ". . . there was a touch of the 'king-maker' about him, a pleasure in setting up authorities and in then deposing them. We also met James J. Putnam there, the Harvard neurologist, who in spite of his age was an enthusiastic supporter of psychoanalysis. . . . Another event of this time which made a lasting impression on me was a meeting with William James the philosopher. I shall never forget one little scene that occurred as we were on a walk together. . . . At that time I was only 53. I felt young and healthy, and my short visit to the new world encouraged my self-respect in every way. In Europe I felt as though I were despised; but over there I found myself received by the foremost men as an equal. As I stepped onto the platform at Worcester to deliver my *Five Lectures on Psycho-Analysis* it seemed like the realization of some incredible day-dream: psycho-analysis was no longer a product of delusion, it had become a valuable part of reality." [1]

It is thus clear that a turning point in the life of Sigmund Freud and the history of psychoanalysis occurred by his participating in the 20th anniversary celebration of Clark University. It constituted the first public recognition of his professional contribution to psychology, psychiatry and the other behavioral sciences—a recognition that in Europe had been meager and largely negative.

The strong support since 1906 of C. G. Jung, the energetic young psychiatrist of Zurich, Switzerland, was a marked exception, and was very encouraging to Freud. He was therefore delighted when Jung, too, was invited a little later to participate in the Clark sessions. A third member of the party was Sandor Ferenczi, whom Freud invited. Ferenczi, a Hungarian, was an ardent disciple and friend of Freud whose support was unspoiled by rivalry or personal ambition. Jung, an outspoken champion of Freud during the time of the American expedition, entertained ambivalent doubts about both the doctrine and the master, and, in the ensuing three years, these developed into an open breach.

Hall's orientation to Freud differed from that of both the Hungarian Ferenczi and the Swiss Jung. Though an American, Hall was well schooled in European physiology and scientific psychology. He spent six years on the continent in three stints, the last being primarily in Berlin and Leipzig. In the latter city, where he worked for almost two years, he studied with Wilhelm Wundt for two semesters just at the time when the first laboratory of experimental psychology in the world was being established. Since he arrived there after taking his doctor's degree at Harvard in 1878, he was a postdoctoral student. He attended the lectures of Wundt, participated in his weekly seminar and acted as an experimentee in the dissertation research of Wundt's first two doctoral students in experimental psychology. He also studied during this sojourn with such eminent physiologists as Carl Ludwig, Hermann Helmholtz and du Bois-Reymond. While working and living in Leipzig in 1879-1880, he lived next door to the then aged originator of psychophysics, G. T. Fechner. Hall's *Founders of Modern Psychology* was a firsthand account of some of these historic figures. [2]

But Hall had also worked during 1876-1878 with the pioneer American philosopher and psychologist William James at Harvard University. This part of his career appears to have been largely an unplanned interlude. As Hall explains in his autobiography, he had left his job at Antioch College intending to go to Europe and work with Wilhelm Wundt. But he only reached Cambridge, where he was offered an instructorship in the English department at Harvard. He reluctantly accepted it in the hope that he might acquire a foothold to teach philosophy later. Hall studied philosophy and psychology under James; under Dr. Bowditch at the medical school he performed his dissertation research. In 1878 he was awarded the first American Ph.D. in psychology.

Hall then carried out his earlier intention. He embarked for his second stint in Europe, this time to work with Wundt at Leipzig. It is striking and historically quaint to find Hall listed as one of the four experimentees *(Reagierende)* in an experiment on word association performed by one of Wundt's doctoral candidates in 1880 and published three years later. [3] This investigation was Wundt's follow-up of Galton's classical studies of word association—a method that would be adapted by Jung in 1904-1906 for the first experimental confirmation of Freud's theory of neurosis; and it was this work that justified Jung's invitation to lecture at Clark along with Freud. In the spring of 1909 the method played a part in the research Hall and his assistant Amy Tanner performed on Mrs. Piper, the renowned psychical medium who was a protegé of William James. By then, however, the procedure had evolved so far in the direction of Freud's theory that these investigators called it "the Jung-Freud method." [4]

Hall recognized Freud as a new and powerful reinforcement of his own genetic approach to human behavior. Like Freud, Hall derived his psychology largely from the theory of evolution and sexual selection. Unlike William James, Hall attributed an outstanding place to sexuality in human development. And for this reason he welcomed Freud's publications from their earliest appearance. Indeed, Hall had experimented with courses at Clark on the topic of human sexuality as early as 1904, and by 1908 he was conducting a regular seminar on the subject. His invitation to Freud to participate in the 1909 celebration was a continuation of this deep interest.

But Hall differed not only from William James but from the majority of Freud's European colleagues who regarded the theory of infantile sexuality and the dynamic unconscious with much skepticism. Yet Hall was by training an experimental psychologist who had published in that vein (as well as in other areas) as early as 1878, the year of his Ph.D. at Harvard. [5] William James, educated in the elements of medicine but better grounded in philosophical psychology, was not by inclination a laboratory experimenter. He introduced instruction in experimental psychology at Harvard as early as Hall's work there, but his own special commitment was to the field of psychical research and parapsychology. To him, not

Wilhelm Wundt but Frederic Meyers, the champion of scientific spiritualism, was the ideal leader.[6] While Hall, like Freud, reached down to the biogenetic roots of human behavior, James, particularly in the last years of his life, reached up to the mystical realm of human consciousness. There were accordingly two quite different formulations of the nonconscious: for Freud (and Hall) there was the "unconscious," in the sense of depth psychology; for Meyers, there was "subliminal consciousness" of paranormal clair-voyance, telepathy and a spiritual afterlife. The latter formulation was the one endorsed and elaborated by James in his later writings in which he depicted the godhead as a cosmic multiple personality.

These resemblances to and differences from Freudian theory pervaded the Clark conference, notably in the lectures of Freud and Jung, in the brief and informal participation of James at the conference, and in the post-conference events at the Putnam camp in Keene Valley to which Dr. Putnam had invited Freud, Jung and Ferenczi for a five-day sojourn. James, who had earlier owned this camp with Bowditch and Putnam (from about 1876) was not there with the group in September 1909, but he probably recalled his numerous associations with the place during the short walk with Freud in Worcester that Freud alluded to in his autobiography.

By the time of the Clark celebration in the fall of 1909 psy-choanalysis had achieved its major theoretical maturity, indicated by Freud's publications. As Freud implied in his Clark lecture, the basic approach was already implicit in Breuer and Freud's *Studies on Hysteria,* published in 1895,[7] and in the following year Freud first used the term "psychoanalysis" (1896).[8] In the next decade, and in rapid succession, he published *The Interpretation of Dreams* (1899), *The Psychopathology of Everyday Life* (1904), *Jokes and Their Relation to the Unconscious* (1905), and *Three Essays on the Theory of Sexuality* (1905). In the year of the Clark conference appeared the first two of Freud's classical case histories: "Analysis of a Phobia in a Five-Year-Old Boy," published in March 1909, and "Notes upon a Case of Obsessional Neurosis," published in October. This latter case came to be known as that of the Rat Man because of the rats in the primary obsession of the patient.[9]

While, as already stated, Freud's theories had, in general, a mixed reception in Europe, the response of the Swiss psychiatric group at the Burghölzli Mental Hospital in Zurich was clearly favorable. In that setting Jung had, beginning in 1904, performed his research on "complexes" revealed by the word-association method. His studies were directly influenced by Freud's theories of neurosis as a result of sexual conflict and repression. Largely on the strength of this research the correspondence between Freud and Jung began in 1906, and their first personal meeting occurred in Vienna in the spring of 1907. With characteristic energy Jung soon undertook to organize the first international conference of psychiatrists interested in Freud's psychological theories. It convened in Salzburg, Austria, in April 1908 and represented the first public recognition of Freud's contributions by colleagues from several countries. In a different way the participation of Freud and Jung at the Clark celebration was also a first—a first recognition of Freud's contributions as significant enough to be accorded a place among similarly outstanding contributions in other scientific fields.

What Jung had done for the Salzburg conference G. Stanley Hall did for Freud at Clark. As a psychologist and educator he had been closely following the publications of Freud and his disciples so that by 1908, the time of the planning of the 20th anniversary of Clark's opening, Freud had become a revolutionary figure for him. Though the celebration would include many other distinguished behavioral scientists and eminent scholars in the physical, biological and social sciences, Freud was to Hall the leading light of the celebration. After some vacillation Freud responded in kind: Hall's invitation came as a welcome sign of a new turn of the wheel of fortune, a thought that he repeatedly expressed in his letters to Jung, particularly after Jung was also invited to participate.

It should be recognized from the start that the cast introduced above was by no means the entire array at the Clark fall celebration. In addition to Freud and Jung, there were 27 other invited lecturers, all of whom received honorary degrees as a token of their contributions to the fields they represented. This fact has often been overlooked, sometimes by distinguished historians such as E. G. Boring (1965). Complementarily, the presence of the psychoanalysts has been stressed. In Chapter VI, indicating the full range of the lectures, the scope of the scientific fields will be described though the emphasis will be on the behavioral sciences. These were naturally favored by Stanley Hall. Moreover, in keeping with the theme of this volume, indicated by the title, the contributions by

Freud and Jung will be primarily considered, along with the response of William James to Freud's contribution, which will be considered in detail.

It remains to note, partly from correspondence with E. G. Boring, the preeminent historian of psychology, that the granting of special favors extended by Hall to the psychoanalytic contributors was not accidental. To quote from a letter received from Boring: ". . . I think it is important that you should explain why it is that the Clark celebration got to be considered as psychoanalytic. It was not at the time. I came into psychology [from Cornell] in September, 1910, only a year after this celebration, and a half a year after the publication of the papers in the AJP [American Journal of Psychology]. We knew what was going on in the satellites and talked about it a lot, and our impression at Cornell was that the great event at this occasion was not the general celebration but the introduction of the psychoanalysts to America." [10]

Repeatedly throughout this book Hall's special interest in Freud's psychoanalytic writings, practically from their inception in 1894, has been noted, and his personal identification with Freud's purpose of making up for the neglect of human sexuality in the investigations of psychologists will become clear. As President of Clark University, Hall could, without much fear of rebuke, indulge to some extent his own preferences, and he did so without apology by entertaining Freud and Jung as his house guests for the duration of their stay in Worcester. That he accorded the same courtesy to William James made it possible for the interesting interaction between Freud and James considered in some detail below.

Chapter II

The Invitations

The Setting for the Invitations

Clark University in Worcester, Massachusetts, 40 miles west of Boston, was founded and endowed by Jonas Clark in 1887 and opened for classes in the fall of 1889.[1] The founder, son of a farmer, never had the benefit of a college education but wanted to offer this advantage to future generations of young men. As it turned out, this goal was to cause perennial conflict between him and the first president, Granville Stanley Hall, pioneer American psychologist and educator, until Clark's death. At the insistence of Hall and under his presidency, Clark University began and continued for its first 12 years as an exclusively graduate school. Hall believed that at the time a greater contribution could be made by training scientists, scholars and teachers in preference to undergraduates, for there were no schools then devoted solely to the education of such specialists. An undergraduate college was, indeed, added in 1902, after the death in 1900 of Jonas Clark, who had explicitly provided for it in his will and designated that it not be under Hall's administration.

A mark of Hall's success in his own special goal was the large number of advanced degrees in psychology granted during his tenure as head of psychology and president of the University. In those 31 years, ending in 1920, degrees were awarded to 110 doctors of philosophy, including six women, and to 81 masters of art, including 11 women. With this record, Clark University stood for many years in first place among American institutions of higher learning. This result bespoke Hall's influence even more eloquently than did his published articles and books. Among the eminent pyschologists trained at Clark were William Lowe Bryan, James Leuba, Edwin Starbuck, Henry Goddard, Phyllis Blanchard,

19

Florence Mateer, Arnold Gesell and Lewis M. Terman. The various graduates ranged over a variety of subdisciplines in psychology, pure and applied. Because Hall constantly allied psychology with pedagogy—as education was then called—these specialists were well prepared for teaching and the training of teachers. Moreover, Hall trained teachers as such and worked cooperatively with educators at local and distant schools.

The University enjoyed the services of a distinguished Board of Trustees with whom Hall was able to work successfully despite some conflict with the founder, Jonas Clark, and the faculty. He devoted special attention to medical psychology by enlisting the cooperation of nearby Worcester State Hospital, one of the oldest in the country, established in 1833. Adolf Meyer, its pathologist, who later became a leader in American psychiatry as well as the psychiatry department chairperson at Johns Hopkins, was a personal friend of Hall. At the time of the decennial celebration in 1899 Meyer was head of the subdivision of psychopathology at Clark, and in 1909 he was one of the honored participants.

The founding of the University had first been commemorated at the decennial on a modest scale. Even then the event reached out to distinguished scientists world-wide. There were five invited lecturers, including two in the behavioral sciences. The group consisted of Émile Picard, Professor of Mathematics at the University of Paris; Ludwig Boltzmann, Professor of Theoretical Physics at the University of Vienna; Santiago Ramón y Cajal, Professor of Histology at the University of Madrid; Angelo Mosso, Professor of Physiology at the University of Turin, and August Forel, former Professor of Psychiatry at the University of Zurich and Director of the Burghölzli Mental Hospital. The conference was memorialized in a handsome volume with chapters on the history of the University, reports by department heads, and the lectures of the scientists. [1a] At this time the psychology department consisted of five divisions: general psychology, headed by E. C. Sanford; psychopathology, by Adolf Meyer; anthropology, by A. F. Chamberlain; pedagogy, by W. H. Burnham; and philosophy, by G. Stanley Hall.

It is noteworthy as a precedent that the celebration in 1899 occurred on July 5-10. The July date is specifically indicated as marking "the completion of the 10th academic year of the University." The point is significant because, in contradistinction, the 20th anniversary celebration presently to be discussed was described in the resulting publication edited by Hall as marking "the twentieth anniversary of the opening of Clark University." [2]

Lectures were presented on the first four days; honorary degrees conferred on July 10, 1899. The honored guests stayed at the homes of various members of the Clark faculty and Board of Trustees. It thus fell to President Hall to serve as host for the physiological psychologist Professor Angelo Mosso. This precedent was followed in 1909 when Hall invited Freud and Jung to be his house guests.

The plan for the 20th anniversary celebration was far more ambitious than that for 1899. [2a] The participating departments were mathematics, physics and chemistry, biology, history, psychology and pedagogy. There were 29 invited lecturers and all were awarded honorary degrees. Psychology and Pedagogy (the behavioral sciences) was represented by eight lecturers: Franz Boas, anthropology; Leo Burgerstein, education and school hygiene; Sigmund Freud, psychology and psychiatry; H. S. Jennings, biology; C. G. Jung, psychology and pedagogy; Adolf Meyer, psychopathology; William Stern, personality and forensic psychology; and E. B. Titchener, experimental psychology. These sessions occurred in the period September 6-11, during the second part of the vigentennial.

Following the decennial precedent, the first part of the psychology celebration was held in July 1909. It was devoted to child research and welfare. This general area of child development had for most of Hall's professional life been of special importance to him and by 1909 he was well known as an expert in this field. Because this emphasis in the early planning of the celebration played a significant part in Freud's being invited to participate, as well as for its intrinsic importance in Hall's career and reputation, a summary of his devotion to the area is appropriate here.

Hall had embarked upon this specialization in 1883 while still at Johns Hopkins. His first publication was entitled "The Contents of Children's Minds" (Hall, 1883). In it he outlined the various topics that appeared to be promising for serious investigation. These topics were actually pursued by him and his students during the next 30 years, largely by the questionnaire method. Though the method was later widely criticized for its lack of precision, it was much imitated and its disclosure of children's knowledge about life in the real world had a great influence.

Looking back at his life work one sees that, implicitly or explicitly, child development was a complement to Hall's establishment in the same year of the first systematic American laboratory of experimental psychology. For Hall, the laboratory was to the science of psychology what the child study movement was to pedagogy (or education).

But the decade prior to Hall's coming to Clark University was chiefly devoted to experimental psychology. Child study was not pursued assiduously until after he had lived through the first few years of administrative organization and some conflict. Then, by 1893, he was able to turn to this type of work in earnest. In that year he had been a prime mover in organizing the National Association for the Study of Childhood, and in that same year he published a paper containing a detailed outline of his investigative plans entitled "Child Study: The Basis of Exact Education" (Hall, 1893). Ten years of extensive child research followed, and at the same time he pursued his reading and thinking with the resultant publication of his two-volume, major work *Adolescence* (Hall, 1904a).

Concomitantly with this publication a national movement had been taking shape under the leadership of labor leaders and social workers concerned mainly with the evils of child labor. They established the National Child Labor Committee in 1904 under the chairmanship of Felix Adler, founder of the Ethical Culture Society. Largely through the influence of this committee President Theodore Roosevelt in 1909 called the first White House Conference on the welfare of children. Three years later a Children's Bureau was established in the U. S. Department of Commerce.

In 1909 Hall saw the possibility of combining the fruits of the child labor movement and the child study movement. In the latter he had been one of the chief architects. It was in terms of this integration that he thought of organizing the early part of the celebration of the twentieth anniversary of the founding of Clark University. Hence he organized and held at the University a national conference on child study and care. There were five days of meetings with 15 sessions of nearly 50 addresses by representatives of 27 child welfare societies. During these sessions a new organization (The National Child Conference for Research and

Welfare) was formed, its constitution drawn up, and its first officers elected. Hall was elected President. The intention was to hold such conventions annually, and the second was held at Clark University in 1910. The contributions of 1909 were published as *Proceedings of the Child Conference for Research and Welfare held at Clark University in connection with the Celebration of the Twentieth Anniversary, Worcester, Massachusetts, July 6-10, 1909.* [2b]

In anticipation of the 1909 summer events, Hall had formulated a plan for a Children's Institute at Clark and sought the support of the Board of Trustees. By the following spring he had prepared a Prospectus. It was an ambitious enterprise, including a new building for which preliminary architectural plans were drawn up. Hall had successfully persuaded the Board (at a special meeting on June 17, 1909) to take action. The minutes of the meeting succinctly convey what Hall was to do at this time.

"Upon the recommendation of the Committee upon the subject, appointed at the last meeting, it was voted that the Trustees appropriate from the current, unused income of the University funds, five thousand dollars ($5,000) a year for three years beginning September 1, 1909, to establish an Institute for the collection, diffusion and increase of the scientific knowledge of childhood and for its practical application to child welfare; this Institute to be organized and directed by Dr. Hall under the guidance and control of the Board of Trustees, to be a department of the University, and to be located in the new building." (Minutes of the Board, p. 248).

It is in this setting of Hall's early plans for the vigentennial that one must seek to understand the first invitation he extended to Sigmund Freud. Hall was apparently at this point in 1908 attempting to enlist Freud to further his aims in the establishment of a Children's Institute. He saw Freud as a developmental psychologist whose views on early childhood, including sexuality and the unconscious, were crucial for understanding the child below the surface of everyday observation.

Freud's Invitations

Freud received two invitations to participate in the 20th anniversary Clark celebration—the first dated December 15, 1908, which he declined; the second, dated February 16, 1909, which he accepted. The differences between the two invitations, as well as his different reactions, are more than casually instructive. In the first invitation, Clark's president G. Stanley Hall, after introducing himself in terms of a profound and long interest in Freud's work, proposed a group of four to six lectures, either in German or English, "setting forth your own views" to be presented during the first week of July 1909 on the occasion of the 20th anniversary of Clark University's founding. Hall proposed "an honorarium of four hundred dollars or 1600 marks, to cover expenses." (It is of some interest that on the same date Hall invited Wilhelm Wundt, his former teacher and the founder of the first experimental laboratory of psychology, to whom he offered $750 [3000 marks].) When Freud declined in a letter dated December 29, 1908, he acknowledged the honor with appreciation but could not accept the invitation for the reason that at the proposed date he would lose three weeks of private practice which continued to July 15, then resumed at the end of September. As a prelude to his statement of regret, Freud mused, "I do not know how the following difficulty can be overcome." When Hall wrote again two months later, the obstacle was removed: the honorarium was raised to $750 and a postponement was made to the second week of September. Moreover, an honorary degree was now promised Freud. When Freud accepted the second invitation, in a letter dated February 29, 1909, he not only noted the increase in "travel expenses" but mentioned the honorary degree. It was in these four letters of December 15, 1908 through February 29, 1909 that the correspondence between the two men began, and it would continue, more sparsely at the end, until 1923, the year before Hall died. (See Part Two.)

This statement of the facts regarding the two invitations received by Freud requires now to be supplemented by a consideration of the motivation that had presumably led Freud to decline the first one almost impetuously but to accept the second with distinct enthusiasm. From an examination of Freud's contemporary correspondence with Jung, as well as with other colleagues, e.g., Karl Abraham, one learns that both decisions were accompanied by a penumbra of interpersonal and intrapersonal motives that go far toward explaining other aspects of the American visit. To pause on the threshold and consider these circumstances in some detail will make it possible more fully to comprehend later events at

Bremen, New York, and Worcester, and in the aftermath of the
Clark celebration.

Three days before declining Hall's first invitation Freud had
written to Karl Abraham, a disciple in Berlin. The occasion was
the rejection by Morton Prince, editor of the *Journal of Abnormal
Psychology*, of a paper on sexual trauma by Abraham that Prince
had earlier seemed interested in receiving. Without mentioning
Hall's invitation, Freud commented about the situation in America
with some reflections that he must have had in mind when he
wrote to Hall: "The hostility by which we are surrounded bids us
hold together. Morton Prince, who has always been a kaleido-
scopic character, is this time really lamentable. Where do the
Americans expect to get with this fear of public prudery?. . .
He [Prince] always begins by over-compensating for his cowardice
and then withdraws into it. In fact he intended to come to
Salzburg." [3]

For the Salzburg conference, April 26, 1908, Morton Prince
had announced a paper "Psychogalvanic reactions in a case of
multiple personality," but in the end he was unable to attend.
This vacillation on Prince's part was not lost on Freud who guarded
his cause with care and zeal. [4]

Freud, therefore, had misgivings about America that entered
into his prompt declination of Hall's first invitation apart from
financial considerations. Writing to Jung the day after he declined,
he told him the good news about the invitation but explained that
he had declined "without even consulting you" for the "crucial
reason" that a loss of "several thousand kronen" would have resulted. He concluded, "I don't really believe that Clark University,
a small but serious institution, can postpone its activities for three
weeks." [5] Nevertheless, it is clear from this statement that when
Freud declined, he had meant to leave open the possibility of a
postponement. In the event, he must have felt elated because
Hall ostensibly complied. Freud did not realize that the whole
celebration had not been postponed until September.

Resuming the question of Freud's having turned down the first
invitation, we find a second letter to Jung that repeated the negative
appraisal of America. After mentioning that Brill and Jones had
communicated some positive aspects of the American response to
psychoanalysis, Freud added: "I also think that once they discover
the sexual core of our psychological theories they will drop us.

Their prudery and their material dependence on the public are too great. That is why I have no desire to risk the trip in July." [6]

There is a revealing bit of contretemps at this point in the correspondence. In Freud's letter of mid-January Jung detected a slip of the pen criticizing Jung's sexual attitudes. In response, Jung wrote: "We have noticed this prudishness, which used to be worse than it is now; now I can stomach it. I don't water down the sexuality any more." [7] Jung's hypersensitivity is singular because in this letter of his for the first time the parallel between Freud's patient, Little Hans, and Jung's disturbed young daughter Agathe came to the fore. He explicitly observed at the end of it that the girl was aware of the "beautiful bottom" of her little brother and underscored this observation by a long gloss about children's words for the cloacal and genital areas. He concluded with the statement that the child was plainly referring to these areas. In view of the special importance of the "castration threat" to Little Hans (by Freud's interpretation), Jung's statement implied that the little girl had noticed the difference between her bottom and that of her new brother. And a week later the parallel between the two cases in this regard was noted by Freud with stress on the nucleus of the neurosis. [8] However, when Jung recounted the case at Clark in September, he omitted this point.

As for Prince's prudishness, there was no abatement. His hostility to Freud's ideas persisted. That is probably why he did not attend the Clark celebration in the fall. But he wrote to Freud in advance to explain that he was committed to be in Europe at that time—to which Freud quipped, "so that he will miss me on both continents, etc. I shall be just as glad not to see him." [9]

In a special sense Prince epitomized what Freud perceived as the entrenched American resistance to psychoanalysis. Hence it required a strong antidote for Freud to change his mind; and Hall provided it in his second invitation with its extraordinary concessions. He seemed to sense, as if by a personal sympathy, what Freud needed—an identification that perhaps reflected his own differences with Prince and, as will presently appear, with Prince's mentor, William James.

One thus arrives at the question of how Freud overcame his concern about American prudery when, on February 29, he accepted Hall's second invitation. The increase in the honorarium coupled with the new date (that enabled Freud to continue his practice until mid-July and to resume at the end of September) surely entered into his decision. But probably even more significant was Hall's promise that Freud would receive an honorary degree. That promise assured Freud that at least Hall and his associates did not entertain reservations. A friendly reception could be expected in Worcester.

That Freud did not overprize the honorary degree was borne out by later events. This was the only such degree Freud would receive though he attained great renown during the remaining 30 years of his life. Hall caught the contemporary significance for Freud in a synoptic article he published about the 20th anniversary soon after the celebration: "It was remarked at Clark several times by his chief European pupil, Professor Jung of Zurich, who was with him, that the invitation to America, the honorary degree bestowed upon him, and especially the sympathetic attitude of those who heard him, came at the psychological moment for him personally as well as for his views." [10]

Another factor that may have influenced Freud to accept concerned Pierre Janet. In inviting Freud to participate, Hall in his first letter held out the inducement that the distinguished French psychopathologist, a rival of Freud in respect to the theory of neurosis, had previously visited America and given a series of lectures which had had a profound influence. Hall wrote: "We believe that a concise statement of your own results and point of view would now be exceedingly opportune, and perhaps in some sense mark an epoch in the history of these studies in this country." [11] Janet's lectures were given in 1906 on the occasion of the inauguration of new buildings of the Harvard Medical School in Boston. When these lectures were published the next year, the book was dedicated to James Jackson Putnam, Professor of Neurology at the Harvard Medical School. [12] Putnam's subsequent support for Freud, during and after the Clark celebration, indeed did, as Hall had surmised, represent a clear gain for psychoanalysis vis-à-vis Janet's views. Hall may also have been thinking of Janet's earlier visit to the U.S.A. when he addressed the Congress of Arts and Science in St. Louis at the widely-known World's Fair of 1904. On that occasion Morton Prince also spoke. [13] Prince's opposition to Freud has been noted; it may now be added that Prince was an adherent of Janet in formulating a structural theory of dissociation. Both Janet and Prince differed from Freud in his espousal of a dynamic theory emphasizing the repression of sexual conflict.

In addition to the rational and conscious factors that appear to have brought about Freud's rapid acceptance of Hall's second invitation, there was a further influence that arose from very private aspects of his idioverse. In these terms Freud's expressed earlier reservations were overcome by an accrual of unconscious motives which explain aspects of the journey that the rational grounds do not. One can discern some of this dynamic contribution from the correspondence with Jung, especially Freud's letters of March 9 and April 16, 1909, the one before Jung visited Freud in Vienna (the second visit) and the other, 18 days after that visit. [14] Here we have Freud's own free associations—essentially a part of his continuing self-analysis.

In the letter of March 9, Freud told Jung that he had accepted Hall's second invitation and "that the festivities had been postponed to the week of September 6." He continued: "In 1886, when I started my practice, I was thinking only of a two-month trial period in Vienna; if it did not prove satisfactory, I was planning to go to America and found an existence that I would subsequently have asked my fiancée in Hamburg to share. You see, we both of us had nothing, or more precisely, I had a large and impoverished family and she a small inheritance of roughly 3000 fl. from her Uncle Jacob, who had been a professor of classical philology in Bonn. But unfortunately things went so well in Vienna that I decided to stay on, and we were married in the autumn of the same year. And now, twenty-three years later, I am to go to America after all, not, to be sure, to make money, but in response to an honorable call!" [15]

This passage indicates that the now accepted invitation to America had a longstanding meaning for Freud. Hence it meant more to him than "anything that has happened in the last few years" and, as he stated, he could think of nothing else. That he entertained a plan to emigrate to America if his practice in Vienna did not prove successful is, however, only part of what particularly happened in 1886. There is substantial ground for the view that just prior to his marriage, while serving as a military doctor during maneuvers in August-September at a locale about 40 miles west of his own birthplace (Freiberg), Freud experienced a regressive personality disturbance quite similar to that of his later patient the

"Rat Man." [16] Though the full details for this hypothesis cannot be presented here, it is essential to take advantage of Freud's reminiscences to explore this hypothesis. One can then comprehend better a number of odd incidents during the journey: for example, the fainting episode at Bremen and the attack of prostatitis during the trip to Columbia University, discussed in Chapters III and IV. It thus becomes possible to interpret the deeper currents of the Freud/Jung "mutual enchantment."

The "Rat Man" was the convenient name for a case of obsessional neurosis analyzed by Freud in 1907-1908, in which rats played a prominent part in the obsessions. The patient came to Freud for treatment in October 1907. He was a lawyer, age 29, whose initial complaints consisted of fears that some injury might befall his father and/or his lady friend, to both of whom he was very attached. His complex feelings toward his father were dominated by hostility, including death wishes. The patient was superstitiously concerned about questions of death, particularly of relatives whose demise he often seemed able to predict. He was therefore sometimes called "carrion crow." Hostility towards his father and others was often deflected to himself. Thus he experienced suicidal compulsions, such as the temptation to cut his own throat with a razor. During childhood he also believed that his father was able to read his thoughts and that his own thoughts (or wishes) were often transformed into reality by a kind of magic ("omnipotence of thought").

Freud soon discovered that two incidents during recent army maneuvers had brought the patient's symptoms to the fore and led to his being consulted. One of these involved the recounting to the patient by a fellow officer, whom he called the "Cruel Captain," of a form of punishment, practiced in the East, in which a pot containing live rats was strapped to a man's buttocks. The Captain seemed to derive a sadistic satisfaction from the telling. (One surmises that the Captain was allusively threatening the patient with such punishment on account of some offense, but this intent is not spelled out.) The patient was fascinated by the "Cruel Captain's" narrative. It appeared to Freud that some homosexual attraction (*and* revulsion) was involved. The second special incident during maneuvers concerned the patient's losing his pince-nez. Again, the "Cruel Captain" was in some way implicated in the confusion that arose in the payment of 3.80 kronen due at the post office upon the arrival of a replacement of the glasses from Vienna.

In attempting to reconstruct the early influences that had contributed to the symptoms, the patient's biting of a sibling (as a rat might do) during childhood stood out. He felt implicated in the death of a sister (Katherine) who was three-and-one-half years old. Severe punishment of the patient by the father, including a dire prophecy about the future of the miscreant (a "castration" threat), lay at the root of the illness. Not only jealousy between siblings but infantile sexual misdeeds, including masturbation, were involved.

Freud presented the case as the keynote address at the first psychoanalytic congress, which occurred at Salzburg, April, 1908. The analysis was then still in progress. The treatment lasted for about a year, until September 1908, at which time the patient seemed to be cured of his major complaints. But the publication of the case did not occur until the middle of 1909, and during the interim Freud was able to mull over the details of the analysis.

It was Freud's practice to destroy the notes and drafts he had used in preparing any publication, including his five classic case histories, but in the case of the Rat Man, he made an unexplained exception. A portion of the current treatment record was found among his papers after his death. Though most of the notes were absorbed in the published account, the following points, among others, were omitted: that the patient had been "confined to barracks" for a three-week period during his compulsory military career; and three direct or indirect allusions to his having one undescended testis (unilateral cryptorchism), a condition that entered into his dream life and into his relationship with his lady (who had at one time had an ovariectomy). In view of these omissions, it is noteworthy that at one point in the original record, after Freud had mentioned incidents connected with the death of the patient's sibling Katherine, he wrote: "My uncertainty and forgetfulness on these last two points seem to be intimately connected. . . . (They were forgotten owing to complexes of my own.) . . . Death was brought close to him by his sister's death, and he really believed that you die if you masturbate" (*Standard Edition, 10,* 264).

As above stated, Freud began the treatment of the Rat Man in October 1907 and continued it until September 1908. He remained in touch with him for some time afterwards; thus we learn from the letters Freud wrote to Jung that the Rat Man had married in the fall of 1910. During 1909, notably after Jung's second visit to Freud in Vienna, Freud, despite other obligations and considerable fatigue, resolved to write up the case. Thus on June 3, 1909 he told Jung that he had the sudden impulse to write up the case history. He wrote: "I suddenly feel like writing up the Salzburg Rat Man, and if you like I can give you the piece for the second number [of the *Jahrbuch*]. It will not be long because in print I shall have to be much more discreet than in a lecture. But here is a case that will enable me to throw full light on certain aspects of the truly complicated phenomenon of obsessional neurosis. I am no longer tired, I shall have a full schedule in June, but shall only be working half time during the first two weeks in July and am confident of being able to complete the article before the summer holiday." [17]

By the end of the month he again referred to the case history. He confessed that his energy was "pretty well exhausted, except for one undertaking": "This one undertaking is my paper about the Rat Man. I am finding it very difficult for it is almost beyond my power of presentation; the paper will probably be unintelligible . . . outside our immediate circle. . . . Unfortunately this paper . . . is becoming too bulky. It just pours out of me, and even so it's inadequate, incomplete and therefore untrue. A wretched business. I am determined to finish it before leaving and to do nothing more before setting sail for our America" (p. 238). This description of the process of composition—the resolve to finish the business, the difficulties encountered though the material poured out but was "incomplete and therefore untrue"—suggest that he was not only being discreet with respect to the private life of the patient but was probably omitting much of its resemblance to his own life.

With these considerations in mind the earlier disclosures about 1886 that Freud made to Jung may be viewed as perhaps paving the way for the composition of the Rat Man case. Was he perhaps now recording in the composition of this case, even if obliquely, events and fantasies similar to those he had entertained for much of his troubled life—fantasies that will reveal themselves to the prepared reader of *The Interpretation of Dreams* and Freud's various other contributions (e.g., the Leonardo essay)?

It should, of course, be understood that Freud was not actually the obsessional neurotic that he presented to his readers in the long case history published in 1909. There was a contemporary patient whom he treated in 1907-1908. But in keeping with the scheme he used in common with many creative writers, Freud's chief case histories expressed three levels of communication. At the recondite (the inframediate level)—the most personal—he used himself or some well-known relative or friend as a prototype. At the next (intermediate) level came the observed patient and, finally, at the immediate level of the narrative, a rough blend of the other two levels was presented. For this reason the history of the actual patient when known usually exhibits gaps which it is possible to fill from below, as it were. Reciprocally, one can read the case presentation as a partial communication of the inframediate level. [18]

To return now to the case itself, we now know that there was an obsessional neurotic, Ernst Lanzer, who came to Freud for treatment in 1907. But what has not hitherto been recognized is that this contingency resembled in essence what Freud himself had experienced in 1886 at Olmütz, Moravia. Freud appears to have had a serious personality disturbance toward the end of the army maneuvers which lasted from August 9 to September 10. By this hypothesis Freud, in his writing of Lanzer's case history in 1909, drew also upon his own experience of 1886, particularly when he felt the need to fill the gaps in his patient's narrative.

This process is clarified by the second letter from Freud to Jung mentioned above, dated April 16, 1909. Allusion to it opens the extended discussion of Freud's identity as Rat Man and leads into confirmatory evidence of the identity hypothesis. [18a]

The reasoning involved will appear strange to conscious ratiocination, but one cannot expect to understand the thinking of a Rat Man by sticking to conscious logic. In the world of the obsessional neurotic, who has a particular history, one must exploit the "compliance of chance," explained in Note 18a, to patch up discrepancies and repair failing friendship by exercising inge-nuity. By composing the Rat Man case history in the following weeks, Freud would try to accomplish this feat and perhaps also give the feat a certain permanence. Hence his resolve, as we have seen, to perform the task before leaving for America in August. With that journey he would enter a new phase of his unconsciously determined life, and appear on the lecture platform in Worcester as if by the "omnipotence" of his own thought and wishes he was fulfilling an "incredible daydream."

Freud's remark at Clark about this realization of an "incredible daydream" lends itself to idiodynamic interpretation. Not only should one consider that portion of his idioverse in which he is identified with the Rat Man (cf. "omnipotence of wishes"), but one should take into account a theoretical formulation that he set forth at this time. It appeared as an unsigned interpolation in a monograph by Otto Rank (1909) entitled, *The Myth of the Birth of the Hero: A Psychological Interpretation of Mythology*. It consisted of six pages (ibid., 63-68), later included in the *Standard Edition* under the title "Family Romances." (The German original included the further words "of Neurotic Individuals," which the translator infelicitously omitted.) To Rank's psychoanalytic interpretation of the myths of such heroes as Oedipus, Moses, Jesus, Siegfried and Tristan, Freud added his very own formulation of the theme. In it he invoked the personal mythologies of certain talented neurotic patients in whom the Oedipus complex is unconsciously elaborated to include the elements of mysterious birth, often accompanied by congenital and social handicaps which are compensated in fantasy by eventual greatness. This contribution by Freud (and Rank) at this point in the history of psychoanalysis has a peculiar relevance to Freud himself as just such a neurotic hero who in 1909 received the vocation to international fame by the invitation of Stanley Hall. With it came the historic turning point in the fate of Freud's Oedipal theory and, simultaneously, of his own neurotic fantasies. Little wonder that both Freud himself and some unsympathetic critics referred to psychoanalysis as a Freudian mythology. But from the Freudian standpoint (as expounded by Rank and Freud in 1909) social epochs have often been an expression of a leader's private and "neurotic" fantasy projected to become a social reality, with historic effect, fortunate or unfortunate for humanity. Yet as William James (1902, pp. 6-21, 374-378) has maintained, the origins of a belief do not constitute the best criteria for judging its validity. Nevertheless, they do provide a guide for the understanding of its nature or shape. Thus the exploits of military leaders like Alexander and Napoleon or religious leaders like Moses and Jesus have had unconscious meaning that Rank and Freud could quite pertinently attribute to an Oedipus complex, and they thus explained in psychoanalytic terms the significance of the hero myth. At the stage of the history of psychoanalysis that was involved in the visit to America in September 1909, Freud was, in terms of his own neurosis as well as of his social mission, not only enacting a biographical event but was simultaneously corroborating his theory of the unconscious. Hence his sense of realizing an "incredible daydream" as he stepped on the lecture platform at Clark University in a galaxy of internationally recognized scientific leaders such as the physicists Ernest Rutherford, Albert Michelson and Robert W. Wood.

Jung's Invitation

While the evidence for Freud's invitations to participate in the Clark vigentennial is quite explicit, Jung's invitation is veiled in something of a mystery. That he was invited is in itself surprising because he was only 34 years old—the youngest of all the invited lecturers—and his record of publications was then neither lengthy nor unusually impressive. It is true that Hall was acquainted with Jung's work on word-association which he employed conspicuously in his study of Mrs. Piper, the medium, conducted in collaboration with Amy Tanner in the spring of 1909 (as discussed at length in Chapter V below). But Hall called it the "Jung-Freud tests" and thus linked Jung to Freud although Jung had independently used this method (of Francis Galton) to explore the validity of Freud's theories. The implication is that Hall did not consider Jung an important scientific innovator in his own right.

But the mentioned enigma does not arise from Jung's status as a tyro in science. It exists because none of the extant contemporary correspondence of Hall, Jung or Freud mentions the initial invitation. Yet there is a voluminous file of correspondence between Freud and Jung (cf. the *Freud/Jung Letters*) and a supposedly complete file of the correspondence between Freud and Hall concerning the visit (published in Part Two of this volume). No correspondence between Hall and Jung has been found though it has been assiduously sought in both the Jung Archives in Switzerland and the Hall Papers at Clark University in Worcester.

The first mention of Jung's invitation to Clark is a retrospective reference in a letter from Jung to Freud dated 12 June 1909. Jung alluded to the invitation in the words, "Isn't it splendid about

America?" In a footnote the editor added, "Jung evidently had sent Freud the news of his invitation to Clark University, but the telegram or letter is missing." He then stated that Freud wrote Pfister, the Swiss pastor-psychoanalyst, on June 13 about Jung's invitation and implied that by then Pfister probably had the news from Jung. The editor continued that though, according to Jung's autobiography, Jung and Freud had been invited "simultaneously and independently," this assertion could not be verified because it had not been possible to document Hall's invitation to Jung. [19]

The consistent omission of letters in contradiction to normal expectations recalls "Silver Blaze" by Conan Doyle with the curious incident of the dog that didn't bark in the night— missing evidence that Holmes interpreted to mean that the thief was not a stranger to the dog. The theft did prove to be an "inside" job. In the present instance, the absent letters similarly suggest design. Did Hall, Jung and Freud agree not to reveal the initial circumstances of the invitation to Jung?

A search for corroborative evidence about the invitation in related contemporary papers preserved at Clark University brought some limited results. There was only one mention of Jung in the extant minutes of the meeting of the Clark University Board of Trustees whose approval Hall needed for the anniversary plans. It appeared under the date June 15, 1909, at which time it was included in a list of invited lecturers recommended for honorary degrees. Freud's name was also on that list, but it had appeared previously in the minutes of the Board on February 15, 1909, a day before Hall's second letter of invitation to Freud. However, the name of an Ernst Meumann occurred repeatedly in the minutes until June—when Jung was first listed.

In the minutes of the faculty meetings in June 1909, which contained lists of proposed participants, Jung's name appeared under Pedagogy, along with that of Leo Burgerstein, and in the same list under Psychology the names of Sigmund Freud and William Stern occurred. Meumann was no longer listed. It is thus possible to infer that Jung was invited as a replacement for Meumann and, like Meumann, he was intended to represent the field of Pedagogy (education). Yet Jung had no particular expertise in that area. In fact, the faculty committee on honorary degrees appears to have had some doubt about his suitability on other grounds. He was a youngster in comparison with the other candidates. His name did not appear in *Wer Ist's* (the German equivalent of *Who's Who*), which the committee conscientiously consulted for age and other vital facts. It was presumably on the strength of Hall's insistence that Jung did finally receive a Doctor of Laws, designated as in Pedagogy and School Hygiene.

Ernst Meumann was included in the Preliminary Announcement of the Second Decennial Celebration of the Opening of Clark University containing the September program, dated May 15. He was listed as a lecturer, but a note at the bottom of the page stated that he would not be able to attend. But though there is considerable surviving correspondence concerning other invited lecturers who declined, none of the letters between Hall and Meumann have been found. One does not therefore know the conditions under which Meumann's name was withdrawn.

We have derived from archival research at Clark some significant new information. Jung's invitation was delayed until June because he was invited to replace a previously invited lecturer on pedagogy whose name was withdrawn, presumably in May. That Jung was to represent the field of pedagogy is anomalous. As will be shown in Chapter VIII, just one of his three lectures at Clark had a direct bearing on child education, and then only by observations of the emotional development of one child. It would hence seem that factors other than the special expertise of the lecturer entered into his invitation. One such factor was, undoubtedly, his relationship to Freud, Hall's favored guest. The role of sexuality in childhood, newly stressed in Freud's theories, was clearly of interest to Hall. But the anomaly of the selection of Jung as a participant remains.

Can further light be shed on the topic by examining the extant correspondence of Freud with his adherents and friends during the period of Jung's invitation?

As has already been indicated, Freud communicated with his Swiss friend Dr. Pfister on the day after Jung wrote Freud about the American prospect. Freud wrote: "You too must have been impressed by the great news that Jung is coming with me to Worcester. It changes my whole feeling about the trip and makes it important. I am very curious to see what will come of it all." [20]

But it is perhaps even more instructive to discover when and what Freud told Karl Abraham. [21] He faithfully informed this colleague in Berlin about his own two invitations from Hall shortly after each had been received, but Jung's invitation was not mentioned anywhere in the volume of published correspondence. But there was a noticeable gap in the sequence during the most relevant months—June and July 1909. An attempt was therefore made to fill it. By this effort it was eventually discovered that Freud did refer to Jung's invitation, not immediately but in retrospect. It was alluded to in the context of a possible meeting between Freud and Abraham on Freud's way to or from America, perhaps at Bremen, the port from which Freud would embark. Thus on July 7, 1909—a month after Jung's invitation was settled—Freud wrote to Abraham: "Ferenczi will be with me [in Bremen]; whether Jung, who, as you know, was also invited will meet us at the ship or beforehand is not yet decided." There is, however, no previous (extant) letter in which Freud told Abraham about Jung's invitation, and that there was indeed none is confirmed by Abraham's reply six days later (July 13) in which he remarked: "I knew nothing at all about Jung having been invited." Abraham was clearly piqued that Freud had not imparted this very interesting news. Had Freud withheld it because he knew of the long-standing problematic relationship between Abraham and Jung? Abraham would surely not have encouraged Jung's closeness to Freud by a visit to America. If Freud had played some part in the arrangement of Jung's invitation, he would have had additional reason for avoiding the entire matter. There will be more about Abraham and Freud in relation to Jung in the sequel.

An obvious source of information about Jung's invitation is his own statement of the matter in his autobiography written toward the end of his life and posthumously published. The relevant paragraph reads as follows: "During the years 1904-5 I set up a laboratory for experimental psychopathology at the Psychiatric Clinic. I had a number of students there with whom I investigated psychic reactions (i.e., associations). Franz Riklin, Sr., was my collaborator. Ludwig Binswanger was currently writing his doctoral dissertation on the association experiment in connection with the psychogalvanic effect, and I wrote my paper 'On the Psychological Diagnosis of Facts.' There were also a number of Americans among our associates, including Carl Petersen and Charles Ricksher. Their papers were published in American journals. It was these association studies which later, in 1909, procured me my invitation to Clark University; I was asked to lecture on my work. Simultaneously and independently of me Freud was invited. The degree of Doctor of Laws *honoris causa* was bestowed on both of us." [22]

The salient fact about this statement is the inverse order of the events that Jung creates for the reader. By starting with his own research on word association, then mentioning American collaborators who published in American journals, Jung arrived at the next step: that these association studies brought about his invitation to America in 1909. With that backdrop he then asserted: "Simultaneously and independently of me Freud was invited." And he concluded with the equalization of the two invitations by citing the honorary degrees awarded them both.

Autobiography written toward the close of a lifetime will notoriously be unreliable and in this instance the writer by his chosen title acknowledged that he was combining memories, dreams and reflections. A comparison of Jung's statement about the invitations with the presently known facts is revealing. First, it is not true that Jung was invited simultaneously with Freud. As previously indicated, Freud had been invited twice (in December 1908 at which time he declined, and again in February 1909, when he accepted) before Jung was invited. It is clear from Jung's letter to Freud dated June 12, 1909 that he received the invitation a few days prior to that date—more than three months after Freud. One is then struck by the other adjective he coupled with simultaneous: "independently of me Freud was invited." The impression is conveyed that Freud's invitation was secondary to Jung's when, in fact, the opposite was the case. When independence is linked with the error about simultaneity it, too, becomes suspect. Is this additional claim an attempt to nullify whatever part Freud may have had in the arrangement of Jung's invitation?

Several hypothetical scenarios for Jung's belated invitation are possible though none at this point can be proved. The simplest is that during Jung's visit to Freud at the end of March 1909 a tentative plan for Jung to accompany Freud, as Ferenczi was going to do, was concocted. In such a venture Jung would presumably have paid his own expenses. [23]

The significance of the eventual invitation for Jung is readily apparent. Not only was the Clark celebration momentous for Freud and psychoanalysis but it marked for Jung a sudden emergence into international prominence that he had apparently craved for a long time. An honorary degree at the early age of 34 was extraordinary.

What was Jung's imaginative preparation for this great event? First we know that he had had a secret yearning for a journey to America which beckoned as a land of promise—a land where his special abilities would be recognized and where he might acquire wealthy patients. In his monograph, *The Psychology of Dementia Praecox* (1906), which he sent to Freud on publication at the beginning of their relationship, Jung included a lengthy analysis of the dream of a young husband who revealed just such an ambition. When Freud commented to Jung about the book, he surmised that Jung was the dreamer and made some astute observations about what the dream meant. It is interesting that, as with later correspondence touching on sensitive points about Jung's life and personality, this letter is missing from the volume of the *Freud/Jung Letters;* but Jung's reply is available and from it one gleans not only that Jung was indeed the dreamer but that the yearning for an American journey was a distinct part of his contemporary personality. [24] When at the end of December, 1908 Freud told Jung that he had declined Hall's (first) invitation Jung responded that it would have been good "to speak in America if only because of the echo it would arouse in Europe." Reverting to the topic at the end of the same letter, he added: "About America I would like to remark that Janet's travel expenses were amply compensated by his subsequent American clientèle. Recently Kraepelin gave one in California for the [tidy sum] of 50,000 marks. I think this side of things should also be taken into account." This observation by Jung stressing the potential of a lucrative result of becoming known to the American elite is characteristic. As is now recognized by Jung's various biographers, wealthy patients from America, particularly women, did indeed hold a large place in his subsequent practice.

Jung's fantasy was complemented by Freud's search for a successor and for that reason he eagerly welcomed Jung's positive response to psychoanalysis and his eventual invitation to Clark. With an ingenuously implied high self-esteem, Freud called Jung his "crown prince." After correcting the proofs of his article on Little Hans, which had been sent to Jung as the editor of the journal in which it was to appear, Freud wrote: "We are certainly getting ahead; if I am Moses, then you are Joshua and will take possession of the promised land of psychiatry, which I shall only be able to glimpse from afar." [25] The fact that this statement is made in the context of Freud's invitation to America bespeaks the germ of a fantasy for Jung to accompany him on such a journey.

But Freud's plans about a suitable successor had a special condition that Jung peculiarly satisfied. Though by this time Freud had a number of pupils and followers, these were almost exclusively Jewish, a situation that did not fully satisfy him. The fact that Jung was a gentile and connected with the prestigious Burghölzli Hospital in Zurich had profound significance for Freud. Freud was concerned because he anticipated and, indeed, did evoke decided opposition to his ideas about repressed sexuality in early childhood as the key to adult neurosis. The pending publication of the Little Hans case, in which Freud first fully described the castration complex, was bound to be offensive to a culture in which children were perceived as little angels rather than as little animals. And Freud's markedly biological conception of child development would, he felt, be rejected out of hand. For these views to be endorsed and championed by a vigorous young Protestant psychiatrist from Switzerland ideally fitted Freud's felt need. For that reason he was willing to overlook Jung's doubts about psychoanalysis which could readily be explained as "resistance" that had to be analyzed away. And Freud helped the analysis along in their voluminous correspondence and occasional personal contacts. In the beginning, Jung welcomed this discipline; it was appropriate for an acolyte. For Freud the science of psychoanalysis was built on a foundation of self-analysis that could only be conducted by overcoming resistance in oneself, to be followed by passing on such insights to others who came as patients or as pupils. Because Jung offered himself at the outset as an eager pupil and as a subject for analysis, Freud was unable to recognize Jung's orientation for what it really was: a blend of neurotic self-doubt and a good measure of opportunistic ambition, the latter of which would, in the end, undermine their professional affiliation.

That Jung encouraged Freud in his wishful thinking about the ideal successor is, in retrospect, easy to discern. Early in their relations Jung willingly undertook to become Freud's spokesman in the International Congress of Psychiatry, Neurology and Psychology at Amsterdam, September 1907 where he debated the outspoken foe of psychoanalysis Gustav Aschaffenburg. [26]

The next year Jung initiated and organized the first international meeting of psychoanalysts and psychiatrists, convened at Salzberg. Without Jung it is doubtful that such a meeting would have occurred, certainly not with its favorable results, including the plan to publish the first psychoanalytic journal, of which Jung became the editor. [27]

It must also have augured with special cogency for Freud that Jung in 1908-1909 undertook and reported to him in their correspondence the careful, continuous observation of a four-year-old girl who was puzzled by her mother's pregnancy. It was recognized by both Jung and Freud that this situation afforded a good parallel to Little Hans—an opportunity to confirm Freud's pending publication of that case. Moreover, this child was Jung's own daughter! His willingness—indeed his eagerness—to study and report her behavior over many months could not but encourage Freud's belief that he had indeed found the right successor. This series of observations was not only part of Jung's indoctrination; it unwittingly paved the way to Worcester, for Jung eventually presented this case as his third and final lecture at Clark. All things considered, it was only natural that Freud might entertain the fantasy, once he himself had accepted Hall's invitation, that Jung might on some basis accompany him to Worcester.

It is necessary to return briefly to Freud's special condition for a non-Jewish successor so as to adduce some explicit evidence on this point. It is found in Freud's own words as a constant motif in correspondence with his above-mentioned colleague Karl Abraham of Berlin. Abraham had spent three years (1904-1907) working at the Burghölzli in Zurich as a colleague of Jung. After the Salzburg meeting in 1908, he developed a conflict with Jung in the latter's new leadership role. Abraham left Zurich partly because he felt handicapped by his Jewishness. Not unnaturally Freud could discuss with him the Jewish implications of psychoanalysis. But, unlike Abraham, Freud thought of Jung as an unprejudiced gentile who could help emancipate psychoanalysis from being perceived as limited in its applicability or scope.

Freud's first statement to this effect is found in his letter to Abraham dated May 3, 1908 in which Freud avers that "it was by his (Jung's) appearance on the scene that psychoanalysis escaped the danger of becoming 'a Jewish national affair.' " [28] Freud spoke openly to Abraham explaining that "you are closer to my

intellectual constitution because of racial kinship." On this basis
Freud was attempting to mediate between Jung and Abraham in
their current conflict over professional matters. On May 11
Abraham made his only response to this thesis; he conceded
that there was a "Talmudic" element in psychoanalytic thought.
But it is clear that Abraham was not in agreement with Freud's
main argument about the Burghölzli group. Instead, on July 16,
he wrote about Bleuler's concealed "grandiose tendencies" hidden
behind "exaggerated modesty." And he remarked that Jung
seemed to be "reverting to his former spiritualistic inclinations." [29]

On July 27 Freud made the most remarkable of his several
statements about psychoanalysis as a Jewish movement. He was
anticipating a visit to the Jungs in Zurich in September and
promised personally to mediate the continuing misunderstanding
between Abraham and Jung. Freud continued: "I have nothing
to reproach you with; I nurse a suspicion that the suppressed anti-
Semitism of the Swiss that spares me is reflected in reinforced
strength on you. But I think that we as Jews, if we wish to join
in, must develop a bit of masochism, being ready to suffer some
wrong. Otherwise there is no hitting it off. Rest assured that if
my name were Oberhuber, in spite of everything, my innovations
would have met with far less resistance." [30]

At the end of the year Freud again expressed his regret that
Abraham was at loggerheads with Jung, then added: "Our Aryan
comrades are really completely indispensible to us. Otherwise
psychoanalysis would succumb to anti-Semitism." [31]

The context for these continuing ethnic reflections is found in
a forthcoming article by Freud: "I expect a huge defensive din to
arise from the case history of the boy of five [Little Hans] which is
to be the first paper in the *Jahrbuch;* I have the proofs here for
correction. German ideals threatened again!" [32] By this time
Freud was probably aware that there lay at hand from Jung
himself a counterfoil to this controversial case in the observations
Jung had begun making of his four-year-old daughter.

That Freud was so conscious of the Jewish question in relation
to psychoanalysis may come as a surprise to some readers but
the point is explicitly made in Freud's correspondence with this
Jewish colleague. Abraham was having a problem with Jung but
not avowedly on any ethnic basis. Nevertheless, it is striking
that it was Freud, not Jung, who first made a point of the ethnic

orientation of psychoanalytic theory. One must, however, qualify this comment by recognizing that Freud was not meaning to detract from the universal and scientific validity of his observations or concepts. On the contrary, he objected strongly to any attempt to limit the universal validity of psychoanalysis. But he did believe that it was more difficult for those with a different background (he actually said "constitution") to originate or accept these ideas. Jews, he thought, lack the "mystical" way of thinking, and are hence freer to observe the facts of human biology. [33]

These private indications of Freud's need for Jung as his non-Jewish successor came to public professional notice at Nuremberg early in 1910 when the Second International Psychoanalytic Congress was in session. Ferenczi, primed by Freud, made the proposal for an international organization and nominated Jung as life president. Jung's authority would include the decision about the suitability for publication of all papers written by members. That Jung was to be elevated to that status for life was more than the core membership—the Viennese Freudians—was ready to accept and in protest a group of them met privately to make plans. One of that number, Fritz Wittels, who would become Freud's first biographer, described the episode as follows: "On the afternoon of this memorable day, the Viennese analysts had a private meeting in the Grand Hotel at Nuremberg to discuss the outrageous situation. Of a sudden, Freud, who had not been invited to attend, put in an appearance. Never before had I seen him so greatly excited. He said: 'Most of you are Jews, and therefore you are incompetent to win friends for the new teaching. Jews must be content with the modest role of preparing the ground. It is absolutely essential that I should form ties in the world of general science. I am getting on in years, and am weary of being perpetually attacked. We are all in danger.' Seizing his coat by the lapels, he said: 'They won't even leave me a coat to my back. The Swiss will save us—will save me, and all of you as well.' " [34]

The eventual solution included the election of Jung as president but for only two years. He was also appointed editor of a new publication, a monthly bulletin (Korrespondenzblatt), intended to keep members informed about Association developments. A second scientific journal, in addition to the Jahrbuch of which Jung remained editor, was established (Zentralblatt für Psychoanalyse). The directors were designated as Bleuler and Freud but the working editors were to be Alfred Adler and Wilhelm Stekel, the two Viennese who had been the chief organizers of the protest meeting. While Jung still remained the foremost official of the now formally organized Freudians, the seeds of discontent had been sown. It would still take three years before Freud's full and painful recognition of his misbegotten choice.

With present knowledge and even with the limited availability of the Freud/Jung correspondence, but with aid from the letters between Freud and Abraham and Freud with Sandor Ferenczi, one can arrive at a plausible picture of what may have transpired regarding Jung's eventual invitation to Clark in June. In particular, one can reconstruct what happened during Jung's second visit to Vienna March 25-30, 1909. By this time Freud had accepted Hall's second invitation, i.e., what Jung called Freud's "American triumph" had come to pass. Freud had invited Ferenczi to accompany him to America and that invitation had been enthusiastically accepted. This point is significant as indicating Freud's need for support at this critical juncture in his career and of his psychoanalytic cause. That his brother Emmanuel had in early March also volunteered to make the journey with Freud and Ferenczi reinforces this interpretation. [35] In this context one may conjecture what Freud had chiefly wanted to discuss with Jung during the latter's visit and what he meant by saying in anticipation: "There will be much to discuss about the American journey when you come here." In brief, Freud may have broached a plan at that time by which Jung, his non-Jewish "crown prince" and successor, would join the party to lend an ecumenical cast to the representation. That Emmanuel did not in the event make the trip helped give the representation a better balance.

Jung's fitness for his role in Worcester had been predetermined from the moment that he became Freud's representative at the International Congress in Amsterdam in September 1908 which, again, had been planned, at least partially, during Jung's first visit to Vienna in April 1907. But this time Jung had painted himself into the picture by his careful and continuous observation of his four-year-old daughter "Agathli," a perfect foil to the case of the five-year-old boy Little Hans.

That Freud could make such political plans for his cause is evident from the letters he wrote to Hall about Ferenczi at the time he was preparing his five Clark lectures for publication in the April

1910 issue of the *American Journal of Psychology*, edited by Hall. Indeed, Freud's motion in that direction was seconded by Hall, and a contribution by Ferenczi did appear along with those of Freud and Jung in that historic issue of the *Journal*. To round out the picture, the paper presented by Ernest Jones at the meeting of the American Psychological Association in Cambridge, Massachusetts in December 1909 was published, not with others presented at the APA in Prince's *Journal of Abnormal Psychology* but in this April issue of Hall's *Journal*. Freud was marshalling his forces and Hall gladly accepted the role of adjutant. Hall might later appear to Freud as only a "king-maker," but at this stage he was very ready to aid Freud with the "crown prince" and other courtiers.

In this context one should consider Freud's arrangement with Ferenczi to accompany him to America about which one had confirming evidence in Freud's letter to Abraham dated March 9, 1909. This is the same date on which Freud first wrote to Jung to convey the news about his acceptance of Hall's second invitation. From these circumstances the hypothesis arises that Freud may have tried during Jung's visit at the end of March to persuade him to join Ferenczi and himself in making the journey to America. Freud's need for Jung as a champion and Jung's longstanding desire to go to America support this conjecture. If there was such a plan, it may have merged into the later invitation extended by Hall in early June after Meumann declined.

Other Invitations

As has already been shown, the slot occupied by Jung in September had originally been intended for Ernst Meumann, who withdrew around May 15. Who was this distinguished psychologist?

Ernst Meumann (1862-1915) was Professor at the University of Münster in 1909. He was a specialist in the field of experimental pedagogy, a pioneer area of research that marshalled the earlier knowledge and made new investigations of learning and memory as applied to childhood education. A former student of Wundt, Meumann was a leader in this field. In 1905 he founded and edited the *Zeitschrift für experimentelle Pädagogik*. He had published several monographs on learning, memory and time perception and was the author of a two-volume work of introductory lectures on experimental pedagogy (1907-1914). One of his books was translated into English under the title *The Psychology of Learning* (Meumann, 1903). It is evident that this authority in experimental psychology and education was a highly desirable participant who was invited early. By his withdrawal after the printing of the preliminary announcement, a vacancy was created.

In this context it is relevant to observe that in the above-mentioned English work by Meumann (pp. 17-18, 381), Jung's work on word association was cited. His name was joined with those of Riklin, Bleuler and Freud in relation to "the much disputed Freudian theories" on which his experimental studies of "complexes" were based. [36]

In addition to Ernst Meumann, several other leading figures in the behavioral and biological sciences invited by Hall had to decline for various reasons. [37] These included John Dewey, Hermann Ebbinghaus, Jacques Loeb, Élie Metchnikoff, August Weissmann, William Morton Wheeler, and Wilhelm Wundt. Loeb, the famous physiologist, on May 1, 1909 wrote to decline because of a prior commitment, then added these words of appreciation for Hall's work: " . . . I have often realized that the foundation of Clark University was, perhaps, the beginning of the epoch of true universities in this country. You for the first time gathered the phalanx of scientific men who have in all these years represented the highest type of creative scientists in America. When the history of universities in America is written this fact will not be overlooked and you may be sure that sooner or later I shall avail myself of the opportunity of stating this fact in a forcible way."

When Hall, on December 15, 1908 (the same date on which he first invited Freud) invited Wundt, his former professor, the Clark celebration was scheduled for early July 1909. Wundt declined because of a conflict with the 500th anniversary of the University of Leipzig scheduled the last week of July.

Hall apparently did not extend a second invitation to Wundt as he did to Freud for the September date. The exchange between Hall and Wundt is of historical interest and, in the present context, sheds light on Freud's two invitations from Hall. The exchange of letters will hence be quoted.

Professor Wilhelm Wundt,   December 15, 1908
University of Leipzig
Leipzig, Germany

My dear Professor Wundt:

The first week in next July marks the twentieth anniversary of the founding of this University, which we wish to celebrate by a congress of American psychologists, at which we are extremely anxious to have you present.

Not only, as you know, have many American professors been your own personal students (and I have always been very proud of having been the first and oldest), but the influence of your thought in this country has been profound and far-reaching.

Moreover, we are now having occasion to greatly refresh our sense of obligation to you, our master, by the efforts being made to cooperate in the approaching celebration of your anniversary at Leipzig, in a way that shall be worthy of you and of us.

Under these circumstances, it has seemed to my advisers and to myself that we may appeal with unusual cogency to you to now visit this country, and allow those psychologists who have, and the far larger number who have not, seen or heard you to have the stimulation of that experience.

As you know, the voyages are now made very easy, quick, and comfortable. We have chosen the best season for temperature and weather here, and hope to be able to give you the best audience the country can afford.

The topics could be either new or old, or anything to suit yourself, and be presented either in German or in English.

We are able to attach an honorarium, to cover all expenses, of $750, or 3000 Marks, together with entertainment as long as you remain in this city.

I am, with great respect,

> Sincerely yours,
> (signed) G. Stanley Hall
> President

The reply, translated from the German, follows:

Leipzig 5. January, 1909

Dear and Honored Professor Stanley Hall!

Please accept my heartiest thanks for your very friendly invitation to the 20th anniversary celebration of Clark University. I would so gladly come over the ocean to this celebration, especially since I would have the opportunity to see not only you but many other American friends at this single event. But there are two reasons which make it completely impossible for me to accept this enticing invitation. First, I have now reached the stage in life at which such long journeys are not a simple matter, especially when, like me, one is no longer accustomed to such trips. Secondly, our University will be celebrating its 500th Jubilee immediately after your celebration, with a very short period between the two events. Added to this is the fact that I have been requested to give the Jubilee Address on that occasion, a duty which I am afraid could not readily be well discharged if I have just come back from a long journey. My regret in declining is that much greater because I would so much have enjoyed this opportunity to see you again as well as the other American friends who at various times visited the previous Psychological Institute and carried out work there.

Please accept my congratulations on the successful completion of the second decade of Clark University under your direction, and my wishes for its further success, especially in the disciplines of psychology and pedagogy.

With best greetings.

Yours,
(signed) W. Wundt.

Two further facts need to be recognized in order for the declination by Wundt to be better comprehended. First, there is the fact that ten years earlier Hall had invited Wundt to participate in the celebration of the Clark decennial of 1899. Then, too, the fact that the long journey was too much for him at his age [he was 66] caused him to decline. Hall's letter of invitation has not survived but Wundt's reply of February 23, 1899 is extant. Five months later Wundt wrote a second letter to Hall, presumably on request and in lieu of his influential presence at the celebration. In it he addressed Hall as "Highly esteemed Mr. President" and stated that he had heard many good things about Clark from competent sources and had gained the impression from papers in the *American Journal of Psychology* that the Psychology and Pedagogy Department at Clark must be counted among the outstanding institutions of its type. [38]

The second fact concerns the 500th anniversary celebration of the University of Leipzig held in the summer of 1909, an event that contributed to Wundt's declination of Hall's invitation of 1908. In a reciprocal friendly spirit Hall sent his colleague Professor Edmund C. Sanford, director of the psychology laboratory, as a representative from Clark to the University of Leipzig celebration. [39] Sanford was, incidentally, not only a very gentle and congenial person but was an outstanding experimental psychologist, one of Hall's Ph.D. graduates at Johns Hopkins in 1888, and in 1902 he had been the President of the American Psychological Association. Sanford recalled this journey to Europe, particularly his stay in Leipzig, with great pleasure. Wundt, in turn, appears to have reciprocated by mentioning in the *Festschrift* volume of the 500th anniversary of Leipzig University, which contained a 15-page account of the Leipzig laboratory, that "Dr. G. Stanley Hall, now President of Clark University in Worcester, Mass. . . . [was] one of the first participants in the experimental research of this laboratory." [40] From these indications it is reasonable to infer that the relationship between Hall and Wundt at the time of the 20th anniversary Clark celebration was cordial. To infer, to the contrary, that Hall was deeply frustrated by Wundt's declination in 1908 appears to be untenable. [41]

A paradoxical coda: The declination by Wundt was followed by Hall's enhanced second invitation to Freud, which Freud then accepted. Similarly the withdrawal of Meumann (a Wundtian) enabled Hall to invite Jung, who gladly complied. In both these critical instances a Wundtian loss became a Freudian gain.

Chapter III

Lunch in Bremen and the
Ocean Voyage

Meeting in Bremen

In planning the trip to America, Freud considered two routes: the first, via the Austro-American Line, leaving from Trieste, and the second, via North German Lloyd departing from Bremen on August 21. He liked the former route which included Palermo and other parts of Italy on the scenic Mediterranean but it took 14-15 days and would have brought him to New York only a day or two before the opening of the celebration on September 6. The second route was selected by the middle of May, with reservations for Freud and Ferenczi on the *George Washington*. After Jung was invited in early June, he booked a cabin but, as he told Freud, could only get first-class accommodations at that late date. [1,2]

From Freud's Diary and letters home we learn that he arrived at Bremen in the early morning of August 20. He had had an uncomfortable night with little sleep on the train, made worse because he inadvisedly drank some beer en route. At Bremen he met Ferenczi for breakfast. Then he began to discover Bremen with the help of Ferenczi's Baedeker. They explored the inner city with the domed city hall, old churches and several distinguished houses. Ferenczi had studied the guidebook in advance and supplied the dates and other relevant details about the history of the city, many of which Freud recorded. Ferenczi also had "a large bundle of dirty notes with him which were black on one side and green on the other, and which have a picture in the middle like that of a buffalo or of some other animal. These are dollar bills, each worth 10 or 50 dollars. With this money he paid the rest of

51

our fare. The dollar is worth 4.17 marks." Freud and Ferenczi then took out travel insurance policies—Freud in the amount of 20,000 marks, Ferenczi for 10,000. They received mail from home, including a postal card from Jung saying that he would arrive on the evening of the 19th. Freud's Diary then continues: "A few minutes later he himself appears, beaming as he always does." Jung obtained a letter of credit for America. They all then went to the train station to deposit their luggage for the ship and obtain tickets for the special train to Bremerhaven.

Jung already knew the city so he led a tour of the chief sites including the cathedral, which had a Bleikeller (a lead basement) with a famous history. Freud explained that 400 years ago a workman who had accidentally fallen from the roof was buried in this cellar and many years later was discovered to have been preserved like a mummy, in this lead environment. Other individuals later arranged to be buried in this basement. This situation was confused by Jung in his autobiography. He confounded it with the preservation of some human remains in bogs in parts of Germany and Scandinavia.

Fateful Lunch

The trio stopped for lunch at the renowned old Essinghaus Restaurant. When wine was ordered by Freud, Jung unexpectedly declared that he had decided to abandon his previous abstinence from alcohol—an abstinence that dated from the temperance crusade of August Forel, a former director of the Burghölzli, which was endorsed by Bleuler and others of the Hospital staff including Jung. Jung's new resolve probably indicated to Freud another token of Jung's allegiance to him and may have excited him to partake of the wine more liberally than usual.

We now learn from Freud's Diary, and thus for the first time in Freud's own words, about his having fainted on this occasion. This event has repeatedly been described by others in different versions, including that by Jung in his autobiography. The following is Freud's account: "Jung mentioned, to our great satisfaction, that he has decided to give up his abstinence, and he begs us to encourage him. We toast with an excellent wine. Whether because I drank too fast or was disturbed by the [previous] sleepless night, it happened that when I was eating the salmon

I broke into a bad sweat with a feeling of faintness. I had to forgo the other courses of the meal. I didn't trust myself to drink any more. Jung will now take care of the drinking for me. Of course, the whole attack was soon over."

Jung's version supplied details about how he carried Freud to a couch until he recovered and describes the condition as having lasted longer. In particular, Jung stressed a mealtime conversation in which he talked about corpses discovered in bogs near Bremen. Jung believed this account contributed to Freud's attack because Freud interpreted Jung's lively comments on the subject as expressing a death wish toward Freud. Freud, however, says nothing on the topic. From what he does say about the sudden sweating and the feeling of faintness, and his having to forgo the rest of the meal and further drinking, it is safe to infer that a state of anaphylactic shock with loss of consciousness did indeed occur.

The significance of this incident is, of course, a matter of interpretation but, in psychoanalytic terms, Freud's mention of over-indulgence in wine and the effects of the sleepless night are inept, too banal for the founder of psychoanalysis. More to the point is his next Diary comment: "Jung remarks, 'Naturally we will not let Papa pay for us anymore,' and they [Jung and Ferenczi] divided the other expenses of the day between them." The implication is that the attack of fainting and his advanced age [53 years] had inspired a patronizing attitude in Jung, which Freud resented.

Whether Freud had actually attributed a death wish to Jung in so many words or whether Jung made that inference is questionable, particularly since Jung admits that he had confused the circumstances of the mummification in the Bleikeller with the bog corpses he had discussed during lunch.

Since Freud again fainted in Jung's presence three years later, attempts have been made to account for this behavior. Ernest Jones was present on the second occasion, in 1912, and he described it in his biography of Freud.[3] The place was the Park Hotel in Munich at the time of a stormy psychoanalytic Congress when the friendship between Freud and Jung was all but over. Jones explained that during lunch Freud was chiding Jung and Jung's friend Riklin for not citing Freud by name in their publications. Jones commented that Freud seemed oversensitive in this regard. In the course of the conversation Freud fainted. Jones continued: "The sturdy Jung swiftly carried him to a couch in the lounge, where he soon revived. His first words as he was coming to were strange: 'How sweet it must be to die'—another indication that the idea of dying had some esoteric meaning for him."

Jones then quoted a letter from Freud to him dated December 8, 1912: "I cannot forget that six and four years ago I suffered from very similar though not such intense symptoms in the same room of the Park Hotel. I saw Munich first when I visited Fliess during his illness and this town seems to have acquired a strong connection with my relation to that man. There is some piece of unruly homosexual feeling at the root of the matter. When Jung in his last letter again hinted at my 'neurosis,' I could find no better expedient than proposing that every analyst should attend to his own neurosis more than the other's."

The discussion in Jones cited above indicated Freud's awareness of the possible relation of his fainting attacks to unresolved guilt concerning the death of his sibling rival in infancy, his younger brother Julius who died at age six months when Sigmund was less than two years old. That Freud carried this burden unconsciously to the time of his own death is demonstrated in a paper "The day of Freud's death," that day being the Day of Atonement in 1939. [4] The relation of this seeming coincidence to Freud's obsessional character is only hinted at in that brief publication but in the present context it should be considered in its wider implications with at least a little of the supporting evidence.

At Bremen after lunch on Friday, the 20th, Jung hired an automobile to continue the tour. Freud wrote: "We meet a military unit which is coming back from the maneuvers and it, of course, has to be carefully inspected by the Captain of the Swiss army." This ironic observation so early in the journey may lend some support to the speculation (below) that Freud may have seen in Jung some resemblance to the Cruel Captain of the Rat Man case. Freud's fainting in Jung's presence rooted in Freud's "bit of unruly homosexuality" also supports this speculation.

The automobile dropped the trio off at the Vienna Cafe. After enjoying coffee, they took a walk along the Weser River and through the Park. They talked a good deal about Europe and America and Freud stated that he had learned for the first time, presumably from Jung, about the other guests invited to Worcester who are to be on the boat: "A Viennese who is a Professor of Pedagogy, named Burgerstein, [5] and a man from Breslau called

Stern who, through his work on the psychology of testimony, has become well known. [6] But he is a stinker ["Ekel"—repulsive person] who has set himself in opposition to us, and if he is going to be on the *George Washington,* he will not find us hospitable. The company does not now appear to be brilliant."

Freud's hostility to Professor William Stern, who had also been invited by Hall, continued, as will be seen, throughout the journey. He considered Stern to be pushy but the specific and probably more important reason for Freud's antagonism was a review of Freud's *The Interpretation of Dreams* that Stern had published in 1901. [7] The reviewer had expressed doubts about Freud's treatment of the subject as dubiously scientific. He believed that Freud's uncritical treatment of the topic would lead readers "to join in the author's play of ideas to end up in complete mysticism and chaotic arbitrariness." It was characteristic of Freud to regard criticism of his work as a personal affront, which was, no doubt, an indication of his high degree of ego-involvement in the subject matter. But Freud did know about Stern's work on the psychology of testimony, which had much in common with Jung's word-association studies for investigating complexes. The bridge was provided by the early contributions of Wertheimer and Klein who employed the word-association method as a means of validating the honesty of witnesses in courts of law—the earliest version of the lie detector. [8]

The Diary records that Freud had seen the passenger list of the *George Washington* at the Lloyd office earlier that day and that when he obtained his identification card for the journey, he found his name had been misspelled as "Freund." He disliked this error, particularly when it was repeated in the newspaper listing the passengers when the ship landed in New York.

The Crossing

The three travelers boarded the *George Washington* at noon on Saturday the 21st. Freud gave a detailed description of the boat in his Diary. He praised the elegance of the cabins and the other fine accommodations. Mail was being held, including what Freud called "the great event of the day," a *bon voyage* gift of a box of rare orchids sent Freud by a female patient at Nassau. He prized the bouquet highly and had the steward place it in a vase on the table the trio shared in the dining room. A generous tip assured that the flowers would be provided with fresh water as needed.

Later on Saturday the ship left Bremerhaven en route to Southhampton and Cherbourg. The landing at Southhampton was at 2:00 P.M. on Sunday, the 22nd, and at Cherbourg in the evening of the same day.

In a letter to the family that Freud mailed from Southhampton he described the ship with its beautiful appointments and stated that there were 2400 passengers, with 500 in first class. Freud, Jung and Ferenczi were traveling in that class.

Describing the departure on the 21st, Freud dwelled on the cold and rainy weather—a dismal beginning. He concluded the entry by remarking, "I wonder whether it will stay that way." He then wryly quoted a line in French:

"Ça va bien pourvu que ca dure."

[It goes well as long as it lasts.]

to which he added a line to form a couplet:

Said the roofer as he began to fall.

The French line is a well-known saying of Napoleon Bonaparte's mother Letitia who had forebodings about her son's growing eminence. [9] She did not rejoice at his coronation in 1804 and, in fact, chose not to attend it. She was, of course, in the end proved right: her son had reached too high and a few years later fell from his elevated position and was sent into exile. The quotation and Freud's wry addition afford a good example of his ironic humor. It is possible that in the context it indicated some specific foreboding about Jung's ambivalence, perhaps sensed by Freud at lunch the previous day before he fainted. The joke about the roofer might have been inspired by the accidental fall of the workman who had gone to his death and was then preserved in the mummifying soil of the Bleikeller. Jung's dominance when he took over the expenses for the meal from "Papa," and Freud's comment about the inspection of the troops returning from maneuvers may have figured in the forebodings as the ship left Bremen in the dismal weather. More on this theme will appear below in describing the walk of Freud and Jung in Central Park, New York City, and Freud's indisposition at the Palisades.

Shortly after the ship had got underway on Tuesday, the 24th, there was an unpleasant incident described by Freud as follows:

"Professor Stern has quite early announced himself—bespoke himself to Jung and took possession of him while he turned his back on us [Freud and Ferenczi]. I watched this for a while and then called out to Jung: 'Now, Doctor, when are you going to bring that conversation to an end?' Whereupon the shabby Jew in embarrassment departed."

As the "crown prince" and his "sovereign" thus leave Europe for the "coronation" in America, one is struck by this unpleasant evidence of Freud's intolerance. Though not intended for publication, this incident remained in his mind to be compulsively recorded and remembered. One is dismayed by this display of deliberate rudeness. Was the act a projection—an attempt to rid himself of his own self-image as a Jew? That he had promised himself to treat Stern in this way only adds to the starkness of the behavior and suggests a sadistic trait complementing the masochistic quality of the fainting spell. From a new angle, one wonders about the analogy with the obsessional character of the Rat Man whom Freud had portrayed as anal-sadistic, especially toward rivals.

In terms of that paradigm, the behavior becomes more comprehensible. Professor Stern had not only rejected Freud's major work as unscientific but now he was here on the boat en route as an invited lecturer at Clark on an equal footing with Freud. He was, indeed, a rival, and an intolerable one because he had put himself above Freud in his unqualified opposition to the psychoanalytic approach. Moreover, he was now attempting to lure away Freud's chosen successor, C. G. Jung, who had been invited to lecture on word association at Clark. And Stern was scheduled to speak on the psychology of testimony, one component of which was the technique of word association. In the circumstances Freud could not regard Professor Stern as an objective critic. Instead Stern aroused from a deeper layer of Freud's unconscious a complex that expressed itself in utter rudeness regardless of consequences. The "reality principle" was neurotically displaced by the egoistic short-term "pleasure principle."

After a week at sea Freud noted that the weather had been almost consistently misty and rainy. Heavy fog was added on the approach to Newfoundland. The travelers enjoyed continuous conversation. "It was really the redeeming feature of the journey for the weather and the ocean were not friendly and the uplift in mood through the sea air did not occur as I had surmised." Freud mentioned that they were counting on Dr. Brill, when they dis-embarked, to serve as their guide in seeing New York City. Freud mentioned for a second time the dollar equivalent of the mark and that the price of hotel accommodations and taxis quoted in Baedeker "frighten one to death. In my pocket a regular pantheon is holding sway: crowns and marks and that power God, the dollar."

Arrival in New York

The ship anchored at Hoboken, New Jersey on August 29 and Freud promptly sent a telegram to his family announcing the safe arrival. In a letter to his family on the 30th he described an in-terview with the *Staats-Zeitung.* He remarked that the interview was "probably arranged by that awful character Stern who today already has everything in the paper including the titles of his lectures; this was followed by Professor Fre*und* with his friend Jung who were much less communicative." [10]

Freud explained to his family that Dr. Brill, a practicing psychoanalyst in the city, would be their host and guide. A loyal disciple, he was translating a volume of Freud's papers which would be Freud's first book to appear in English translation. He added that "the translation should be coming out in two weeks." [11]

Due to official regulations Brill was not allowed on the ship but he arranged for a colleague, Dr. Bronislav Onuf, who had recently moved to New York from Switzerland and who was now Consultant in Neuropsychiatry at Ellis Island, to greet the visitors on the boat. [12] Onuf helped the travelers through the various inspections at disembarkation, formalities that lasted for over two hours. On the dock Brill was waiting to greet them. "He immediately led us into the subway, the railroad under the level ground, then to the electric car, then by foot through an endless route to the hotel to which we had already sent our luggage." This was the Hotel Manhattan where they registered on August 29. They got to bed that first night at 11:30. The next morning they read the interview in the German-language newspaper above mentioned and began a busy day of sightseeing and visiting. Freud described the famous "skyscrapers" along Broadway and remarked that they were certainly not beautiful. The city as a whole reminded him of London. As if entertaining the thought of a move to America, he says: "It is really very expensive here and some of the necessary comforts for us would be quite lacking. But if one becomes oriented, one could get along." In his letter the next day he added: "Gradually one gets used to this city. In a week one could get settled." [13]

Chapter IV

A Walk in Central Park

The six days that followed the arrival in New York and preceded the departure for Worcester were occupied with sightseeing and visits. The Synoptic Chronicle (Chapter XIII) lists these events and, since most of them do not bear significantly upon the mission or consequences of the journey, these will not be discussed here in further detail. It may be noted incidentally that Freud's antagonism to his brother-in-law Eli Bernays, the husband of Freud's sister Anna and the brother of his wife Martha, found expression in a letter to his family. He went in a hired automobile to the Bernays address at 121 West 119th Street but found everything locked up tight. The occupants were still on holiday. He continued: "Perhaps I can get to see them on my way back. For Eli alone who perhaps is in the city I will not take even one [further] step." (Unpublished letter to the family, 31. August, 1909.) On returning to New York for the departure to Europe at the end of the month, the Bernays family were at home, and a picture postal card of Central Park was mailed to Frau Martha Freud, September 20, signed by Anna and each of her children as well as Rose Brill, Dr. Brill's wife. Eli's signature is not present.

Two significant incidents during the first four days after the arrival will now be singled out for discussion because they shed light on the relationship of Freud and Jung which, even as early as the day in Bremen, had begun to show its seamy side. The events must have depressed Freud but he appears to have suppressed (repressed?) them.

Jung's Aryan Dream

The first incident occurred on Monday, the day after the arrival. It is known to us from letters which both Freud and Jung wrote home. In the afternoon they took a walk in New York's Central Park for several hours. One aspect of their conversation is ominous.

Freud, describing how he spent that afternoon, tells about his unsuccessful attempts, first to visit a former Viennese medical friend, Dr. Lustgarten, and then the Bernays family. Both were still away on vacation. He then continued: "After that I went with Jung to Central Park—an endless landscape in the style of English parks, but with beautiful garden plots, full of children and women, and with tame squirrels which have grey tails instead of red, and act as if they were the masters of the place. Signs are posted which, besides being in English, are in German, Italian and Yiddish with Hebrew lettering. The park swarms with Jewish children, large and small, and often I thought I caught a glimpse of Martha and Hella [Bernays] who by now must be much bigger. We then took tea, which was delicious, in a small restaurant quite similar to those in the Vienna Prater [public park] and, of course, there were various couples who met there in rendezvous, while American music was playing. In the evening we were invited to Brill's and met his lovely wife—taller than he, quite American— gracious and slim. . . . " (Unpublished letter of Freud, August 31, 1909.) No mention is made of the long walk with Jung and the discussion between them. Instead, the ethnic diversity in the park, including the Yiddish signs and Jewish children, is depicted.

On the same evening as Freud did, Jung wrote to his wife, Emma. After a brief general opening, he continued: "Yesterday Freud and I spent several hours walking in Central Park and talked at length about the sociological problem of psychoanalysis. He is as clever as ever and was extremely touchy; he does not like other sorts of ideas to come up, and, I might add, he is usually right. He certainly has the most comprehensive and rigorous biological point of view one could imagine nowadays. We spoke a good deal about Jews and Aryans, and one of my dreams clearly pointed up the difference. But one can't really go very deep into anything here, because the general hustle and bustle is so overwhelming. However, those few quiet hours in the park did me good. Afterwards we went to Brill's for supper. He has a nice, uncomplicated wife (an American)." [1,2]

One is struck by Jung's description of the very long walk with Freud and the subject of their conversation. The stress on Freud's "comprehensive biological point of view" apparently means Freud's adherence to a universally applicable human biology. In that context Jung contrasts his own position concerning a notable difference between Jews and Aryans. Freud said nothing about this conversation. Instead he described the ethnic diversity observed during the walk. For that conspicuous diversity Jung came up with a racist dichotomy. The distinction was so important to him that it was the focus of one of his dreams. It is remarkable, not hitherto noticed, that the difference between Aryans and Jews was important to Jung as early as 1909.

In telling his wife about the conversation, Jung mentioned that Freud was "touchy." From the comment that Freud "has the most comprehensive and rigorous biological point of view," one gathers that, despite Freud's recognition that psychoanalysis has some Jewish cultural characteristics, he evidently did not accept a biological difference between Jews and Aryans as here stressed by Jung. It is well known that Freud later insisted, rightly or wrongly, on the biological universality of such conceptions as the Oedipus complex. He appealed to Darwin's notion of the "primal horde" to develop the theory that during early human evolution a possessive polygamous father asserted his exclusive rights to the women of the tribe against the rival sons. The sons rebelled, were expelled and thus began the practice of exogamy. This Freudian view, not explicitly published until 1912, may have entered into the conversation with Jung. Apart from theory, it is plausible that the ethnic diversity so conspicuous in Central Park brought to the fore the question of racial differences. Freud had Jewish friends like Dr. Lustgarten and his disciple Dr. Brill and relatives like the Bernays family who had sought new opportunities by emigrating to the New World. But the chief point here is that Jung generalized the difference between Jews and Aryans and considered the matter significant enough to tell his wife about it in a letter sent across the ocean.

Freud's Jewish Nightmare

The second incident above mentioned occurred on Thursday, September 2, during a visit by the group to the Psychiatric Clinic at Columbia University to which Dr. Brill was attached as a clinical assistant, a position that he occupied as a supplement to his private practice. This Clinic was located near Riverside Drive and commanded a view of the Palisades overlooking the Hudson River. In that situation Freud experienced a personal mishap involving his bladder or prostate—an accident that revealed to Jung the frailty of the master. The details are available for the first time here and derive from an interview the writer had with Jung in 1951.[3]

During several years before that date I had had the experience of teaching at Clark University in Worcester and had become interested in the 1909 visit of Freud and Jung to participate in Clark's 20th anniversary celebration. It was this interest that in part actuated my request for an interview with Jung but there were other reasons stressed in my letter: I was a former student of Jung's disciple H. A. Murray of the Harvard Psychological Clinic and had been a research associate at the State Hospital in Worcester. I wanted better to understand Jung's place in the history of psychoanalysis and his present orientation toward personality theory. At the beginning of the session Jung inquired about my background and experience, and I asked questions about his studies of word association, the origin of the concept of the complex, and his views of frustration in relation to the creative process. I then broached the topic of the visit to America in 1909. At first Jung appeared a bit reluctant but the hesitancy was brief, and he was soon rather eagerly discussing the topic. He appeared to be deriving some special satisfaction from the disclosures he was making about Freud.

He described one aspect of the American journey in detail. Shortly after the arrival in New York City, there was a visit arranged by Dr. Brill to the Columbia University Psychiatric Clinic, where Brill had studied and was now a clinical assistant. While looking at the Palisades Freud suffered a personal mishap. He accidentally urinated in his trousers and Jung helped him out of this embarrassment.[4]

It was, morever, soon evident, said Jung, that Freud

entertained a fear of similar accidents during the time of the lectures at Clark University. So Jung offered to help Freud overcome this fear if Freud would consent to some analytic intervention. Freud agreed and Jung began "the treatment." In due course Freud produced a dream the interpretation of which appeared to require some intimate personal associations. When Jung asked for these details, Freud paused, thought carefully, and then declined, declaring that he could not "risk his authority" by such disclosures. So, concluded Jung, "I lost, and this incident started the break between us."

Jung had already told Freud that the enuretic symptom concealed a conflict about an inordinate degree of ambition that was expressed regressively by an impulse to urinate—and thus attract attention to himself at all costs—despite the adult need for continence. Jung believed that Freud considered the opportunity to lecture at Clark to be a fulfillment of unconscious fantasies about greatness. But Freud denied his ambitiousness; he maintained that, in fact, he was the least ambitious of all psychoanalysts. This denial, said Jung, contributed to the enuretic symptom. [5]

Is there any direct evidence from Freud himself regarding the embarrassing mishap described by Jung? The question has a special interest not only in its own right but because, as above noted, the disturbing conversation with Jung during the long walk in Central Park was not mentioned in the letters written by Freud to his family. Was there a similar omission concerning the second incident, this time more understandable in view of the personally disturbing nature of it? A brief answer is that Freud did, indeed, omit the specifics of the incident but a fuller consideration of the evidence tends to confirm Jung's statement that there was such an episode.

This evidence is found in a fairly long unpublished letter dated September 2-3, 1909. It was included in material released to me from the Freud Archives at the Library of Congress together with Freud's Travel Diary of 1909. This letter was begun on the evening of September 2 and completed the next day. After apologizing for not being able to write for at least two days and explaining that "New York has us in its clutches," Freud outlined the plans for Saturday when the group would go by boat to Boston. He mentioned that reservations for the return journey to Europe had just

been made for September 21 on the *Kaiser Wilhelm der Grosse.*
He continued: "We have seen everything. Brill puts himself entirely at our disposal. . . . In a few weeks I shall be back home
and would not want to leave again." He mentioned the indigestion
that they have all been suffering and which has led to their taking
turns at fasting. ("Day before yesterday was the turn of Fer[enczi]
to go without food, yesterday Jung, today my turn. . . .") He then
described several excursions during the preceding two days, including Coney Island, and continued: "In addition, the museums,
parks, streets—they all make a strong impression. Also Columbia
University, where Brill studied, belongs in that category. . . . Now
I must rest for half an hour. New York makes one weary." There
are no details about the visit to Columbia University earlier that
day but his general weariness and the need for rest led to an interruption—the letter here breaks off, without signature or ending. (Did something occur at the time of the Columbia University
visit which Freud preferred not to describe?) But then, under the
date 3. September, he resumed: "Only a few more words. Today
is quite warm. It is Jung's turn to eat nothing, as we are both
well." Freud then went back to describe some of the events of
yesterday [September 2], but he said no more about Columbia
University.

As previously with the unpleasantness in Central Park, nothing
is communicated about the mishap in the environs of Columbia
University. The omission itself is not surprising, but the style—
the break after a stated need for rest, and a continuation the next
day with further details about *other* events the day before—leave
the impression that Jung's description of the incident is reliable. [6]

It is illuminating to compare Jung's account during the interview with the comparable passage in his autobiography published
ten years later (1963, p. 158). There he stated: "The trip to the
United States which began in Bremen in 1909 lasted for seven
weeks. We were together every day, and analyzed each other's
dreams. At the time I had a number of important ones, but Freud
could make nothing of them. . . . But then something happened
which proved to be a severe blow to the whole relationship. . . .
Freud had a dream—I would not think it right to air the problem
it involved. I interpreted it as best I could, but added that a great
deal more could be said about it if he would supply me with some

additional details from his private life. Freud's response to these words was a curious look—a look of utmost suspicion. Then he said, 'But I cannot risk my authority.' At that moment he lost it altogether. That sentence burned itself into my memory; and in it the end of our relationship was already foreshadowed. Freud was placing personal authority above truth."

Two points are here notable. First, the reticence that Jung displayed in his published autobiography concerning Freud's unmentionable problem was, with only a little hesitancy, overcome by him in the interview situation. In fact, he appeared rather eager to divulge this information about the problem at the Palisades. The enuretic mishap probably did occur but there is reason to question the degree to which Jung conducted specific therapy with Freud. And if, indeed, Freud was uncooperative how did it happen that the so-called therapy succeeded sufficiently to prevent a recurrence of the symptoms at Worcester less than a week later? Second, Jung's conclusion after Freud's uncooperativeness—a conclusion common to both the interview and the autobiography—seems forced and illogical. In what sense did Freud "place personal authority above truth"? The term "truth" as here employed presumably means truth in the abstract but the truth in question involved a disclosure of personal facts about Freud's life. Even if it is granted that Freud was in the role of a patient of Jung at this time, which is itself a matter of interpretation, Freud was not withholding an abstract truth. He simply declined to share a confidence. During the preceding two years, by correspondence and visits, Jung, indeed, was in the role of pupil and patient. For example, he consulted more than once with Freud about problems he was having about intimacy with his female patients. Now Jung apparently sought to reverse their roles but, with a pretense of naiveté, he concluded instead that Freud had subordinated truth to the importance of his personal authority. In fact, the conclusion that appears more consistent with the known circumstances is that, though they may have been mutually interpreting dreams during this period, Freud, even after the problem at the Palisades, never put himself in the role of a patient to be treated by Jung. A more likely interpretation is that Freud conducted some further self-analysis, including his excessive countertransference to Jung, and a favorable effect resulted.

Common Denominator

This speculation about the self-analysis is strongly supported by aspects of it disclosed by Freud in *The Interpretation of Dreams* ten years earlier. Indeed, Jung may actually have drawn upon this public source for his own interpretation of the mishap at the Palisades. The dream that Jung said arose from that mishap may have been in large part a repetition of an earlier one—the dream of Count Thun—which more than any other in Freud's book bristles with the dreamer's awareness of anti-Semitism. [7,8]

The occasion for a repetition had been established by Jung himself during the walk in Central Park when, as we have seen, he focused on the anti-Semitic dichotomy of Aryans versus Jews. Freud must have been astonished by the highlighting of this subject in a dream of Jung at this apogee of their relationship, on the threshold of the promised and prized reward at Clark University. For Jung to put the fly into the ointment right after the arrival in the New World was, to say the least, undiplomatic unless, by an effort of objectivity, one looks upon the incident as implying that Jung was here offering Freud an opportunity to analyze one of his dreams possibly derived from an unconscious complex. In this best possible light one would need to give a new construction to Jung's remark in the letter to his wife that the "hustle and bustle" in the New York environment did not lend itself to a full discussion and resolution of the question.

In this hypothetical light, let us return to the above-mentioned dream of Count Thun. It had occurred in mid-June 1898 during the 50-year Jubilee of the Coronation of the Austro-Hungarian Emperor Franz Josef. The dream and its various ramifications occupied approximately 20 pages of Freud's book—one of the two or three longest examples in the volume. As already stated, anti-Semitism and the Pan-German movement resounded through it and reflected Freud's sensibilities concerning his minority plight. In that context Freud's own "Cruel Captain" (in his prototypic role as Rat Man) played a prominent part in the cryptic cast of the dream. And now in viewing the Palisades Jung may have constituted, at least subliminally, a contemporary edition of that ambivalent figure.

Though a detailed discussion of the dream is not possible here, some of its major features need to be recalled for the understanding of the alleged analogy—the recurrence of it or of a variant on the occasion of the visit to Columbia University. It should be noted that just as the Palisades overlooking the Hudson River served as a landmark for Jung's narrative about Freud's mishap, the Count Thun dream had occurred, as Freud explained in his associations, shortly after an excursion to the Wachau. The Wachau was a scenic region along the Danube River in the environs of Vienna including points with steep banks or bluffs occupied by historic edifices. This resemblance in landscape could not have escaped the ever-vigilant Freud, particularly after the recent discussion with Jung of Aryans vis-à-vis Jews. Hence it is here assumed that the dream to which Jung referred was some variant of the Count Thun dream. [9]

The likelihood that Freud vividly recalled the dream of 1898 is strengthened by the fact that he completed the second edition of *Traumdeutung (The Interpretation of Dreams)* in November 1908, less than a year before the journey to America. As published, the edition was dated 1909. The new edition involved many revisions and extensive additions. Freud told Jung about this accomplishment and promised to send him a copy when he wrote to him on November 8, 1908. (*Freud/Jung Letters,* 1974, p. 175.)

The Count Thun dream had prominently involved an urge to urinate which, Freud stated, was a somatic stimulus for the dream. As soon as Freud awoke from the dream, he went to micturate. In his associations he described two childhood incidents of incontinence that had elicited from his father a dire prophecy as to the boy's unpromising future—a prophecy that haunted the son thereafter. In his adult achievements he felt himself to be disproving the prophecy. Here is the ambitiousness that Jung says Freud denied.

Regardless of interpretations, one must agree with Jung's own statement that already at this early stage of the American visit his relationship to Freud had begun to deteriorate. The conversation in Central Park three days before the visit to Columbia University had disclosed the depth of Jung's need to challenge Freud. In these circumstances it is less remarkable that Freud regressed to an earlier neurotic symptom (as he viewed the Palisades) than that he was able to carry on, following these experiences with Jung, and perform as successfully as he obviously did at Worcester with Stanley

Hall and, later, with Dr. J. J. Putnam in Keene Valley. One surmises that he thus succeeded by continuing his self-analysis, rather than through any therapy administered by Jung. But the beginning of the end of his father-son (master-successor) relationship with Jung had indeed begun. The Rubicon—call it Hudson, call it Danube—had been crossed.

Synchronicity in Vienna

To grasp the ultimate significance of the two episodes above recounted requires a recognition of Jung's encounter with the Nazis in the 1930s, by now a well-known part of the Jung legend. What is unknown, or at least unrecognized, is the early origin of Jung's Aryan bias as disclosed here. While it would be inappropriate to consider at length Jung's later role in the history of the Third Reich, a brief examination is essential for appreciating the 1909 predisposition.

One may begin with Thomas Campbell's line, "Coming events cast their shadows before," and in those terms ask what was burgeoning in Vienna while Freud and Jung were touring New York. For seeds were, indeed, being planted that would, in the next generation, bear historic but blighted fruit. An unknown youth of 20 resided in Vienna as an aspiring but unsuccessful student of art who earned his meager living by painting post cards. A burdensome feature of his life in that period (1907-1913) was his aversion to military conscription, an evasion which he accomplished by repeated changes of residence. When in 1913 he moved to Munich, Germany, it was as a final effort to avoid service in his native Austria.

There was, however, a more abiding aspect of Hitler's experience in Vienna. In part it arose from his lack of success as an artist. He had ample leisure, as he would later explain, and thus could devote himself assiduously to self-education. [10] He read voraciously. As his friend and roommate August Kubizek observed: "Books were his whole world." [11] With the rest of his free time he explored the city in all directions. Once he took his friend to visit a red-light district which they viewed from the street where at open house windows scantily dressed girls were on display. Another time they visited a Jewish synagogue where a wedding was in progress.

Vienna was officially anti-Semitic. The mayor, Karl Lueger, was the leader of the anti-Semitic Christian Socialist Party. He occupied this position from 1897 to 1910, the year he died. The city was fatefully well qualified for Hitler's future calling. In this ambience he progressively and decisively confirmed his hatred of Jews. He saw at first hand, he later recalled, the prostitution and white slave traffic promoted by Jews as part of their natural avarice and usury. [12] Having achieved a full appreciation of the "Jewish evil," he returned to his room one day in 1908 to announce to Kubizek that he had reached a crucial moment of his life: "Today I joined the Anti-Semitic Union." [13] From his friend's reminiscences and Hitler's own autobiography, it is clear that it was in Vienna during the early part of the period 1907-1913, including, of course, 1909, that Hitler crystalized his rabid anti-Semitism. And largely from this bias there sprang, a generation later, some of the most heinous conduct recorded in human history: the genocide of six million Jews and numerous other "undesirables" considered unfit even for the slave labor employed in the war effort.

Did Hitler read Freud during 1907-1913 while he was so conveniently living in the city of psychoanalysis? The question has not previously been raised though several books in addition to that by Kubizek have been devoted wholly or partly to Hitler's Vienna years. [14] We know that this was a period of extensive reading and self-education. Under the circumstances during the period when Freud published several of his most popular and influential books, could Hitler have avoided hearing about Freud, particularly after Freud gained an international reputation through his invitation to Clark University and his participation there? The evidence, though not conclusive, favors this hypothesis.

In 1904 the popular *Psychopathology of Everyday Life* appeared; in 1905, the *Three Essays on the Theory of Sex,* and, in the same year, *Jokes and the Unconscious.* In 1910 the five introductory lectures on psychoanalysis (which Freud had delivered at Clark University in 1909) were published. Potentially most significant for Hitler's reading was Freud's book on Leonardo da Vinci which appeared in May 1910. As a painter Hitler would have had special sensitivity for this book. In it Freud for the first time applied the psychoanalytic method to biography. He extravagantly depended on one of Leonardo's childhood reminiscences which he interpreted as reflecting a mother fixation with implications for

Leonardo's alleged homosexuality and oral sexuality. This reading, which affronted most of Freud's intellectual contemporaries, would particularly have offended the unstable Hitler who, by all accounts, was a sexually confused neurotic. And even if Hitler did not read the book itself, he very probably knew about it from fellow artists. In either case, he would have had only one possible reaction: to recoil in disgust. Here was a fertile source for his rabid anti-Semitism. For by such utterances from a prominent Viennese Jewish medical psychologist the pure Germanic soul would, in Hitler's eyes, have been debased in just that pernicious manner which he later ascribed to all Jewish influence. [15]

From all these volumes, which respectable Vienna at that time generally scorned, Hitler could readily have acquired a significant part of his anti-Semitism. If so, not only did he learn in Vienna about the evil commercial practices of Jews but he became acquainted with the "Jewish psychology," as Jung later called Freud's message, that would have horrified him.

There is at this point something of an enigma that needs to be addressed. Why is neither Freud nor psychoanalysis ever mentioned as such in *Mein Kampf* if this source played an important part in the formation of Hitler's philosophy? The key may lie in another source—Karl Marx and the communist movement. It was, again, in Vienna that Hitler painfully learned about it under the label "Social Democracy," and he fanatically repudiated it throughout his subsequent career quite openly. At least twice in *Mein Kampf* he wrote "the Jew, Karl Marx" (pp. 382, 391) for Marx and Marxism would be constantly associated in his book with Jewishness—a Jewish international movement intended to conquer the world. It is plain that in Hitler's rabid crusade two blended evils had to be overcome: the Jews, hence anti-Semitism, and Marxist communism, a Jewish cause. The common denominator was Jewishness. But while anti-Marxism as a social and political cause could and, indeed, had to be treated as public policy, which openly linked Karl Marx as a Jew with communism, Hitler's anti-Semitism, which also crystalized in Vienna, derived, in part, more privately from Freud's psychoanalysis. But this impact would have been too intimate to be openly avowed.

If, as Robert Waite has argued in *The Psychopathic God* (1977), Hitler was a prime example of Freud's psychopathology— intense mother fixation, ambivalent father complex (Oedipal), castration anxiety complicated by monorchism—his reading of Freud during the "saddest period of my life" (ibid., p. 211) may have reached unbearably to the quick of his unconscious idioverse and so may have undergone automatic repression. If this was, in fact, the manner in which Hitler assimilated Freud, a compensatory counterthrust against Freud as a Jewish thinker could have aroused anti-Semitism as "the return of the repressed" (a reaction formation). Thus the pan-Germanism Hitler was absorbing from the theories of Schönerer and the practices of Lueger would, in the form of anti-Marxism, have merged with the more private impact of Freud's psychoanalysis in a compound of fanatical anti-Semitism. The National Socialism Hitler would later aggressively espouse in Munich in 1919 would thus have been a blend of an open political element and a private, unacknowledged one. If this reconstruction is valid, "the Jew, Karl Marx" would, in part, have done duty for Freud, the Jewish Faust, who had tried to steal Adolf's Germanic soul by a too intimate awareness of the fire consuming it in the secret depths. Freud's name would then have been automatically expunged by some apotropaic means. [16]

If, indeed, Hitler did read Freud in the period 1907-1913, there was a remarkable synchronicity in Vienna because in precisely those years C. G. Jung was becoming increasingly entranced with Freud's theories and had been chosen by Freud as his successor and "crown prince." The parallel is there despite the fact that Hitler detested what he observed while Jung for the nonce was enraptured; but in both cases the result by 1913 was a rejection of things Jewish. When this negative result reached its culmination Jung's reaction was so intense that, after the official break a year or so later, he experienced a psychological collapse. This was largely induced by Freud's sardonic repudiation of him and his Zurich associates in the essay on the history of the psychoanalytic movement published in 1914. As part of his recovery, Jung developed his theory of "analytical psychology" which not only repudiated Freud's materialistic sexual theory but included the seeds of a racial orientation. In particular, he contrasted the Aryan with the Jewish outlook. This point, to be developed shortly, is mentioned here only to signal why Jung's psychology, in contrast with Freud's, was so congenial to Nazi psychiatrists like Matthias M. Göring, cousin of the highly placed political leader Hermann Göring. This fitness of Jung's ideas to the Nazi orientation and Jung's connection with the Nazi regime are concisely expounded and documented in the book by Cocks, *Psychotherapy in the Third Reich.* [17]

A second synchronicity occurred on this very basis in Berlin when on May 10, 1933 thousands of books by Jewish authors, including Sigmund Freud, were burned by Hitler's order in the streets of the city. And a month later—in June 1933—Jung was named President of the International Medical Society for Psychotherapy, previously known as the German Society for Psychotherapy. Its president, Ernst Kretschmer, had resigned and Jung was drafted for the post. Jung also became chief editor of the Society's journal, the *Zentralblatt für Psychotherapie und ihre Grenzgebiete,* and in 1936 Matthias M. Göring was appointed coeditor with Jung. Not until 1940 did Jung totally sever his Nazi connection. But in the early days of the affiliation Jung published several papers that clearly identified him with the Nazi cause although he insisted later that he had been interested only in the preservation of professional psychiatry and psychotherapy and the protection of Jewish practitioners.

The most revealing evidence that, despite these protestations, Jung identified with the Nazi cause in 1933-1934 is found in a direct comparison of what he wrote in his first important paper after assuming the editorship of the *Zentralblatt* and what Hitler had written in contrasting Jews and Aryans in *Mein Kampf.* It must be understood that though Hitler had published his book in 1925-1927, it was not widely read until he came into power. As the *Oxford Companion to German Literature* succinctly states: "After 1933 this work, which has justifiably been called the Bible of National Socialism, was distributed in enormous quantities; up to 1940 the total . . . reached 5,000,000." [18] One should add that it was required of every Nazi partisan to read and embrace the principles enunciated by the Führer in that book. That Jung conformed to this expectation is demonstrable.

In the above-mentioned article, "The state of psychotherapy today," published early in 1934, Jung wrote: "Freud and Adler have beheld very clearly the shadow that accompanies us all. . . . As a member of a race with a three-thousand-year-old civilization, the Jew, like the cultured Chinese, has a wider area of psychological consciousness than we. Consequently it is *in general* less dangerous for the Jew to put a negative value on his unconscious. The 'Aryan' unconscious, on the other hand, contains explosive forces and seeds of a future yet to be born, and these may not be devalued as nursery romanticism without psychic danger. The still youthful German peoples are fully capable of creating new cultural forms that still lie dormant in the darkness of the unconscious of every individual—seeds bursting with energy and capable of mighty expansion. The Jew, who is something of a nomad, has never yet created a cultural form of his own and as far as we can see never will, since all his instincts and talents require a more or less civilized nation to act as host for their development. . . . In my opinion it has been a grave error in medical psychology up till now to apply Jewish categories—which are not even binding on all Jews—indiscriminately to Germanic and Slavic Christendom. Because of this [error], the most precious secret of the Germanic peoples—their creative and intuitive depth of soul—has been explained as a morass of banal infantilism, while my own warning voice has for decades been suspected of anti-Semitism. This suspicion emanated from Freud. He did not understand the Germanic psyche any more than did his Germanic followers. Has the formidable phenomenon of National Socialism, on which the whole world gazes with astonished eyes, taught them better?" [19]

If one now turns to Hitler's *Mein Kampf,* one reads: ". . . the Jewish people, despite all apparent intellectual qualities, is without any true culture, and especially without any culture of its own. . . . the Jew possesses no culture-creating force of any sort, since the idealism, without which there is no true higher development of man, is not present in him and never was present. . . . Since the Jew never possessed a state with definite territorial limits and there-fore never called a culture his own, the conception arose that this was a people which should be reckoned among the ranks of the *nomads.* This is a fallacy as great as it is dangerous. The nomad does possess a definitely limited living space, only he does not cultivate it like a sedentary peasant, but lives from the yield of his herds with which he wanders about in his territory. . . . Probably the Aryan was also first a nomad settling in the course of time, but for that very reason he was never a Jew! No, the Jew is no nomad; for the nomad had also a definite attitude toward the concept of work which could serve as a basis for his later development in so far as the necessary intellectual premises were present. . . . He is and remains the typical parasite, a sponger who like a noxious bacillus keeps spreading as soon as a favorable medium invites him. And the effect of his existence is also like that of spongers: wherever he appears, the host people dies after a shorter or longer period." [20]

The similarity between Jung's and Hitler's characterizations of Jewish culture is unmistakable. The lack of a Jewish potential for new cultural creativity is stressed in both and contrasted with the Aryan potential. The suspicion that Jung was influenced by Hitler rises almost to a certainty when one observes that in both the Jew is compared to the *nomad*. While Hitler rejected the comparison and instead flatly denounces the Jew as a parasite, Jung was more cautious, but he agreed with Hitler that the Jew has no autonomous culture.

For Jung, Freud's psychology, being Jewish, was, therefore, not applicable to the "Aryan soul." To meet that need a different— a more spiritual ideology—was required. And Jung's theory satisfies this requirement. For basic to the distinction was Jung's postulate that fundamental racial differences exist which require different psychological conceptualizations. Nevertheless, Jung soon withdrew from his commitment. The details of that development are beyond the scope of the present discussion but its essence and end are patent in the essay he published in 1945 under the title "After the catastrophe." There he frantically denounced National Socialism and diagnosed Hitler as suffering from *pseudologia phantastica,* an extreme form of hysteria, and then extended the diagnosis to the German people as a whole who, he believed, were infected by their frenzied leader. [21]

Paul Stern's synopsis of Jung's relation to Nazism is cogent: "His antisemitic sounding statements can in turn be attributed largely to the floods of resentment that periodically inundated him—the labile and constricted neurotic—and then overshot their intended target. In the present context this target was undoubtedly Freud, the spiritual father he loved and hated. When his smoldering animosity against Freud erupted, from the very depths of his personality, it swept like lava over anything in its path. Blinded by the intensity of his personal passion, Jung may have failed to realize fully to what extent his denunciations of 'Jewish' psychoanalysis played into the hands of men whose goals were far more ambitious—and bloodier—than the defeat of Freudian psychology's claims to validity." [22]

The conclusion seems warranted that Jung was not anti-Semitic in the ordinary negative sense (his numerous loyal Jewish disciples, notably Aniela Jaffé, [23] attest to this fact); but he did have a longstanding pro-Aryan bias. Moreover, his overweening ambition made him an easy prey to the romantic myth of Aryan superiority when in the 1930s he was still smarting under Freud's utter rejection of him. Hence, the selective nature of Jung's memories, his tendentious dreams, and the limited scientific validity of the reflections on life he exhibited in his autobiography.

****

During a busy week the group from Europe made various pleasant excursions to museums, theaters and special parts of the city such as Chinatown and the Jewish ghetto. Ernest Jones, just returned from Europe, joined them on Saturday, September 4. The entire company, now including Freud, Jung, Ferenczi, Brill and Jones, left New York on Saturday by night-boat to Fall River, Massachusetts. On Sunday they travelled by rail via Boston to their destination, Worcester.

President G. Stanley Hall's home in Worcester, where Freud and Jung were house guests during the Clark Conference

Chapter V

At the Home of the Host

Upon arrival in Worcester the three weary visitors registered at the Stanish Hotel and rested for several hours. At six in the evening they visited G. Stanley Hall at his home for dinner. After a very pleasant evening they returned to the Hotel to spend the night. The next morning Freud and Jung moved to the Halls', where they remained as house guests for the duration of the Conference.

Jung wrote three letters to his wife from Worcester.[1] In the first of these, composed "at Professor Stanley Hall's" dated Monday, September 6, the first day of the Conference, he described his host and hostess and their quaint home as follows: "He is a refined, distinguished old gentleman close on seventy who received us with the kindest hospitality. He has a plump, jolly, good-natured, and extremely ugly wife who, however, serves wonderful food. She promptly took over Freud and me as her "boys" and plied us with delicious nourishment and noble wine, so that we began visibly to recover. . . . The house is furnished in an incredibly amusing fashion, everything roomy and comfortable. There is a splendid studio filled with thousands of books, and boxes of cigars everywhere. Two pitch-black Negroes in dinner jackets, the extreme of grotesque solemnity, perform as servants. Carpets everywhere, all the doors open, even the bathroom door and the front door; people going in and out all over the place; all the windows extend down to the floor. The house is surrounded by an English lawn, no garden fence." He described the University as "richly endowed . . . but distinguished and [it] has a real though plain elegance." After the hectic week in New York with the digestive problems Freud and Jung now found themselves refreshed and revived. Freud's lectures were to begin the next day (Tuesday) and Jung's, two days later.

William James Arrives

The next important house guest was Hall's old friend William James. When Hall learned, probably from Dr. J. J. Putnam, with whom James was staying at Cotuit from September 1 to 4 before Putnam himself went to Worcester, that James was planning to attend some of the sessions, Hall on September 7 wrote and invited James to be his guest. He tempted James by mentioning that he would thus "meet Freud and Jung who are with us." When James replied in a letter the next day he accepted Hall's invitation and stated that he would arrive Thursday on the 5:55 P.M. train, drive directly to Hall's house and stay overnight, but would have to return Friday evening since he needed to go to his summer home in New Hampshire on Saturday. [2]

From letters of William James to his wife Alice who was at their summer place while he was at the Putnam's in Cotuit, we learn that in the week previous to the Clark Conference James had planned to attend the last four days (Wednesday through Saturday). But when he wrote her on Wednesday he indicated that he planned "to spend Thursday night with Stanley Hall and the German guests." One reason for his change in plans was the death of Professor Child's wife, whose funeral he wished to attend. [3]

He now mentioned to Alice that he planned to be in Worcester from Thursday evening for one day: "Probably I shall have got all that I require of it by Friday P.M." So he planned to be at Chocorua by Saturday afternoon. What had occurred to dampen his interest and lead him to omit Saturday, as well as the earlier part of the week, at the Conference is not clear. That he had made his plans for the longer attendance while he was staying with Dr. Putnam at Cotuit may have made some of the difference; as we know from later events, Dr. Putnam had a very serious interest in psychoanalysis.

The arrival of James at Hall's was dramatically described by Jung in a letter recalling the event 40 years later. [4] As Jung states, it was anticipated that James would be bringing with him "papers concerning Mrs. Piper" (the medium with whom James had been working for many years in his psychical research), but before delivering these to Dr. Hall James played a little trick on his host. James had put his hand into a breast pocket to produce the expected papers which, however, turned out to be a wad of dollar bills. With a profuse apology he then put his hand into his other pocket and produced the "real papers." Jung explained the hoax by mentioning that Hall had a reputation for cultivating the material welfare of Clark University, of which he was President. What Jung failed to note was Hall's skepticism about the validity of any medium's communication with spirits. James, knowing it well, may have been parrying in advance Hall's probable response to the report he was delivering: Hall did not believe in the spirit world but he greatly respected the world of Mammon!

We know from other information that what James brought to Hall was the just-published article on Mrs. Piper's Hodgson-control—a report on the series of seances in which she was controlled by the deceased former secretary of the American Society for Psychical Research, who died suddenly, at an early age, on December 20, 1905. James had the task of digesting and summarizing the numerous sessions with various sitters in which Hodgson communicated with the survivors via his former friend, the professional medium Mrs. Leonore Piper. This report had appeared in the June 1909 *Proceedings of the American Society for Psychical Research* so James was able to bring a reprint to his host, the skeptical Stanley Hall. [5]

But for Jung in the brief description in his letter concerning the delivery of the "papers" about Mrs. Piper, she was described as an adept in "extrasensory perception"; so he wrote of interesting discussions that he had with William James on two evenings at Hall's home (presumably Thursday and Friday) concerning "parapsychology."

Before proceeding further it is important to cast a backward glance at the long years of ambivalent friendship that had existed between the two great pioneers of early American psychology—William James and G. Stanley Hall—in their quite diverse views of psychology as science. That relationship had begun in 1875 at Harvard University and had weathered the vicissitudes of experimental psychology in relation to psychical research for the following 34 years. Only if we know at least in essence what had transpired in that checkered relationship can we hope to understand the meaning of this final encounter at Hall's home on September 9-10, 1909. Strangely, the occasion was provided by the visit of Freud and Jung, which for 24 hours brought about a face-to-face encounter under the improbable auspices of psychoanalysis and its revolutionary approach to the psychology of sex.

Hall, James and Psychical Research

The conflict between James and Hall as to the role of psychical research in psychology constituted a strain between them that, for the most part, did not obtrude itself to disturb the friendship that had begun in 1875 when Hall studied at Harvard and eventually completed a Ph.D. dissertation with James as the nominal sponsor in 1878. His dissertation research was published in *Mind* under the title "The Muscular Perception of Space" in that same year.[6] Already it is evident that while Hall was pursuing physiological psychology at the Medical School, James was nurturing his interest in spiritualism, as shown by a review of *The Unseen Universe* in *The Nation* in 1875. (The earliest published item by James on spiritualism is a review of *Planchette* by Sargent that appeared in 1869.) To what extent these two pioneers discussed the topic of spiritualism as a fit subject for scientific investigation during the long walks they are supposed to have taken in 1875-1876 and the vacation they spent in the Adirondacks in 1877 appears not to be known. But Hall's clear primary interest in experimental psychology, like that which he pursued with Bowditch, was evident. Even when he left his professorship at Antioch late in 1876 he had already become interested in Wundt's *Grundzüge der physiologischen Psychologie,* first published in 1874, and resolved to go for a second time to Germany and enter Wundt's laboratory. His work with Bowditch at Harvard and his Ph.D. in 1878 constituted a kind of unplanned interlude but did not blunt his earlier purpose. He went to Germany, first to Berlin, then to Leipzig where Wundt in 1879 opened the first scientific laboratory of modern psychology. By the delay Hall had unintentionally brought it about that he was both student and subject in experiments conducted in this first laboratory. These experiences he brought back with him to America when he returned in 1880. As Wundt recalled in 1913, in his 82nd year: "Stanley Hall was the first to introduce experimental psychology into America, the first to recognize its significance for pedagogy. That in the year of its foundation he was one of the co-workers in the Psychological Institute of Leipzig remains one of the most precious memories."[7]

It is an interesting coincidence that in 1879, the very year of the founding of Wundt's Psychological Institute, the founder went on record decisively opposing spiritualism as a proper subject for scientific investigation. An open letter defending this thesis appeared in *The Popular Science Monthly.* The occasion was the appearance of the American spiritualist performer Henry Slade in Leipzig and elsewhere in Europe before popular audiences and select scientific groups, some of the latter of which had become convinced of the genuineness of his allegedly supernatural feats. What particularly disturbed Wundt, as he indicates at the end of his letter, was that such performances have a harmful influence on academic youth who would thus become diverted from a serious interest in science by spectacular performances purporting to emanate from supernatural forces with no serious scientific standing. [8]

Hall brought his well-established interests and newly acquired skills in experimental psychology to an appointment at Johns Hopkins University in Baltimore, where in 1883 he established the first systematic research laboratory in the United States. There have been historically oriented and somewhat controversial papers as to whom credit should be given for the first laboratory of experimental psychology in America—a topic that there is no intention of reviewing here—but it seems indisputably clear that to Hall must go the credit for creating the first systematic research and teaching laboratory, although James would find it hard to accept this fact, as will presently be shown. It will also there be shown that there may have been more than strictly historical grounds on the specific points that actuated James in his protest.

To his skills in experimental psychology on Wundt's model Hall added an innovative recognition of the significance of experimental psychology to pedagogy. It was probably this combination of his expertise in experimental psychology and his expressed intent to apply this new scientific knowledge to the field of education that led to his appointment as President at the newly-founded Clark University in Worcester in 1888. After devoting much of the first year of his presidency, with full salary, to visits to foreign universities selected for their excellence in educational methods, he returned to Worcester for the opening of Clark in October 1899. Among the five departments established at this phase of the University, psychology loomed large and included pedagogy as a new field of instruction and research.

A glance at the development of James's interests in the years after Hall left Harvard to study in Europe and then to teach at Johns Hopkins in Baltimore shows an unmistakable difference in their interests and their conceptions of psychology as a scientific field. During the decade 1880-1890 James gradually accumulated the chapters of his later classic *Principles of Psychology*. Beginning around 1885, at which time he met the medium Mrs. Leonore Piper, his interest in spiritualism was transformed into systematic pursuit of psychical research as a field of scientific investigation. In 1884 the American branch of the British Society for Psychical Research was established with headquarters in Boston. Early in 1887 Richard Hodgson came from England to the U.S.A. to become secretary of the American organization and served as the leader of its research program. Much of this work, in collaboration with William James, was done by conducting seances with the trance medium Leonore Piper.

Also relevant here are the facts of William James's own experiences of death in the family during the first half of the 1880s. Both his mother and his father died in the same year, 1882, and, in July 1885, James's son Herman died before his second birthday. It was shortly after this last event that William James first visited Mrs. Piper, in the fall of 1885. He knew about her because his mother-in-law Mrs. Gibbens had visited her shortly before and had been impressed by her knowledge of Gibbens family affairs, especially Christian names of the members. To what extent the death of his parents three years earlier influenced his interest is a matter of surmise, but there is less doubt that the death of his son had a direct influence. It figured in one of the communications, allegedly involving the spirit of Herman, which Mrs. Piper conveyed to him, in typical mediumistic disguise, as from "Herrin." James stated: "A child Herman (whom we had lost the previous year) had his name spelled out as Herrin." [9] What is signified that James displaced the date of the death by a year is open to interpretation: it may have sprung from a defensive attempt to distance his visit to the medium from the poignant event that probably actuated it. It is also revealing that in this same report of 1890 he mentioned "a hearty message of thanks from my father" for having "published the book." He explained that he had, indeed, published *The Literary Remains* of his father [in 1885, the year in which he met Mrs. Piper], but he was unable to elicit the title from the medium. He seemed not to have been much impressed by the message, perhaps because it concerned public information that Mrs. Piper could have learned incidentally or casually obtained from one of the proud family members, e.g., Mrs. William James or Mrs. Gibbens, William's mother-in-law, both of whom were friends of Mrs. Piper. [10]

In any event, James was now embarked on his career as an acknowledged leader in psychical research. That his two-volume *Principles of Psychology* appeared in 1890, the same year as the report describing the achievements of Mrs. Piper, and that the *Principles* concentrated on the nature of consciousness, of the self (which included the condition of mediumship), and even the concept of the soul, makes it evident that the orientation of psychical research had, during the preceding decade, established itself firmly in James's approach to psychology. His quest for knowledge would soon include a frank avowal of interest in matters of religion and philosophy. Hence in 1902 he published *Varieties of Religious Experience,* and it was as a philosopher that his final major works appeared in the years 1907-1909 before his death in 1910. [11]

Mrs. Piper, The Medium: Hall vs. James

In the meantime the work of the American Society for Psychical Research, under Dr. Hodgson's guidance since 1887, had been progressing with Mrs. Piper as the chief subject of investigation. William James's interest since his first encounter with her in the fall of 1885 had continued under the auspices of the Society and his friendship with Hodgson. Even a summary of these activities is unnecessary here, but the later years of Hodgson's career are of special interest in the present context. Hodgson was a bachelor and a scholar who lived on Beacon Hill in Boston where the headquarters of the Society were located. He had time to assist in the research of Dr. Morton Prince, who was interested in both psychical research and, more directly, in hysteria as an expression of dissociation. Prince followed the views of Pierre Janet who emphasized structure rather than dynamics (in the sense of sex and aggression), though conflict was, of course, involved both in his theories and that of the rising psychoanalytic school under Sigmund Freud. In 1898 an opportunity arose for Prince to study intensively the case of a young lady who later appeared in his writings as Miss

Beauchamp and about whom he published an entire book at the end of 1905. [12] In this work Dr. Hodgson, whom the patient called "Dicky" and who is not otherwise identified in the book as Dr. Hodgson, assisted Dr. Prince by attending the patient as the need arose when Prince was absent from the city. The appearance of Prince's book was therefore an important occasion both for the author and for Richard Hodgson, and it came as a considerable shock that almost simultaneously with the publication of the volume in December 1905 Hodgson died suddenly and prematurely from a massive heart attack. But for psychical research this disaster also provided an opportunity: Mrs. Piper began being visited subconsciously by her former friend and colleague Dr. Hodgson. It therefore soon was resolved by the Psychical Research Society, and with the active concurrence of William James, to conduct sittings with Mrs. Piper as trance medium, with Hodgson as the control who communicated with the sitters through her. This investigation was continued intensively for over three years, with a voluminous record of the sessions in some of which William James himself sat. And it was to him that the duty of digesting and summarizing was assigned. He performed the task with qualms about the enormity of it but succeeded in producing the desired report for publication in June 1909. As previously noted, it was this report that James handed to Hall at the beginning of the visit on Thursday, September 9, 1909. What has not previously been remarked and must now claim our attention is the study of Mrs. Piper by Hall, assisted by Amy Tanner, in the spring of 1909, almost simultaneously with the publication of James's report on this medium as a vehicle (or control) for Hodgson. [13]

A prelude to Hall's work with Mrs. Piper was a popular article he published in *Appleton's Magazine,* December, 1908, under the title, "Spooks and Telepathy." [14] In the *Appleton* essay, Hall complained that he had unsuccessfully attempted for years to get permission to study Mrs. Piper; presumably he had not yet obtained that permission at the time of writing this article, but the complaint also made it clear that the author was interested in verifying certain serious doubts about the validity of her mediumship. He maintained that findings from such sittings were usually received uncritically by investigators who were ill equipped to detect the devices regularly employed by professional magicians. He, however, was familiar with these devices. For the past decade he had purchased a series of conjurers' tricks that he then mastered by careful practice. He commented on an encounter he had had with a dedicated and intelligent spiritualist to whom he attempted to explain a device for which he had paid five dollars and by means of which he could produce a spirit message written between two sealed slates. He demonstrated the trick and explained it in detail only to be told that he had performed the feat not by the trick method, but by the intervention of spirits in which he himself did not believe. Hall continued: "He had the invincible 'will to believe,' and so believe he would. Very likely he got more out of his faith than I out of my doubt. And so, if pragmatism is true, he was right and I wrong" (p. 678). The allusion to James's doctrines is unmistakable.

This was his verdict: "Spiritism in its cruder forms is the very sewage of all the superstition of ages, and it is the common enemy of true science and true religion. Culture of every kind began in the denial of its claims. To clear up its dense jungles and to drain its fetid morasses is one of the chief endeavors of science" (p. 679).

Hall concluded with a practical challenge: "I have now a modest fund at my disposal and a committee, and we will welcome and reward anyone who will come to us and demonstrate either spirits or telepathy. But they must conform to our conditions and not impose their own . . ." (p. 683).

With the attitudes and presuppositions set forth in this article, it is indeed surprising that Mr. Dorr, Mrs. Piper's manager at this time (as the successor of Dr. Hodgson) would agree to allow her to be investigated by Hall. Whatever the reasons (which included Mrs. Piper's fee of $20 per seance—a fact noted in the Tanner/ Hall book), six sessions were scheduled for the investigation in early 1909 (before the Clark celebration). These and other studies by Amy Tanner (and Dr. Hall) were reported in the book *Studies in Spiritism.* In a sense this investigation was a continuation of the previous three-year series of the Piper-Hodgson control, the report of which James brought to Hall on September 9, even though the results of Tanner's work would not be published until the next year. The point is significant in its bearing on the time of James's visit and on the role of psychical research in the long, somewhat troubled James-Hall relation.

The book opens with a 20-page Introduction by Hall at the start of which he recounts his own history with respect to his observation and participation in mediumistic phenomena. The history is impressive. It had begun in his boyhood which, one recalls, co-incided with the rise of spiritism in America following the myste-rious feats of the three Fox sisters in 1848. Hall, born in 1844, as an impressionable adolescent "became familiar with table-tipping and levitation, slate-writing, inspirational speaking and all the phe-nomena of seances" which could be readily observed at the resort of Lake Pleasant near his birthplace in Ashfield, Massachusetts, where camp meetings were held every summer by a spiritualist sect (p. xv). As a mature student in Germany he made the acquaintance in Leipzig of a trio of famous scientists—Professor Theodor Fechner, who, as a panpsychist, held that both "plants and planets were besouled"; E. H. Weber, famous physiologist, and J. C. F. Zöllner, the astronomer, all of whom had become converts to spiritism. At Johns Hopkins University in Baltimore, in the 1880s, Hall had witnessed a wave of interest in spiritism. The English Psychical Research Society was founded in 1882, and William James, in 1884, after a visit to Europe, initiated the organization of the American branch. In his *American Journal of Psychology,* Hall reviewed at length the first 15 years of the Proceedings of the English Society. He became a member of the Council of the American branch when it started so that, as he states, he "passed through every stage from pretty complete boyish credulity to no less preponderating adult disbelief. . . . I have long felt a strange combination of aversion from and attraction to all the works and ways of believers" (p. xvi). He knew that something serious and useful could be learned from a careful study of spiritistic phenomena. Hence he undertook, with Amy Tanner, the inves-tigation of Mrs. Piper's trances when finally his application was successful.

As one peruses *Studies in Spiritism,* one finds that Tanner and Hall had used the "Jung-Freud tests" (the method of word asso-ciation) as an important tool in their methodology. [14a] In partic-ular, this method was employed to determine to what extent the alleged control was truly different from the primary personality of the medium. An Appendix reproduces the word lists, the re-sponses, and reaction times in detail. A digest of the results casts doubt on the independence of the control as a separate personality. There is also an interesting discussion of the 19 words with possible sex reference. While the sexual references in the normal and the trance conditions were nearly identical, in both states Mrs. Piper revealed conflict in this area. But the conflict was more evident in the normal state than in the trance.

Incidentally, the inclusion of the Jung-Freud word-association method in early 1909 reveals Hall's acquaintance with Jung's earlier use of it, mainly to validate Freud's theories. The choice of Jung to occupy the place vacated by Meumann in the Conference program is thus easier to appreciate, though this contribution may still be questioned as a sufficient basis.

One finds a large part of Chapter XVII, "The Medium in the Bud," devoted to the case of a young girl who claimed to have powers of spirit communication and whom Hall intended for his colleagues from Europe to observe. It bespeaks Hall's special regard for Freud that Freud's diagnostic comment is mentioned in this early account of the case; and more significant, perhaps, is the stress on the girl's "repressed desire" for a man to whom she was sexually attracted and wished to impress by her special powers. [15]

The major portion of the book, devoted to the investigation of Mrs. Piper, is notable for its negative findings. This result is in marked contrast to James's appraisal of her accomplishments. In the Preface by Amy Tanner she confesses that her former bias to believe in telepathy and spirit communication was completely refuted by the outcome of this work. Alluding to James's report on the Piper-Hodgson control, she explicitly names Professor James and quotes his figure of the "marsh of feebleness" surrounding Mrs. Piper's veridicality. She then asserts that it is time for this negative side to be shown the public. The limited "stream of veridicality," stressed by James, has, she states, "undermined science for him" (p. vii).

From the standpoint of spiritism the chief conclusion arrived at by Tanner and Hall was that even the genuineness of the alleged trances of Mrs. Piper was questionable and the messages she communicated could not be shown as originating from deceased persons. This outcome was, of course, no surprise to Hall, and committed believers repudiated it as a product of bias. Future writers on psychic research either ignored the Tanner/Hall book or made a passing reference to its unreliability. [16]

Perhaps the most unique feature of the book as regards Mrs. Piper is the frank discussion of her gynecological history in relation to her accomplishments as a medium (Chap. III). We learn that her special gifts appeared during a session with a blind medium named Dr. Cocke whom she first consulted in 1884 at the persuasion of her father-in-law, a Spiritualist. She went for advice about an ovarian tumor that had developed apparently as a result of an accident nine years earlier. In the meantime she had married and had had a child. At the second or third consultation she fell into a trance and appeared to be in communication with spirits similar to Dr. Cocke's own alleged spirit communications. A year or so later Mrs. Piper had a second child. Then between 1893 and 1895 she underwent several gynecological operations for the removal of diseased Fallopian tubes and ovaries, and a year later surgery was performed to correct a hernia. Her gifts as a medium seemed to coincide with her gynecological anamnesis. As she is approaching the climacteric, she is less successful. This history is later reviewed in an attempt to develop a theory of Mrs. Piper's mediumship (Chap. XIX, p. 301f.). [17]

Both Dr. Hall in his Introduction (p. xxxi) and Dr. Tanner in the text (p. 301f.) express the view that Mrs. Piper's mediumship represented a case of secondary personality, the manifestations of which were mystically interpreted by a "will to believe." Dr. Tanner directly compares the secondary personality to Prince's case of Sally Beauchamp. [18] The splitting of the personality is traced to some psychological shock (cf. the views of both Freud and Janet on the origin of hysteria). Tanner and Hall accept Freud's emphasis on sexual conflict in the neurotic. It is only when the manifestations of mediumistic trance are wishfully construed that they appear to be supernormal—as telepathy, clairvoyance or spirit communication.

This interpretation by the authors is a prelude to the now familiar derogatory conclusion which Hall strongly restated at the end of his Introduction: "Spiritism is the ruck and muck of modern culture, the common enemy of true science and of true religion, and to drain its dismal and miasmatic marshes is the great work of modern culture. The passion to know whether if a man dies he shall live again . . . will never find satisfaction or solution in this wise. But . . . science is now advancing into this domain more rapidly than ever before, and . . . the last few years have seen more progress than the century that preceded. The mysteries of our psychic being are bound ere long to be cleared up. Every one of these ghostly phenomena will be brought under the domain of law." [19]

It is poignant and somewhat ironic that Hall's Introduction with its foregoing conclusion was signed and dated at Clark University, Worcester, Mass., July 10, slightly over a month before William James died at his country home in New Hampshire on August 26.

Hall and Experimental Psychology

While James was devoting himself to this series of activities with psychical research as an essential ingredient, Hall had steadily moved forward in his dedication to experimental psychology. It is impressive that, while Hall had studied at the Union Theological Seminary in New York and had received from it a Bachelor of Divinity degree in 1871, he never served as regular pastor of a church. He did show continuous interest in religion and religious psychology though it never predominated over other topics in his work or writings. (Cf. Vande Kemp, 1992.) The only substantial expressions of his continuing interest in religion were the establishment of the *American Journal of Religious Psychology and Education* in 1904 (which lasted through 1915) and the publication of his *Jesus, the Christ, in the Light of Psychology,* one of the least successful of his works. [20] James, on the other hand, who started with the background of his father's Swedenborgian "ideas," which probably contributed in his twenties to his neurotic doubts about the will, escaped temporarily from the dilemma by taking up painting as a vocation. He then entered medical school but never practiced, and was soon employed at Harvard in the Department of Physiology, then Philosophy. The latter first meant for him psychology. Quite early, however, he evinced an interest in psychical research, and that grew rapidly after his marriage in 1876 and lasted until the end of his life. Philosophy as a profession engaged him soon after the publication of his *Principles* in 1890. By the middle of the '90s he was developing the philosophy of Pragmatism and the "radical empiricism" which combined with psychical research. He ended in what was essentially a return to the problems of religion which had implicitly engaged him from the beginning. In a word, while both Hall and James began with religious concerns, Hall moved from religion to experimental psychology and philosophy, supplemented by a dedication to the field of pedagogy (education). [20a] James moved from painting through medicine, physiology, and psychology to philosophy which, as early as 1869, was supplemented by an interest in or pursuit of psychical research.

In later years a similar difference of departmental orientation was present: At Harvard, philosophy and psychology were joined in one department until psychology achieved its independence in 1936, while at Clark, from the very beginning, psychology and pedagogy (education) constituted one department—as was true in 1909—and the separation occurred in 1949. Thus, for James, philosophy was a natural partner to psychology, while for Hall, psychology, strongly oriented toward the experimental at its core, was joined to education as its natural supplement.

After his two-year sojourn in Europe, Hall returned to America and shortly received an appointment at the new Johns Hopkins University in Baltimore. In 1883 he established a laboratory of psychology which was the first in America to function systematically and productively with students and colleagues. In 1887, the year before his appointment as President of Clark University and while still in Baltimore, he founded the *American Journal of Psychology*, the first in its field in English, which published primarily in the area of experimental (physiological) psychology. Its editorial position implicitly excluded reports of original work in psychical research as unsuitable from the standpoint of scientific investigation, but in the book reviews which were regularly included, publications in that area were faithfully covered.

But Hall's establishment of the *Journal* in 1887 converged at one point with spiritualism as a movement in the United States. When the American Society for Psychical Research was founded in 1884, the Council included G. Stanley Hall and R. Pearsall Smith along with William James and others. Reminiscing about the founding of the *American Journal of Psychology* 30 years later, Hall (1917b) stated that while he was still at Johns Hopkins (in 1886 or 1887), he was visited one Sunday afternoon by Pearsall Smith of Philadelphia, whom he here called "a wealthy stranger." [21] Having heard about Hall's new department of psychology, Smith suggested that Hall start a new journal and, as an earnest of his proposal, gave him "on the spot" a contribution of $500 with an intimation of more later. "This was the origin of the *American Journal of Psychology*" (p. 299). Hall added that when, during the first year of publication, the *Journal* took a negative view of psychical research, no further contributions were received from Smith. Moreover, a number of other subscribers withdrew. In 1921, on the occasion of his turning over the editorship of the *Journal* to E. B. Titchener, Hall again mentioned the "alienated patron" (without naming Smith) but now stated that the contribution was accepted "on the assumption, as it afterward appeared, that the *Journal* would favor this cult [psychical] research" (Hall, 1921a, p. 21). This version makes it appear that, in accepting the original contribution from Smith, Hall did not know what field of psychology was of primary interest to the donor. However, in view of Smith's part in the organization of the American Society for Psychical Research only three years before the *Journal* started and of Hall's coordinate rank with Smith in that organization, the accounts of both 1917 and 1921 appear to be disingenuous. Pearsall Smith was no *stranger* to Hall when he visited in 1886-1887, nor could Hall have been unaware of what the purpose of the gift for the proposed journal was. That Hall repeatedly recalled Smith's visit—he did so again parenthetically in his *Life and Confessions (op. cit.,* p. 228) without acknowledging his culpability—shows a paradoxical obtuseness that some of his colleagues perceived in other situations.

There is incidental but eloquent evidence that in 1890 William James had a very high regard for Hall's psychology department and its laboratory in Worcester. This testimony has survived from a contact between William James and Mary W. Calkins in the spring of that year when she was exploring various schools to select one where she might begin study with emphasis on the new physiological or experimental psychology. She conferred with James in the hope of studying with him and Josiah Royce at Harvard. There was a special condition attached to her plans: she wanted a location near her home in Newton, Massachusetts, where she lived with her parents, for whom she felt some responsibility. Hence she had told James that she did not wish to take up residence at a distant school. But obstacles soon arose that prevented enrollment at Harvard because she was a woman. James had consulted President Charles Eliot in her behalf but was told that the rules were definitely opposed. In writing to her in May 1890, James conveyed the decision with regrets, then suggested an alternative: "Can't you get to Worcester about as easily as to Cambridge?

Stanley Hall's Psychological department ought to be the best in the world." Thus one sees that just months before his *Principles of Psychology* was to appear in the fall of 1890, James had the highest regard for Hall's department. [21a]

This judgment accords with an event that occurred two years later. In the summer of 1892, Hall was the moving spirit in the founding of the American Psychological Association. He assembled leaders of American psychology at Clark University on July 8 to discuss this proposal. Though James was named to the organizing committee, it is evident that he did not attend the meeting, for he was then in Switzerland on a sabbatical leave. The first annual meeting of the Association was held in Philadelphia on December 27, 1892, with Hall the elected first president. [22] It is instructive that at that meeting the first scheduled paper was by G. Stanley Hall, under the title, "History and Prospects of Experimental Psychology in America." The discussants were designated as Professors Ladd and Baldwin. [22a]

The only public breach in the friendly relations of James and Hall appeared in 1895, when James took offense at an editorial by Hall in the *American Journal of Psychology* which to James implied that Hall was claiming to have been the first to establish a laboratory of experimental psychology in America. [23] James not only published a protest in *Science* but was joined by several of his colleagues who wrote similar comments for the same issue of the periodical. James also wrote to Hall directly and asked him to retract the statement that the laboratory at Harvard was founded under the influence of a Clark man. He reminded Hall that Hall's own earliest psychological experimentation had been done at Harvard— but he omitted the fact that Hall had done this research with Bowditch at the Medical School, not at Harvard College with James.

Most of the controversy dissolves if, as has been stated earlier, the *productivity* of the laboratory of experimental psychology established by Hall at Johns Hopkins in 1883 is observed and accepted as the criterion. To argue otherwise is to get lost in the definition of experimental psychology, of laboratory versus demonstration unit, and other rather pointless issues. The most thorough and reliable examination of the earliest laboratories question is that recently published by Cadwallader (1992) in the centennial history of American psychology. His conclusion regarding the Hall/James priority issue agrees essentially with the one above given. But the details shed further important light on the development of experimental psychology in America.

There was a complication added to the offending editorial: simultaneously with it in the October issue of the *Journal* appeared a collective review, signed G. S. H., devoted to seven current publications on psychic research (Hall, 1895b, *op. cit.*). The description of the research is detailed and the comment is highly critical in Hall's characteristic fashion. James, who must have read or, at least, scanned this review, would have considered the judgments unjustifiably negative. In fact, James himself had reviewed three of the items in Hall's collective review—Parrish, Podmore, and Sidgwick—in the *Psychological Review* in the same year and came to quite different conclusions. (Cf. James, 1895a.) Moreover, reading in the light of Hall's editorial, James would have been reminded that Hall did not regard psychic research as a proper part of experimental psychology, with insult thus added to injury.

Were there predisposing events that perhaps prepared James for the precipitating one in 1895 to which he responded so intensely? There are two possibilities. In 1892 Hall, as has been noted, founded the American Psychological Association and was elected its first president. James was not present but that he did not oppose the plan to organize is evident from his acceptance of the presidency in 1894. Nevertheless, Hall's ambitiousness and his bid for preeminence in 1892 could not have escaped James's competitive notice.

There was, however, another, more telling incident. In 1895 James found it convenient to claim that he was only defending the honor of Harvard in repudiating Hall's unjustified claim to priority. This displacement suggests that something more directly personal might have provoked him. Just such an incident occurred in 1891. When in the previous year James published his *Priniciples of Psychology,* the result of a decade of work, Hall had had the temerity to compose a very long and severely critical review of it. [24] While Hall praised many of James's brilliant and original pages, he seriously challenged the book as a solid contribution to psychology as science. James's stress had been far too subjective, not only in the many interesting personal revelations, but in the stress on issues like conscious states, self, and soul, which were more matters of philosophy than of laboratory investigation. Hall offered the gist of his criticism in these pithy lines: "That he is even unconsciously all through the book only building a new stage and setting a fit scene in modern science-town for the old timeless, spaceless, deathless soul of eschatology, we have no right to say in view of the many unwonted, masked reserves, but every intelligent reader will see not only that there is nothing inconsistent with this view, but that this is the only possible standpoint from which the book has unity or cohesion. Deny the knowledge of passing thought, a matter left very dark by the author, and we must have a soul to mediate union between psychic elements. *Seelensucht* is the key to what is left undone as well as to what is done. His abhorrence of mindstuffists and associationists, the slight treatment of instinct, memory, and the lower senses, the special lines of interest to which he confines himself in treating vision, hypnotism and automatism, the almost total omission of pleasure and pain, of hearing, touch, taste and smell, and of anthropological psychology, and the strange neglect of fundamental biological principles, etc., are now all explained. Some of the most lusty branches of the psychological tree are neglected or mutilated in the interest, consciously or unconsciously, of the author's strong undertow of animistic propensities. We, too, believe in soul, but not in a way which interferes with causation or the conservation of energy. As consciousness, he thinks, need only tip molecules, so soul needs, it is pleaded, only to prolong the fixation time of spontaneous attention. If consciousness can tip molecules, what of the 'chasm' so orthodoxly emphasized between brain and psychic state; may it not tip a table, at least if it be accurately enough balanced; and how is its force applied, or is the brain 'boxed and blanketed' like a medium's cabinet to cunningly defy our peering curiosity; was it with this consciousness that physical miracles of old were wrought; can it act telepathically? There is at least nothing against any or all of these. To appeal to consciousness as a physical cause is to invoke the chaos and the old night of spiritualism. Holding firmly to the views of it we expressed in the first number of this journal (see vol. 1, No. 1, p. 145), we cannot accept the smallness of this baby (I, 144), as any excuse for its illegitimacy or its depraved heredity." In fewer words, Wundt had arrived at a similar judgment of *The Principles:* "It is literature, it is beautiful, but it is not psychology." [25]

A precipitating event in the Journal controversy of 1895 was very probably the new psychological periodical edited by psychologists unhappy with Hall's policies for the *American Journal of Psychology*. It was called the *Psychological Review* and appeared in 1894 with Baldwin and Cattell as primary coeditors and with William James on the editorial board. There had been some preliminary negotiations in an attempt to get Stanley Hall to merge his journal with the proposed one, but the negotiations had ended in failure. It was not James, but Baldwin, Cattell and Münsterberg who apparently conducted the negotiations, but they kept James closely advised. A fruit of this negotiation process is a judgment of James about Hall that broaches the question of integrity, which, as will appear, loomed large in Hall's rejection of psychical research. In August 1892 James wrote to his colleague Münsterberg: "I have already written to Baldwin and Cattell about the Journal, asking Baldwin to send the letter to you so . . . I will be brief now. . . . I am not altogether surprised that you have all come to grief in your negotiations with Hall; his personal psychology is a very queer and tortuous one. Containing, however, sincere devotion to truth. He hates clearness—clear formulas, clear statements, clear understandings; and mystification of some kind seems never far distant from everything he does. Yet I think he does not mean to deceive, nor is he a liar in any vulgar meaning of the term. He shrinks with an instinctive terror from any explanation that is definitive and irrevocable, and hence comes to say & do things that leave an avenue open to retreat—at bottom it is connected with timidity in him—as a *dreamer* he is bold, when it comes to acting, he wills-and-wills-not. But what I least like in his journal and other writings of his as President [of the Psychological Society] is the religious cant he finds it necessary to throw in. Yet in a certain sense even that is not insincerely meant! He has too complicated a mind!"[26] Yet a decade earlier James had given his wife Alice a quite different and very positive evaluation of Hall after meeting him and resuming their friendship in Heidelberg in 1880. He characterized Hall then as: ". . . a remarkable being. Such a simple craving for truth and boundless power of acquisition with such absolute modesty."[27,28] The difference clearly points up the effect of the Journal controversy and, perhaps, Hall's critical review of *The Principles*.

Monday Seminar Room in Hall's home

To round out James's appraisals of Hall's personality one might profitably consult the various comments by Hall's students and colleagues collected by L. N. Wilson (*op. cit.,* 1925a, pp. 57-96). Characteristically they stress Hall's impressive qualities as a teacher and lecturer who brought out the best in his students despite their remarkable diversity in background, age and previous experience. He had an extraordinary capacity to impart his own enthusiasm for research in psychology, especially by the weekly seminars held every Monday evening at his home over a period of 30 years. A typical evaluation is the statement by Professor Lewis M. Terman of Stanford University, who was awarded his Ph.D. at Clark in 1905:

"On first entering the University, the student was always advised by President Hall to sample all the courses he thought he might be interested in, and to drop those he cared least for. . . . I think the Clark situation . . . was of almost crucial importance in my development. I have never worked well under restraint of rules and regulations, and it is hard to imagine a régime that would have been better adapted to my temperament than the one I found at Clark, if régime indeed it could have been called. Because I was placed absolutely on my own responsibility, I was able to give my best with unalloyed enthusiasm. . . . The laboratory facilities, in psychology at least, were hardly less generous in proportion to the demands upon them. There was unlimited room, and apparatus was available for almost any type of experiment a student might want to undertake. All this meant much less to me than did the library, where I spent so much more of my time. For me, Clark University meant chiefly three things: freedom to work as I pleased, unlimited library facilities, and Hall's Monday evening seminar. Any one of these outweighed all the lectures I attended. . . . When Clark students of the old days get together, their conversation invariably reverts to Hall's seminar. All agree that it was unique in character and about the most important single educational influence that ever entered their lives. No description could possibly do it justice; its atmosphere cannot be conveyed in words. . . . It might be either a summary and review of the literature in some field or an account of the student's own investigation. When the report was finished Dr. Hall usually started the discussion off with a few deceivingly generous comments on the importance of the material that had been presented, then hesitantly expressed just a shade of doubt about some of the conclusions drawn, and finally called for 'reactions.' . . . Hall would sum things up with an erudition and fertility of imagination that always amazed us and made us feel that his offhand insight into the problem went immeasurably beyond that of the student who had devoted months of slavish drudgery to it. Then we were herded into the dining room, where light refreshments were served, and by 9:30 or so we were in our chairs listening to another report. Sometimes the second half of the evening was even more exciting than the first half, and we rarely got away before eleven or twelve o'clock. I always went home dazed and intoxicated, took a hot bath to quiet my nerves, then lay awake for hours rehearsing the drama and formulating the clever things I should have said and did not. As for Dr. Hall, he, as I later learned, always went upstairs to his den and finished his day by reading or writing until 1:00 A.M. or later. So inexhaustible was his energy! . . . If there is any pedagogical device better adapted to put a man on his mettle than a seminar thus conducted, I do not know what it is" (Terman, 1932, pp. 313-316).

A complementary evaluation of Hall, not by a former student but by a distinguished colleague, the famous Professor E. B. Titchener of Cornell, Hall's fellow editor of the *American Journal of Psychology*, will close this section. In 1924 when Hall died, Titchener wrote (in part):

"I was in fairly close touch with Dr. Hall for nearly thirty years. Looking back, however, I find that I must say what others have already said,—that it was impossible to be intimate with him. . . . Almost from the first he seemed to treat me as—how shall I put it?—a sort of professional or psychological son; and my own regard for him has always had an element of quasi-filial affection. Yet, somehow or other, one never got quite inside him. There was, of course, the difference of age and status; but that did not account for it; I have felt myself 'inside' Burdon Sanderson and Wundt in a way that I have never felt with Stanley Hall. It was as if he never fully gave himself; as if, however courteously interested he might be in your conversation and however appreciative of your company, he was still busy, at the back of his mind, with something quite foreign to his present topic. It was not, either, a matter of simple absent-mindedness; the

part-withdrawal seemed to be conscious, even if it were not volun-
tary. Sanford and I were discussing this trait only the other day,
and Sanford confessed himself as much baffled by it as I had
been. . . . it must not be forgotten—and Dr. Fisher's recent paper
in the *Journal* has reminded us—that Dr. Hall began his psychological career as an experimentalist and never completely lost contact with experiment; sometimes, in his later years, he spoke a
little wistfully of the laboratory, almost as if he wished himself
again in the field that he had so often decried as narrow and
overtilled. . . . Sometimes, however, Dr. Hall rose in lecture to the
full height of his personality; and far oftener in conversation. I
have left his house at the end of many evenings with the feeling
that I had been in the company of a very great man,—a man
far greater than his books show him. Genius is a lofty
word, but it is not too high to apply to Dr. Hall at the times
when, fronting a sympathetic audience or with two or three friends
about him, he was at his very best" (Wilson, 1925a, *op. cit.*, pp.
91-92).

William James was contending with a pioneer figure of the new
psychology whose opinions about psychical research and other current issues might be openly ignored but could not be summarily
dismissed.

Concluding Appraisals of Psychical Research

William James's final message on the topic appeared under the
title "Confidences of a 'Psychical Researcher' " the month after his
visit to Worcester but before the Tanner/Hall volume was published. [29] It ends in a hedged confession of faith: ". . . I personally
am as yet neither a convinced believer in parasitic demons, nor a
spiritist, nor a scientist, but still remain a psychical researcher
waiting for more facts before concluding" (p. 374).

Earlier in the article James had revealed that, like some mediums, he had "cheated shamelessly" during a popular lecture in
Sanders Theater at Harvard (around 1878) when, as an assistant
to Newell Martin, Professor of Physiology, he was in charge of a
turtle's heart the enlarged shadow of which appeared on a screen
so that the lecturer could demonstrate the heartbeat in response to
stimulation of certain nerves. But when the Professor came to his
ultimate demonstration, the turtle's heart had come to the end of

its tenuous life. "Presiding over the performance I was terrified at the fiasco, and found myself suddenly acting like one of those military geniuses who on the field of battle convert disaster into victory. There was no time for deliberation; so, with my forefinger under a part of the straw that cast no shadow, I found myself impulsively and automatically imitating the rhythmic movements which my colleague had prophesized the heart would undergo. I kept the experiment from failing and not only saved my colleague (and the turtle) from a humiliation that but for my presence of mind would have been their lot, but I established, in the audience the true view of the subject. The lecturer was stating this; and the misconduct of one half-dead specimen of heart ought not to destroy the impression of his words. . . . even now as I write in cool blood I am tempted to think that I acted quite correctly. I was acting for the *larger truth* . . . . To this day the memory of that critical emergency has made me feel charitable toward all mediums who make phenomena come in one way when they won't come easily in another" (pp. 364-365). So James asserts: "Fraud, conscious or unconscious, seems ubiquitous throughout the range of physical phenomena of spiritism, and false pretense, prevarication and fishing for clues are ubiquitous in the mental manifestations of mediums" (p. 365). To overrate this fraudulent element, as many literal-minded scientists tend to do who then dismiss all the rest as "rot" or "bosh," is a case of misapplied objectivity. [30]

It is to this literal-mindedness and lack of sympathetic participation that James attributes most of the current hostility to psychic research. Admitting his bias in the opposite direction, James goes on to consider the case for the validity of mediumistic conduct. He goes on record as believing that there is a natural tendency for individuals toward "a crazy will to make believe." He thinks that there is "some curious external force impelling us to personation" (p. 372). Again, he goes on record that despite the presence of occasional humbug there is some "really supernormal knowledge" available to us from mediums. To comprehend this totality one must allow for "an interaction between slumbering faculties in the automatist's mind and a cosmic environment of *other consciousness* of some sort which is able to work upon them. If there were in the universe a lot of diffuse soulstuff, unable of itself to get into consistent personal form, or to take permanent possession of an organism, yet always craving to do so, it might get its head into the air, parasitically so to speak, by profiting by weak spots in the armor of human minds, and slipping in and stirring up there the sleeping tendency to personate. It would induce habits in the subconscious region of the mind it used thus, and would seek above all things to prolong its social opportunities by making itself agreeable and plausible. It would drag stray scraps of truth with it from the wider environment, but would betray its mental inferiority by knowing little how to weave them into any important or significant story" (p. 373).

This conception of the process of mediumistic communication is intelligible only if one accepts the possibility that beyond the individual mind "our lives are like islands in the sea . . . there is a continuum of cosmic consciousness, against which our individuality builds but accidental fences, and into which our several minds plunge as into a mother-sea or reservoir" (p. 374). In terms of this panpsychic metaphysical view James insisted that one must put up even with the elements of humbug that occasionally mar the facts that appear to come through. "It is through following these facts, I am persuaded, that the greatest scientific conquests of the coming generation will be achieved" (ibid., p. 375).

Hall's final statement on psychical research, except for what he wrote in his autobiography of 1923, was made in a 1918 article based on an event that occurred on the last full day of Freud's visit.

From Hall's point of view the vagaries of psychical research, in contrast to the methods of experimental psychology, were epitomized in the case of a 20-year-old girl whom he called "a medium in the bud." [31] She appeared at his home in early 1909 and asked for an interview with the Professor for whom she had a message from the spirit world. Hall was just about to leave for a lecture but arranged for her to return the next day, at which time there would be present in addition to himself, a mature woman, his assistant, Dr. Amy Tanner, and a former Ph.D. of Hall's sponsorship, Dr. Edward E. Weaver, who had a special interest in faith healing and related topics. The sessions with this young lady were coincidental with the studies of the medium, Mrs. Piper, above reported. Moreover, since she lived in a neighboring town and was available on request, Hall arranged for her to visit his home while Freud and Jung were guests there so she could demonstrate her powers to them and he could benefit from their appraisal of her.

From one of Jung's letters to his wife written from Worcester on Saturday, September 11, 1909, we learn that this session occurred in the evening of that day, though, in Jung's words, it was a "private conference" on the "psychology of sex." [32] Jung's description undoubtedly reflects Hall's own interpretation of this young lady's talents—or symptoms—though it is somewhat surprising to find Jung delivering the information to his wife without any mention of psychic mediumship. Regardless of this oddity, the case as studied by Hall, including her appearance at the time of Freud and Jung's visit, was published at length in the *American Journal of Psychology* nine years later and, as mentioned, it served as a final appraisal by him of the phenomena of psychical research in general. It suggested, as he there states (p. 154), an analogy to the patient, St. Martin, with the open stomach that made possible the direct observation of the digestive process (by Dr. William Beaumont). In the case of this "medium in the bud," the naive and still immature girl similarly revealed to the prepared observer the way in which her thwarted sexual needs and fantasies found expression in remarkable powers to communicate with spirits in the other world. She reported this to the Professor and his colleagues almost compulsively and with no apparent suspicion of their pathological origin. But in his 1918 article (p. 156) Hall reports some embarrassment: "The erotic motivation was obvious and the German savants saw little further to interest them in the case, and I was a trifle mortified that now the purpose so long hidden from us was so conscious and so openly confessed. They suspected a possible incipient dementia praecox, which we were a little loathe to accept. . . ." But when Hall planned to see her for the last time she called to say very briefly "that she had fallen in love with another and very different kind of man, and that neither he nor she cared to have anything more to do with spiritism." She now avowed that she had never really believed in her powers without reservations and "was now very happy" (p. 156).

In a word, she had been unable to gain admiration and sexual satisfaction because of religious and other scruples, and had hence resorted to indirect means even if these involved self-deception and distortions of reality by projection. Since her sexual needs were now being promised direct satisfaction, these methods of spiritism were no longer necessary.

Summarizing his inferences about the case, Hall stated:

"Psychic researchers to-day represent the last potent stand of about all the old superstitions of the past, against which science has contended. The next generation will be hardly able to believe that prominent men in this [century] wasted their energies in chasing such a will-of-the-wisp as the veracity of messages or the reality of a post-mortem existence, which they no more prove than dreams of levitation prove that man can hover in the air at will" (ibid.).

The Role of Sexuality

The great difference between Hall and James regarding the role of psychical research in psychology was largely a function of the contrast between them regarding the significance of sexuality in human life and its conceptualization. That this contrast will now be discussed against the background of Freud's visit is unintentionally germane.

Hall was interested in the problem of sexuality for many years previous to Freud's visit in 1909.[33] He stated in 1909 that for 20 years he had accumulated books on sexuality that covered half-a-dozen shelves of his library. He discussed the topic at length in his autobiography.[34] He commented on the range of the subject, which extended from biology, with man as a procreative animal whose sexual needs are "in excess of the needs of procreation," to anthropology and the history of culture, to aesthetics, and religion. In this vein he stated: ". . . the advent of Freudianism marked the greatest epoch in the history of our science" (p. 409). Though he believed that Freud may have overemphasized sexuality, he regarded the exaggeration as "a natural reaction to the long taboo and prudery that would not look facts in the face." He then briefly reviewed the achievements of the Freudian approach to the new understanding of childhood, the interpretation of dreams, the nature of behavior disorders, and the extension of these insights to the domain of biography, history, literature, religion, sociology and art. These views, he confessed, "came to me to seem almost like a new dispensation in the domain of psychology, so that from 1909, when Freud visited us, it [sex] and its wider implications became of central interest to me" (p. 410). In that connection he deprecated Jung's mysticism as transcending the legitimate bounds of science but, at the other extreme, the search for sexual meaning of all

behaviors by the followers of Freud could be harmful. Nevertheless, he concluded, "I have the deepest appreciation of the service
Freud has rendered our specialty by doing more to popularize and
give zest to it among all sorts and conditions of intellectuals than
any other man in the history of science" (p. 411).

It therefore comes as no surprise that by 1909 Hall offered
a course at Clark University entitled "The Psychology of Sex"
which was described in the University *Register* (under the date
March 1909, p. 79) as including "fatherhood, motherhood, marriage, sexual errors and disease, sexual morality, divorce, shame
and modesty, prostitution, abortion, illegitimacy, fecundity, eugenics and race suicide, periodicity, the psychological differences
between the sexes, sex éclaircissements, school instruction in these
subjects."

In his previous writings, Hall had recognized and dwelt upon
the importance of sexuality. Five years before the 20th anniversary
sessions, in his two-volume work *Adolescence,* he had devoted
an entire chapter to "Adolescent Love." It occupied 50 pages.
He there cited the work of Breuer and Freud on hysteria (1895),
and quoted as follows from an 1896 paper by Freud: ". . . from
whatever side and from whatever symptom we start, we always
unfailingly reach the region of the sexual life. . . . At the bottom
of every case of hysteria, and reproducible by an analytic effort
after even an interval of ten years, may be found one or more facts
of previous sexual experience belonging to early youth. . . . I regard this important result as the discovery of a *caput Nili* of
neuropathology." [35] But Hall did not consider sexuality as limited
to abnormal psychology. He hence explored its relevance to everyday adolescent life, its great significance in the understanding of
marriage, and its paramont role in the religious experiences of
youth. In an entire subsequent chapter he discussed the psychology
of religious conversion and there stressed its part in the adolescent's
special experience of sexuality. At this point in a long footnote
Hall criticized William James's *Varieties of Religious Experience*
(which had appeared two years earlier) as failing to recognize the
importance of sexuality and he pointedly rejected James's "dicta
concerning sex." [36]

In this context it is instructive that when Hall sent William
James a copy of his *Adolescence* on publication in 1904, James
read it selectively, as one can infer from the cut and uncut pages.

On examining the pages that were cut, and presumably read, one finds that these dealt largely with the topic of sexuality, including the role of sexuality in religious conversion. On this latter subject, Hall cited and criticized James, as noted above, and James had cut those pages.

By such statements Hall incurred, as Boring later said, the "Odium sexicum." [37] Boring may have had in mind E. L. Thorndike's critical review of *Adolescence* in which the reviewer took issue with Hall's derogation of James's *Varieties of Religious Experience.* [38] He rejected Hall's characterization of James as a "brilliant litterateur" [who] "throws scientific caution to the winds." Recommending scientific caution, Thorndike then spoke for James by strong disagreement with Hall's confidence in the questionnaire method through which many of the latter's findings had been obtained. In this argumentative stance—and as a former student of James at Harvard—the reviewer failed to recognize the various other sources employed by Hall in his depiction of the sexual life of adolescents.

The impact of the 1909 vigentennial conference, along with the extensive interests of Hall in problems of sexuality, is evident in one of Hall's major works, *Educational Problems,* published in 1911. [39] Though primarily a contribution to education or "pedagogy" (in the academic vernacular), it ranged not only over the various levels of education—from kindergarten to secondary schools and special fields of higher education—but devoted an extensive chapter of 150 pages to "The Pedagogy of Sex." This exposition included a survey of infantile and childhood sexuality, perversions and social vice, and the great importance of sexual education as a part of civilized culture. Hall referred specifically to Freud's contributions, in particular, his study of the five-year-old boy with a phobia rooted in a sexual orientation, and gave a very detailed abstract of Jung's presentation of the emotionally disturbed four-year-old girl that constituted his third lecture at the Clark Conference (pp. 443-445). He then continued: "The chief evidence of active sex life in young children . . . rests upon the results of psycho-analysis, which has led Freud and his now rapidly growing school to the conclusion that nearly all neuroses, if not most of the psychoses of later life, rest back upon and have their ultimate origin in some lesion or trauma of the *vita sexualis* before puberty, perhaps averaging about the age of eight or nine"

(p. 445). Hall then described in some detail Freud's theory of sexual development beginning in infancy, both normal and abnormal, and lauded psychoanalysis as having ushered in a new era in the whole domain of psychology. It "gives sex, which had been rejected by all contemptuously and dismissed by some psychologists as of the slightest significance, its rightful and dominant place" (p. 447). The next 90 pages were devoted to the problems of sexual education which needed to be explicitly confronted, and he referred to specific studies and remedies being made in America and abroad. He considered the questions of the consanguinity of parents as a possible unfavorable influence on children, the effects of "masculine insufficiency," and the problems of menstruation and pregnancy. He dwelt on cultural practices such as infanticide and abortion. This chapter is a veritable treatise on the topic of human sexuality addressed in a direct and bold fashion.

In the practical purview, apart from Hall's writings, it is noteworthy that in 1908-1909 he served as President of the New England Watch and Ward Society, an organization chiefly concerned with sexual waywardness in adolescence. One of its major concerns was the prevalence of prostitution for, as Hall mentioned in a memorandum written at this time, there were 200 "bad houses" known to be operating in the Boston area. From this work Hall must have learned a great deal not only about sex but about alcoholism, cocaine abuse, and other social evils in adolescence and youth. He approved of a forthright approach and expressed disgust for the "kid gloves method for handling these questions" (Hall Papers).

While Stanley Hall was serving as President of the New England Watch and Ward Society a remarkable coincidence occurred: the Viennese-born Bertha Pappenheim, now a social work leader, was lecturing in the United States on prostitution and white slavery among Jews. [40] She was the real-life patient whom Josef Breuer had treated in 1880-1882 and called "Anna O." in *Studies on Hysteria* (Breuer and Freud, 1895). Freud, in opening his Clark lectures, referred at some length to this important case of hysteria as the fountainhead from which the method of catharsis sprang and from which, in turn, psychoanalysis developed. Freud so strongly felt the need to emphasize this beginning that he even called Breuer the originator of psychoanalysis, then later, in *The History of the Psychoanalytic Movement,* retracted the exaggeration. But the contribution of the patient herself was not exaggerated. As if by historical determinism, Bertha Pappenheim was in North America in 1909 just as Freud was. She had come to attend the International Women's Conference in Canada in August and stopped, by invitation, to lecture in Chicago and New York. In this field she had been a German-Jewish pioneer for a decade largely because Jewish leaders, unlike their Protestant and Catholic counterparts, were loathe to admit such evil amongst themselves through fear of augmenting anti-Semitism. Like Stanley Hall, whom she never met, Pappenheim attributed neurotic adjustments and social evils involving sexuality primarily not to unconscious conflicts but to quite conscious ones between classes of citizens who tolerate poverty, inferior education and economic exploitation. These were the more basic causes. Thus arose for girls and women the evils of prostitution, white-slavery traffic, and family discord. These problems demanded socio-economic reform, public education and religious instruction. Though she practiced orthodox Judaism, she worked hand in hand with Catholic and Protestant groups who had similar social aims.

Sociologists and social historians in recent years have tended to agree with Bertha Pappenheim more than with Sigmund Freud in the analysis of psychological and social maladjustment, particularly as concerns the abuse of girls and women. From this point of view, the dislocations in family life and social adjustment may entail internal conflict and attendant mental illness, but even when these are cured by psychotherapy, the more basic social abuses continue. Psychoanalysis may even serve as a palliative or anodyne to divert attention from the degenerative social practices that require correction from the bottom up.

In this purview Stanley Hall shared to some extent. He was aware of the social basis of psychological disorder—he was professionally not only a psychologist but an educator. In contrast, William James moved through psychology to philosophy and religious idealism. Yet, peripherally, James also recognized and responded on occasion to the need for reform. For example, he lent his moral and financial support to Clifford Beers in the founding and fostering of the National Committee for Mental Hygiene in 1909. But it is noteworthy that James himself in one of his letters to Beers (January 17, 1910) confessed, "I inhabit such a realm of abstractions that I only get credit for what I do in that special empire." He was therefore grateful that he could, in this instance, do something practical by helping the reforms that Beers had initiated.

From this standpoint one will better appreciate Hall's later attempt to supplement Freud's theories by those of Alfred Adler who not only emphasized the "inferiority complex" but looked for basic causes in social abuses. Adler was, in fact, an ardent socialist; he was married to a Russian woman who, as a friend of Trotsky, had some part in the early preparations for the Russian Revolution of 1917. (See Jones, *op. cit.*, *2*, 134.)

In the context of President Hall's major role in planning the 20th anniversary celebration to which Freud and Jung were invited, it is remarkable that at this very time he was serving as president of a local organization devoted to the reform of sexual mores. It becomes evident that Stanley Hall was not interested merely in the theoretical psychology of human sexuality but was applying himself actively to the understanding and improvement of social practices. It is not improbable that some of his academic critics may have viewed this kind of activity as an expression of prurience. In that light it is the more remarkable that Freud was received at Clark and in New England generally with as much approval and favorable notice as is apparent from the detailed newspaper accounts. It is similarly significant that William James put aside the reservations he may have entertained and attended the Clark celebration, precisely to hear Freud. Did this resolve reflect, as above noted, the influence of James's friend Dr. J. J. Putnam, as well as his own partial awareness of his neurotic involvement in matters of sexual adjustment?

G. W. Allen, one of the best of James's biographers,[41] contrasts the experiences of Stanley Hall and William James during their respective travels in Europe before either of them had been married. He describes Hall's intimate acquaintance with James in 1875-1876 when they knew each other at Harvard, took long walks together and discussed their earlier experiences. While Hall had used his European opportunities to associate with the opposite sex without inhibition, James had had a quite different set of experiences. He had not felt free to be intimate with the German *Fraülein* despite, or because of, his exposure to his father's espousal of François Fourier's doctrine of "free love." As Allen states, "William had grown up with exalted ideals of chastity" (p. 212). It is evident that James had a great deal to overcome in the way of prevailing American and British prudishness in the middle of the 19th century.

There was, however, a peculiarly personal side to James's sexual orientation during his journeys in Europe and, for that matter, while he was home in America. From his diaries and letters it is now an open secret that throughout his youth he had suffered from neurotic symptoms that he attributed to a family diathesis. During his twenties he suffered from states of despair and depression including a fear of psychosis, a syndrome at that time designated as neurasthenia. James himself was acutely aware of his inadequacies and drew the conclusion that not only he but also his five siblings were unfit for marriage because of an inherited nervous instability that, in particular, manifested itself in what he called a "dorsal infirmity." A letter to his brother Bob (Robertson) written on November 14, 1869, on the occasion of Bob's engagement to be married (which William tried to discourage) reveals these views of William that reflect his own neurotic condition. [42] Following Strouse, we note the circumstances that elicited the letter here in question. [43] In the fall of 1869 Robertson had fallen in love with his cousin Kitty Temple and had become secretly engaged to her. But Bob did not keep his secret from William. The letter William wrote to Robertson reads in part as follows: "After all, what results from every marriage is a part of the next generation, and feeling as strongly as I do that the greater part of the whole evil of this wicked world is the result of infirm health, I account it as a true crime against humanity for anyone to run the probable risk of generating unhealthy offspring. For myself I have long since fully determined never to marry with any one, were she as healthy as the Venus of Milo, for this dorsal trouble is evidently a thing in the blood. I confess that the flesh is weak and passion will overthrow strong reasons, and I may fail in keeping such a resolve, but I mean not to fail. I want to feel on my death bed when I look back that whatever evil I was born with I kept to myself and did so much towards extinguishing it from the world. This is an ideal, which it wd. be wrong for me to expect either you or Harry to follow, granting that this dorsal complaint succeed in developing itself in you. But your present enterprise is so peculiarly certain to be fraught with bad results that I feel it would be wrong for me not to beg you to pause and consider them before doing any thing further." As the letter further indicates, James was supported in his view by current scientific literature on the inheritance of ill-defined, presumably nervous ailments that could only be eliminated from future generations by abstinence from marriage and childbearing. One should add that though William stresses what he calls the family's "dorsal trouble," he was influenced by more than just this infirmity. He knew states of depression, fatigue and indecision as well as backache.

Two months after this 1869 letter to Bob, there was no more talk of Kitty Temple. But Bob's nervous troubles continued. As Strouse explains, he wrote in 1872 complaining of exacerbated physical troubles such as backaches, poor digestion, constipation, nocturnal emissions and fear of becoming impotent. William, now an M.D., prescribed remedies: iron, moderate exercise, painting the back with coats of iodine until the skin peeled off, and a stiff upper lip. Later, he made light of Bob's sexual fears: "Your case as you describe it belongs to the most trifling class, amenable to treatment in some form, and if continuing in spite of medical treatment, ready to cease when sexual intercourse begins regularly." But these remedies and reassurances had little effect on Bob's troubles. Strouse comments that William was trying even in the late '60s to find a philosophy to overcome his own psychological torments. He gave up the idea of practicing medicine almost immediately after graduation and looked to research to counteract his horror of a wasted life. From these letters we learn about William James's concerns, not only regarding Bob, but about his own problems. In later years these would lead him continually to consult mental healers in America and to visit health spas in Europe.

The letters of 1869 and 1872 have been cited here because they convey in James's own words the burden of his neurasthenia and melancholia as shared with his nearest kin in their common destiny. But William and his younger brother Henry managed to transform this diathesis creatively in ways that have made their names memorable. [44]

That by 1876, several years after these letters to Bob, William tried to convince himself, as well as his fiancée, that one could justify marriage of unhealthy persons, demonstrates that passion did indeed "overthrow strong reasons," but one should perhaps qualify even this explanation. James's need for a companion to overcome his instability was probably the ultimate pragmatic ground that prevailed. No doubt, Alice's need and her willingness to enter a marriage with him reflected the practical and social advantages that must have outweighed for her the liabilities that he portrayed. That two years later she accepted the prospects of this anomalous marriage is not only a tribute to her self-confidence but to her competence; and it perhaps represents a comment on the cultural expectations of upper-class married women in the Victorian era.

In connection with James's recurring sense of inadequacy and his spells of depression, it is important to note his recourse to injections of testicular compounds, frequently mentioned in his correspondence with Théodore Flournoy. [45] In 1894 he refers to this medication as "Brown-Séquards's famous injections" which, unfortunately, resulted in an abscess that kept him in bed for five weeks. (It is perhaps relevant that Brown-Séquard had briefly been Professor of Physiology at the Harvard Medical School during James's student days. A concrete memorial of this contact—notes from a lecture by Brown-Séquard dating from around 1866—can still be seen at the Countway Library Archives in Boston.) The purpose of these injections was rejuvenation or, at least, reinvigorization. Though at first the therapy failed, James made more successful attempts for eight to ten years during the last decade of his life with the Roberts-Hawley lymph compound. In 1908 he wrote Flournoy a detailed account of the treatment and sent him a supply so that he could attempt a similar series. He was actuated to do so by the favorable results he had obtained over a period of eight years: "In a week all symptoms begin to improve, fatigue diminishes, sleep improves, digestion ditto, courage and aggressiveness replace pusillanimity, etc. etc." (September 16, 1908, p. 200). James affirmed his belief that "I have owed my power to do effective work in the past 7 years essentially to my semi-annual dosage with this remedy" (pp. 200-201). That this compound, like Brown-Séquard's, included materials from animal testicles (e.g., bulls) may well have had a symbolic psychological effect in addition to any physiological one—which, incidentally, had never been convincingly established. Flournoy regretfully reported to his friend seven months later that the compound, carefully injected according to prescription twice a day for more than four weeks, produced no favorable effects. He stated his conclusion that results were not capable of changing the normal temperament of the individual and that the lymph thus produced different effects on different individuals. But he was, of course, grateful to his friend James for extending this generous help. But James was not personally discouraged, for in June of 1909, acknowledging Flournoy's report, he told him that he had in mind trying the remedy again to overcome a bad condition of fatigue and hoped for "the usual improvement of symptoms" (p. 216). Speaking of his cardiac condition in the next paragraph, James then described it as primarily functional since the pain associated with it occurred mainly "whenever I exert myself strongly or rapidly, or whenever I get into any mental hesitation, trepidation or flurry. Apparently it is predominantly a neurosis, but it makes me pusillanimous . . ." (ibid., 216-217). It is striking that James has juxtaposed his condition of fatigue, for which he proposes to use the Roberts-Hawley remedy, with his cardiac condition, a neurosis that makes him "pusillanimous." That was the word he had used to Flournoy to describe the symptoms that the lymph compound seemed to cure for him.

Against this background of James's experiential involvement in sex, one is in a better position to consider his views about sexuality as expressed in his published writings. In his *Principles of Psychology,* written over the 1880-1890 decade, he failed to recognize the full significance of the sexual drive, and when he begins a brief treatment of the topic emphasizing its primitive impulsivity, he at once brings in inhibiting factors such as early habits and others that, he believed, continuously check sexual expression. Among the latter he singles out "ordinary shyness . . . and what might be called the *anti-sexual* instinct, the instinct of personal isolation, the actual repulsiveness to us of the idea of intimate contact with most of the persons we meet, especially those of our own sex." [46] The strong part played by coyness in women, which has to be overcome by wooing, and the aversion to contact between men occupy a larger place in his brief discussion than the more positive aspects of sexual attraction and fulfillment. In the fiction of his brother Henry this "anti-sexual instinct" would loom. The influence is surely less a reflection of William's writings than of his personal relationships to Henry and to the rest of the James family—a largely unconscious expression of the Freudian theory of libido and "the family romance."

But it is essential in the interest of fairness to give James the opportunity to state his case more fully than has been done up to now. To that end one may turn to his famous *Varieties of Religious Experience* (1902) in which, as in no other place, he has argued the limited relevance of sexuality not only with respect to religion, but, by implication, to the whole conception of personality. One needs to quote at some length to do justice to his position.

James squarely confronts the issue in the following: "A more fully developed example of the same kind of reasoning [by assigning a lowly origin to spiritual values] is the fashion, quite common nowadays among certain writers, of criticising the religious emotions by showing a connection between them and the sexual life. Conversion is a crisis of puberty and adolescence. The macerations of saints, and the devotion of missionaries, are only instances of the parental instinct of self-sacrifice gone astray. For the hysterical nun, starving for natural life, Christ is but an imaginary substitute for a more earthly object of affection" (ibid., p. 10).

Under the derogatory epithet "medical materialism" James adds some colorful examples: "Medical materialism seems indeed a good appelation for the too simple-minded system of thought which we are considering. Medical materialism finishes up Saint Paul by calling his vision on the road to Damacus a discharging lesion of the occipital cortex, he being an epileptic. It snuffs out Saint Teresa as an hysteric, Saint Francis of Assisi as an hereditary degenerate. George Fox's discontent with the shams of his age, and his pining for spiritual veracity, it treats as a symptom of a disordered colon. Carlyle's organ-tones of misery it accounts for by a gastro-duodenal catarrh. All such mental overtensions, it says, are, when you come to the bottom of the matter, mere affairs of diathesis (auto-intoxications most probably), due to the perverted action of various glands which physiology will yet discover" (ibid., p. 13).

In a lengthy footnote, essentially a short essay, he makes a rebuttal: "It seems to me that few conceptions are less instructive than this re-interpretation of religion as perverted sexuality. It reminds one, so crudely is it often employed, of the famous Catholic taunt, that the Reformation may be best understood by remembering that its *fons et origo* was Luther's wish to marry a nun:—the effects are infinitely wider than the alleged causes, and for the most part opposite in nature. It is true that in the vast

collection of religious phenomena, some are undisguisedly ama-
tory—e.g., sex-dieties and obscene rites in polytheism, and ecstatic
feelings of union with the Saviour in a few Christian mystics. But
then why not equally call religion an aberration of the digestive
function, and prove one's point by the worship of Bacchus and
Ceres, or by the ecstatic feelings of some other saints about the
Eucharist? Religious language clothes itself in such poor symbols
as our life affords, and the whole organism gives overtones of
comment whenever the mind is strongly stirred to expression"
(ibid., p. 11, note 1).

Then as an ultimate refutation, James concludes: "The plain
truth is that to interpret religion one must in the end look at the
immediate content of the religious consciousness. The moment one
does this, one sees how wholly disconnected it is in the main from
the content of the sexual consciousness. Everything about the two
things differs, objects, moods, faculties concerned, and acts impelled to. Any *general* assimilation is simply impossible: what we
find most often is complete hostility and contrast. If now the
defenders of the sex-theory say that this makes no difference to
their thesis; that without the chemical contributions which the sex-
organs make to the blood, the brain would not be nourished so as
to carry on religious activities, this final proposition may be true
or not true; but at any rate it has become profoundly uninstructive;
we can deduce no consequences from it which help us to interpret
religion's meaning or value. In this sense the religious life depends
just as much upon the spleen, the pancreas, and the kidneys as on
the sexual apparatus, and the whole theory has lost its point in
evaporating into a vague general assertion of the dependence, *somehow*, of the mind upon the body" (ibid., p. 12, note 1).

James epitomizes his position by an appeal to an early New
England religious authority: "By their fruits ye shall know them,
not by their roots. Jonathan Edwards's Treatise on Religious Af-
fections is an elaborate working out of this thesis. The *roots* of a
man's virtue are inaccessible to us. No appearances whatever are
infallible proofs of grace. Our practice is the only sure evidence,
even to ourselves, we are genuinely Christians" (ibid., p. 20).

Surprisingly, one finds here a source of the doctrine of "pragmatism" that James espoused in this book as a continuation of his
"will to believe" (James, 1896c). He had introduced the doctrine
in a philosophical paper published four years earlier (James, 1898)

but the real-life implications were spelled out in the *Varieties,* which is rarely invoked as the forerunner that it was of his epistemological doctrine. At the end of the volume (p. 444), he explicitly cites "an American philosopher of eminent originality, Mr. Charles Sanders Peirce," and, following him, defines "pragmatism" as based on Peirce's article published 24 years earlier (Peirce, 1878). That Peirce would later disclaim the tribute of this citation was lost on James, who had just drawn from his predecessor what he needed to assuage his religious doubts. Peirce later emphatically repudiated this attribution and even went so far as to rename his principle by coining the variant term "pragmaticism," which, he said, was "ugly enough to be safe from kidnappers." Peirce was actually closer in his philosophy to the idealist Josiah Royce than he was to William James. Stanley Hall, without the developed philosophic grounds of Peirce, likewise repudiated James's doctrine, particularly in alluding to the adherence of James to psychical research.

It is therefore not surprising that Hall commented unfavorably on James's derogation of sexuality in *The Varieties of Religious Experience.* He noted the lack especially in James's treatment of adolescent religious conversion. The difference here between Hall and James probably reflects not only differences in rationale but differences of endowment and personal experience during their quest for a scientific psychology. The orientation toward sexuality was, of course, only one of the differences between them, but it was crucial because it entailed other differences, including their regard for psychical research as an area of scientific endeavor.

Freud, Jung, and Hall the King-Maker

The lecturers in the Behavioral Sciences. *Left to right:*
Burgerstein, Freud, Titchener, Jung, Boas, Meyer, Stern, Jennings

The Art Room at Clark University, where Freud and Jung lectured

Chapter VI

The Scope of the Lectures

There were in all 29 distinguished lecturers at the 20th anniversary celebration in Worcester. Of that number, 21 received honorary degrees on the evening of Friday, September 10, and the other eight, on the following Thursday. The entire gamut of the sciences was represented: mathematics, physics, astronomy, chemistry, biology, psychology, education, anthropology, and history. Among the lecturers were two Nobel laureates, A. A. Michelson, the physicist, who had investigated the nature of light and was honored in 1907, and Ernest Rutherford, pioneer investigator of radioactivity and the structure of the atom, who received the prize in 1908. The other lecturers, complementing the eight behavioral scientists considered below in detail, were as follows: in *astronomy,* Percival Lowell, Massachusetts Institute of Technology; in *mathematics,* E. H. Moore, University of Chicago, W. F. Osgood, Harvard University, James Pierpont, Yale University, and E. Van Vleck, University of Wisconsin; in *physics,* Carl Barus, Brown University, Vito Volterra, University of Rome and Robert W. Wood, Johns Hopkins University; in *chemistry,* M. T. Bogert, Columbia University, Arthur Michael, Tufts College, Arthur A. Noyes, Massachusetts Institute of Technology, William A. Noyes, University of Illinois, Theodore W. Richards, Harvard University and Julius Stieglitz, University of Chicago; in *biology,* H. C. Bumpus, Director of the American Museum of Natural History and Charles O. Whitman, University of Chicago; also André Debierne, Director of Research, University of Paris; Ernest F. Nichols, President of Dartmouth, and Lebbens R. Wilfley, First Judge, U. S. Court in China. All these participants were selected because of internationally recognized contributions to knowledge. Hence it is not surprising that Freud, as he started to lecture at

Clark in such a galaxy, saw himself as realizing an incredible daydream.

The Behavioral Scientists

Eight of the lecturers were behavioral scientists who represented experimental and clinical psychology, psychiatry, biology, anthropology and education. It is important to notice the six besides Freud and Jung in order to appreciate the scope and cogency of the total purview. [1]

Take, for instance, the lecture of Franz Boas (1853-1942), Professor of Anthropology at Columbia University who, on coming to America from Germany, served as professor at Clark. He dwelt on the definition of race and the notion of racial purity— topics that over the next 20 years he would more fully develop. Unfortunately his views had no deterrent effect on Germany in the 1930s.

A glance at his book *Anthropology and Modern Life,* published in 1928, only two years after Adolf Hitler published *Mein Kampf,* is paradoxically noteworthy. Boas expounded the interrelationships of race, nationalism and culture, and, focusing on the prevailing mixture of races, stressed the dangers of nationalism when unjustifiably equated with racial purity. He emphasized the striking effects of education and culture in diminishing the significance of the hereditary aspects of racial types. In particular, one may note his timely statement: "The idea of the great blond Aryan, the leader of mankind, is the result of self-admiration that emotional thinkers have tried to sustain by imaginative reasoning. It has no foundation in observed fact" (p. 80). Boas stressed that race, nation and language are divisive concepts that, when politically manipulated, bring conflict and war. He concluded that the federation of nations was the next necessary step in the evolution of mankind (p. 93). But these prophetic words still represent a distant goal of effectiveness.

In a similar vein, the lecture by Professor Adolf Meyer (1866-1950), "The Dynamic Interpretation of Dementia Praecox," de-emphasized heredity as a basis for understanding the disease and stressed critical events that are valuable clinical units or "reaction-types." He proposed that mental illnesses like dementia praecox be regarded as "experiments of nature" which do not follow fixed laws of a fate-like character affording little opportunity for treatment. Instead he recommended more constructive concepts for prognosis and practical handling. In that context he paid the following tribute: "We owe to our European guests, Professor Freud and Dr. Jung, the demonstration that what is at work in the centre of the stage is a complex or group of complexes consisting of insufficiently balanced experiences in various ways modified by symbolism. Their ingenious interpretations have made possible a remarkable clearing up of many otherwise perplexing products of morbid fancy, in ways the discussion of which, no doubt, I had better leave to their lectures" (p. 389). Dr. Meyer preferred not to rely on heredity or toxins to explain why only few persons develop these same complexes with a disastrous outcome. He stressed "habit-conflicts" that affect the balance of the personality, the sum total of "mental metabolism," and the capacity to regulate behavior in emergencies.

William Stern (1871-1938), professor at the University of Breslau, gave four lectures, the first pair devoted to the psychology of testimony, the second, to the study of individuality. He outlined methods of studying testimony, e.g., by examining the accuracy of witnesses in reporting events that they had by prearrangement previously observed. From his various methods of observation he outlined a series of typical errors in testimony: apprehension, expectation, confabulation, and sheer fantasy. He discussed the consequences of these findings for public education and for testimony in courts of law.

In the third lecture, Stern described empirical methods for the study of individuality. He appraised the use of mental tests and other quantitative devices for constructing "psychographs." In such charts all possible characteristics that may come into consideration in the study of an individual are listed and graded for the particular person without reference to a priori assumptions as to whether these are essential or not. This comprehensive approach permits the recognition of unique traits. In his final lecture Stern explored the individuality of the child at different stages of development and, in that context, commended the Binet Scale of Intelligence employed in school psychology. It is of historical interest that two years later (1911) Stern introduced the concept of the "Mental Quotient" (the ratio of mental age as measured by test to known chronological age) which, in 1916, L. M. Terman adopted for the widely used Stanford-Binet scale and relabeled it the "Intelligence Quotient" (IQ).

Professor Leo Burgerstein (1853-1928), of the University of Vienna, offered three lectures in the fields of education and school hygiene. Unlike Ernst Meumann, who had been unable to participate and would have represented the experimental psychology of pedagogy, Burgerstein presented findings in applied aspects of secondary education. He discussed coeducation—a then novel approach—and such aspects of school hygiene as sanitation and the salutary relation of body and mind to be achieved by the use of supervised games and recreation, exercise, planned diet, and the management of sleep to avoid fatigue. In these ways the best conditions can be provided for the learning experience. He presented specific empirical results to support his generalizations by surveying the work of educators in Germany, Scandinavia and America, in addition to the presentation of his own findings.

H. S. Jennings (1868-1947) in his lecture on the study of behavior in lower organisms stressed the synthetic approach as opposite to the analytic. "Thus in this method we begin with the complex organism and attempt to analyze its behavior, proceed to simpler and simpler determining factors, till we get the simplest that can be reached" (Jennings, 1906, p. 354). By emphasizing the importance of studying the organism as a whole and, further, the biological interrelationships of organisms, he anticipated what was later called "ethology." He opposed the exclusive stress on the physico-chemical approach of Jacques Loeb and the emphasis on tropisms. He similarly—at the other extreme—opposed teleology, finalism or vitalism, then in fashion, maintaining that such explanations are unnecessary if one empirically studies the whole organism, in particular, seemingly spontaneous responses. He emphasized the arrangements of energy, process and activity, not merely the physical and chemical arrangements of substances. The outcome of this approach pointed up the individuality and diversity of organisms. In this vein he stressed the importance of understanding the past history of the organism for a better comprehension of present activity. Hence, he dwelt on the need to probe the formation of habits.

Some of these ideas had previously been expounded in his book *The Behavior of the Lower Organisms,* published in 1906, three years before the Clark Conference. In the years to come some of these same arguments supported the innovations of Gestalt Psychology. The emphasis on a new empiricism helped to inspire the approach of B. F. Skinner. That influence is not often recognized though it peeks through in Skinner's choice of title for his first book, *The Behavior of Organisms* (1938).

In his lecture "The Past Decade in Experimental Psychology," E. B. Titchener (1867-1927), Professor at Cornell University, gave a pithy account of recent developments in Europe and America. His orientation was rigorously scientific—too rigid for some of his colleagues. But he had an elegant self-consistency. Thus he referred, in passing, to the three European experimental psychologists—Meumann, Ebbinghaus and Wundt—who had been invited by Hall but who had for one or another reason been unable to attend. He paid particular tribute to Hermann Ebbinghaus, who had died earlier that year at the age of only 59. Titchener referred to his "promised address from this platform—an experience that should have remained a lifelong memory." He praised the qualities of this pioneer of the psychology of memory as being ideally scientific, i.e., independent of philosophy. He extolled the special capacity of Ebbinghaus for brilliantly expounding the facts he had acquired.[2] Ebbinghaus was the example so much needed at this time when psychology still appeared to be "helplessly entangled with theory of knowledge . . . ; when theory is impatient of fact, and the facts themselves are scattered and incoordinate." He called attention to the work of Wundt's student Meumann in establishing the (German) *Archiv für die gesamte Psychologie* in 1903 and for opening it to studies in applied psychology. He likewise credited William Stern for beginning in the same year, 1903, the publication of his *Beiträge zur Psychologie der Aussage* which, by 1907, had developed into the *Zeitschrift für angewandte Psychologie.* In this context Titchener mentioned Jung's first volume of studies in word-association, published in 1906. Though usually known as a champion of pure experimental research, this lecture clearly attests Titchener's endorsement of applied psychology when founded on experimental research. But in that vein he made an adverse comment on psychoanalysis for its stress on the unconscious, a conception he deplored as a stumbling block in the way of scientific advance.

He devoted the latter part of his lecture to a review of various systematic topics, such as attention, memory and affection (feeling), which he surveyed on the basis of the newly accomplished results. He then stressed the importance of individual psychology approached experimentally, and "first systematized by Stern in 1900." He praised this innovation as furnishing the key to "many otherwise inexplicable differences that increasingly appear in the results" of general psychology. And he similarly commended the experimental study of the behavior of the lower organisms as having a wholesome influence on the investigation of human behavior. He concluded by a vigorous defense of what he termed the analytic approach in experimental psychology; it was not objectionably "atomistic" because science is of necessity analytic. But apart from this special pleading at the end, one is impressed by the breadth of Titchener's outlook. It contradicts the common view that his definition of psychology was too narrow. [3]

Before proceeding to the major lectures—those on psychoanalysis by Freud and Jung—a word of appraisal concerning these other six behavioral scientists is appropriate. There is a remarkable freshness about their contributions viewed in their interrelatedness: a stress on the significance of the individual, as organism and as person, and the importance of the empirical procedure as a safeguard against hasty and prejudiced generalizations. One is impressed by the cogency of the messages delivered in 1909, still all-too-relevant in the world of the 1990s. Our planet continues, perhaps even more desperately, to need these invigorating insights. And to some degree this continuing timeliness reflects the orientation of G. Stanley Hall, the chief organizer of the vigentennial, who was particularly responsible for the choice of lecturers in the fields of psychology, psychiatry and education.

Chapter VII

Freud Introduces Psychoanalysis

Freud gave a series of five lectures at Clark University, Tuesday, September 7, through Saturday, September 11, 1909. The lectures were spoken, not read, in German. They were presented at 11:00 A.M. This assigned hour bespeaks Hall's identification with Freud. Upon his retirement in 1921, Hall wrote: "For more than 40 years I have lectured at 11 o'clock and cessation of this function leaves a curious void . . . ." [1] Freud's first two lectures were given in the auditorium of the main University building, the last three, in the Art Room on the third or top floor of the Clark Library building. [2] Since the complete lectures are presented in a new translation as Part Three of this volume, only a synopsis will be included here.

As a preliminary, however, it is important to understand that there were important differences, presently to be described, between the lectures as published and the lectures as delivered on the occasion. The following synopsis is based on the published translation that followed the manuscript Freud submitted to Hall some weeks after the Conference. To grasp the historical situation, however, it is essential, if possible, to discover the content and sequence of the lectures at the time vis-à-vis the evidence of the published version. With a synopsis of that version as a basis, the reader will better appreciate these differences as described below.

Freud's Lectures as Published

In the first lecture Freud modestly accorded the origin of psychoanalysis to his senior Viennese colleague Josef Breuer. (In the 1924 edition of the lectures he modified this statement by acknowledging his own "unrestricted responsibility" for psychoanalysis.)

In this context he outlined the case of Breuer's patient Anna O.—
a case of hysteria with symptoms of paralysis, impaired vision,
nausea, etc. These symptoms had been traced to earlier traumatic
experiences including, in particular, the death of the patient's father, whom she painstakingly nursed in his last illness. The "talking cure" by which Breuer treated these symptoms was described
as both exploratory and therapeutic. Freud claimed that such hysterical symptoms had never before been understood and treated so
successfully.

In the second lecture Freud began by contradicting the theory
of hysteria advocated by the French psychopathologist Pierre
Janet, in which hereditary weakness or degeneracy was stressed.
Freud argued that patients like Anna O. did not suffer from
hereditary or otherwise impaired mental abilities. The use of hypnosis by both Janet and Breuer, Freud maintained, was sometimes
an obstacle to the understanding of the case, and he recommended
instead the conscious exploration of the patient's history. Such
exploration revealed conflicts between personal wishes and ethical
or aesthetic values which caused intolerable mental pain and were
hence defensively repressed, only to be replaced by symptoms. By
the recall and resolution of such conflicts symptoms could be re-
lieved. The wishes involved often could be realized by sublimation—their transformation into a higher goal—if these wishes
were not rationally repudiated as no longer relevant for the mature
adult.

In the third lecture Freud described the technical innovation
of free association and its essential use in the analysis of dreams,
in slips of the tongue and other bungled acts. He stressed the
importance of the strict determinism of such seemingly uncaused
events and pointed out how, by the technique of free association,
such lines of determination could be recovered with the recognition
of unconscious meaning. In this connection, he described the experiments on word association carried out by Dr. Carl Jung and
Dr. Eugen Bleuler of Zurich, Switzerland, by which means unconscious constellations of emotionally charged ideas, designated
as "complexes," could be recovered. Freud then developed his
theory of dream interpretation in detail. Dreams are not absurd
and senseless, as most people, including psychiatrists, tend to
believe. Indeed dreams afford a royal road to the understanding
of the unconscious determinants of behavior, both normal and

abnormal. He distinguished between the manifest content and latent thoughts inherent in dreams, and stressed the not uncommon symbolic connection between the two. A recognition of this symbolism was essential to the understanding of dream life. Myths and legends were often intelligible as the experience of the group—a symbolic repository of group wishes and conflicts that could be unravelled by the understanding of similarly constructed individual dreams. He then briefly outlined the Oedipus complex as a dramatic representation of a universal family drama in which children are in conflict with parents. These conflicts were intuitively recognized as far back as Greek mythology, but they are prevalent in everyday contemporary life. Freud argued that critics of psychoanalysis repudiate these keys to human motivation from ignorance, because they refuse to enter into the kinds of self-searching and research that disclose and explain what is ordinarily unconscious and seemingly meaningless.

In his next lecture, the fourth, Freud introduced and explored the most controversial of his theories—the development of sexuality beginning in infancy. He deplored current sexual taboos, which need to be overcome by the physician or other investigator in order to discover the existing state of affairs during childhood when these taboos are instilled as part of civilized culture. Freud defined sexuality more broadly than is customary: he included sensitive body areas—the mouth, the anus, urethra, the skin— before the genitalia themselves become dominant. The earlier stages of sexual life undergo repression in the educational process in which shame and disgust, in the name of morality, mask the existence of sexual impulses. In adolescence the genitals assert their primacy but the complex process of development frequently distorts the normal progression. Neurosis or perversion, including autoerotism, homosexuality and various infantile fixations, arise and interfere with a mature expression of sexuality. He set forth the thesis that every neurosis stems from an arrest or distortion of sexual development, usually involving some aspect of the Oedipus complex. In this complex sons are sexually attracted to their mothers, daughters to their fathers, in a rivalry with the other parent. An ambivalent attachment results, which can be overcome only by the recognition and analysis of the complex.

The final lecture dealt largely with the social or cultural aspects of sexuality in civilized society. Freud repudiated customary attitudes toward sex which are largely responsible for the existence of neurosis and other maladjustments. In attempted adjustment, fantasy replaces reality to an abnormal extent. However, the artist, by a process not yet well understood, sometimes transforms such fantasy into creative products that form a successful bridge to reality. Freud described the nature of "transference" that exists in psychoanalytic therapy by which a reenactment of childhood attachments and hostilities can be dissolved or transformed. He repeated the importance of the strictly determined nature of personality development, by the recognition of which the patient may achieve a new level of maturity. Civilized conditions—the claims of modern society—make life too hard for most individuals. By the recognition of such facts society gains more than it loses; for in this process libidinal impulses, instead of being repressed, may be sublimated and contribute to the culture, professionally and artistically. A reform in conventional sexual ethics is required and the theories and methods of psychoanalysis can help to accomplish it.

Freud's Lectures as Delivered

Since the bibliographic information regarding the editions and translations of Freud's lectures is given in detail below, in the Introduction to Part Three preceding a new translation of the five lectures, these details will not be included here. It is, however, necessary to supply some other particulars regarding the preparation of the lectures and the difference in the content and order of the lectures in the published version as compared to the original delivery. At least three such differences are significant for understanding the impact of the lectures *in situ,* and these will be considered in detail.

From what Freud stated in his obituary of Sandor Ferenczi, it would appear that the preparation of the lectures was finalized just before the eleventh hour.[3] The subject matter for a given lecture was chosen and outlined during a walk that Freud took with Ferenczi before each lecture. In the context of a necrology Freud may have somewhat exaggerated out of gratitude to a friend and disciple who had met an untimely death. But the statement does at least indicate that Freud was free to select the lecture topics in the current situation. On that basis one may surmise that when, while living as a guest at Hall's home for the week of the Conference, Freud learned that the famous William James would be coming to Worcester for just one day, Friday the 10th of September, he chose to expound his theory of dreams on that date. As early as June 3-4, three months previous, Freud, Jung and Jones had corresponded about the most appropriate topics for the Clark lectures and, because psychologists, rather than professional psychiatrists or medical specialists, were expected to constitute the majority of the audience, the psychology of dreams was proposed by Freud as perhaps the best suited for the entire series. In the end, this idea was dropped as being not "practical" enough for an American audience. [4]

But James was not a typical American, and for the lecture on the one day of his attendance, Freud again probably decided that the topic of dreams would be particularly appropriate. In any event, the impact of Freud's theory of dreams upon the attentive William James was momentous, as will clearly appear below.

We come thus to the above-mentioned difference in the order and content of the delivered lectures as compared to the published version. In sending Hall his third lecture for publication in the *American Journal of Psychology,* Freud (letter 19 F, November 21, 1909) asked permission to make some changes in the published version and Hall in his immediate reply stated that such liberties were not only permissible but customary. Given Freud's own intention, starting with the third lecture, one is impelled to discover these modifications. Luckily the quite detailed newspaper coverage of the Clark celebration, including Freud's lectures, makes the effort profitable. An important change in the order of topics thus emerges. Freud shifted essential aspects of the third and fourth lectures from delivery to publication: he moved the topics of dream interpretation and free association from the fourth to the third lecture, and that of sexual development, including infantile sexuality, from the fifth to the fourth. Some topics covered in the fifth delivered lecture were not included in the published version and others were added.

By recognizing the changes in order, two important results are achieved. We learn for the first time that William James, present at the Conference only during Friday, September 10, heard Freud discuss the subject of dream interpretation and psychic determinism rather than the details of sexual development. It will be shown below that the inference as to what James heard affected his allusions to the lecture in two extant letters written to friends after his attendance: in both he singled out the topic of dreams and made a negative comment. With the published fourth lecture (on sexual development) as the reference point, one would encounter difficulty in explaining these comments.

The second point of difference concerns the shift from the fifth to the fourth lecture. As delivered, sexual development, in particular infantile sexuality, was the topic of the last lecture—the one on Saturday, September 11. On that day, two hours earlier, Jung delivered his third lecture, which focused on the sexual curiosity of a four-year-old girl. As we have already seen regarding Freud's choice of topic for Friday, one may similarly infer that Freud deliberately chose sexuality for Saturday to highlight the corroboration of his colleague, Carl Jung, on this most controversial of his views presented at the Conference. In fact, Freud himself referred to his colleague's earlier lecture that same morning.

For confirmation, the newspaper accounts of Freud's fourth and fifth lectures will now be briefly examined. Freud's fourth lecture, presented on Friday, September 10, was most fully reported the next morning in the *Worcester Telegram* (September 11, p. 4, col. 4) with the headline: "Tells of Dreams: Dr. Freud Tells How to Interpret Them." The text explained that Freud emphasized the importance of the infantile element in the dreams of neurotic individuals and stressed the significance of dreams in general for the understanding of personality. He described free association and the technical methods of interpreting dreams and offered several illustrations. Dreams disclose "infantile inclinations" preserved in the unconscious. Anxiety dreams occur when, despite the dream work tending toward wish-fulfillment, the problem or conflict present in the dream-thoughts breaks through to awareness.

Again referring to the *Worcester Telegram*—the only Worcester paper that had a Sunday edition—one finds a quite detailed outline of Freud's Saturday lecture. The main topic was the psychology of sex. Pointing out that repressed sexual impulses usually are found at the root of all nervous troubles, Freud discussed in detail the course of sexual development with emphasis on sexual impulses in young children. He cited the study of Dr. Sanford Bell

of Denver University, a former student of Dr. Hall, who had examined reports of emotional attachments among a very large group
of children three years old and above. Freud emphasized the value
of this independent American research. In considering the forms
of sexuality in childhood, Freud described thumb-sucking and
rhythmic rocking as examples. He discussed the natural curiosity
of children about the origin of babies, ordinarily not honestly explained to the child. In that context he reported the case of a five-
year-old boy (Little Hans) who, in relation to the birth of a sibling,
developed a phobia based on partial and distorted information and
wrong inferences regarding parental sexual activities. He then referred to the case of the four-year-old girl whose sexual development
Dr. Jung had discussed in this same lecture room earlier that morning. Freud maintained that sexuality needs to be controlled in the
life of the child without being distorted by misinformation, if neurosis is to be avoided and channels opened up for the sublimation
to higher goals. From this newspaper account it is clear that practically every aspect of the fourth *published* lecture was included in
the fifth, *delivered* the following day, Saturday. (See *Worcester
Telegram,* September 12, p. 4, col. 6.)

With this preparation, one can proceed in the next chapter to
examine the lectures delivered by Carl Jung at the Conference, in
particular, his third and last lecture, that concerning "Little Anna"
(Agathli), presented on Saturday, September 11 at 9:00 A.M. As
will be shown, Freud plainly intended to deliver his account of
Little Hans two hours after Jung had described the case of the
four-year-old girl who displayed similar sexual curiosity. In this
way Freud's radical innovations regarding the existence of sexuality
in the young child would fall on prepared ears, with the shock
buffered.

There is a third difference between Freud's lectures as published
and as delivered. *The Worcester Sunday Telegram,* reporting
the Saturday (fifth) lecture of Freud, stated that he discussed
"race suicide" in terms of the difference between fertility rates
in the Occident and in the Orient, and the devastations of war-
fare in eliminating the best and the strongest young men as future
fathers. He referred, in particular, to the loss of 2,500,000 men
in the Napoleonic Wars. Freud spoke of eugenics as essential
for the future of society. These social aspects of sexuality and
reproduction were, however, omitted in the lectures as published

and, specifically, they are not found in either the fourth or the fifth published lectures.

That Freud touched on these topics is not surprising—there is independent evidence of his interest in them—but their omission in the published version raises the question whether the audience in Worcester lent itself to their discussion, though he was not willing to give them permanent importance in the subsequent publication. A possible explanation that covers both these two aspects concerns the presence at the lectures of the notorious Emma Goldman. She was a radical socialist reformer whose interests in precisely these topics was well known through her insistent propaganda.

The evidence for Miss Goldman's presence in Worcester appears not only in the local Worcester newspapers—the *Telegram* and the *Gazette*—but in the *Boston Evening Transcript*. From the Worcester papers it is evident that she was present in the city for a week beginning Saturday, September 4. Her presence at a session devoted to education appeared in the *Transcript*. Referring to the afternoon of Thursday, September 9, that report read: ". . . conspicuous in front seats at the afternoon conference on education as a college subject were Emma Goldman, Anarchist, and Dr. Ben Reitman, 'the king of the hoboes.' Miss Goldman, who seems to be distinctly unpopular with the chief of police, proposes to speak in Worcester tomorrow night, if she has to proclaim her convictions from some sympathizer's doorstep. Meanwhile she seeks amusement and instruction, and though on this occasion she experienced boresome moments and turned a trifle fidgety, the rose that nestled at her belt seldom vibrated under stress of such unflattering emotion. Plump of person, demure of manner, chastely garbed in white and bedecked with rimless glasses, she might have passed as a visiting teacher—much more successfully than her comrade, Dr. Reitman, a tall, swarthy, slouchy person, who looked like a good-natured pirate" *(Boston Evening Transcript,* September 10, 1909). (Dr. Ben Reitman was the paramour of Miss Goldman for many years and collaborated in her activities as a reformer.)

Towards the end of the session Miss Goldman joined in the discussion with several rhetorical questions: "'Is not pedagoguery today filling the mind of the child with predigested food, instead of aiming to bring out his individuality?' Miss Goldman demanded. 'Is it not most important that he should learn his own ability and be equipped to understand his relation to the world about him? Do not women's colleges neglect to take up the most important subject, that of sex psychology, and so unfit their graduates, who become teachers, to get in touch with pupils? Does not successful teaching depend on individuality rather than method?'" (Ibid.)

It may appear improbable that Freud would have been influenced in his choice of topics by the presence of this unpopular radical, but several considerations appear to favor this conjecture. As already observed, Freud's lectures were not written out in advance but were largely improvised just before delivery. Moreover, there was a distinct similarity between Freud's and Miss Goldman's views regarding civilized sexual morality, including education, and even her notorious political anarchism was not beyond the scope of his unconscious interests. [5] Miss Goldman appears to have known Freud years before the Clark Conference—as early as 1896 when she heard him lecture in Vienna and, as she later noted, strongly agreed with his novel outlook. (Goldman, 1931, p. 173.)

As a footnote to history, her opinion, based upon astute observation, is worth recalling. In the following she is referring to the effect on her of Freud's lectures as she heard them in Vienna: "His simplicity and earnestness and the brilliance of his mind combined to give one the feeling of being led out of a dark cellar into broad daylight. For the first time I grasped the full significance of sex repression and its effect on human thought and action. He helped me to understand myself, my own needs; and I also realized that only people of depraved minds could impugn the motives or find 'impure' so great and fine a personality as Freud" (ibid.).

After hearing him in Worcester, she wrote: "The most important event of our Worcester visit was an address given by Sigmund Freud on the twentieth anniversary of Clark University. I was deeply impressed by the lucidity of his mind and the simplicity of his delivery. Among the array of professors, looking stiff and important in their university caps and gowns, Sigmund Freud, in ordinary attire, unassuming, almost shrinking, stood out like a giant among pygmies. He had aged somewhat since I had heard him in Vienna in 1896. He had been reviled then as a Jew and irresponsible innovator;   now he was a world figure;   but neither obloquy nor fame had influenced the great man" (ibid., 455-456). In the latter part of this comment, she is presumably alluding to Freud's appearance on Friday evening, September 10, when she was present at the convocation for the awarding of honorary degrees.

Chapter VIII

Jung Supports Freud:
The Case of Agathli

Word-Association Studies

Jung gave three lectures at Clark, on Thursday, Friday and Saturday at 9:00 A.M. in the Art Room of the Library. The first two lectures were on his word-association studies; the third, on problems in the mental life of a four-year-old girl. As Jung told me in 1951, the topic of word-association had been proposed to him when he was invited; he added the second topic on his own. However, since we now know from the formal program that Jung was expected to lecture on child psychology and mental hygiene, and that his honorary degree was designated to be in the area of pedagogy, his choice of the disturbed child was no mere happenstance. Moreover, as has already been shown, Freud must have planned with Jung for the lecture on the case of the four-year-old girl to corroborate Freud's just-published case of the five-year-old boy with a phobia rooted in sexual development. From Freud's standpoint, Jung's first two lectures afforded experimental confirmation of the psychoanalytic theory of unconscious complexes, and the third supported the Freudian view of the important place of sexuality in childhood.

Before the Clark conference Jung had published only one short monograph of his word-association studies. It appeared in 1906; a second volume was published in 1910, the year after the Clark lectures. But in 1907 Jung had published a journal article on word-association among members of the same family which significantly contributed to his second Clark lecture. The third lecture was based on observations not hitherto published though, as will presently

135

appear, Jung had shared them in correspondence with Freud as the observations were being made during many months prior to the Worcester conference.

Jung's lectures were reported in some detail in the Worcester newspapers and the *Boston Transcript*. As usual, the *Worcester Telegram* gave the longest and best reports. The method of word-association, as we know from these articles, was outlined in the first lecture. The detection of "complexes" was attributed to various indicators, such as abnormally long reaction times to the stimulus words or very unusual content in the response words. Such complexes pointed, allegedly, to the unconscious (repressed) conflicts in neurosis. As the lecturer explained, these conflicts reached beyond what the patient could communicate directly. In the second lecture, the topic was continued with supplementary data obtained from family members of the patient. The familial responses extended the significance of the results beyond the single individual and validated the psychoanalytic theory of hysteria.

As was shown in Chapter V, the familial parameter of the word-association technique had recently been utilized in an intensive investigation by Stanley Hall of the personality of the famous psychic medium Mrs. Leonore Piper, a protegée of William James. In his investigation Hall had employed the technique to validate claims of the medium that during trance she was speaking not individually but for other personalities that controlled her behavior. The word-association results supported other methods in casting doubt on these claims by demonstrating the similarity of her own responses to those of the control.

The Case of Anna (Agathli)

The consideration of Jung's third lecture—by far the most important—may begin by reviewing the report of it in the *Worcester Telegram* the next morning (September 12). It was there stated that the child enjoyed perfect health up to the age of four when she began to display aberrant fears and fantasies tied to sexual curiosity aroused by the birth of a sibling. She displayed insatiable curiosity about the origin of babies and the relationship of the parents in the process. It was evident from the newspaper account that the girl's anxieties derived not only from the presence of a new sibling, but reflected concern about the secret activities of the parents about which she developed many bizarre fantasies.

The further discussion of Jung's third lecture will follow the sequence of his own published versions of this case because, as will be seen, it is a bellwether of the Freud/Jung relationship from zenith to nadir. To supplement the report in the contemporary *Worcester Telegram,* we turn first to the full report of the entire lecture as it appeared in the *American Journal of Psychology* six months after the Clark conference. [1] The title of the lecture read, "Experiences Concerning the Psychic Life of the Child." The opening paragraph announced: "In today's lecture I should like to give you some insight into the psychic life of the child through the analysis of a four-year-old girl. It is much to be regretted that there are, no doubt, few among you who have had the opportunity to read the analysis of 'Little Hans' (Kleiner Hans), which has been published by Freud during the current year. I should properly begin by giving you the content of that analysis so that you could compare for yourselves the results obtained by Freud with my findings, and to observe the marked, even astonishing, similarity between the unconscious creations of the two children. Without a knowledge of the fundamental analysis of Freud, much in the report of the following case will appear strange to you, incomprehensible, and perhaps unacceptable. I beg you, however, to defer final judgment and to enter upon the consideration of these new subjects with a kindly disposition, for such new work in virgin soil requires not only the greatest patience on the part of the investigator but, also, the unprejudiced attention of his audience. Because the Freudian investigations appear to involve an indelicate discussion of the most intimate secrets of sexual life, many have had a sense of revulsion and have thus rejected everything as a matter of course without any actual proof. Hitherto this has unfortunately almost always been the fate of Freud's doctrines. For if one approaches the consideration of these matters with the firm conviction that they do not exist, it readily results that, for the prejudiced, they really do not exist. One should therefore for the moment assume the author's point of view and investigate these phenomena under his guidance. Only in this way can the correctness or incorrectness of our observations be affirmed. We may err, as all human beings do. But the continual holding up to us of our mistakes—perhaps they are worse than mistakes—does not help us to see things more distinctly. We should prefer to learn *wherein* we err. That demonstration should be given us in our own sphere of experience. Thus far, however, no one has succeeded in meeting us on our own ground and in providing us with a different conception of the things which we ourselves have observed. We must still complain that our critics are persisting in complete ignorance and without the slightest notion of the matters in question. The sole reason for this state of affairs is that our critics have never taken the trouble to become thoroughly acquainted with our method; had they done this, they would have understood us." [2]

There follows an account of the observations made on the four-year-old girl as reported by her father to the lecturer. It is of interest that the observations of Little Hans had been similarly made by the father of the boy and reported to Freud with permission to publish them. The lecturer emphasized throughout the analogy between Freud's case and that of "Little Anna," as the girl was called. And the lecturer pleaded for an unbiased attitude toward both cases, which involved novel and delicate matters, in particular, the area of infantile sexuality. That Freud and Jung had planned the presentation of the two cases to be made on the same morning (Saturday, September 11) is clear from Freud's own reference to Jung's lecture "in the same room two hours earlier." Incidentally, this fact is not supported by the sequence of Freud's five lectures, as *published,* but it is confirmed by the contemporary evidence of the newspaper reports.

With a preliminary apology for not being able to offer a more systematic account at this early stage of child psychoanalysis, Jung then presented a loosely organized series of diary-like conversational observations related to the birth of a new sibling, a boy. These observations showed the girl's hostility toward the new sibling and curiosity about the origin of babies and the relations of the father and mother in the process. A series of anxieties arose about these secret happenings and the significance of these events for the child: anxieties about her own existence and about the death of old people like her grandmother which, she thought, might be connected with the arrival of the new baby as a replacement. Eventually she questioned the truthfulness of the parents in their explanations of these matters, for example, the part played by the stork in bringing new babies. She created fantasies of her own instead. But everything was thrown into confusion and grave doubt by the occurrence of a great earthquake (at Messina, Sicily, December 28, 1908) which the adults for many days were talking about. Her anxieties were now displaced from the question of the parents' (sexual) activities to earthquakes and to volcanoes about which she had been told. But her curiosity was so extreme that she could not get enough of these explanations. She was shown books with pictures of volcanoes which she wanted to look at again and again. The global upheaval was plainly now a vehicle for the anxieties she had earlier experienced about the secret activities of the parents. To indicate the strictly Freudian nature of this lecture, a footnote by Jung is remarkable. It read: "This wish to sit up with the father and mother until late at night often plays a great part later in a neurosis. Its object is to prevent the parental coitus." [3]

Anna next entered a phase of increased sexual curiosity. She wanted to know what the *father* does to produce new babies. Her fantasy answer was acted out when she got onto the father's bed and kicked her legs up and down. But being given no satisfactory answer, she could not solve the problem. A period of about five months passed without much change in her general behavior. But then she became more disturbed, as shown by an increasing mistrust of her parents, in particular, the father. She even began to fear that he might drown her in the lake near their residence. During the night she woke and cried out for her mother. Apparently some of the love for her parents, being unsatisfied, was converted into anxiety dreams. The mistrust was concentrated on her father who, she seemed to feel, was secretly doing things that could harm her. It demanded considerable effort to reassure her and allay her groundless anxieties. At the time of the lecture by Jung the end of the disturbances had not fully arrived even though the child had been given a limited amount of the true explanation about the difference between boys and girls, future fathers and mothers, and how, by analogy with the planting of a garden, a new baby was produced by the planting of a seed by the father in the mother.

From all indications, it is clear that Anna was experiencing diffuse anxieties not unlike the focused phobia about horses experienced by Little Hans, even though Jung does not mention this parallel. Jung commented that at the peak of Little Anna's anxieties, after the earthquake at Messina, she returned to demanding her mother's presence during the night, just as she had done during her first insecure year of life. She had then cried if her mother was not present in the room. One infers that the parents found it necessary to let the child sleep at night in their room much of the time during these early years.

In concluding the lecture, Jung alluded to other similar cases of child psychology and children's sexual activities. The question of sex education for children was addressed. Like the introduction above quoted, these concluding remarks need, in part at least, to be quoted verbatim.

"It very often happens that children are wrongly treated as if they were unintelligent and irrational. Thus when I indulgently once remarked to an intelligent father whose 4-year-old daughter had been masturbating excessively that care should be exercised about having her sleep in the same room as the parents, I received the following indignant reply: 'I can absolutely assure you that the child knows nothing about sexual matters.' This statement recalls the distinguished old neurologist who wanted to eliminate the attribute 'sexual' from a phantasy of childbirth as represented in a dream.

"On the other hand, a child with a neurotic tendency may be mismanaged by over-solicitous parents. How easy and tempting, as it would be in the present case, to admire, excite, and prematurely develop the child's eager desire for learning. One could thereby develop an unnatural *blasé* state and a precociousness that masks a neurosis. In such instances the parents must consider their own complexes and neurotic tendencies and not indulge themselves at the expense of the child. The idea should be at once dismissed that children are to be kept in bondage or treated as toys of their parents. Children are all individual and unique creatures. In the matter of enlightenment on things sexual, it is common for parents to suffer from the preconceived belief that the truth is harmful. Many neurologists are of the opinion that even for grownups enlightenment on their own psychosexual processes is harmful and even immoral. Would not these same individuals perhaps refuse to admit the existence of the genitals themselves?" [4]

Whether the lecturer was obliquely referring to Little Anna, who was also a four-year-old daughter, when he alluded above to excessive masturbation and perhaps did so to avoid attributing such indelicate activity to Anna will be considered below. It will there also be proposed that the "intelligent father" in this parallel case was actually the "intelligent mother" for whom the father had been substituted as a disguise.

As above mentioned, Jung communicated his observations of "Little Anna" to Freud in their correspondence over many months before the Clark conference. In that correspondence she was called Agathli, the pet name for Jung's first child, Agathe. Before considering the relation of this original form of the observations to the selection reported in the Clark lecture, it should be made clear that the identity was revealed in the *Freud/Jung Letters,* published in 1974. (See pp. 200, n. 3, 208, n. 3, 212, n. 2, and, especially, p. 348, n. 2.)

It is not necessary for present purposes to collate the numerous reported observations of the four-year-old Agathli in Jung's letters to Freud from January 19 through June 4, 1909 with the presentation of the case at Clark. In the very first explicit report of the case (January 19) which extends over two printed pages (199-200), Jung ends with a complicated paragraph concerning Agathli's praise of the bottom of her little brother. He expounds in detail her use of the term "Buobefudili" which, he states, refers both to the posterior and sexual areas. He concludes, "A. naturally means the genitals." This observation is not found in the Clark lecture. Again, in the last of the explicit observations Jung communicated to Freud (August 5, p. 243) before the sessions at Clark, he describes a dream of Agathli about urinating men among whom Papa is present. On his return from a journey to Munich "She stuck a stick between her legs. Asked Mamma if her (A.'s) genitals should be planed off. She had seen the carpenter planing drawers that didn't fit." This observation was not included in the lecture.

But these omissions are of interest because they recall the parallel with the case of Little Hans whose concern about the genitals, both male and female, was of frequent occurrence. The castration complex of Little Hans surely has something in common with the little girl's concern about the genital area. The urination dream and the carpenter's plane played a much larger part in Jung's observation than he communicated to Freud on August 5. The rest of the observation is reproduced in the final version of the case (included in Jung's *Collected Works, 17,* pp. 29-30). In that place it is made clear that the child was still searching for knowledge about the process of birth and was speculating about whether her baby brother had emerged from the mother's posterior. (A similar anal birth fantasy had been described by Freud.)

Jung and Freud had repeatedly discussed the parallel between the cases of Little Hans and Agathli in the course of their correspondence. Freud had made the first such comment (January 25, p. 203): "Your Agathli is really charming. But surely you recognize the main features of Little Hans's story. Mightn't everything in it be typical? I am setting high hopes in a neurotic nuclear complex which gives rise to the two chief resistances: fear of the father and disbelief towards grownups. . . ." The parallel of Agathli and Hans was again remarked in the letters of March 9 and 11, 1909.

An even more revealing line of evidence about the difference between Jung's original observations as reported to Freud and the more circumspect version presented at Clark comes into view from indications that the little girl's "conflicts" probably began weeks or even months before the actual birth of the brother (on November 28, 1908). After a visit to Jung at the Burghölzli, where Freud shared Jung's apartment with him (September 18-21, 1908) while Jung's family was away on vacation, Freud wrote to Jung on October 15. Looking back on these "auspicious days" that he and Jung had spent together and that had "left me in high good humour" (p. 172), Freud added, "Please tell your dear wife that one passage in her letter gave me particular pleasure." (The editor of the *Freud/Jung Letters* adds a footnote here regarding the letter of Emma Jung: "Missing.") But it would appear that this part of Emma's letter was elsewhere preserved by Freud. In his essay on the case of Little Hans, composed for publication in the first number of the *Jahrbuch* (March 1909), Freud included a footnote about a three-and-one-half-year-old girl. (Note that at this time Jung's daughter, who would serve as the subject of Jung's third lecture at Clark, was three years, eight months old. She was born December 26, 1904.) The passage in question as paraphrased by Freud occurs in the case history of Little Hans. It amends the report of an incident that had been communicated to Freud by the father of Hans in the following dialogue:

"Hans, four and a quarter. This morning Hans was given his usual daily bath by his mother and afterwards dried and powdered. As his mother was powdering round his penis and taking care not to touch it, Hans said: 'Why don't you put your finger there?'

Mother: 'Because that'd be piggish.'
Hans: 'What's that? Piggish? Why?'
Mother: 'Because it's not proper.'
Hans (laughing): 'But it's great fun.'"

Freud's footnote to this dialogue reads as follows:
"Another mother, a neurotic, who was unwilling to believe in infantile masturbation, told me of a similar attempt at seduction on the part of her three-and-a-half-year-old daughter. She had had a pair of drawers made for the little girl, and was trying them on her to see whether they were not too tight for walking. To do this she passed her hand upwards along the inner surface of the child's thigh. Suddenly the little girl shut her legs together on her mother's hand, saying: 'Oh, Mummy, *do* leave your hand there. It feels so lovely.'"[5]

This striking similarity between the little boy and the little girl is almost beyond question what Freud must have read in the now missing letter of the child's mother, Emma Jung. Note that Freud inserts the comment that this mother was "unwilling to believe in infantile masturbation" but now communicated what Freud calls "a similar attempt at seduction." Through an unexpected set of circumstances, Jung, who was also the editor of the *Jahrbuch* in which Freud published the Little Hans case, permitted Freud to preserve under anonymity a sexual episode which agrees so remarkably with an episode in the life of the four-and-a-quarter-year-old Little Hans.[6]

Let us now return briefly to the conclusion of Jung's lecture about Little Anna. It will be recalled that he there (p. 267) referred to an "intelligent father" who refused to connect his four-year-old daughter's excessive masturbation with the fact that she slept in the same room with her parents and who made the "indignant reply, 'I can absolutely assure you that the child knows nothing about sexual matters.'" With present knowledge we can reasonably assume that Jung substituted "an intelligent father" for "an intelligent mother," i.e., his wife Emma. He was still talking, discreetly, about the same four-year-old, his child Agathli, but even while keeping her identity secret, he could not bring himself to discuss her autoerotism. By a strange double coincidence he was reporting in this appended example what Freud had already reported in his footnote in the case of Little Hans. As the father of the child, Jung was inhibited by natural reservations and behaved with reticence because he knew, even if the audience did not, that the girl in question was his own daughter. (For a comparison in parallel of Freud's case of Little Hans and Jung's case of Little Anna, see Appendix A to this chapter.)

Sabina Spielrein and Agathli

At this point we make a transition from the conflicts of Agathli arising from the birth of her brother to a problem between her parents that may have had an even more direct influence on her. It so happens that Jung published a short essay on effects of this kind. In an Introduction to a book by Frances G. Wickes in 1927[7] he wrote: "Children are so deeply involved in the psychological attitude of their parents that it is no wonder that most of the nervous disturbances in childhood can be traced back to a disturbed psychic atmosphere in the home. This book shows, from a series of remarkable examples, just how disastrous the parental influence can be for the child" (*Collected Works, 17,* 39). In the enlarged Introduction that he provided for the German translation (*Analyse der Kinderseele,* Stuttgart, 1931), he pointed out a lesson for parents that sounds like a derivative of his experience with Agathe in 1908-1909: "There can be no doubt that it is of the utmost value for parents to view their children's symptoms in the light of their own problems and conflicts. It is their duty as parents to do so. Their responsibility in this respect carries with it the obligation to do everything in their power not to lead a life that could harm the children. Generally far too little stress is laid upon how important the conduct of the parents is for the child, because it is not words that count, but deeds. Parents should always be conscious of the fact that they themselves are the principal cause of neurosis in their children" (*Collected Works,* ibid., p. 42).

Though Jung emphasized the parallel between "Little Anna" and "Little Hans" with regard to the role of the mother's pregnancy and the birth of a new sibling in creating Agathe's anxiety as reflected in her excessive interest in sexual matters, there was in her case another relevant parameter. It involved an extramarital problem that was concurrent with the wife's pregnancy, and that problem may have contributed even more directly to Agathe's anxiety and sexual curiosity. For during 1907-1909 Dr. Jung was involved romantically with a young female patient named Sabina Spielrein. He first became acquainted with her in 1904 when he was a resident psychiatrist at the Burghölzli Hospital. Jung's treatment of this 20-year-old patient for what he later described as a psychotic form of hysteria was conducted with Freud's psychoanalytic theory as a model; in fact, this model was so faithfully followed that Jung presented the case as an illustration of his argument at the first International Congress of Psychiatry held at Amsterdam in September 1907. The theme of the paper was a vigorous defense of Freud's controversial theory of hysteria. But in the course of Jung's relationship with this patient, probably around 1907-1908, he developed a more personal interest in Sabina, which by 1909 she took very seriously. She was then a medical student at the University of Zurich but continued her relationship with Jung as a friend. Intimacy developed, with complications, so that by March 1909 Jung appealed to Freud in their correspondence for catharsis and advice (*Freud/Jung Letters*, p. 207). At first Jung blamed only the patient, but events of the next few months revealed his complicity. On June 4, 1909 Jung summarized the situation in these words: "She was published in abbreviated form in my Amsterdam lecture of blessed memory. She was, so to speak, my test case, for which reason I remembered her with special gratitude and affection. Since I knew from experience that she would immediately relapse if I withdrew my support, I prolonged the relationship over the years and in the end found myself morally obliged, as it were, to devote a large measure of friendship to her, until I saw that an unintended wheel had started turning, whereupon I finally broke with her. She was, of course, systematically planning my seduction, which I considered inopportune. Now she is seeking revenge. Lately she has been spreading a rumour that I shall soon get a divorce from my wife and marry a certain girl student, which has thrown not a few of my colleagues into a flutter. What she is now planning is unknown to me. Nothing good, I suspect, unless perhaps you are imposed upon to act as a go-between. I need hardly say that I have made a clean break" (*Freud/Jung Letters*, pp. 228-229).

The patient had, in fact, by then written to Professor Freud to act as a mediator. She stated: "My dearest wish is that I may part from him [Dr. Jung] in love." [8] She confessed her "infatuation" and expressed the hope that Freud would help her overcome it. On June 11, she wrote Freud the details: "Four and a half years ago Dr. Jung was my doctor, then he became my friend and finally my 'poet,' i.e., my beloved. Eventually he came to me and things went as they usually do with 'poetry.' He preached polygamy, his wife was supposed to have no objection, etc., etc. Now my mother receives an anonymous letter that minces no words, saying she should rescue her daughter, since otherwise she would be ruined by Dr. Jung. . . . To make a long story short, my mother writes him a moving letter, saying he has saved her daughter and should not undo her now, and begging him not to exceed the bounds of friendship. Thereupon his [Jung's] reply: 'I moved from being her doctor to being her friend when I ceased to push my own feelings into the background. I could drop my role as doctor the more easily because I did not feel professionally obligated, for I never charged a fee. This latter clearly establishes the limits imposed upon a doctor. You do understand, of course, that a man and a girl cannot possibly continue indefinitely to have friendly dealings with one another without the likelihood that something more may enter the relationship. For what would restrain the two from drawing the consequences of their love? A *doctor* and his *patient,* on the other hand, can talk of the most intimate matters for as long as they like, and the patient may expect her doctor to give her all the love and concern she requires. But the doctor knows his limits and will never cross them, for he is *paid* for his trouble. That imposes the necessary restraints on him.

'Therefore I would suggest that if you wish me to adhere strictly to my role as doctor, you should pay me a suitable recompense for my trouble. In that way you may be *absolutely certain* that I will respect my duty as a doctor *under all circumstances.*

'As a friend of your daughter, on the other hand, one would have to leave matters to Fate. For no one can prevent two friends from doing as they wish. I hope, my dear and esteemed Madame, that you understand me and realize that these remarks conceal no baseness but only experience and self-knowledge. My fee is 10 francs per consultation.'"[9]

This letter from Dr. Jung to Sabina's mother has been quoted at length because it reveals an incredibly indiscreet naiveté but demonstrates as well that Jung had himself confessed his extra-professional role because he was not "paid for his trouble." One can thus begin to understand Jung's letter to Freud, dated

12. June 1909, in which, admitting he had been "too stupid," he pleads for Freud's help (*Freud/Jung Letters,* p. 232).

In Freud's reply (June 18, pp. 234-235), he mentions his correspondence with Fräulein Spielrein: "My reply was ever so wise and penetrating; I made it appear as though the most tenuous clues had enabled me Sherlock Holmes-like to guess the situation (which of course was none too difficult after your communications) and suggested a more appropriate procedure, something endopsychic, as it were. Whether it will be effective, I don't know. But now I must entreat you, don't go too far in the direction of contrition and reaction."

Freud does not here appear in an admirable light. In fact, he enters into a conspiracy with Jung at the expense öf the patient. He deliberately downplays Jung's complicity and treats it as a misinterpretation by her. But in view of Jung's letter to Mrs. Spielrein above quoted (which Freud had apparently seen by June 18), one can only conclude that Freud's need for his chosen successor—who by this date has also been invited to Clark—is so great that he connives at Jung's involvement and grants him absolution.

While this description of Jung's indiscreet relationship with his young patient is biographically revealing in itself and throws light on the collusive relationship of Jung to Freud, at this juncture the purpose is to discern how Jung's relationship with Sabina must have affected his wife Emma with anxiety that young Agathe could have sensed. Quite apart from the contribution made by the mother's pregnancy and the arrival of the new sibling in arousing the little girl's great interest in the origin of babies, and the part played by the relationship of the parents in reproduction, there appears to have been a much more direct source for the child's sexual curiosity and for her mistrust of the father as a reflection of the mother's mistrust of her husband. It would appear to be more than a coincidence that the extreme mistrust of the father in June 1909, noted in both the Clark lecture and in the first German edition of the Agathe case, should have occurred precisely at the time when the scandal about Jung's relationship to Sabina had reached its climax. Let us therefore reexamine this mistrust by Agathe as reflecting the mother's anxiety conveyed by empathy to the child. It will be recalled that the earlier mistrust concerned the origin of babies—the truth of the stork explanation, etc.—but now a change had occurred.

After a standstill of five months, Jung reported, the anxiety of "Little Anna" assumed the form of a severe mistrust of the parents, especially of the father. This phase is reported in detail in the Clark lecture, in the German adaptation published a few months later, and in the final version included in the *Collected Works*.[10] In this last, Jung's words are: "This time the mistrust was directed not against the mother, but against the father, who she was sure must know the secret, but would never let anything out. What could the father be doing or keeping up his sleeve? To the child this secret appeared to be something very dangerous, so obviously she felt that the worst might be expected of the father. (This childish fear of the father is to be seen particularly clearly in adults in cases of dementia praecox, which takes the lid off many unconscious processes as though it were acting on psychoanalytical principles.) Hence Anna had arrived at the apparently nonsensical notion that her father wanted to drown her" (p. 26). These words in the first instance refer to the child's curiousity about the role of the parents in creating a baby and at the same time may express another threat arising from the father. Did the mother's anxiety about the father's secret relation with another woman pass by empathy to the child? As already mentioned, this decisive mistrust of the father became evident in June 1909, precisely at the time that the scandal involving Sabina had become a serious threat to Jung—disturbing enough for him to seek help from Freud (*Freud/Jung Letters*, June 4, 1909, p. 228).

That Emma Jung, the wife, was a party to the problem is evident from Jung's disingenuous confession to Freud at the first mention of the episode: ". . . I have learnt an unspeakable amount of marital wisdom, for until now I had a totally inadequate idea of my polygamous components despite all self-analysis. Now I know where and how the devil can be laid by the heels. These painful yet extremely salutary insights have churned me up hellishly inside, but for that very reason, I hope, have secured me moral qualities which will be of greatest advantage to me in later life. The relationship with my wife has gained enormously in assurance and depth" (March 7, 1909, p. 207).

It is inconceivable that Emma's response to the affair was as adaptive and mature as Jung seemed to imply. Her mistrust of her husband, whose infidelity had intruded itself so soon after their marriage (in 1902), must have seriously upset her. Her anxieties were then implicitly conveyed to Agathe, who sensed the strain in the relationship between her mother and father. [11]

To round out the discussions of the Sabina influence on Agathe, we note an additional observation by Jung that occurs in his book, *Transformations and Symbols of the Libido* (1911-12, p. 190). There, in the context of a discussion of children's interest in the act of defecation as providing a possible route for the emergence of the newborn into the world, he alludes to "Psychic Conflicts in the Child." The child of that case, he states, "had a well-developed anal birth theory, like Freud's 'Little Hans,' (and) later contracted the habit of sitting for hours on the toilet. On one occasion her father growing impatient, went to the toilet and called: 'Come out at once! Whatever are you doing?' Whereupon the answer came from within: 'I'm doing a little cart and two ponies!' So the child was 'making' a little cart and two ponies, things she particularly wanted at that moment. In this way one can make whatever one wishes. . . . From a patient I got a parallel fantasy dating from her childhood: in the toilet there was a crack in the wall, and she used to imagine that a fairy would come out of this crack and give her everything she wished for."

It is quite likely that this patient was none other than Sabina Spielrein whose case Jung had presented (without identifying her, of course) at the Amsterdam Congress in 1907, as above noted. In his account of the origin of her symptoms in the childhood years her fixation on defecation was stressed and was related by him to Freud's theory of the anal stage of infantile sexuality. That Jung here connected that case with the observations of his young daughter by the common theme of anal erotism, and that both are seen as providing support for Freud's account of Little Hans indicates how, in ways not mentioned in the published letters of Jung and Freud, the case of Agathe and that of Sabina were interwoven in the thought of the father/therapist. The reconstruction of this parameter of Agathe's anxieties—Jung's relationship with Sabina—gains a certain confirmation from this (inferred) reference to her in 1911.

The tension between Carl Jung and his wife Emma continued and even intensified after the influence of his relationship with Sabina Spielrein receded. The new influence was Carl's connection with Antonia (Toni) Wolff, another Jewish girl in her early twenties. She also had come to him as a patient and he successfully cured her of a schizoid type of ailment. The intimacy apparently developed by 1911-1912, the year after Sabina withdrew. However, this extramarital affair attained a permanent status when, at Jung's insistence, Toni became an acknowledged member of the family circle, e.g., by her regular presence at Sunday dinner. The Jung children called her "Aunt," and Emma, after enduring the situation for a long period under protest, yielded to it as a necessary condition of her husband's mental health. It is now generally acknowledged that Jung's psychological disorder, which began in 1913 and posed a serious problem, with psychotic symptoms at times, was engendered, in part, by the rupture with Freud, and was aggravated by the conflict between Carl and Emma over his intimacy with Toni. Emma for a period of months sought the guidance of Sigmund Freud through a correspondence some of which survives and has been published in the *Freud/Jung Letters.* Toni was apparently regarded by Carl as an indispensable complement to Emma as a "femme inspiratrice," (an anima projection), while Emma served the more conventional roles of wife and mother.

It is not unlikely that Emma's published monograph entitled "Animus and Anima" (E. Jung, 1957) was largely an expression of her effort to rationalize and reconcile herself to the complicated marital situation.

Emma Jung made an ingenuous confession that supports this interpretation. She is quoted as having said just before she died: "I shall always be grateful to Toni for doing for my husband what I or anyone else could not have done for him in a most critical time" (van der Post, 1975, p. 177). One may infer that Emma, in the end, considered Toni as a necessary condition of Jung's psychic stability—doubtless an echo of Jung's own demand.

It is repeatedly mentioned by biographers that Jung had a following of female patients who became his adulatory and protective guard over and above these two instances of sexual intimacy. This conspicuous aspect of his entourage, including the Toni Wolff relationship, is well described by Paul Stern (1976) and Vincent Brome (1978). Interpretively new light is shed on the role of women in Jung's therapeutic and investigative endeavors by the essay of Claire Douglas (1989). In it she bespeaks the independence of many of Jung's female patient-disciples who, like Christiana Morgan, asserted their autonomy from the orthodox, male-dominated dispensation of Jung himself. (See Appendix B.)

Agathli in Later Editions

Leaving the observations of Agathli by Jung in the *Freud/Jung Letters* before the Clark Conference, we go forward now to the first German version of the case published by him after the Conference. It will be recalled that, though the lectures were presented in German (as were Freud's), the first printing of the lecture was in English, in a translation by A. A. Brill of a German version supplied by Jung, for publication in the *American Journal of Psychology* (April 1910). The German original of this translation has not survived. Moreover, in two Forewords to subsequent German editions, Jung bypassed it. He referred to the German version published in the *Jahrbuch für Psychoanalyse,* vol. 2, August 1910, as if it were the very first. Thus the Foreword for the "Second Edition" (dated 1915) was followed by a reprinting of the *Jahrbuch* version. Apparently Jung preferred not further to acknowledge some aspects of the lecture as it was presented at Clark. Historically, however, the article translated by Brill best reflects what actually happened in Worcester in September 1909 when Jung was still serving as Freud's disciple. By July-August 1910 the relationship had deteriorated and, as has already been seen, the decline had apparently begun as early as the conversation in Central Park on September 2. It is for that reason that detailed attention has been accorded above to the version first published.

A notable difference in the *Jahrbuch* version is the change in title. As published in the *American Journal of Psychology* the lecture had been called "Experiences Concerning the Psychic Life of the Child" (the German original is not available), but the new title "Über Konflikte der kindlichen Seele" replaced the more general "Experiences" with the more specific term "Conflicts." (The English translation in the *Collected Works* reads "Psychic Conflicts in a Child.") In view of the actual content, one might have expected the word "Anxieties" instead of "Conflicts" to reflect the actual symptoms. But that choice would perhaps have mirrored the parallel to the phobia of the five-year-old boy which, by then, Jung was less inclined to stress.

Another striking difference from the lecture is the omission of the prologue (above quoted) in which the lecturer beseeched the audience to listen without prejudice and to note the astonishing similarity to Freud's recently published case of the five-year-old boy. The other conspicuous omission is the epilogue that followed the diary-like observations, in particular, the example of another four-year-old daughter of an "intelligent father"—a father who refused to recognize the child's behavior as masturbation. Since this point has been discussed above, the omission is here merely noted.

It is important, however, to note that, while in his correspondence with Freud before the journey, the last report about Agathe was in the letter dated August 4, 1909, in the *Jahrbuch* Jung added observations from the next half year. These involved further enlightenment of the child about the nature of reproduction, the birth process, and the relationship between the parents.

Most of the observed details, especially the child's fantasies, were retained. A telling exception concerns the fable of the stork, which in the Clark version was attributed to the father, but which was now said to "have been told to Anna." The allusion to the *other* four-year-old girl who masturbated was omitted, as was the scornful disapproval of those who would omit all things "sexual" in dealing with children. It is obvious that Jung, instead of using the opportunity to fortify Freud's position on infantile sexuality, has taken a more neutral stance. Later he would go further and offer a nonsexual explanation of the child's fantasies.

Having observed the child through her fifth year of life, Jung now recounted what happened after she was given further sexual information. In essence he found that she experienced no harmful effects; but he also comments that she accepted the new knowledge without entirely abandoning her own fantasies—a result that he commends.

The impact of this first published German version upon Freud was clearly reflected in an exchange between him and Jung immediately after the August *Jahrbuch* appeared. On receiving that issue, Freud wrote: "I have reread with pleasure the charming story of the children (cf. Worcester, Anna and Sophie) but regretted that the scientist did not entirely overcome the father;

it is a delicate relief when it might have been a vigorous statue, and because of its subtlety the lesson will be lost on most readers. . . . The analogies with Little Hans are developed only here and there; you forget that the reader is by definition a simpleton and deserves to have his nose rubbed in these things" (*Freud/Jung Letters*, p. 348).

Though Freud tactfully thus refrained from open criticism of Jung's article and made no direct comparison with the original version at Clark, his dissatisfaction is but thinly veiled. His deft metaphor concerning the difference between a delicate relief and a three-dimensional, vigorous statue is notable. He even tried to mitigate the shortcomings of the article by excusing the *father* who had to hide behind the *scientist.*

In his apologetic reply Jung grasped at this straw: "I knew of course that I could not quite disown the father when writing about my Agathli, but I don't think this personal note will worry the initiates. The analogies with Little Hans should have been developed if only it had been possible to keep these explanations short. I had the feeling that I would have had to say very many things I wanted to avoid. The thicker a work is the less it is read. Finally, one must after all leave something to the reader's imagination" (ibid., p. 350).

It is all too evident that Jung is disingenuously rationalizing for having played down the analogies with Little Hans. His reasons are lame, e.g., the excuse that reporting at length might have bored the reader. One discerns that he is restive and one questions the total sincerity of the presentation of the case at Clark. Some of the skepticism that he had shown to Freud in New York was more openly asserting itself but with a veneer of diplomacy.

To judge from the number of different editions he devoted to it over the years, Jung must have attached special significance to the essay on Agathe. There were five editions. Two appeared in 1910, the first in the English translation by Brill (April 1910), then the first edition published in German (August 1910) in the *Jahrbuch.* The latter was a revision of the German version that Jung had supplied to Brill. But Jung regarded this *Jahrbuch* edition as the first; he ignored the actual first edition (translated by Brill) when he published what he called a "second edition" as a separate brochure in 1916 and, again, a "third edition" of the

brochure in 1939. This last version served as the basis for the
English translation that appeared in Jung's *Collected Works, 17.*
As we have seen, he reported the original observations in letters to
Freud during the first eight months of 1909. One may reasonably
infer that Jung was in conflict about the presentation of this quite
special case, the case of his own daughter. For us it is a bellwether
of Jung's waxing and waning intimacy with Freud. [12]

It was, of course, Freud's conception of infantile sexuality that
had served as the context of Jung's original observations. As early
as 1909 and as late as 1946 he was attempting to come to terms
with it. His revision of Freud's entire approach first appeared in
Jung's book on the libido (1912) but his revision of Freud's conception of infantile sexuality as portrayed in the case of Agathe
appeared four years later. Jung announced his declaration of
independence in the Foreword to the second edition (1916) of the
essay and, again, with some variations, in the Foreword to the
third edition (1939). This position was epitomized in a Supplement, now available in the English *Collected Works, 17.*

What was the thesis of this declaration? Jung formulated it as
the "polyvalent germinal disposition" of the child, a phrase patently
designed in counterpoint to Freud's "polymorphous perverse
disposition" (cf. Freud, 1905a). Jung's formulation follows:

"The basic hypothesis of the view advanced in this work is that
sexual interest . . . plays a not inconsiderable role in the nascent
process of infantile thinking, a hypothesis that should meet with
no serious opposition. . . . [But] I also lay stress on the significance
of *thinking* and the importance of concept-building [by the child]
for the solution of psychic conflicts. . . . the initial sexual interest
strives only figuratively towards an immediate sexual goal, but
far more towards the development of thinking. . . . I do not
regard . . . thinking . . . as just a makeshift function of sexuality
which sees itself hindered in its pleasurable realization and is
therefore compelled to pass over into the thinking function;
but, while perceiving in infantile sexuality the beginnings of a
future sexual function, I also discern there the seeds of higher
spiritual functions. . . . The fact that adult sexuality grows out
of this polyvalent germinal disposition does not prove that
infantile sexuality is 'sexuality' pure and simple. I therefore
dispute the rightness of Freud's idea of the 'polymorphous-
perverse' disposition of the child. . . . Even though a child may be

preoccupied with matters which, for adults, have an undoubtedly sexual complexion, this does not prove that the nature of the child's preoccupation is to be regarded as equally sexual." (*Collected Works, 17,* 4-7.)

This formulation first appeared as a Supplement to Jung's last revision of the Agathe article. There he postulated the child's innate autonomy to employ the thinking function at a time coinciding with the beginnings of sexuality. He compared children to primitive peoples who, knowing the basic facts of human sexuality, still often prefer a mythological explanation. In that regard he wrote: "Side by side with the biological, the spiritual, too, has its inviolable rights. It is assuredly no accident that primitive peoples, even in adult life, make the most fantastic assertions about well-known sexual processes, as for instance that coitus has nothing to do with pregnancy. . . . It is not hard to see that in these facts, so frequently observed among primitives, there lie the beginnings of *abstraction,* which is so very important for culture. We have every reason to suppose that this is also true of the psychology of the child. . . . We must assign a separate principle to the thinking function, a principle which coincides with the beginnings of sexuality only in the polyvalent germinal disposition of the very young child. To reduce the origins of thinking to mere sexuality is an undertaking that runs counter to the basic facts of human psychology" (*Collected Works, 17,* 34-35).

In this context it is illuminating to observe that in the Foreword to the second edition Jung briefly returned to consider the significance of masturbation, which he had discussed by an example at the end of his Clark lecture (preserved in the Brill translation but not included in later editions). Jung states (*Collected Works, 17,* 4-5, Foreword, dated December 1915): ". . . we know from experience that the infantile beginnings of sexuality can also lead to real sexual functioning—masturbation—when the conflicts are not resolved. The building of concepts, however, opens out to the libido a channel that is capable of further development, so that its continual, active realization is assured. Given a certain intensity of conflict, the absence of concept-building acts as a hindrance which thrusts the libido back into its initial sexuality, with the result that these beginnings or buddings are brought prematurely to an abnormal pitch of development. This produces an infantile neurosis."

One sees here that Jung regards childhood masturbation as unnatural—as symptomatic of the damming up of the spiritual (conceptual) fantasies that the child builds up for him/herself under normal conditions. In diametric opposition to Freud, who used sublimation as a refinement (by analogy with chemical sublimation) of biological sexuality, Jung asserts that the primordial behavior of the child is spiritual—an expression of the soul—and it is only when this expression is blocked that gross sexual behavior occurs in the child. It has seldom been so clearly stated by Jung that his opposition to Freud's infantile sex theory was so radical that it would seem to some scientific observers as a reversion to a religious psychology. No wonder that Jung was never quite comfortable with this regressive position after he had formerly given unqualified support to the sexual theory as Freud's chief accomplishment. One suspects that even in his later, more fully evolved theories concerning the collective unconscious, the archetypes, anima and animus, and the various imagos, Jung was not quite convinced of his emancipation from the "materialistic" position of Sigmund Freud. In fact, the transition from his earlier adherence to Freud to his own later theoretical formulations after 1913 involved a psychotic experience with hallucinations, delusions and other symptoms. In other terms, it constituted a religious conversion—in essence, a reversion to the Christianity of his father. But in Jung's version, Christian theology is modernized to become compatible with the demonic—the pagan demands of the collective unconscious.

Was it this tendency that attracted Jung to the Teutonic ethos in Hitler's National Socialism? Just as Hitler thought of the Jew as without soul—as grossly materialistic and thus an enemy of the Aryan spirit—Jung, for a brief period, at least, found himself in agreement with the doctrine of *Mein Kampf.* Jung, too, repudiated Jewish materialism, in particular, the doctrine of infantile sexuality. In this sense, Jung's alleged anti-Semitism is not prejudice against individual Jews but is rather an alignment with a spirituality that, as he states in the chapter of his autobiography dealing with Freud, is totally incompatible with Freud's philosophical orientation.

A concluding glance at the case of "Little Anna" will hence model itself on Jung's own thoughts as he recalled his rift with Freud and reconstructed it in the autobiography published a year after his death (1962). Referring to his 1912 book on the "libido," he wrote: "When I was working on my book about the libido and approaching the end of the chapter 'The Sacrifice,' I knew in advance that its publication would cost me my friendship with Freud. For I planned to set down in it my own conception of incest, the decisive transformation of the concept of libido, and various other ideas in which I differed from Freud. To me incest signified a personal complication only in the rarest cases. Usually incest has a highly religious aspect, for which reason the incest theme plays a decisive part in almost all cosmogonies and in numerous myths. But Freud clung to the literal interpretation of it and could not grasp the spiritual significance of incest as a symbol. I knew he would never be able to accept any of my ideas on this subject." [13]

If one reads this passage in the historical perspective of Jung's own experience with the case of "Little Anna," the first German edition of which appeared in the summer of 1910, and of his book on the libido, which appeared 1911-1912 in its periodical form, it is evident that these two events were intertwined. The book was in significant part a reaction to his close observation of the early development of his daughter Agathe. These observations were conducted under the scrutiny of Freud, a part of Jung's self-analysis under Freud's guidance. Freud's theory of infantile sexuality was being put to the test by Jung's observations of his first child which, Freud hoped, would confirm his just-published case of "Little Hans." In a modified sense, Jung was offering his daughter as a sacrifice to the inspiring master, Sigmund Freud, who had adopted him as "son and heir." [14]

The analogy with the biblical sacrifice of Isaac by Abraham as a test of faith is compelling if one recognizes Jung's own later reinterpretation of the Agathe case, in particular, his insistence upon the symbolic as opposed to the literal meaning of incest. True, he himself, in his 1912 book, emphasized mother/son rather than father/daughter incest; but this difference is easily read as a displacement from the current relationship to his little daughter. Jung's reinterpretation of the "incest barrier" must, in part, have been a defensive attempt to extricate himself from his dangerous involvement with Freud's materialistic world view. In this light it is easy to read Jung's description of his departure from Freud's sexual theory as an allusion to the personal sacrifice that was entrapping him. He had to escape by redefining Freud's concept of libido, the Oedipus complex and incest. This rescue was important enough to warrant the price of Freud's friendship. But while Jehovah at the last moment spared Abraham the sacrifice of Isaac and accepted a scapegoat, Freud was a more jealous god! He would not forego his theory of the libido for what he regarded as a regression to precisely the occult or mystical view of human nature that his bold observations had challenged and overturned.

Let us turn to Jung's own account of his difference from Freud in the chapter called "The Sacrifice" (Chapter 8) to test the above interpretation. Having discussed the creation of the world according to the *Rig-Veda,* Jung continued: "It is evident that by this is meant not a physical, but a psychological cosmogony. The world comes into being when man discovers it. But he only discovers it when he sacrifices his containment in the primal mother, the original state of unconsciousness. What drives him to this discovery is conceived by Freud as the 'incest barrier.' The incest prohibition blocks the infantile longing for the mother and forces the libido along the path of life's biological aim. The libido, driven back from the mother by the incest prohibition, seeks a sexual object in place of the forbidden mother. Here the terms 'incest prohibition,' 'mother,' etc. are used metaphorically, and it is in this sense that we have to interpret Freud's paradoxical dictum: 'To begin with we knew none but sexual objects.' This statement is not much more than a sexual allegory, as when one speaks of male and female electrical connections, screws, etc. All it does is to read the partial truths of the adult into infantile conditions which are totally different. Freud's view is incorrect if we take it literally." [15]

A little later Jung argues against the literal view in these words: "Freud's incest theory describes certain fantasies that accompany the regression of libido and are especially characteristic of the personal unconscious as found in hysterical patients. Up to a point they are infantile-sexual fantasies which show very clearly just where the hysterical attitude is defective and why it is so incongruous." [16] From the view that it is precisely the neurotic who not only exemplifies but suffers from the Freudian type of sexual obsession, Jung returns to the Vedic hymn of creation and now relates it to the "Christian mystery" of sacrifice. "Even as the world is created by sacrifice, by renouncing the personal tie to childhood, so, according to the teaching of the Upanishads, will be created the new state of man, which can be described as immortal." [17]

In Freud's early conversations with Jung as reported in *Memories, Dreams, Reflections* (p. 154), Freud is said to have feared "the black tide of . . . occultism." In contrast, as Jung explains: "The stories of the [Holy] Grail had been of the greatest importance to me ever since I read them at the age of 15, for the first time. I had an inkling that a great secret still lay behind those stories. . . . My whole being was seeking for something still unknown which might confer meaning upon the banality of life." This quest was the essence of Jung's conceptions of the collective unconscious, the archetypes, etc., in which sexuality was transformed by the symbolism of his system to discover the "chthonic spirit" which represents "the dark side of the God-image." [18] He was not abandoning sexuality, he insisted, but, instead, seeking to discover and reveal its true significance as the other side of the divine. It is in these terms that one must approach Jung's latter-day portrayal of traditional Christianity. After a decade of dangerous flirtation with the materialistic Freudian theory, Jung would spend the rest of his life making converts to his own vision of numinosity. In that quest the observations of "Little Anna" under Freud's influence would be transformed by the "polyvalent germinal disposition" that he shared with her.

The American expedition, including Jung's third lecture at Clark University when fully understood, represented an aspect of his own self-realization. And it may, in fact, be seriously questioned whether during this process Jung had ever seriously accepted or even conscientiously attempted to accept Freud's psychoanalytic theory—as he pleaded with his audience at Worcester to do. His experience with Freud, as reflected in the case of Agathe, was a means to an end—an end that from the outset did not permit him to satisfy Freud's dire need for a non-Jewish successor.

Appendices to Chapter VIII

A. Little Hans and Little Anna

The recognition that Jung's Little Anna in his third lecture at Clark University was his own daughter Agathli is not unique in the annals of child analysis. It is now also possible biographically to identify Freud's Little Hans. The extent of the parallel between these two cases is historically of considerable interest and warrants a comparative synopsis.

Little Hans was Herbert Graf, the son of Max Graf, a Viennese musicologist. This fact is known from a portion of Herbert Graf's biographical interview in *Opera News,* vol. 36, Feb. 1972, pp. 25-26. He was the Grafs' first child, born April 10, 1903. In later life, from 1936-1949, Herbert Graf was Stage Director of the Metropolitan Opera Company, New York.

Little Anna was Agathe Jung, the first child of Dr. Carl G. Jung, who was born December 26, 1904. In both cases the arrival of a new sibling appeared to be related to the major symptoms. For Hans, that sibling was the sister Hanna, born October 4, 1906; for Agathe, it was the arrival of a brother, Franz, born November 11, 1908.

In both instances the father made the developmental observations and reported them to Freud as consultant. Freud was not the direct therapist.

A question exists as to the possible role of suggestion in the observations and symptoms, especially regarding the child's intense sexual curiosity, as reported by the father. Freud, in his article on Little Hans, stated that he had encouraged his pupils carefully to observe the early sexual development of their offspring because the topic had hitherto been ignored or even "cleverly overlooked" (*Standard Edition, 10,* p. 6). Since Max Graf was a friend of Freud and a member of the professional circle who eventually organized the Vienna Psychoanalytic Society in 1907, with meetings held in Freud's apartment on Wednesday evenings, his observations of the boy were, no doubt, partly due to Freud's encouragement. Did he intensify the child's sexual curiosity by his expectations? Moreover, the mother of Herbert had been helped therapeutically by Freud "in her girlhood," i.e., before marriage (ibid., p. 141). Max Graf, the father of Herbert, also mentions Freud's therapy of a lady acquaintance as a result of which Graf became interested in Freud and met him personally (Graf, 1942, p. 467). From the context one may infer that the lady in question was the future Mrs. Graf, and the treatment occurred around 1901-1902. It was Hans's mother, as Freud explained, who first induced the boy's "castration complex" (when he was three-and-one-half) by her naive threat to call in the family doctor if the boy continued to touch his "widdler" (penis). Was the boy led to pay more, rather than less, attention to the genital area by this threat? And did she make this innocent mistake because in her own therapy with Freud he had disclosed some early sexual etiology? However, Freud did not criticize her for admonishing the child, perhaps because he believed that castration fear was an inevitable part of a boy's Oedipus complex.

In the case of Little Anna, the father was making his observations of his daughter during the time of Freud's greatest influence upon him as a young psychiatrist. Moreover, he had personal problems for which he was reaching out to Freud for guidance. In a sense, his careful observations of Agathli were part of his own self-analysis. This fact does not necessarily invalidate the observations—a view that Jung himself appeared to hold despite his later rejection of Freud's sexual theory. Otherwise Jung would not have continued for years to report the empirical data though he gradually revised his interpretation of them.

It is possible that Freud's involvement in the case of Little Hans had an influence upon Jung's contemporary observations of his daughter. Freud was writing up the case of Little Hans in 1908; he published it in 1909. These are the relevant dates. On August 5, 1908, Freud submitted the manuscript of the Little Hans paper to Jung; Jung was the Editor of the *Jahrbuch* in which the article would appear in April 1909. On January 17, 1909, Freud told Jung that he had corrected the proofs of the article (*Freud/ Jung Letters*, pp. 166 and 196). The first observation of Agathli was sent by Jung to Freud in the letter of January 19, 1909, two days after Freud's comment to Jung about correcting the Little Hans proofs. (There is reason to believe that Jung had made earlier observations of Agathli reported in letters that have not been published.) In any event, Jung's awareness of the Little Hans case was keen while he made his observations of his young daughter. Repeatedly in the letters the parallel between Little Hans and Agathli was noted by both Freud and Jung, once with the semi-humorous comment that Agathli knew nothing about Little Hans.

Returning now to the observations of Little Hans by his father, we should consider a remarkable biographical fact not hitherto noted. In an article by Max Graf of reminiscences about his relationship with Sigmund Freud (*Psychoanalytic Quarterly*, 1942, vol. 11), the author, gratefully remembering Freud's friendship, mentions (p. 474) that on the third birthday of his son Freud went to the trouble of carrying up the four flights of stairs to the Graf apartment a rocking horse brought as a present for the child. (Nothing in the article refers to "Little Hans" or Freud's treatment of Graf's son.) Now consider the published case: Freud stated that the first reports "date from a period when he [the boy] was not quite three years old" (*Standard Edition, 10*, p. 7). At that time Hans was already showing a "peculiarly lively interest in that portion of his body which he used to describe as his 'widdler'." The mother of Hans made her ill-advised "castration threat" when the child was three-and-one-half years old. The first observation involving a horse, according to the diary, occurred when Hans was four-and-a-quarter, and the earliest phobic symptoms concerning horses came six months later.

What influence did the gift of the rocking horse from the admired family friend on the third birthday of Hans play on later developments? That the gift was impressive is attested by its recall after a lapse of 40 years by the father; it must also have made a special impression on the child at the time. Was it a sheer coincidence that the present was a horse? Or was there a determining relationship? One possibility is that the child had exhibited some concern about horses before the symptomatic behavior first included in the father's diary. If so, was Freud, in presenting the rocking horse, doing a commonsense "behavioristic" bit of therapy—an attempt at desensitization concerning horses by offering some positive reinforcement? But if there was such an attempt, it might have boomeranged. By the rhythm of the rocking horse the boy might have incidentally stimulated himself—at a very susceptible age, according to Freudian views about masturbation. In that event, play with the horse might have heightened his sexual awareness and increased oedipal fantasies.

Though Joseph Wolpe and Stanley Rachman knew nothing about the rocking horse, it is remarkable that in 1958 Wolpe published his now classic work *Psychotherapy by Reciprocal Inhibition*, essentially desensitization, and in 1960 he and Rachman published a critique of Freud entitled "Psychoanalytic 'Evidence': A Critique Based on Freud's Case of Little Hans." Had they known about the rocking horse, they would have had a compelling piece of evidence to report. At the date of their writing, however, the identity of Little Hans as Herbert Graf was unknown, so that even if they had read the paper by Dr. Graf, it would not have provided the relevant information.

Let us now return to the evidence for the identity of Little Anna and to the original observations of her by her father under her real name, Agathe (Agathli). Jung had considered these observations important enough in their own right to deserve publication even before he was invited to Clark. Thus he states in a letter to Freud dated June 4, 1909 (*F/J Letters*, p. 230): "My Agathli will appear in the August number [of the *Jahrbuch*]; I haven't written it up yet for lack of time. I'll get to it next week." One week later we learn that Jung has just been invited to lecture at Clark. A year later Freud (writing to Jung, April 26, 1910) sends regards to Jung's wife and to his child "Anna." The editor of the *Freud/ Jung Letters* explains in a footnote concerning "Anna": "The case name for Agathli in 'Psychic Conflicts in a Child.'" A reference is then given to Letter 209 F, note 2, August 18, 1910, where it is stated that this is the new title adopted by Jung for the third of his lectures at Clark. In the interim Jung had presented that lecture, undoubtedly by agreement with Freud. For Freud had foreseen the furious opposition to his forthcoming publication on Little Hans, the first detailed example of infantile sexuality, the Oedipus situation, and the "castration complex." It should not be surprising to learn that Freud's need for this contribution by Jung entered into the (still) enigmatic negotiations with Hall that, by June 12, 1909, had brought about Jung's invitation to lecture at Clark. But until the missing letters concerning these negotiations are found and published—if they still exist—we can only conjecture about the influence of Freud in that invitation and the possible role of the case of Agathli.

B. An Analogue

There is some question about the stability of this emancipation. The doubt arises, in particular, from the reading of a recently published book (Robinson, 1992) which largely concerns the career of this former patient of Jung, Christiana Morgan. The details of her life course are of interest here in more than one respect.

Jung's therapy with married female patients appears to have had its effect partly by liberating them and their paramours from sexual inhibitions. At any rate, this inference seems to be warranted and is strikingly illustrated in the above cited book, *Love's Story Told: A Life of Henry A. Murray*. Henry (Harry) Murray was a professor of psychology at Harvard University, who, after a long life of 95 years, died in 1987. His mistress for 40 years was Christiana Morgan. Nearly 20 years before his death, Murray planned this book with Forrest Robinson. He cooperated with his future biographer by holding frequent and frank conversations with him during those years and by giving him unlimited access to the diaries that he and Christiana (Chris) had kept to describe in detail the beginning, development and vicissitudes of their unusual sexual relationship. That liaison was not only outside the limits of conventional marriage but inside the realm of sheer sexual abandon. Murray maintained that he required this license in order to overcome his otherwise hampered literary creativity. He desperately wanted to write without impediment. Perhaps (one may surmise) this intense need sprang from a speech impediment that he thought resulted from an eye operation performed on him during childhood to correct a squint. The Adlerian formula of "organ inferiority" that may entail "psychical compensation" with the aid of a "guiding fiction" seems made to order for the case of "Murr" (Murray's pseudonym) in his contribution to *The History of Psychology in Autobiography*.

Moreover, this untrammeled sexuality was meant to serve as a laboratory—an observatory for a book which, as a "dyad," the lovers would jointly produce. The volume would describe objectively but from the inside the revelations of uninhibited libidinal expression. There was also another book, one that had been planned by Murray shortly after the time of his first meeting Christiana in 1923. In 1924, when Harry was 31 and Chris,

27, they travelled to England with their families. Harry and Christiana's husband Will were going for a period of study at the University of Cambridge. During the ocean voyage Harry read Melville's *Moby Dick* for the first time and, according to the Murray legend, he became instantly infatuated with its author.

It may be significant that Robinson, following Harry, alludes repeatedly in the biography to Murray's involvement not only with *Moby Dick*, but with *Pierre, Mardi*, etc.; yet, surprisingly, no mention is made of Melville's last novel *Billy Budd*. The protagonist of that story suffers from a stammer—a hallmark that leads him involuntarily to a (reflex) thrust with his arm resulting in manslaughter. After a court martial, Billy is sentenced to be hanged. I have long thought that this book of Melville, rather than *Moby Dick* or *Pierre*, decided Harry's identification with Melville. The omission suggests that Harry repressed the root experience as too revealing.

Interrupting his year of study at Easter 1925, Harry, already in the toils of his attraction to Christiana, went to Zurich for consultation with C. G. Jung. Soon afterwards Christiana followed suit. From that time forward, Jung became their guru. Their liaison was molded not only by the Analytic Psychology of Jung, but by the model of Jung's own life. As above noted, Jung had had extramarital relationships with female patients, at least one of whom (Toni Wolff) became a distinguished therapist and an "aunt" in the Jung household. This prototype was well known to the dyad, as Robinson notes (Robinson, pp. 122-126).

In the course of her self-study under Jung, Christiana painted a series of visions that Jung later used for seminars in which they served as the materials for instruction through interpretation and discussion with the seminar members. (A book based on these visions is presently being prepared by Claire Douglas to be published as one of the continuing volumes of Jung's *Collected Works*.)

In keeping with Murray's Melvillian dedication, Robinson has constructed the biography, presumably with Harry's help, on the model of Melville's writings: *Moby Dick, Pierre* and *Mardi*. These books became Robinson's scaffold for the composition and provided the titles of the various chapters. A chief objective of the biography was to portray the life style of the dyad—an objective that partly carries out their own uncompleted project. The result is "the undraped spectacle of a valor-ruined man," Melville's words though not quoted by Robinson.

Harry and Chris constructed and acted out a private mythology that ignored and increasingly defied the conventions—in secret, of course. In that never-never land, he was Mansol and she, Wona. The story, a mixture of fact and fantasy, is frankly told: it teems with detail from the diary sources, so much so that one sometimes strains to perceive the nominally dominant Jungian conception of the libido. For, denying the all-powerful biological sexual drive as formulated by Sigmund Freud, Murray replaced it with the more transcendental Jungian one, yet Mansol and Wona paradoxically unfold to the reader a love story the core of which is polymorphous sexual indulgence. By 1936 this behavior had taken the form of literal sado-masochism ("The Whip of Slavery"), in the beginning the whip being wielded by Harry but, at a later stage, by Chris. By this time the dyad was unable to experience sexual arousal without recourse to this mode of overstimulation. But they had a convenient rationalization for resorting to these "exertions." It was a necessary part of the research for the writing of the book on love, by now referred to as "The Proposition" (ibid., pp. 250-254).

Even more instructive than the mythology of Mansol and Wona is Harry's not-so-secret identification with Lucifer. This was a guiding fiction that he expressed—even flaunted—on occasion in his writings. Thus, on the centenary of Melville's *Moby Dick* (1851) he published an essay "In Nomeni Diaboli" (In the Name of the Devil), one of his two significant contributions to the Melville literature. The title commemorates an expression used by Melville in writing to Hawthorne about the evolving composition of *Moby Dick*. He declared that the book was broiled in Hell-fire and baptized, not in the name of the Holy Ghost, but in that of the Devil. Even more forthrightly expressing Harry's identification with Lucifer was his presidential address in 1962 to Division 8 of the American Psychological Association. It bore the title "The Personality and Career of Satan." The meeting was held in St. Louis, the city of my residence, and before the session Harry visited at my home. He took the opportunity briefly to examine my library— we had a longstanding common interest in collecting books. I vividly recall the moment when he took from one of the shelves, with a grunt of satisfaction, the volume called *The Devil: A Historical and Medical Study.* (The work was authored by Garcon and Vinchon, and it appeared in 1929. Harry had apparently not seen a copy previously.) These are but three representative instances of Harry's abiding interest in the kindred spirit of the great Adversary (cf. Robinson, 313, 320, 343-344).

In the end both literary projects foundered—and the Melville, not of *Moby Dick,* but of *Pierre* began to provide the key to what was transpiring. *Pierre,* originally published in 1852, a year after *Moby Dick,* is a book about a failed writer. And, as if to express this modified identification, Murray, with the assistance of his daughter Josephine, in 1949 published a new edition of that novel. The editors supplied a long expository Introduction and abundant explanatory notes. It was Harry's major contribution to Melville scholarship and was the closest he ever came to writing his big Melville book. He himself considered this contribution as a first step toward the original project which, in 1946, he foresaw as consisting of two volumes, entitled "The Development of Herman Melville" (ibid., p. 314). As things turned out, *Love's Story Told* is, in essence, and with appropriate modifications, a reification of *Pierre or the Ambiguities.*

But the modifications are, of course, the quintessence. Mansol and Wona moved from the heights of ecstacy to the depths of despair. And, after conflict and disillusionment, the whole enterprise finally failed. Chris became a devotee of Bacchus—a hopeless alcoholic—and at last yielded herself to eternity. It happened on St. John, one of the Virgin Islands, to which the two had gone for a vacation in 1967. Early one morning Harry found Chris lying dead in the shallow water on the beach by their cottage.

The projected books were never to be written. Instead, about three years after the death of Chris, Harry began cooperating with Robinson for this biography. By now Murray accepted incompletion as his destiny; he also was willing to accept the help of another to portray the dynamics of the incompleteness. He might thus even make a virtue of his fault by having it frankly described in a unique biography! And he might thus also achieve a pseudo-Satanic immortality—a continuation of what his mortal life had become.

As a former assistant of Harry Murray at the Harvard Psychological Clinic on Plympton Street during the heyday of its beginning (1930-1934), and as a friend of Chris Morgan, I keenly read this unusual biography. As I read, I recalled the Delphic motto engraved on an elegant bronze medallion distributed to one and all the faithful at a Clinic festival: "Let not him who seeks cease until he finds and when he finds he shall be astonished."

But the major lesson that I learned from these vivid pages as they recreated those years for me concerned not only Harry and Chris, some of whose secrets I already knew, but also concerned the illustrious figure of C. G. Jung, who had served from the beginning of the enterprise as Harry's guide and model. Jung had had extramarital relations with female patients but Jung's marriage had weathered the storm. The dyad of this book was not so fortunate. Yet in a parallel, Jung provided for them an analog of Pierre's Rev. Mr. Falsgrave, albeit in a more robust version than Melville fashioned. For as the quest faltered, Chris, in her diary, had more than once pondered the doubtful benefits of Jung's guidance. Harry, however, appears to have been more steadfast. His allegiance and admiration were attested by an event in 1936. In that year Harvard celebrated its founding 300 years earlier and, as at the 20th anniversary of Clark in 1909, numerous notables were assembled to lecture and to receive honorary degrees. For psychology, not Freud, still alive though ailing, but Jung, was selected, with Murray's strong recommendation. The choice of Jung vis-à-vis Freud is discussed in Robinson's book (page 229).

Ruminatingly, one recalls the classic allegory of Bunyan's *Pilgrim's Progress,* published in 17th century England shortly after the founding of Harvard University. There, too, Pilgrim pursues a beleaguered quest—a quest for the Celestial City. The story is forged in a homely, graphic and compelling style that has given it a permanent place in the history of literature. The protagonist of the First Part is named Christian; that of the Second, published six years later, is his soul-mate, Christiana. In Robinson's biography there is also a Christiana, but Harry, the Narcissist (ibid., 190, 384), could hardly have borne the name Christian: more than once, as already demonstrated, he had (cryptically) portrayed himself as a regular Beelzebub, a reveling pagan. Robinson's "Pagan's Progress" is a veritable inversion of Bunyan; it is reminiscent of Hogarth; but it only mimics Melville. Old Harry, guided by the Old Man (Jung), leads the feckless Christiana to a tragic denouement in a Caribbean Eden.

Soon after the death of Chris Morgan, Harry wrote me to say that "your friend Chris is gone." She walked out for an early swim before he was up. She "feinted" (a Freudian slip), Harry wrote, and because of an earlier operation on her sympathetic nervous system (of which I was aware), she was unable to rise without assistance. That was Harry's reconstruction of what had happened. He also explained that he and Chris had planned to be married in two months—in May. But this posthumous forecast was a fiction told to many of Harry's friends—*after* the death of Chris (ibid., p. 358).

****

In retrospect, Jung proved not to be a safe and stabilizing counsel for this dyad, at least not for the female partner. (See ibid., 205-208.) Sabina Spielrein was followed by a series of other women who fell in love with this charismatic therapist to a greater or lesser degree—a not infrequent effect of psychoanalytic therapy. Freud recognized the phenomenon as early as 1899, at the close of his book on dreams; he there called it "transference." But unlike Jung, Freud was quite restrained in responding with "counter-transference." Jung exceeded what Freud regarded as the permissible limits of the analyst's role.

Portrait of William James, 1909

Chapter IX

James's Day at the Clark Conference

As has been shown, William James arrived in Worcester at the end of Thursday afternoon September 9, 1909, went straight to Stanley Hall's home and spent the night there. In the present section we examine James's day at Clark with focus on Freud's recall of meeting him in Worcester. Freud wrote in his autobiography: "Another event of this time which made a lasting impression on me was a meeting with William James the philosopher. I shall never forget one little scene that occurred as we were on a walk together. He stopped suddenly, handed me a bag he was carrying and asked me to walk on, saying that he would catch up with me as soon as he had got through an attack of *angina pectoris* which was just coming on. He died of that disease a year later; and I have always wished that I might be as fearless as he was in the face of approaching death." [1]

It is of some consequence to determine just when this walk with James occurred. Other aspects of this unique encounter can then be related to James's impression of Freud upon hearing and meeting him in Worcester.

It is reasonable to assume that on the morning of Friday, September 10, James listened to Jung's lecture delivered at 9:00 A.M. in the Art Room of the Clark University Library. It was Jung's second lecture and was concerned with the word-association method. At 10:00 a lecture by William Stern on the psychology of the individual was presented. More important than either of these two lectures was Freud's fourth as delivered at 11:00 A.M. As already explained, this lecture as later published was not the one that Freud presented at Clark as the fourth in a series of five. He had delivered the lectures from notes and changed

171

the order when he wrote them out for publication. But it seems safe to infer from collation with the contemporary newspaper reports that the lecture on September 10 was similar in content to the one delivered the previous day. It dealt largely with the theory of dreams and, less fully, with slips of the tongue and other examples of unconsciously determined "accidental" behavior. That Freud's discussion of the psychology of dreams was, indeed, the main thrust of the lecture is further confirmed, as will presently be shown, in James's own words in letters to friends written soon after the event. For the moment let us follow James through the rest of the day.

It must have been around noon that the well-known group photograph of the participants, lecturers and audience, in the Friday morning sessions devoted to the behavioral sciences, was taken. The photograph shows the group assembled in rows on the steps of the Library building, which housed the Art Room. That it was taken then is certain because William James is prominent in the front row, and he was available for such a photograph only on Friday, September 10.

Lunch followed, and the sessions of the Conference resumed at 2:00 P.M. One learns from the *Worcester Telegram,* Saturday morning, September 11, that Freud on the previous morning discussed the interpretation of dreams with stress on "infantile inclinations" reflected in them and that Jung continued his lecture on word association with special reference to responses by members of the patient's own family; also that an afternoon session, under the Department of Psychology, was devoted to the topic "Elementary Psychology in the College." This symposium focused on the course offered to sophomores. In the chair was Professor Carl Seashore of the University of Iowa who introduced Dr. E. F. Buchner, Professor of Education at Johns Hopkins University, to discuss "The Preparation of the Student." Professor E. B. Titchener of Cornell University continued with "The Aim of the Course." He spoke not only about the course for sophomores but about his own particular interests in psychological investigation as basic to his instruction of students. He described the two scientific attitudes toward the world of experience—that of physics and that of psychology—each quite different in point of view. Even the elementary student should be taught this difference in orientation and method from the beginning instead of attempting to impart information about psychological facts. After two other papers, by Dr. Steven Colvin and Dr. Joseph Jastrow, "Dr. William James of Harvard University spoke briefly on the papers which had been given, as did Professor Mary W. Calkins of Wellesley" (*Worcester Telegram*, p. 4).

James's Walk with Freud

We know from the letters of James to Hall before the Conference that James intended to return to Cambridge Friday evening. After 4:00 or 5:00 P.M., James was apparently free of obligations, but it is clear from a letter written by Jung to Virginia Payne on July 23, 1949 that James spent two evenings at Hall's house during which Jung talked with him. [2] The first evening was obviously that of Thursday, September 9, when James had arrived there; the second must have been that of his departure, Friday, September 10. But since Hall, Freud and Jung had to participate in the convocation for the awarding of honorary degrees scheduled for 8:00 P.M. on Friday, Jung must have been referring to some time after 5:00 and well before 8:00 P.M. From a particular in the account by Freud describing his walk with James, it would appear that around 6:00 to 7:00 P.M., Freud, by invitation, walked with James toward or to the Union Depot, a mile and a half from Hall's house, where James would take the train for Boston. What is the particular that supports this probability?

It is the incident of the "bag"—the bag that Freud said James handed to him during the walk. But the word "bag" by itself does not carry the point. In Freud's German original of the autobiography he used the term *Handtasche,* which was freely translated by the English "bag". [3] Luckily, however, James himself seems to have supplied the more correct translation—the word that should have been used by the translator. In his letter to Hall written from Cambridge on September 8, 1909, the day before he took the train for Worcester, James said, "I shall drive [by cab from the depot] with my gripsack straight to your house." Is it not likely that this gripsack—James's overnight travel bag—was the bag he had with him on the walk with Freud? James was presumably now returning to the depot—with that same bag. It is unlikely that he would have carried the gripsack on any other walk he would have taken with Freud during his brief 24 hours in Worcester. According to this construction, the walk with Freud occurred when James invited Freud to accompany him on foot to the depot. This inference is strengthened by the supposition that James was seeking an opportunity to talk with Freud alone—an opportunity that he would not readily have had at Hall's house in the presence of the various other guests. To support this supposition we have James's statement (in a letter to Flournoy quoted at length below): "I went there [Worcester] for one day in order to see what Freud was like."

William James's Dreams

Shortly after the Clark Conference, James shared his impression of it with two colleagues. To Professor Mary Calkins of Wellesley, who had been present and participated with James in the Friday afternoon symposium, he wrote as follows: ". . . My day at Clark University was very enjoyable, not only in meeting you, but in seeing new faces; especially Titchener's, whom I had never met, and who made on me a very pleasant impression. I strongly suspect Freud, with his dream theory, of being a regular *halluciné* [deluded individual]. But I hope that he and his disciples will push it to its limits, as undoubtedly it covers some facts, and will add to our understanding of 'functional psychology.'"[4]

Having written to Mary Calkins on September 19, James, nine days later, shared his impressions of the Clark events, especially of Freud and Jung, with Théodore Flournoy: "Speaking of 'functional' psychology, Clark University, of which Stanley Hall is president, had a little international congress the other day in honor of the twentieth year of its existence. I went there for one day in order to see what Freud was like, and met also Yung [sic] of Zürich, who professed great esteem for you, and made a very pleasant impression. I hope that Freud and his pupils will push their ideas to their utmost limits, so that we may learn what they are. They can't fail to throw light on human nature, but I confess that he made on me personally the impression of a man obsessed with fixed ideas. I can make nothing in my own case with his dream theories, and obviously "symbolism" is a most dangerous method. A newspaper report of the congress said that Freud had condemned the American religious therapy (which has such extensive results) as very 'dangerous' because so 'unscientific.' Bah!"[5,6]

In this context it is illuminating to discover in the Diary of William James for March 17, 1909—seven months before the Worcester celebration—that he has noted "an attack on us by Witmer." James is disturbed about this publication. A day later he again alludes to Witmer's "attack" and confers with an unidentified "M–g," and adds the conclusion, "no action to be taken." Consulting the bibliography of Lightner Witmer, one finds a three part paper, published in the *Psychological Clinic* under the title "Mental healing and the Emmanuel movement" (Witmer, 1909). Freud in September was, therefore, a *second* source of irritation to James in regard to the Emmanuel movement.

But the remarkable aspect of this Diary entry is in the earlier of the two just-quoted passages. There the mention of the attack by Witmer is preceded by the comment "pectoral symptoms returned," and after the second allusion to Witmer's attack, in the first entry for the next day, one finds "very bad, pectorally." The final comment for the day is "*Horrible* day precordially." One infers that the criticism of James, including his support of the Emmanuel movement, evoked notable cardiac symptoms.

One should observe in that context that during the preceding months and for some months afterwards James was himself being treated by a Dr. James Ralph Taylor of Boston, a homeopathic physician, for his heart ailment and the accompanying neurosis. From March 1908 to May 1909 there were nearly 200 sessions, each carefully noted in the Diary with an appropriate number, along with fee payments at the rate of $2.00 per hour!

The relevance of these Diary entries and their association with James's cardiac symptoms lies in the parallel between James's attack of *angina pectoris* (or mental lapse) during his walk with Freud, described in this chapter, and the severe cardiac symptoms in response to Witmer's critique. In this latter case the connection is demonstrable; it thus tends to support the hypothesis that James's response during the walk in September was also instigated by a complex aroused during the conversation with Freud.

The article by Witmer began in the issue of December 15, 1908, and was concluded in the issue of February 15, 1909. In the third and final installment the heading refers to mental healing "As a System of Psychology and Philosophy" (p. 282), and in that discussion Witmer severely and at length criticizes William James as the leading authority upon whom the faith healers of the Emmanuel movement depend. Witmer contrasts James with Wundt and Hall, two leaders of experimental psychology. Hall is cited as having established the first American laboratory of experimental psychology, at Johns Hopkins University, and is contrasted with James who is a distinguished "literateur." "The art of William James resembles that of his brother Henry, although the medium in which they give expression to their thought and feeling differs greatly. William James may be something far better than a psychologist. [But he is not a scientist in the accepted sense of the word.] . . . William James has won recognition as our leading American psychologist through sheer force of personality. Nothing but a realization of the danger to the public and of the injury to psychology, which result from his using his professional authority to build up a modern occultism, would justify us in questioning this authority. The spoiled child of American psychology, exempt from all serious criticism, and the beau ideal of a large and cultured circle, Professor James, since the publication of his 'Principles of Psychology,' has apparently relaxed the intellectual inhibition which every man should exert over his desires" (pp. 294-295). Four pages later the writer lashes out: "If any supporter of the scientific 'slush' whose outpouring Professor James predicted flings at us such stones of rhetoric and false logic as 'materialism' and 'soulless psychology,' we appeal, in reply, to the practical outcome of our psychology—the social forces with which we believe ourself to be aligned." Witmer then commends the Emmanuel movement as a spiritual, moral and social force and couples it with the YMCA and other philanthropic organizations. These, like the church and the labor movement, do a great deal of good. And he announces that the editorial policy of his journal, *The Psychological Clinic*, stands for everything "that the Emmanuelists advocate *except* the unbridling of our intellectual inhibitions, the depreciation of science and of the human intellect, the recrudescence of occultism, the popularization of hypnotism, and the practical developments of the theory of subconsciousness . . ." (pp. 299-300).

It is evident from these quotations that James had a good basis for considering himself to be under "attack." That he responded with marked cardiac resonance is idiodynamically significant, and makes more plausible the hypothesis underlying Chapter X.

It was in other terms that Jones had recorded James's comment to him at the Conference. "He was very friendly to us and I shall never forget his parting words, said with his arm round my shoulder, 'The future of psychology belongs to your work'— a remarkable saying when one reflects on his puritanical background" (Jones, 1953, I, p. 57). Despite the happy effect on Jones made by this unqualified praise, he, as a psychoanalyst, should perhaps have suspected the superlative.

It is significant that James, in writing to both Calkins and Flournoy, selected Freud's dream theory for criticism—it was chiefly on dreams that Freud had lectured on Friday the 10th— and that he (James) repudiated the theory for its extravagance, especially in respect to symbolism. In the letter to Flournoy, James pointedly related the theory negatively to himself with the words, "I can make nothing in my own case with his dream theories. . . ."

A third statement by James on the topic of dreams while not mentioning Freud by name was an implicit repudiation of his theory. James's view was contained in an article entitled "A Suggestion About Mysticism," which appeared five months after the Worcester Conference (February 17). [7]

From James's Diary one learns that his article was rapidly written on December 16-17, 1909, three months after the Clark Conference, and mailed on the 17th of December. It appeared on February 17, 1910, six months before his death in August. The contemporary memorandum in which James had noted down his peculiar dreams was dated "San Francisco, February 14, 1906." It referred to the dreams as having occurred on the nights of February 11-12 and 12-13.

This article is not an essay explicitly on dreams, but it is chiefly based on some of James's dreams and cognate personal experience. It is a unique, autobiographical statement in which James revealed a type of his experience that he called "pathological." He had had such an experience on four occasions, all during the preceding five years. In each case there was a peculiar lapse of consciousness that "broke in abruptly upon a perfectly commonplace situation and lasted perhaps less than two minutes. In one instance I was engaged in conversation, but I doubt whether the interlocutor noticed my abstraction." (James, 1910b; 1978, p. 160).

These lapses applied to three waking experiences, the first of which, as just indicated, had occurred during the conversation James had with an unidentified person. He continued, "My fourth experience of uncovering had to do with dreams." Despairing, as he stated, of giving the reader any "just idea of the bewildering confusion of mind into which I was thrown by this, the most intensely peculiar experience of my whole life," he then reproduced a memorandum about a pair of dreams written a couple of days after the experience, dated 1906. It is clearly on the basis of these dreams that the article was now published as seeming to shed light on the nature of mystical experience and "as a contribution to the descriptive literature of pathological mental states."

But to the current recall of his dreams, James added a comment that compared them with a just-published article in the *Open Court* for December 1909. That article described "a fit of ether-mysticism" in which the writer's consciousness had been enormously enlarged after an infusion of ether administered for a surgical operation. Frederick Hall, the author, as he was losing consciousness had a vision of the real but unseen world. "I was, in the phrase of one of Jack London's heroes, 'all there.' I had no dread of pain, so far as I was concerned the surgeons might have begun their work that moment. . . . All of us feel, sometimes, I imagine, that there *ought* to be a world different from and better than this one . . . I would ask for myself or for my loved ones no better realization of the Christians' Heaven." [8]

By contrast James's pair of dreams that constituted "the most intensely peculiar experience of my whole life" conveyed to the dreamer a "bewildering confusion." In one of the dreams there was a strong sense of the "tragic"; in another "a sort of nightmare . . . had to do with soldiers." The dreamer "began to feel curiously confused and *scared*" and tried to waken himself only to find that he was already wide-awake. "Presently cold shivers of dread ran over me . . . ." [9] It is evident that while Frederick Hall had entered a kind of Nirvana under the early influence of ether, James in his pathological dream states was experiencing a nightmare world—a world of indeterminate anxiety. Yet in a footnote to the *Open Court* article, the writer, having raised the question of whether he could with any certainty return to the world of his ether vision if he had a second ether inhalation, quoted an answer sent him in a letter received from William James: "You would doubtless get something similar if you tried ether again."

James was enough impressed by the article to write Frederick Hall about it. Partly on the basis of this article, James was apparently stimulated to respond to Freud's dream theory by recalling and publishing some of his own dreams which were not, in his view, explained by Freud's theory, but accorded better with Frederick Hall's experience. A larger frame of reference was required—larger than the mundane individual life that Freud invoked. There was a subliminal realm suggestive of the mystical to which James's dreams and other of his experiences appeared to him to belong. A reductive theory of crude sexual strivings failed to satisfy James—as a little later it failed to satisfy Jung. In James's view there was a cosmic consciousness in which the petty conflicts of the individual were subsumed by a universal spiritual realm. It was a strenuous region of coexisting states of split consciousness. Paradoxically, the pragmatist James, toward the end of his life, advocated a pantheistic but pluralistic conception of reality—a multiple personality writ large.

Before further discussing these dreams, there is a special question—a hypothesis—that demands consideration. James referred to one of his states of abstraction as having interrupted a conversation he was having with someone. His exact words need to be quoted in full. "I seemed all at once to be reminded of a past experience; and this reminiscence, ere I could conceive or name it distinctly, developed into something further that belonged with it, this in turn into something further still, and so on, until the process faded out, leaving me amazed at the sudden vision of increasing ranges of distant fact of which I could give no articulate account. The mode of consciousness was perceptual, not conceptual—the field expanding so fast that there seemed no time for conception or identification to get in its work. There was a strongly exciting sense that my knowledge of past (or present?) reality was enlarging pulse by pulse, but so rapidly that my intellectual processes could not keep up the pace. The *content* was thus entirely lost to retrospection—it sank into the limbo into which dreams vanish as we gradually awake. The feeling—I won't call it belief—that I had had a sudden *opening,* had seen through a window, as it were, distant realities that incomprehensibly belonged with my own life, was so acute that I can not shake it off to-day" (James, *op. cit.,* p. 160).

Was James here alluding to the conversation with Freud three months earlier? We know from Freud that during that peripatetic conversation James paused and asked Freud to walk on while he (James) stayed behind briefly. Did James, as Freud inferred, have an attack of *angina pectoris* and/or did he experience the aura of a peculiar lapse of consciousness *(petit mal)* that developed into a chain of free associations? If one answers in the affirmative, it may have been something said by Freud during the conversation that triggered this response. Knowing, as we do, that Freud was at this time on the verge of leaving Worcester for a sojourn at Dr. Putnam's camp in the Adirondacks, and, knowing further, that this camp had begun in 1876 as a joint venture of Drs. Putnam, Bowditch and James himself, it becomes plausible that it was the mention of it which aroused James's dissociative state. The hypothesis gains credibility if one is aware of the scope and wealth of James's associations with that camp. It was there that he spent his honeymoon in 1878. And, as will be shown, it was there in 1898 that he contracted the coronary ailment to which Freud referred. That critical event, with later associations, would have been indelibly imprinted on James, and this chain of reminiscences was ready to emerge at the mention of the place by Freud. If, indeed, James did suffer an attack of *angina pectoris* in conjunction with the lapse of consciousness—a *combination* not ruled out by his own description of these pathological states—the attack could have begun by the arousal of a "complex" centered in the circumstances of 1898. And Freud's lecture on dreams a few hours earlier might already have stirred up this "repressed" material. Moreover, this surmise would be significantly substantiated if it could be demonstrated that the dreams of 1906, reported in the 1909 manuscript, were also linked to the circumstances of the 1898 crisis. On the hypothesis of just such a convergence, an idiodynamic reconstruction of James's dreams will now be attempted.

Chapter X

A Reinterpretation of Dreams

To ease the way, a synoptic restatement of the hypothesis may be helpful: (1) James had a complex about a romantic (sexual) episode in the vicinity of the Putnam camp that included the origin of his heart ailment. (2) Freud in a lecture on the morning of September 10—the one lecture of Freud's heard by James—developed the view that dreams of neurotics are apt to arise from wishes rooted in just such complexes. (3) Anxiety dreams may reflect a failure of such wish fulfillment. (4) James's complex was alerted as he listened to Freud. (5) When during the walk in Worcester, to which James had probably invited Freud, Freud made mention of his prospective sojourn at the Putnam camp in the Adirondacks, this served as a stimulus that fully aroused the complex. (6) Thus was started the attack of *angina* and/or the dissociated state of consciousness described by James in his article. (7) But James, according to Freud's theory, would have denied any such connection, precisely because of the resistance offered by the complex. (8) After the Clark Conference James wrote to his friends Mary Calkins and Théodore Flournoy about Freud, especially his dream theory, which made no sense ("in my own case"). (9) Three months later James rapidly composed and published a paper based on some of his own dreams ("the most peculiar experience of my whole life") that had been recorded in a contemporary memorandum in 1906. (10) But in this publication he offered an interpretation of the dreams that implicitly repudiated Freud's theory.

With this setting, we shall reexamine these dreams and attempt to reconstruct their origin on the premise that, instead of refuting Freud's theory, they lend support to it.

William James and Pauline Goldmark

The detailed reconstruction must start with young Pauline Goldmark whom James met in 1895 when she was 21 and he was 53. They were in the Adirondacks, a region she loved like a dryad. Usually she was in the company of her brother, sisters, and their young friends. The impression she made upon James at their first meeting is succinctly conveyed in a letter from Beede's Lodge to his wife Alice which began: "I have been happy, *happy, happy!* — with the exquisite imperishable beauty of the place, the place I know so well. Nature has made it for falling in love in, passing honeymoons and the like. There is a perfect little serious rosebud of a Miss Goldmark . . . who climbs cliffs like a monkey. . . ." [1] This ecstatic outburst sounds like love at first sight—the impact can be great at age 53!—and the metaphor of the rosebud bespoke the courtship of a swain that lasted to the end of James's life, 15 years later.

Pauline was also probably present a few months later when, on February 9, 1896, William James lectured by special invitation to students at Bryn Mawr. On that occasion he wrote to his brother Henry: "I came here yesterday P.M. to give an 'address' at Bryn Mawr College, the gilt edged feminine institution of the country. There is something quite intoxicating in this addressing of young girls—they look so pretty and are so electrically responsive." [2]

Who was Pauline Goldmark? She was the daughter of Joseph Goldmark, a physician who in his early manhood took part in the Vienna revolution of 1848, then fled to the United States in 1850. In America he was a successful chemist and industrialist with a family of ten children. Of these children, his daughter Alice married Louis D. Brandeis, the later Supreme Court Justice; Helen was the wife of Felix Adler, founder of the Society for Ethical Culture. The youngest of the children, Josephine, was a well-known social investigator and writer who assisted Louis Brandeis in some of his early social reform. She is included in *Notable American Women* (1971). Her sister Pauline (1874-1962), whose vocational interests were close to those of Josephine, is of special interest here for she was the particular friend of William James. The Goldmark family had a summer home in the Adirondacks, a half mile from the Putnam camp of which James was then part owner. In the late summer of 1895 the young Harvard philosopher Dickinson Miller first brought William James to this home. Pauline was then in her last year at Bryn Mawr. Since early childhood she had spent her summers there in the woods and mountains, and this fact became the common bond of their friendship. His interest in her was expressed by James through occasional visits and, especially, by a continuous correspondence of which 63 letters from him to her, dated 1897 to 1910, have survived. Pauline's vocation was in the field of social work and labor relations, with marked interest in the welfare of women in industry. At one time she served as Secretary of both the New York State and the National Consumers Leagues. But it was her avocational devotion to the out-of-doors that reverberated in James's letters to her. It was as if there was an imprinting of their first habitat in common that revitalized him. He was more than twice as old as she—a difference that seemed to him neutralized by their immersion in the eternal freshness of the mountain scene. But, as will appear, this illusion overreached itself so far that, three years after their first meeting, he outdid himself in a brave display of prowess that left him with a fatal heart lesion.

The mentioned lecture at Bryn Mawr in 1896 was probably the first of a series that Pauline heard James give—lectures to which he repeatedly invited her. Thus, he wrote her on March 2, 1898 concerning a lecture he had been invited to give at Bryn Mawr on April 23 before the Graduate Club. As on other occasions, he used the pretext of other members of her family, in this case, her younger sister, who was still attending Bryn Mawr and for whose sake she might perhaps be there and thus incidentally hear him: ". . . the sight of your face in the audience would communicate a real thrill of satisfaction to the lecturer" (letter of March 2, 1898).

A more consequential invitation was extended to Pauline three months later, on June 29, 1898 when, from the Adirondack Lodge, James wrote to her at her parents' summer home suggesting that she come with "the fair Josephine" and other young family members or friends to share with him the brilliant moon that he had enjoyed for the last four nights. Could you not "come up to the Marcy Camp, where I should meet you, and, after passing the night all of us descend hither for as long as might seem pleasant, you and your sister being my guests, and then go out to Keene Valley by the trail . . . ." The invitation was accepted but it led to the overexertion above noted.

The positive side of the experience is best conveyed in the words of James himself in a letter to his wife Alice from Keene Valley on July 9, 1898. ". . . I have had an eventful 24 hours, and my hands are so stiff after it that my fingers can hardly hold the pen. I left, as I informed you by post-card, the Lodge at seven, and five hours of walking brought us to the top of Marcy—I carrying 18 lbs. of weight in my pack. As usual, I met two Cambridge acquaintances on the mountain top—"Appalachians" from Beede's. At four, hearing an axe below, I went down (an hour's walk) to Panther Lodge Camp, and there found Charles and Pauline Goldmark, Waldo Adler and another schoolboy, and two Bryn Mawr girls—the girls all dressed in boys' breeches, and cutaneously desecrated in the extreme from seven of them having been camping without a male on Loon Lake to the north of this. My guide had to serve for the party, and quite unexpectedly to me the night turned out one of the most memorable of all my memorable experiences. I was in a wakeful mood before starting, having been awake since three, and I may have slept a little during this night; but I was not aware of sleeping at all. My companions, except Waldo Adler, were all motionless. The guide had got a magnificant provision of firewood, the sky swept itself clear of every trace of cloud or vapor, the wind entirely ceased, so that the fire-smoke rose straight up to heaven. The temperature was perfect either inside or outside the cabin, the moon rose and hung above the scene before midnight, leaving only a few of the larger stars visible, and I got into a state of spiritual alertness of the most vital description. The influences of Nature, the wholesomeness of the people round me, especially the good Pauline, the thought of you and the children, dear Harry on the wave, the problem of the Edinburgh lectures, all fermented within me till it became a regular Walpurgis Nacht. I spent a good deal of it in the woods, where the streaming moonlight lit up things in a magical checkered play, and it seemed as if the Gods of all the nature-mythologies were holding an indescribable meeting in my breast with the moral Gods of the inner life. The two kinds of Gods have nothing in common—the Edinburgh lectures made quite a hitch ahead. The intense significance of some sort, of the whole scene, if one could only *tell* the significance; the intense inhuman remoteness of its inner life, and yet the intense *appeal* of it; its everlasting freshness and its immemorial antiquity and decay; its utter Americanism, and every sort of patriotic suggestiveness, and you, and my relation to you part and parcel of it all, and beaten up with it, so that memory and sensation all whirled inexplicably together; it was indeed worth coming for, and worth repeating year by year, if repetition could only procure what in its nature I suppose must be all unplanned for and unexpected. It was one of the happiest lonesome nights of my existence, and I understand now what a poet is."[3]

From an article, "An Adirondack Friendship" about William James and Pauline Goldmark written by Pauline's sister Josephine, one learns that the meeting place was at Panther Gorge "where a small Adirondack camp of rough-hewn logs had been built, open in front, and carpeted with balsam boughs on which perhaps a half-dozen persons might stretch out for the night."[4] Since it is evident from James's letter of July 1898 that there were seven in the party who spent the night in this cabin, one may safely infer that William James and his special guest Pauline Goldmark lay side by side. And this part of the experience, anticipated and planned by James, proved too much for his already excited state of mind. Not having slept since 3:00 A.M. of the previous night and having exerted himself by hours of climbing, burdened by a pack, he now slept little if at all. Instead, he wandered under the bright moonlight and indulged in fantasies about the conflict between Christian and pagan Gods portrayed in the *Walpurgisnacht* (witches' Sabbath). Goethe had graphically represented that demonic festival in his *Faust* where it teems with sexual implications. Inquiry reveals that the use of the metaphor by James was more than casual; it was rooted in his thought at that period.[5, 5a]

It was this night that left its lasting imprint and became embodied in the friendship with Pauline. Explicit evidence of the imprinting was to appear nine years later in a letter written to her (September 14, 1907 from Keene Valley): "Hurrah! hurrah! that communication should at last be re-establisht! Your dear letter of the 11th. came yesterday, with its implied prospect of more, and with its breath of your camping days, which maltreated you less rainily than I had been afearing. If I could only go camping with you again, even if for 48 hours, I think the truths so communicable under those conditions would conduce to much appeasement. . . . A party of 14 left here yesterday for Panther Gorge, meaning to return by the 'range,' as they call your 'summit trail.'

Apparently it is easier than when on that to me memorable day we took it . . . ." The implicit evidence of this transforming night appeared repeatedly over the years and had the effect of setting aside any ordinary reserve in admitting the need for this very special friend.

When Henry James, III, the son of William, was collecting his father's letters for publication in 1920, he wrote to Pauline and requested that she send him all the letters she had received from his father so that he might copy them and include some in his book. He did include seven, but the one James wrote to his wife Alice, quoted above, is more revealing about Pauline than any of the seven. Moreover, as editor, Henry omitted a final portion of that letter which dealt with the friendship of Dickinson Miller and Pauline, whom James here characterized as "too simple and childlike mentally for him [Miller], and the immense Jewish alliance would be more than one Christian by himself could stand up under. But she is awfully innocent and good and wholesome, and I confess that I have seriously had conscience now in not having brought her and the Solomons together."

Perhaps even more significant is a comment by the son Henry which, again, was not included in the published letters but which Henry, III apparently considered important enough to preserve with his father's papers. It explained the fatal effect of the experience at Mount Marcy and Panther Gorge in these words: "This adventure was what first strained W. J.'s heart. (See my text in the *Letters*). What isn't mentioned here or in that text is the fact that during this arduous 2nd day W. J. let his guide carry things for the girls and added to his own pack what he had originally engaged his guide to carry for him. So he was heavily loaded. The girls probably had no understanding of the unwisdom of this for a man of W. J.'s age. My mother, who was anyhow unable to find Pauline Goldmark sympathetic, could never forgive her for thus absorbing W. J.'s guide.—H. J." [6]

One here not only learns the origin of W. J.'s cardiac strain but the effect of William's closeness to Pauline upon James's wife Alice, who found that relationship hard to accept. That she blamed Pauline for the heart ailment is, of course, irrational. It was James, not Pauline, who made the decision about the guide. But there were grounds for jealousy even if the husband's expression of his attraction to the nymphlike girl was restrained.

The next significant phase of the relationship between William James and Pauline Goldmark occurred the following spring. Writing to her from Newport on April 18, 1899 at the time of the university spring recess, he talked thus to himself: "'Why . . . don't you run down here, and come and see me. . . !' Well! that sounds natural; but, apart from the lack of dignity it would argue for a man at my time of life to spend the *whole* of his time in running after the girls, there are a number of other reasons too long and subtler to be put down on paper why I must stay here . . . during the April recess."

James then mentioned that he was sending Pauline a copy of his new book.[7] ". . . you are familiar with most of the content already, so you need not read them. There is, however, one Essay 'On a certain blindness,' etc. which I do want you to read, because I care very much indeed for the truth it so inadequately tries by dint of innumerable quotations to express, and I like to imagine that you care for it, or will care for it too." The paper's theme is a paean of praise for love which, fortified by the mentioned quotations from authors like Wordsworth, verges on pantheistic mysticism. Elsewhere James described its message as the unique individuality of every person discernible to others only through the experience of love. That in this essay, thus singled out for her, he was reaching out beyond the boundaries of friendship is conveyed in an early, pithy paragraph: "This higher vision . . . often comes over a person suddenly; and when it does so, it makes an epoch in his history. As Emerson says, there is a depth in those moments that constrains us to ascribe more reality to them than to all other experiences. The passion of love will shake one like an explosion, or some act will awaken a remorseful compunction that hangs like a cloud over all one's later days."[8]

On May 19, having learned about Pauline's plans for a European trip, he helped pave the way for her to be received by his friend, F. C. S. Schiller at Oxford, England who "will attend to you" with special courtesies. Four days earlier he had indeed written a letter introducing her to Schiller.[9] There, with intimate jocularity, he professed his special feeling for Pauline: "Some friends of mine in New York, the Goldmark girls, are about to start for a summer abroad with one or two feminine companions and should be at Oxford for a day or two about the middle of June or a little later. They are friendless and inexperienced and when

Miss Pauline G. was at my house the other day, I told her that I would write to you and you might possibly put her and her sister in the way of seeing something at Oxford that otherwise she might miss. She will, in consequence, probably make bold to send you a card or a note when she arrives. If you have no time to call, all you need do is to write and excuse yourself. They absolutely expect no entertainment or hospitality—just a word of advice. She and her sister Susan (who is lame) are Bryn Mawr graduates and great friends of Miller. Pauline is a biologist, has done practical philanthropy work among the poor in N.Y., is athletic, a tramper and camper, and lover of nature such as one rarely meets, and withal a perfectly simple, good girl, and a beautiful face—and I fairly dote upon her, and were I younger and 'unattached' should probably be deep in love. Be friendly if you can, to however slight a degree, and I will in turn send letters, to precede your arrival, to the presiding dignitaries in the realm of the blest—with whom my influence is peculiarly great. So be a good boy, and thank me for throwing so charming an acquaintance in your way. Would I could be there myself, simultaneous!"

While Pauline and her sister were spending the summer in Europe, William James, after a busy schedule of his own, went to Keene Valley for a much needed vacation. But this vacation was marred by a misadventure that he explained in a letter to Pauline written from the spa in Germany where he went afterwards to recuperate. [10] One day he had started without a coat, food or matches on what was meant to be a slow walk. Somehow he drifted to the top of Mount Marcy and, when he began to descend, found himself on a strange trail. The return trip to the Lodge that should have taken three hours turned into a seven hour scramble during which he fainted twice before he finally emerged in the valley at 10:15 P.M. The misadventure aggravated his heart condition and made him turn urgently to Nauheim for treatment. As he stated to Pauline: ". . . I was an ass and you ought to have been along to steer me straight. I fear we shall ascend no more acclivities together. 'Bent is the tree that should have grown full straight!'"

Do these words imply that he got lost because he was preoccupied in fantasy about Pauline? Was he harboring a secret hope to repeat the exhilerating adventure of the previous July? At that time Pauline had been very much present and, as he now noted, "you ought to have been along to steer me straight." Was he lost in thought about her when he started on the slow walk, hence took the wrong turn and wandered for hours? The experience of 1898 had obviously had an intense effect and, on his return to Keene Valley the next summer, he must have wanted desperately somehow to recapture the former exhileration, but he got lost instead, with further serious consequences.

We have no information about the results of Pauline Goldmark's trip to Europe because her letters to William James have not survived. Despite persistent efforts to find such letters among the numerous literary remains of James at Houghton Library, her letters to him could not be found. This outcome is a bit more remarkable, because, as noted earlier, James's son Henry made a distinct effort to obtain the letters his father had written to her. The son made typewritten copies of everything she sent him—the main source of the quotations in the present account of their relationship; but either William James himself or one of his survivors, possibly Mrs. Alice, did not save the numerous letters Pauline had written to William and to which he often looked forward with great yearning. Whatever the reason for the one-sidedness of the surviving correspondence, it exists and renders the picture of the relationship incomplete.

The above cited article by Pauline's sister Josephine provides little compensation since, though it was written while Pauline was still alive, it was chiefly based, as the subtitle "Letters of William James" explains, on James's letters to Pauline. Apparently Pauline did not save copies of her letters to James but the admiring younger sister, who was one of the group that often met with William, wanted not to let this significant aspect of James's life, intimately involving Pauline, meet with oblivion. Even so, when Josephine wrote to the son Henry James and to Professor R. B. Perry of Harvard, who at the time was working with the James literary remains for his forthcoming work entitled *The Thought and Character of William James*, some restrictions may have been imposed upon her.

In any event, the letters of January 4 to February 13, 1906, to which we now turn, were not included in Josephine's account though they reveal much about James's friendship with Pauline. [11] They come to prominence here because they were written just before the dreams James reported in "A Suggestion About Mysticism." [12]

In that article, published in February 1910, James facilitates the process of reconstruction by dating the two dreams as having occurred at Stanford, California on the nights of February 11-12 and 12-13. In his Diary for the year 1906, potentially relevant day residue or stimuli for the dreams are available. Similar data are to be found in the various biographies of James and in his correspondence, most notably his letters to Pauline Goldmark just mentioned.

Aspects of the two dreams have been quoted above and, with one exception, will not be repeated here. The exception concerns the condition of anxiety—a sense of being lost in the woods, of being in danger, of being scared. It will be necessary to return to this point when the dreams are later examined in the context of Freud's lecture on dreams which James heard at Clark University on September 10, 1909. [13]

From the various sources available, the circumstances that generally existed during the critical days of February 11 and 12, 1906, and that provided what has been termed "day residue" for the two dreams which James stated to be "the most intensely peculiar experience of my whole life," were the following: The most striking feature was severe gout of a foot which began on Sunday, February 4, worsened and interfered with his sleep—all noted in his Diary daily until February 16, at which time he noted, "foot better." During this period he resorted to crutches, mentioned on February 12 ("still on crutches"). On the 13th he has written "still crippled." It is clear that this condition with its insistent pain was present during the days just preceding the dreams of February 11-13 and may well have contributed to their negative qualities.

A less direct stimulus, but one that nevertheless was present, was the death of James's close associate and friend Richard Hodgson, Secretary of the American Society for Psychical Research, who had died suddenly from a heart attack on December 20. James had described this event to Pauline Goldmark in a letter of January 4, 1906. He was involved with Hodgson's lawyer, Mr. George Dorr, in the administration of Hodgson's estate, especially the literary remains, and, in particular, he noted in his Diary of February 12 that he received from George Dorr "a big letter with enclosures" containing "delicious compliments to Alice," who was acting for William during his absence in California. The unexpected and sudden nature of Hodgson's death shook James—

as he explained not only to Pauline but to other correspondents—
for the victim was only 50 years old, a remarkably energetic and
outgoing individual who at the time of his heart attack was actually
engaged in a vigorous game of handball on the court of the Union
Boat Club. James's own heart ailment, which may have been tied
in with the current attack of gout as a symptom of circulatory
disturbance, probably tied together in his mind the sudden death
of his colleague and his own similar but chronic illness. [14] Despite
his generally optimistic temperament—"tenderminded" to use his
own terminology—there was undoubtedly an undercurrent of
depression against which he had to struggle. Much of his formulated philosophy, in particular the doctrine of the will to believe,
reflects this duality. It is instructive and seldom noted that before
he announced this doctrine, he addressed the Harvard Y.M.C.A.
in 1895 on the topic "Is Life Worth Living?" (James, 1895b). In
this address he argued, as he did somewhat later in "The Will to
Believe," that life is worth living if one believes that it is and makes
it so. (Cf. James, 1896c.)

Another prevailing circumstance at this time is James's
loneliness while in California since his arrival there early in
January. He would be away from his wife for six weeks, living
by himself, during which they corresponded incessantly. She did
not join him until February 14. Though he had planned to meet
her at the railroad station in San Francisco, he got only as far as
the St. Francis Hotel where she joined him, herself in a poor condition of health. As above noted, he was still suffering from gout.

Coupled with this relationship to his wife Alice was James's
correspondence with Pauline Goldmark that took a special turn
precisely at the time of the two dreams here being considered.
James had written to her en route from Cambridge to Stanford,
California, while visiting the Grand Canyon in Colorado in early
January, but his letters addressed to her from Stanford on February 8 and 13 are unique in their expression of yearning to hear
from her—in response to an almost desperate need. He addresses
her in these two letters as "Paolina" and in both he is begging her
to write him a letter to assuage his needs and make her response
a little closer to his own expression of friendship toward her. Thus
on the 8th he has received from her a picture post card promising
a real letter to follow, to which he replies immediately: "Peace is
made!—Yours of the 4th comes in! The fact is that your head

of potential letter-writing energy seems to be so much lower than mine that it doesn't explode to me-ward, as mine does to you-ward, on the slightest provocation. You see I must sit down immediately to reply to this little note of yours without awaiting the promised letter to-morrow!"

But five days later, on February 13, he is writing her again with his wish painfully unfulfilled. These are his opening words: "Ah! dear Paolina, how you do dislike to write letters! 'More tomorrow'—and now six tomorrows have come and gone without a lebenszeichen from thee. No matter! You did pretty well when you were in Florence, and it is mean of me to sit down and beleaguer you when it goes so against the grain."

He then continues at once to describe the expected arrival of his wife in San Francisco tomorrow where he will go to "collect" her. And he vividly depicts the gout that is still so bad that he cannot put on his slippers and goes to lecture on crutches. But unlucky as he is in these "minor ways," he is "in major ways, more lucky than I deserve." Then he describes the great virtues of Stanford University whose students are "rustic, but earnest and wholesome more than at Harvard. I have been lecturing on 'Introduction to Philosophy' to 275 now regularly enrolled, and much of the time to 175 visitors standing all round the walls."

The contrast between Pauline's apparent failure to appreciate her yearning and ailing special friend and the adulation of the eager Stanford students struck the writer himself, and he felt it necessary to rationalize it when toward the end of the letter he said, "But I'm writing to you Pauline, as if you were a candidate for a Professorship consulting me as to whether you had better 'accept'."

If we return now to the dreams of February 11-12 and 12-13 we are impelled to advance the hypothesis that the peculiar condition of lost bearings—of being adrift—which in James's interpretation of the dream state suggested mysticism may actually have been a response to his mundane gout, the tragic loss of his friend Hodgson, his loneliness in the absence of his caring wife and perhaps most directly relevant, the unfulfilled longing for the long-promised letter from his cherished friend Paolina. This final point is perhaps at least partly confirmed by Freud's dis-cussion of anxiety dreams, especially neurotic anxiety. To quote from his Clark lecture: "Anxiety is one of the ego's reactions in repudiation of repressed wishes that have become powerful; and its occurrence in dreams as well is very easily explicable when the formation of the dream has been carried out with too much of an eye to the fulfillment of these repressed wishes." [15]

But James himself gave a different interpretation of his peculiar dream states. They were instances of dissociation in which he questioned the identity of the dreamer—whether he himself or someone else had had the dreams as they merged into each other to his great confusion. This dissociation suggested the experience of mystics—an otherworldly speculation far removed from Freud's concept of reminiscences from childhood and unfulfilled wishes seeking for resolution in the dream. A possible reconciliation between these two positions is available if one can discern a current personality conflict that could induce dissociation as a neurotic solution. In the case of William James, a conflict of this kind may have existed in his loyalty to his wife Alice, on the one hand, and his yearning for the younger and more romantic figure of Pauline, on the other.

It is of some interest that the concept of dissociation was very much in vogue in 1906, not only because of the publications of Pierre Janet, who in that year delivered invited lectures on hysteria at the Harvard Medical School from the standpoint of subconscious conflict, but also through the book of Morton Prince *The Dissociation of a Personality,* which actually appeared in December 1905 though the title page bore the date 1906. James had received a presentation copy from his friend Dr. Prince, and he appreciatively acknowledged this valuable contribution to the literature of psychopathology in a letter to the author that he wrote on his return from Stanford in September 1906. [16]

One may also ask again why James chose to compose the article which included his 1906 dreams three years after the occurrence of the dreams. Part of the answer has already been given by citing the paper in *The Open Court,* "An Ether 'Vision,'" by Frederick Hall published in December 1909. But this precipitating occasion was probably not sufficient to account for the writing of the article on December 16-17 (the dates in James's Diary); and, in any event, we have the internal evidence of the paper itself in which James points to experiences of a normal lapse of consciousness, including the pair of dreams at Stanford, during the previous five years. So the question becomes: Why did James choose this date in December for reporting these experiences which primarily included the two dreams recorded at the time on February 14, 1906 at Stanford? It is tempting to believe that James's hearing Freud's lecture on dreams on September 10 when coupled with the subsequent conversation during his walk with Freud instigated James's attack of *angina pectoris* (as Freud wrote) or the lapse of consciousness during a conversation (as James wrote). When James told his friend Flournoy, as we have seen, that he could make nothing of Freud's theory of dreams "in my own case," was he obliquely referring to this contretemps? Hence, he reported his pair of Stanford dreams without any mention of Freud or of repressed wishes.

As for the relevance of James's correspondence with Pauline Goldmark in its bearing on the pair of dreams, we have the contemporary knowledge that in 1909 James had written to her three times before the Clark Conference (February 20, June 22 and September 5) and twice afterwards (October 9 and December 11). However, in none of these letters is there any mention of Freud or of the celebration in Worcester. There is, nevertheless, a resemblance between the yearning so poignantly expressed in his letter to Pauline of February 13, 1906 and that of December 11, 1909, i.e., five days before he started to write the article recalling his dreams of 1906. The letter of 1909 began: "Your piece of cardboard, dearest Pauline, which arrived at noon, when your full presence was lookt for, was a sad substitute. But no matter, I'm resigned in these days to everything! I long to see you, but not cooped up in a room, on a hill or in a forest rather. Yet I see no light as to how that consumation is ever to be accomplisht in the future, for I appear to be condemned by this preposterous angina to a life more cooped up than ever." He ended with the pathetic sentiment: "I've lost your little silver pencil case, oh weh! After so many years of fidelity to my person, it departed at Intervale last summer and never came back. It was my dearest possession."

These words of loss and longing, concretely reiterating the similar sentiments just before the dream of February 12-13, 1906, were more feebly expressed in the next-to-last letter we have from James to Pauline. It was dated May 29, 1910, and was sent from the health spa at Nauheim, Germany. Apart from some information about a Professor Goldstein who was to visit him and consult about translating one of his books, it is primarily notable for the *leitmotif* at the opening that plainly induced the writing: "Beloved Pauline, On this rainy lonely morning, my heart goes out in your direction and I can't help sending you a *Gruss!* [greeting]." It ends: "Well! God bless you, Pauline. Be good and happy—your old friend W. J."

In the meantime, as is indicated in James's Diary, Pauline visited James in Cambridge on January 15, and on March 25 she had lunch at the James's. Since the article "A Suggestion About Mysticism" had just appeared, on February 17, 1910, it is conceivable that he showed her this publication during the luncheon visit.

After Pauline learned about William James's death on August 26, 1910 at his summer home in Chocorua, New Hampshire, she wrote a letter of condolence to Mrs. Alice James of which we learn from the adroit acknowledgement of September 14: "Dear Pauline, I thank you for your letter of sympathy and feeling. As you say, a beautiful life and wonderfully rich in friendship. He delighted in yours.

"But he wanted to go, and departed swiftly as he always has when he made up his mind to move on. He was here only one week, and died in the little front bedroom which I think your mother occupied, when you were here. Please remember me to her most cordially, to your sisters also, and believe me always, Affectionately yours, Alice H. James." [17]

"Tragical Marriage"

To appreciate the tragic aspects of James's 1906 dreams and their identity confusion, one needs not only to know the contemporary circumstances of the dream described above—the conflict between his attraction to Pauline and his devotion to his wife Alice—but the circumstances 30 years earlier when James tried honestly to state for his fiancée Alice the conditions of their proposed alliance. In the summer 1876 during their courtship William wrote Alice a long letter about the kind of marriage he foresaw for them. He contrasted the usual marriage of healthy individuals, well accepted by society, with that of unhealthy persons. Society would regard "all departures from the standard of wholesomeness as crimes against its law . . . ." Hence, "The marriage of unhealthy persons can only be forgiven by an appeal to some metaphysical world 'behind the veil' . . . ." But it would be problematic, "outwardly a social crime . . . and should expect no countenance, perhaps even no tolerance from public opinion." To enter into such a marriage "is in a word to throw yourself upon the *Tragical.*"[18] James was apparently telling his fiancée that should they marry, because of his ill health they could not have a normal and happy marriage—like the marriage of the majority who, according to his later classification in *The Varieties of Religious Experience,* are "healthy-minded." The "sick-minded" by their sensitivity may be even more productive in a special way, but they are poorly equipped to handle everyday life. Again, to use the terms of another dichotomy he described in his book *Pragmatism* (1907), there are the "tough-minded" and the "tender-minded" in the approach to reality.[19] The former are much better attuned to the hardships of the world of common sense. James, by building this contrast into his philosophy of religion and into his theory of knowledge, had apparently drawn upon his own years of nervous ailments that ranged from backache to melancholia.

It is remarkable that a few years earlier, in 1869, he had told his brother Robertson that marriage for members of the hereditarily tainted James brothers should be avoided.[20] At that date he had not yet achieved the rationalization that he tentatively offered to his fiancée in 1876 and it took him another 20 years to turn it by his "will to believe" into a philosophical rationale. While on the surface this seems innocent and frank, when critically examined, it verges on what he termed the "tragical." Hence his endless journeys to German spas, such as Nauheim, during the last 43 years of his life, his recourse to various nostrums of a dubious medical basis (e.g., the Roberts-Hawley testicular-lymph compound), and his continuous consultations with mental healers, ranging from Lydia E. Pinkham in 1887 to Dr. James Ralph Taylor, a homeopathic physician, in 1908-1909, and with a Christian Science healer, L. C. Strang, later in 1909.[21]

It is only against this background of James's personal struggle to achieve mental health that one can appreciate the nature of his philosophical conceptions and of his relationships to special individuals in his life, like G. Stanley Hall, a surrogate sibling rival, and Pauline Goldmark, the beloved friend. It is likely that while, superficially, James may have won over his wife and his colleagues, who intuitively, if not explicitly, empathized with his endless struggle and admired his flashes of wit and insight, they saw, as he did, that he had not achieved solutions; that, in fact, his philosophical formulations from the will to believe to pluralism were attempts to justify the "ever not quite." James had spent his considerable gifts in attempts to rationalize the existential process.

It is, however, doubtful that, had Freud known during the walk in Worcester about the dreams of William James in 1906 and their possible connection with Pauline Goldmark, he would have been satisfied with this extrapolation. The theory of neurotic repression and the anxiety dream comes closer to the tough-minded than to the tender-minded view of "tragical marriage." Freud's admiration for James as expressed in the autobiography was, after all, about how James appeared to be facing death, not how he had construed life and even the hereafter. These latter views were for Freud largely an evasion of the reality upon which Freud insisted, especially in his stress upon biological sexuality.

Putnam's Camp in the Adirondacks (c. 1885)

Chapter XI

Aftermath (First Part)

Honors and Publications

The newspaper coverage of the Clark lectures was remarkably broad and, on the whole, accurate. The fact that Freud and Jung spoke in German did not make the task easier, but it did not prove insurmountable. The most complete coverage was in the *Worcester Telegram,* a morning daily that published the only Worcester Sunday paper. The other Worcester dailies, both of which also reported the conference, were the *Evening Gazette* and the *Evening Post.* In Boston, the *Evening Transcript* reported Freud's lectures daily and published a lengthy interview with him conducted in Worcester on Wednesday by Adelbert Albrecht and published on Saturday, September 11. [1] William James, who by then had returned to Cambridge from his one-day visit to Worcester, was unhappy about Freud's unfavorable comment in the interview regarding faith healing, in particular, the Boston-based Emmanuel Movement. His reaction ("Bah!") was conveyed in his letter to Théodore Flournoy. [2]

Not only the lectures but the other parts of the conference were reported in the newspapers. Both the *Gazette* and the *Telegram* described the ceremonies for awarding 21 honorary degrees on Friday evening, September 10. The *Telegram* described in colorful detail the decorations of the hall and the academic procession connected with the Friday awards. It quoted the citations read by President Hall in conferring the degrees. [3] Eight more degrees were awarded on the following Thursday, September 16, 1909.

The language of the citations for Freud and Jung is quoted from the *Telegram* of Saturday the 11th: "Sigmund Freud of the University of Vienna, founder of a school of psychology already rich in new methods and achievements; leader today among students of the psychology of sex, and of psychotherapy and analysis; Doctor of Laws." The citation for his colleague read: "Carl G. Jung of the University of Zurich, Switzerland, specialist in psychiatry, brilliant investigator by the *Diagnostische Assoziationmethode,* editor and fruitful contributor to the literature of psychotherapy; Doctor of Laws." [4]

The citations reported in the *Worcester Telegram* indicated the University department in which each of the degrees was granted— for Freud, the Department of Psychology, and for Jung, the Department of Pedagogy. It is noteworthy that Professor Edward Bradford Titchener of Cornell was awarded the only Doctor of Letters. Hall, his great admirer, must have had special pleasure in describing him: "*Facile princeps* among experimental psychologists in America; master of lucid exposition, whose writings declare him literateur as well as man of science." [5]

The illustration preceding Chapter XIII portrays 42 of the participants, speakers and audience, attending the behavioral sciences sessions of the vigentennial. Some participants, e.g., J. J. Putnam, were not included, probably because they were not available at the time the photograph was made. It is instructive that William James appears in the first row, and it is, therefore, evident that the photo was taken on September 10.

It is also important that the controversial topic of infantile sexuality, with the illustrative case of the five-year-old boy (Little Hans) which is found in the fourth published lecture, was not presented in the lectures until Saturday, September 11. [6] This point is important because it reflects a deliberate agreement between Freud and Jung to discuss this topic on the same morning when Jung presented the case of Little Anna in his third and last lecture (Saturday). Jung described the conflicts in the mental life of a four-year-old girl as a parallel to Freud's five-year-old boy with the phobia described two hours later in the same room. As is noted in Part Three, Freud, when he published the five lectures, failed to allow for his having covered the topic of infantile sexuality in the fifth, not the fourth, lecture.

The lectures of Freud and Jung appeared in English translation seven months after the Clark celebration. They were published in the *American Journal of Psychology,* April, 1910, along with other articles on psychoanalysis by Sandor Ferenczi and Ernest

Jones. The lectures by Franz Boas, H. S. Jennings, Adolf Meyer, William Stern and E. B. Titchener were also included in the same issue.[7]

The translation of Freud's lectures was made by Harry W. Chase, a fellow in the Psychology Department working with Stanley Hall.[8] In 1910 Chase received the Ph.D. in Psychology and Education, with a dissertation entitled "Psychoanalysis and the Unconscious," published in the *Pedagogical Seminary* in 1910.

The lectures of Jung were translated by A. A. Brill, who had worked for some months with Jung at the Burghölzli Hospital in Zurich two years earlier. As will be recalled, Brill had served as the generous host of Freud, Jung and Ferenczi for the first week of their sojourn in the United States. He was at the time serving as Clinical Assistant in the Columbia University Department of Neurology and Psychiatry and was practicing psychiatry and psychoanalysis privately. His devotion to psychoanalysis, especially to Freud, is demonstrated by his translations not only of Jung's lectures at Clark, but of Freud's first book in English, *Selected Papers on Hysteria and Other Psychoneuroses*, published immediately after the Clark Conference (September 30, 1909). By 1910 he had also translated and published a second book by Freud, *Three Contributions to the Theory of Sex*. This latter contained an Introduction by J. J. Putnam, the Harvard Medical School Professor who was the host of the psychoanalytic trio at his camp in the Adirondack Mountains for three days. That sojourn is discussed in some detail below because it laid the foundation of a relationship between Putnam and Freud that gave a powerful impetus to psychoanalysis in America.[9]

The stay in Worcester came to an end on September 12 when, during the afternoon, Freud, Jung, Ferenczi and Brill left the city by train for Albany and Buffalo. Freud had been interested in visiting Niagara Falls even before leaving Europe, and the group made that tour on Monday, September 13. In a holiday mood Freud sent a picture postal card to his daughter Sophie from the American side of the Falls. After crossing over into Canada the party jointly sent a greeting card to Mrs. Brill, signed by "Abe, Freud, Ferenczi, Jung." It is evident that A. A. Brill was still with the group but he left them before the next stage of the journey.

Interlude at Putnam's Camp

That stage was a notable one for Freud and for the psychoanalytic movement in general. James Jackson Putnam, a friend of William James, had attended the lectures in Worcester and had invited Freud, Jung and Ferenczi to spend several days at his camp in the Adirondack Mountains in Keene Valley, New York. Just when the invitation was extended cannot be determined but it apparently happened in Worcester, after Putnam had heard one or more of Freud's lectures. Fortunately the European group had already planned to remain in America until September 21, as indicated by their booking of a return passage for that date shortly after their arrival in New York. So there was a convenient period of several days for a visit with Dr. Putnam that now transpired.

The camp had been established a generation earlier—in 1876—when land and some rude farm buildings were bought from the Beede family who ran a boarding house there, at which a group of young Boston physicians stayed while hiking in the Valley. [10]

The geographic site of the Putnam Camp is of interest because of its later associations with the life of William James described above. From this vantage point could be seen the rugged summits of Giant Mountain, the Gothics and other peaks. The highest mountain in the Adirondacks, Mount Marcy, was only a day's walk away. Lake Placid was even closer. For the remainder of his life William James went to this region for rest and recreation, often alone after his wife Alice had acquired maternal responsibilities.

The 1876 purchasers of the Beede property were the Putnam brothers—James and Charles—and Dr. Henry Bowditch, who also was a professor at the Harvard Medical School, and William James, then a 34-year-old Harvard College professor still at the beginning of his later famous career. At this camp, which originally bore the humble name "the Shanty," relatives and friends of the owners had for years congregated to spend summer vacations; but it was also a place to which an occasional foreign, distinguished visitor was invited, as now happened with the three psychoanalysts.

The quaintness of this settlement has been frequently described, mainly because of its associations with the famous owners, Dr.

James Putnam, Dr. Henry Bowditch and Professor William James. Freud himself gave a detailed description with some particulars of the group visit in a letter sent to the family on September 16, the day after arriving at the camp. He did not, however, repeat the jest he is said to have made before leaving Europe: that he was really going to America to see a porcupine at last! [11,12]

The significance of Putnam's influence on the establishment of psychoanalysis in the United States can best be indicated by the following comment of Freud. It constituted part of the Preface to a collection of J. J. Putnam's papers on psychoanalysis published in 1921, three years after his death, the opening volume in a series *The International Psycho-Analytical Library* issued by the International Psychoanalytical Press (London, Vienna and New York). [13] Freud stated there that Professor Putnam, "the distinguished neurologist of Harvard University . . . was not only the first American to interest himself in psycho-analysis, but soon became its most decided supporter and its most influential representative in America. In consequence of the established reputation which he had gained through his activities as a teacher, as well as through his important work in the domain of organic disease, and thanks to the universal respect which his personality enjoyed, he was able to do perhaps more than anyone for the spread of psychoanalysis in his own country, and was able to protect it from aspersions . . . all such reproaches were bound to be silenced when a man of Putnam's lofty ethical standards . . . had ranged himself among the supporters of the new science and of the therapeutics based upon it." [14]

A remarkable example of Putnam's support of Freud at a very early date after the Clark Conference is found in an Introduction he wrote for A. A. Brill's translation of Freud's *Three Contributions to the Theory of Sex.* [15] In this essay, dated August 21, 1910, Putnam, after commenting on the paucity of scientific knowledge about human sexuality, continued: "Freud has made considerable additions to this stock of knowledge, but he has done also something of far greater consequence than this. He has worked out with incredible penetration the part which the instinct plays in every phase of human life . . . and has been able to establish on a firm footing the remarkable thesis that psychoneurotic illnesses never occur with a perfectly normal sexual life. . . . It cannot too often be repeated that these discoveries represent no fanciful deductions, but are the outcome of rigidly careful observations which anyone who will sufficiently prepare himself can verify. Critics fret over the amount of 'sexuality' that Freud finds evidence of in the histories of his patients, and assume that he puts it there. But such criticisms are evidences of misunderstandings and proofs of ignorance" (pp. v-vi). This unqualified endorsement of Freud's radical theory of infantile sexuality strongly demonstrates Putnam's ardent support of Freud even in the face of opposition from critics like Morton Prince.

Putnam made what Freud would call a strong transference relationship to him, partly reflected in their correspondence and through personal contacts in which he brought some of his personal problems to Freud's attention for therapeutic analysis. In the latter vein he spent six hours with Freud on the occasion of the International Psychoanalytic Congress in Weimar in 1911, while they were both in Zurich before going to Weimar. From these sessions emerged Putnam's interest in self-analysis, stressed by Freud as a necessity for the analysis of others, and Putnam thereafter devotedly conducted such a self-analysis. [16]

Putnam was a New England aristocrat—member of an old Boston Brahmin family. One of his ancestors had migrated from England to Salem, Massachusetts before 1641, hence before the Salem witchcraft trials of 1692; and in those trials a child named Ann Putnam was an important witness who later retracted her accusations. The writer has established that Dr. Putnam was a second cousin, several degrees removed, of Ann Putnam and her family. It is not unlikely that his interest in hysteria and other neuroses had such ancestral roots. In that context probably belongs Putnam's high ethical standards, mentioned by Freud, perhaps reflecting a reaction formation against a sensitive awareness of "instinctual" strivings that were obsessively controlled. From that standpoint one can better understand Putnam's deep interest in German romanticism and the idealism of this orientation. In this regard Freud found a flaw in Putnam's understanding and applications of psychoanalysis: Putnam's devotion to philosophy which was not helpful to the scientific or empirical stance required by psychoanalysis.

But as Freud indicated even in the few lines above quoted, Putnam's support of psychoanalysis was all the more valuable coming, as it did, from the high moral ground that this Harvard professor of neurology, both professionally and personally, represented to his peers. Moreover, Putnam gave generously of himself both to patients and to professional causes that he espoused. An example of this generous devotion was in the invitation to Freud, Jung and Ferenczi.

Of Putnam's professional relationships, those with William James and Morton Prince are particularly significant in the present context. As above indicated, the Adirondack camp at its beginning in 1876 was a joint property of the Putnam and Bowditch families, also of William James, though James appears to have given up his share of the ownership after only a few years. Moreover, William James's relationship to Dr. Putnam was by no means limited to the camp. James was a personal friend who also consulted Dr. Putnam as a physician. Thus it was Putnam whom James first consulted when he suspected that he had strained his heart in Keene Valley in July 1898—an admission that he was very reluctant to make but with which Putnam, through his professional knowledge and personal friendship, was able to help him.

The relationship of Putnam with Morton Prince was apparently less intimate but very significant for the development of psychopathology in the New England area. Prince was never comfortable with psychoanalysis, even though he offered the pages of his new *Journal of Abnormal Psychology* to Freud and his colleagues when he founded it in 1906. He flirted briefly with the idea of presenting a paper at the first international psychoanalytic meeting in April 1908. Prince did not attend the Clark conference in 1909 but participated as a critic in the meeting of the American Psychological Association in Cambridge, Massachusetts in December that year. He opened his journal to some of the contributions made there in the Freudian symposium, mentioned below. Prince's part in the founding of the American Psychopathological Association in 1910 was largely actuated by his desire to attenuate the influence of psychoanalysis in America.

Several of these trends were reflected in Prince's relationship with Dr. Putnam, whose acceptance of psychoanalysis Prince found to be too generous and unscientific. He perhaps suspected that Putnam had personal grounds for gravitating toward Freud but did not recognize his own similar, but negative, grounds for opposing the Freudian orientation. To this very day the correct balance of psychoanalysis in psychopathology still seeks its true level. Given the mixture of fact and fantasy that Freud's creation brought to the wide spectrum known as psychology, the agenda skillfully outlined for an international audience at Worcester in 1909 is still timely.

The APA Symposium

The first notable repercussion occurred as early as three months later, at the 18th annual meeting of the American Psychological Association in Cambridge, Massachusetts on December 29, 1909.[17] On that afternoon the session was devoted to abnormal psychology, with special reference to the theories of Freud. There was a contribution by James J. Putnam, "Freud's and Bergson's Theories of the Unconscious," in which Putnam's philosophical bent is clearly evident. It is also clear that he favors Freud's emphasis, including the recognition of the sexual drive as having primary importance. A second contribution was by Morton Prince entitled "The Mechanism and Interpretation of Dreams" (Prince, 1910–1911). Prince gave credit to Freud's leadership in the understanding of dreams, especially in their relationship to other psychic phenomena, but he extended the approach to dissociation as found in multiple personality. But he raised several questions concerning the adequacy of Freudian methods. In the next issue Ernest Jones vigorously responded and concluded that Prince's paper had done nothing to refute the basic position espoused by Freud. In the December 29 session Ernest Jones had presented a paper, "Freud's Theory of Dreams," which strongly supported Freud. It was included, along with Freud's five lectures, in the April 1910 issue of Hall's *American Journal of Psychology*.

The fourth paper at the session in Cambridge was by Boris Sidis, a former student of William James, and known for some years to Freud as a critic of psychoanalysis. His contribution,

"Fundamental States in Psychoneurosis" argued that psycho-pathology involved a system-complex acting as a kind of parasite to the main personality. He downplayed the importance of sexual experience and instead emphasized what he called "the fear instinct." He illustrated his position by presenting three cases, all with emphasis of something phobic—a fear of the unknown or the mysterious. [18]

Although William James was not present at the sessions of the American Psychological Association (December 29-31, 1909), he noted in his Diary under the date December 31 that many of those who had attended the meeting had visited him and reported the proceedings. He mentioned that Boris Sidis had told about "Jones's windfall"—apparently using *windfall* to reflect Sidis's rejection of the Freudian theory of dreams as supported by Jones.

The Impetus to Organize Professionally

Another result of the participation of Freud and Jung in the Clark celebration was the impetus given to the psychoanalytic movement as an organized professional endeavor. As Ernest Jones relates, Freud, Jung and Ferenczi used the opportunity of the journey home from America to discuss the possibilities of an international psychoanalytic association. In the ensuing year such an organization was indeed established, with its first formal meeting held in Nuremberg, Germany. [19] C. G. Jung served as president. This choice continued to reflect Freud's hope that Jung would become his successor, despite the above-mentioned minor trials that had occurred in New York. Events at Worcester, and later in Keene Valley, apparently overcame Jung's doubts. In any event, as he said later, he had never taken as seriously as Freud did his adoption by Freud as son and "crown prince." In hindsight it is evident that Jung, from the beginning, was not constituted to play for long the role of follower in any movement in which he was seriously involved. His need for dominance was strong. The only question that remains is the extent to which he kept Freud from realizing this fact so as to benefit as much as possible, for the time being, from the guidance Freud could provide in his complex personal life and professional relationships, in which Freud's seniority and preeminence could serve Jung's ambitions. This question arises here because for three successive terms, often against considerable opposition from his Viennese colleagues, Freud insisted upon Jung's occupying the presidency of the International Psychoanalytic Association.

In this context it is illuminating to consider the role of Ferenczi vis-à-vis that of Jung in the founding of the International Association. As already mentioned, the three psychoanalysts had discussed details of the proposed Association on the way back from America, but Ferenczi, a willing and loyal follower of Freud, was apparently ready to do whatever was necessary to serve Freud's cause. It is thus easier to comprehend why, when the first Congress was held at Nuremberg in March 1910, it was Ferenczi who gave the keynote address under the title, "On the Organization of the Psychoanalytic Movement." [20] In this speech he proposed the formation of an international association by reviewing Freud's courageous and brilliant pioneer efforts for ten years, which he labeled the "heroic age of psychoanalysis." He dated the second period from the appearance of Jung and the other psychiatrists from Zurich. In that context he emphasized the contribution made by use of word association for exploring psychoanalytic theory, but in the next moment he downplayed the "exactness" such an approach paraded as "a kind of self-deception, a cloak to hide one's own emptiness" (Ferenczi, 1955, p. 301) which he believed "can teach us little." Ferenczi believed that psychoanalysis in its inexactness was able to disclose unexpected interrelations into layers of the mind hitherto closed to research. What is mainly interesting here is not Ferenczi's aspersions upon experimental methodology in psychoanalysis, but his deliberately overlooking the opportunity to pay passing tribute to Jung as the chief contributor along these lines. Instead, Ferenczi moved on to stress the dangers of organized groups in their tendency to repeat the conflicts and rivalries characteristic of family life—dangers that often undo the advantages of such organizations. He pointed out the importance of trying to maintain objectivity even about the leaders of the movement who are temporarily in the ascendance. Blind acceptance of leadership can result in serious damage. At the end he made the formal proposal for the founding of an International Psychoanalytic Association with a central executive to encourage the formation of local groups, the preparation of annual international congresses, and the establishment of an official journal. "I have the honor to lay before you draft statutes for the Association." [21]

The American Psychoanalytic Association was founded on May 9, 1911 in Baltimore, Maryland, with James J. Putnam as the first president. [22] This fact adds to the previous discussion of Putnam's role in the establishment and development of psychoanalysis in America. As was true in the case of Jung, Freud must have welcomed Putnam's presidency as a way to dissociate psychoanalysis from its Jewish origins in Vienna. There were, of course, other intrinsic reasons for Putnam's election to that office. While G. Stanley Hall was not, as far as is known, particularly prominent in the founding of the Association, he did serve as its president from May 1917 to May 1919. He was for years the only non-M.D. president of the Association. [23]

Another professional organization of interest here is the American Psychopathological Association. [24] It was founded on May 2, 1910 at the Willard Hotel in Washington, D.C. at the time of the meeting of the American Neurological Association. From the outset it had a much broader base than did the psychoanalytic associations; in fact, it appears to have arisen as a counterforce to the Freudian approach, with Morton Prince as perhaps the most vigorous dissenter. It purported to represent a broad range of psychological and psychiatric interests. Morton Prince was chosen as the first president at the meeting in Washington in 1910. As has already been noted, four years earlier he had founded and begun to edit the *Journal of Abnormal Psychology,* and the papers presented at the American Psychopathological meetings found a ready outlet there.

Chapter XII

Aftermath (Second Part)

The Freud/Jung Estrangement

The 40 days that Freud and Jung were together almost constantly from their meeting at Bremen on August 20, before embarking for America, to September 29, 1909, when they returned to Bremen on the completion of the American expedition, represented a kind of marriage of questing minds. The marriage was preceded by almost three years of accelerating courtship and followed by three to four years of pending separation. Most of the earlier and the later events can be followed in the voluminous correspondence between Freud and Jung that was published in 1974. There are some regrettable gaps in the series and the period of the American visit is naturally not represented there. Freud's partial Travel Diary makes up for some of this lack and the occasional letters written by Freud and Jung to their families are also helpful. In general, however, the published correspondence in the mentioned book is the primary source for reconstructing the rise, flowering and fall of this important phase of the history of psychoanalysis, and several biographies of both men published since that correspondence appear to have made the most of this source. It will, therefore, not be necessary to cover the same ground here but only to touch on certain aspects brought into focus by the visit. To some extent, that obligation has already been discharged in the discussion of the invitations extended to them by G. Stanley Hall and of events during an early phase of the visit, in particular, their experiences with each other in New York City before leaving for Worcester.

Our earlier tracking of Jung's accounts of the Agathe case with its various revisions has served to demonstrate how his relationship to Freud moved through the cycle of stages in that relationship in general. In fact, that aspect of the American expedition, including the prelude and the aftermath, serves as an index of the relationship. It was for that reason that the vicissitudes of the case presentation were described in detail; a repetition of that discussion is, of course, unnecessary.

There is a shred of evidence that Freud had hopefully attempted to avoid the dire outcome by continuing the informal analysis of his prospective successor during the return ocean voyage. None of this intimate interchange found its way into Freud's Travel Diary, but in a letter from Jung to Freud two weeks after the return, Jung wrote: "The analysis on the voyage home has done me a lot of good."[1] Unfortunately that promising result was destined not to last. The process of alienation had taken root and was at work in the still unanalyzed unconscious.

Throughout the relationship Freud's need and hope for a successor to the psychoanalytic movement was a dominant force. That Freud overvalued Jung's non-Jewishness and may even, paradoxically, have thus prejudiced the outcome is not out of the question. Freud himself seemed so to believe when he later said that Jung, out of consideration for his alliance with Freud, temporarily laid aside racial prejudices which he otherwise entertained.

The other side of the friendship—Jung's motivation—is more complex even than Freud's. It may involve not so much a naïveté that Freud seemed sometimes to display in his evaluation of colleagues but elements of disingenuousness. What, however, is unmistakable is Jung's extraordinary ambitiousness since, as he himself frankly avowed in his autobiography, it was not natural for him to take second place. But by openly declaring his choice of Jung as son and "crown prince," Freud was naively disregarding a conspicuous trait of his seemingly ardent disciple. Jung was willing to learn from Freud regarding the conduct of cases in therapy, as the correspondence frequently reveals; and he was not above asking for Freud's help in personal matters as, for example, in his affair with Sabina Spielrein. But to subordinate himself to Freud and the Freudian doctrine as Sandor Ferenczi was ready and willing to do was foreign to Jung's nature.

In this connection and as commentary on Jung's high self-esteem, we have this statement by Stern (1976, pp. 158-159): "With the help of his typological theory of relativity (and extending his typology from persons to theoretical systems), Jung declared psychoanalysis to be an extraverted doctrine, one-sidedly oriented toward the external world and viewing this world as the ultimate touchstone of reality. For a while, Jung thought of his own psychology as the (introverted) opposite of psychoanalysis, but eventually decided to assign this position to Alfred Adler's school. This proved to be a stroke of genius, making Jung's doctrine the superior mediator between the 'extremist,' and hence strictly limited, views of Adler and Freud. Already in 1913, Jung had suggested that 'the most difficult task of the future' would be 'to create a psychology that does equal justice to both types.' Even then it was easy to guess whom he had in mind as the architect of this synthesis." (See also Jung, 1921.)

The question of Jung's disingenuousness arises particularly in the early relationship with Freud before the visit to America. As has been shown, the gaps in the correspondence raise a question, or at least prevent an answer, as to whether Freud did have a part in initiating or supporting Jung's invitation to Clark. And Jung surely tried to convey the exact opposite impression when he described his invitation as being both "independent" of Freud—which it may have been—and "simultaneous" with Freud's—which it clearly was not.

It may be useful to point out the major events in the sequence of the estrangement between Freud and Jung even though the details between these points are not described here. One may begin with a hitherto unrecognized piece of evidence—one that shows Freud's early awareness of the inevitability of the rupture early in 1911. Jung had just embarked on the manuscript which was to become the volume *Transformations and Symbols of the Libido.* On January 18, 1911, Jung was writing to Freud of his concern about Freud's possible criticism of what he, Jung, was at this time writing. Jung describes it as following "an ancestral line of thought. But it is a risky business for an egg to try to be cleverer than the hen. Still, what is in the egg must eventually summon the courage to creep out" *(F/J Letters,* 1974, p. 385). Presumably Jung was here referring to the first part of his Libido book and, if so, he is already explicitly recognizing his retreat to the beliefs of his forebears. With that context in mind, let us turn to a short paper by Freud published in the second half of 1911. [2]

This interesting sidelight shows Freud's dawning recognition that the relationship with Jung was already about to end two years before the announced break at the start of 1913. It is a quite minor publication entitled "Great is Diana of the Ephesians." It derived from a book published by E. Sartiaux, *Vielles mortes d'Asie mineure [Dead Cities of Asia Minor]* published in Paris in 1911. Freud abstracted a section of this volume (pp. 62-106) dealing with the city of Ephesus. At an earlier time it had been a center for the worship of the pagan goddess Diana but with the rise of Christianity, its inhabitants turned to the worship of the Virgin Mary with the same enthusiasm. Without further comment Freud had included this abstract under *Varia* of the *Zentralblatt für Psychoanalyse*, vol. 2, 1911, p. 158. Its significance in the Freud/Jung relationship lies in a historical analogy that it cryptically points up. To Freud, the contemporary break with Jung, as Jung returned to the religion of his forefathers, repeated a similar turn of events in the friendship between F. H. Jacobi and Goethe just one hundred years earlier (1811-1812). Jacobi abandoned the pantheistic philosophy of Spinoza that both he and Goethe had enthusiastically embraced as a new revelation and retreated to an orthodox religious view when he published *Von den göttlichen Dingen und ihrer Offenbarung* (1811). On that occasion Goethe wrote a poem entitled "Great is Diana of the Ephesians" which described an old goldsmith in Ephesus who made effigies of the new goddess, undisturbed by the current events in the city streets. The poem is a subtle and cryptic allusion to Jacobi's religious retreat to which Freud is here calling attention by the phrase with which he titled the abstract from Sartiaux in the *Zentralblatt*. Goethe documented the title of his poem by citing, in an epigraph, its derivation from the New Testament (Acts of the Apostles, 19:28). [3]

The import of Freud's brief paper, published in 1911, is clear only if it is read as a record of his awareness of what was happening in his relationship with Jung months before the public evidence of the rupture. Incidentally the piece indicated Freud's identification with Goethe as a model, both in his writing and in his thought. Freud was very familiar with Goethe's life and writings and was undoubtedly aware of the discussion in Goethe's autobiography, *Poetry and Truth* (Part III, Book 14), of his friendship with Jacobi, though Goethe did not there indicate how the break finally occurred. In this context it is probably not irrelevant that Freud's clear recognition of Jung's "defection" may have crystallized at the time he knew that the next International Congress of Psychoanalysis would be held at Weimar in September 1911; and he knew, of course, that Weimar was the city where Goethe spent the major years of his life.

Concurrently with the writing of Jung's treatise on the Libido, in which he desexualized it along the lines of the philosopher Bergson's *élan vital* (in his *Creative Evolution,* 1907), and changed the generic conception to allow for an autonomous spirituality, the relationship with Freud deteriorated rapidly. Early in this reinterpretation of Freud's psychoanalysis the incest barrier lost its biological connotations and was replaced with views about the mother/child relationship easily reconciled with religious doctrines, not only of Christianity but of Asiatic theology from which Christianity has been recognized to have been partly derived. Perhaps, in part, under the influence of Jung, Freud wrote the essays collected under the title *Totem and Taboo* in 1912, in which the Oedipus complex found an evolutionary foundation in Darwin's concept of the primal horde. Rebellion of the sons against the claims of the primal father to the sole sexual possession of the mother figure was viewed as a basis for the origin of exogamy. Thus, as Jung continued more and more to stress the central role of the Great Mother, Freud extended the role of the Oedipal father in the genesis of social organization, i.e., in biological evolutionary perspective.

But the break in the end did not depend chiefly on differences of doctrine. As in all psychoanalytic psychology, it was personal motivation that affected the course of this history. Jung became openly restive about his privileged role as Freud's successor. When Freud had displayed his dominance in relation to Adler and to Stekel in 1911-1912, Jung bluntly used these precedents as a basis for blatantly accusing Freud of tricks. "You go around sniffing out all the symptomatic actions in your vicinity, thus reducing everyone to the level of sons and daughters who blushingly admit the existence of their faults. Meanwhile you remain on top as the father, sitting pretty. For sheer obsequiousness nobody dares to pluck the prophet by the beard and inquire for once what you would say to a patient with a tendency to analyze the analyst instead of himself. You would certainly ask him: '*Who's* got the neurosis?' . . . You see, my dear Professor, so long as you hand out this stuff I don't give a damn for my symptomatic actions; they shrink to nothing in comparison with the formidable beam in my brother Freud's eye. I am not in the least neurotic—knock on wood! I have submitted *lege artis et tout humblement* to analysis and am much better for it. . . . If ever you should rid yourself entirely of your complexes and stop playing the father to your sons and instead of aiming continually at their weak spots took a good look at your own for a change, then I will mend my ways and at one stroke uproot the vice of being in two minds about you. . . . Adler and Stekel were taken in by your little tricks and reacted with childish insolence. I shall continue to stand by you publicly while maintaining my own views, but privately shall start telling you in my letters what I really think of you. I consider this procedure only decent."[4]

In the reply that Freud wrote Jung on January 3, 1913, there was no attempt at a refutation of the charges—an impossible task in any case—but Freud could not refrain from the obvious retort ". . . one who while behaving abnormally keeps shouting that he is normal gives ground for the suspicion that he lacks insight into his illness." He proceeded at once to the decision: "Accordingly, I propose that we abandon our personal relations entirely. I shall lose nothing by it, for my only emotional tie with you has long been a thin thread—the lingering effect of past disappointments— and you have everything to gain, in view of the remark you recently made in Munich to the effect that an intimate relationship with a man inhibits your scientific freedom. I therefore say, take your full freedom and spare me your supposed 'tokens of friendship.'" Freud assured Jung that Jung need not fear "any lack of correctness" in their common scientific pursuits and ended by expressing an expectation of reciprocity on this point.

So Freud had, somewhat to Jung's chagrin, called an end to the personal friendship. The professional relationships, however, lasted for another year and a half during which time Jung continued to occupy official positions in the International Psychoanalytic Association. Finally he brought the tense situation to an end by resigning its presidency.[5]

On July 26, 1914 Freud was thus able to write to his faithful colleague and friend Karl Abraham: "So we are at last rid of them, the brutal, sanctimonious Jung and his disciples. I must now thank you for the vast amount of trouble, the exceptional clearsightedness, with which you supported me and our common cause."[6]

When at about this very time in 1914 Freud published "On the History of the Psychoanalytic Movement" *(Standard Edition, 14)*, largely under the impetus of his break with Jung, he pithily summarized the course of their relationship. After depicting the problematic position of psychoanalysis in which Freud as its leader was either praised by comparison with discoverers like Columbus and Darwin or "abused as a general paralytic," he continued: "I wished, therefore, to withdraw into the background both myself and the city where psycho-analysis first saw the light. Moreover, I was no longer young; I saw that there was a long road ahead, and I felt oppressed by the thought that the duty of being a leader should fall to me so late in life. . . . I felt the need of transferring this authority to a younger man, who would then as a matter of course take my place after my death. This man could only be C. G. Jung, since Bleuler was my contemporary in age; in favour of Jung were his exceptional talents, the contributions he had already made to psycho-analysis, his independent position and the impression of assured energy which his personality conveyed. In addition to this, he seemed ready to enter into a friendly relationship with me and for my sake to give up certain racial prejudices which he had previously permitted himself. I had no inkling at that time that in spite of all these advantages the choice was a most unfortunate one, that I had lighted upon a person who was incapable of tolerating the authority of another, but who was still less capable of wielding it himself, and whose energies were relentlessly devoted to the furtherance of his own interests" (p. 43).

With this judgment may be coupled Freud's later remark to Putnam, on July 8, 1915. Freud there referred to Jung's "religious-ethical crisis [which contained] at the very same time, lies, brutality and anti-semitic condescension toward me."[7]

Thus over a period of three years was dissolved an intimate professional friendship that had grown up over the preceding five years. It had been a source of great hope for Freud, largely based on illusion, which ended in a sense of betrayal. For Jung it was a time of stimulation and guidance, especially in respect to the American expedition; but it ended in a disillusionment that, according to later reports, released a severe mental disturbance and a psychological rebirth that produced Jungian analytical psychology: the collective unconscious, the archetypes and other structural constructs that replaced or supplemented a core of Freudian doctrine that Jung never did fully disavow.

The difference between Freud and Jung in their handling of a similar attraction to the paranormal helps explain their ultimate incompatability. Freud's neurosis involved a compulsive susceptibility to superstitious belief, but he regarded this inclination as a weakness—a symptom to be overcome by continuous self-analysis. Jung, on the other hand, with an equally strong propensity to the occult, would not denigrate it. Instead he tended to elevate it. He hypostasized the irrational and made a place for it in his system of analytic psychology. For example, remarkable cases of coincidence were not dismissed as a product of chance but appeared to Jung as an expression of "synchronicity," a dimension of the numinous that transcended the phenomenal world of time and place. Jung was thus able to provide his patients with considerable indulgence for their extra-rational proclivities. By the concepts of analytic psychology and the latitude provided by the diversity of personality types, he facilitated therapy into an active participation called individuation. But for Freud, Jung's concepts and methods were no longer within the domain of scientific knowledge and control, and to this domain Freud was, in his own way, committed.

In summary, one is struck by the similarities underlying the manifest differences between the relation of Freud and Jung, on the one hand, and Hall and James, on the other. Between Freud and Jung an initial strong attraction was founded on a father/son model, while between Hall and James the relationship resembled that of a younger and an older brother. (Jung was 19 years younger than Freud; Hall, two years younger than James.) In both instances an early intense intimacy gave way to a decided rupture. In the case of Freud and Jung, estrangement came after a short affiliation of seven years but the bond between Hall and James was forged over a period of twenty years and broken, not quite definitively, in 1895. And in both instances the conception of sexuality was crucially involved. With Freud and Jung, the conception of libido was manifestly central; when in 1911 Jung began patently to elevate sex by equating it, more or less, with Bergson's *élan vital,* Freud grew suspicious that a "heresy" was burgeoning and felt personally betrayed. With James and Hall, the conception of sexuality was more arcane, but the difference in orientations was profound both in life experience and in written formulation. This difference revealed itself in the comparative credence each accorded to Freud's theory. But what is most remarkable in this regard is the manner in which the final divergence expressed itself: in Jung's case, it was by a spiritualistic reinterpretation of the libido and a formulation of the unconscious which, at the deepest level, was collective and noumenal rather than materially biological. For James, sexuality never came to the fore; it was consciousness that evolved from a personal stream to a cosmic ocean. While Hall readily accepted Freud's view of the unconscious, he rooted it even more biologically in phylogeny. James never used the Freudian dynamic concept of the unconscious and, in the end, subscribed to a panpsychic version of consciousness that resembled that of Frederic Myers and G. T. Fechner. Historically it is notable that in the dyadic relations of both Freud/Jung and Hall/James, their terminal views about unconscious mental states were expressions of personal philosophical differences.

Hall the King-Maker

The "Defection" to Adler

Stanley Hall and Clark University had conferred upon Freud the unique distinction of inviting him to participate in the 1909 celebration and awarding him an honorary degree. But four or five years later Hall detracted from Freud's eminence by commending the work of Alfred Adler. That, at any rate, was Freud's perception. The first hint of Hall's "defection" is found, not in any publication of Hall's, but in his letter to Freud dated September 26, 1913 (26 H in Part Two). In it Hall confessed: "I have been trying in a very crude way to apply your mechanisms to the study of children's fears and anger, which seem to me to have plenty of *Verdrängung, Verschiebung*, and most of the rest." The letter continues by objecting to the overextension of sexual symbolism. Hall mentioned both Ferenczi and Stekel as offering useful new concepts to developmental psychology but he did not name Adler. Freud's reply to Hall (27 F, November 21, 1913) passed over the extension of Freudian mechanisms but commented on the question of sexual symbolism. He admitted occasional excesses but, he thought, these would eventually be eliminated while the rest would "stand up to verification." However, when Hall's treatise, "A synthetic genetic study of fear," published in April

1914 in the *American Journal of Psychology,* came to Freud's attention, he encountered Hall's explicit preference for Adler's "work of compensation" vis-à-vis his own view of "castration anxiety" (pp. 165-167). In "An infantile neurosis," written in 1914 though it was not published until 1918, Freud rejected this alternative. [8,9]

The time of Hall's critique was probably of some importance. It came at the end of a crescendo. In 1911 Adler himself had, under pressure, resigned from the Vienna Psychoanalytic Society: in 1912 Stekel had done likewise; in 1913 Jung's alliance with Freud was coming to an end. Now, in 1913-14 Hall was "defecting." It was the "most unkindest cut of all." For Hall had not only offered discipleship but had conferred public honors to assuage Freud's ambition.

Another aspect of the effect lay in the strategic part played by infantile sexuality in Freud's contribution at the 1909 conference. As shown in Chapter II, Freud had been concerned that this portion of his theory would be rejected out of hand by respectable citizens. For that reason he welcomed Jung's presence at Clark. Jung would present the case of Little Anna as a complement to that of Little Hans. (It was in the history of this five-year-old boy that the "castration complex" first appeared with sufficient clarity to justify Freud's introduction of it into his account of psychosexual development.) Freud had planned his collaboration with Jung with some care. The last lecture of Jung on Saturday morning was to be devoted exclusively to the case of the four-year-old girl and that was to be followed two hours later by the final lecture of Freud. There Freud discussed the case of Little Hans and pointedly alluded to Jung's case to confirm the theory of infantile sexuality. In the light of this strategy, Hall's unexpected repudiation of a crucial part of infantile sexuality, i.e., the castration complex, with a distinct preference for Adler's views which stressed inferiority feelings and compensation, would have been especially disappointing to Freud.

Adler's debut into psychoanalysis had been largely through his monograph "Organ inferiority and its psychical compensation" (Adler, 1907) in which the seeds of his later divergence from Freud had actually been planted. Hall's deviation thus involved no incidental aspect of psychoanalysis but went to the very core of Freud's sexual theory.

The historical evidence clearly shows that Hall in 1913 was greatly influenced by the new book, *The Neurotic Constitution*, published by Alfred Adler in 1912. Though he tactfully did not mention this influence to Freud, Adler's book plainly stated the case against Freudian theory in a manner that Hall echoed in his September letter to Freud and, as we shall soon see, in two papers that he presented at professional meetings, one before the letter and one after it. But first let us note Adler's own words in the Introduction to his book: "The sexual trend in the fantasy and life of the neurotic follows the direction of the 'masculine goal,' and is really not a trend, but a compulsion. The whole picture of the sexual neurosis is nothing more than a portrait depicting the distance which the patient is removed from the imaginary masculine goal and the manner in which he seeks to bridge it. It is strange that Freud, a skillful connoisseur of the symbolic in life, was not able to discover the symbolic in 'sexual apperception,' to recognize the sexual as a jargon, a *modus dicendi.* But we can understand this when we take into consideration the more extensive basic error, *i.e.,* the assumption that the neurotic is under the influence of infantile wishes, which come to life nightly (dream theory) as well as in connection with certain occasions in life. In reality these infantile wishes already stand under the compulsion of the imaginary goal and themselves usually bear the character of a guiding thought suitably arrayed, and adapt themselves to symbolic expression purely for reasons of thought economy" (p. x).

The point regarding the exaggeration of sexual symbolism had been emphatically made in a paper presented by Hall at a meeting of the American Psychopathological Association on May 8, 1913 (see Part Two, letter 26 H, note 1). This paper "Sex-symbolism in the psychology of Freud," which was extensively commented upon in the Discussion by Jelliffe, Jones and Prince was, unlike the other papers at the meeting, not published. Did Hall suppress it for psycho-diplomatic reasons derived from inner conflict?

The other point expressed by Adler as even more "basic" is documented in a presentation by Hall at the American Psychological Association toward the end of December 1913 (Hall, 1914a). Again, it was not published in full but appeared in the form of a long abstract under the title "The Freudian child (and ambivalence)." In it Hall vigorously repudiated the picture of the child given by Freud and his disciples, based, however, on only two cases "studied in detail." Hall was apparently alluding to Freud's case of Little Hans and Jung's Little Anna, both of which had been described in the Clark lectures of September 1909, the former published six months prior to the conference and the latter, presented for the first time at the conference. Hall characterized the reconstruction of adult pathology from an imagined infantile sexuality as unconvincing and expressed sympathy with "[William] Stern's protest, presented in the Breslau meeting of physicians, against turning the analyst loose on children" (Stern, 1930, p. 67). He designated the tendency to apply [abnormal traits] to normal children as "the great error of the Freudians" (p. 65). The odd presence of the term "ambivalence" (in parentheses) as part of the title of Hall's paper seems to have been a rhetorical avowal of his own state of mind—a conflict in his adherence to the views of Freud vis-à-vis Adler.

It is instructive to observe in this connection Hall's companion essay to his treatise on fear that appeared the very next year under the title "Thanatophobia and immortality," again, in the *American Journal of Psychology.* [10] That 1915 marked Hall's 70th birthday is, no doubt, idiodynamically significant. A little later, to round out his explorations in genetic psychology, he published (1922) the complementary volume to his well-known *Adolescence* (1904). In this valedictory exploration, the last section, entitled "The psychology of death," at its close inquired whether there was a "true enthusiasm for death," thanatophilia. But Hall oddly omitted any mention of Freud's concept of the "death instinct," described at length three years earlier, though he cited and discussed numerous other authors who had written on the psychology of death.

In 1919, at the age of 63, Freud published *Beyond the Pleasure Principle* in which he put forward his dual conception of the life and death instincts—"Eros" and "Thanatos." [11] These words he chose from Greek mythology, perhaps to indicate that he was promulgating not so much a scientific theory as a personal myth. Was he perhaps implying that these ideas had been largely derived from his own "castration complex"? He had tacitly avowed in the associations to his "Three Fates" dream of 1898 (in his *Interpretation of Dreams,* published the next year), that he, like Laurence

Sterne, felt that he "owed a death to Nature." (Cf. Rosenzweig, 1970a.)

A year after Hall's death in 1924, Freud, on publishing an autobiographical study, was impelled to couple the expression of his gratitude to Hall with a subtle indication of resentment. Remembering Hall's defection to Adler, he noted the invitation to the Clark celebration of 1909, and added, ". . . there was a touch of the 'king-maker' about him, a pleasure in setting up authorities and in then deposing them." [12] He continued, "In Europe I felt as though I were despised; but over there I found myself received by the foremost men as an equal. . . . it seemed like the realization of some incredible daydream: psycho-analysis was no longer a product of delusion, it had become a valuable part of reality." But Freud then deplored the fact that the popularity of psychoanalysis in official psychiatry in America "suffered a great deal from being watered down." Earlier, in "On the History of the Psycho-analytic Movement," he had noted with some surprise that "in prudish America it was possible in 1909 to discuss freely in academic circles the literature of psychoanalysis including matters that in ordinary life are regarded as objectionable." [13]

The incidental characterization of Hall as a king-maker is not just a subjective judgment. As E. G. Boring pointed out, Hall was a "fountain of enthusiasms" which led him to a series of "foundings" including, for example, in 1887 the *American Journal of Psychology,* the first journal of psychology as an experimental discipline, and in 1892 the creation of the American Psychological Association. [14] But Boring's statement that Hall was successively caught up by a series of topics each of which he embraced at the expense of the preceding one is not fully accurate. Indeed, Boring himself supplied an alternative view when he recalled Hall's introduction of the term "synthetic psychology" to characterize a comprehensive conception of the behavioral science. Hall's special devotion to what he termed "genetic psychology" was part of an eclectic general psychology congenial to any significant approach or conception whether it stemmed from Wundt, Freud or Adler. It was to some extent Freud's overweening claims for psychoanalysis that made Hall a "king-maker." But Freud was not entirely subjective in this judgment of Hall. Hall, too, had his complexities, among them an ambivalent identification with Sigmund Freud.

The Ambivalent Identification with Freud

The evidence for this identification extends beyond the permissible length of the present discussion so only three points will be addressed. There is, first, the obvious evidence of Hall's invitation to Freud which grew out of a patent interest in psychoanalytic theory because it reaffirmed the genetic approach to human behavior to which Hall had long been committed. A second, much less obvious circumstance concerns the enigma of Hall's birth date. He assigned it inconsistently to different years and days, especially during the last decade of his life. This variability and the question it raises have been discussed by previous writers (Swift, 1946; Ross, 1972, pp. 5-6). Here it need only be mentioned that in his last 25 years Hall gave his birth year as 1844, 1845 and 1846, a progression that Ross conjectured may have had something to do with the common desire to appear younger as the later years approach. But there is a potentially more compelling reason. Beginning with the first edition of *Who's Who in America* in 1899-1900, Hall not only assigned his birth to 1845, but he pulled "May 6" out of the blue as his day of birth. He continued to list that day through the next three editions of *Who's Who* (1899-1905) though in 1903 he changed the year to 1846. (In 1906-1907 he listed February 1, 1846. In various earlier listings, which are thoroughly reviewed by Swift [1946], the day was consistently February 1. The eventually accepted date of Hall's birth is February 1, 1844.)

Now, May 6 was Freud's birthday and the citing of May 6 by Hall coincided with the period of Freud's initial impact on him in the years of Freud's major work (1895-1905). Can this nexus be mere coincidence? By Freud's own theory, one would have to answer in the negative. It seems probable that, consciously or unconsciously, Hall selected May 6 just because it was Freud's birthday and by this caprice he was expressing an identification with the psychologist who, by the late 1890s, was beginning to examine the questions of crucial interest to Hall that the strict methods of Wundtian experimental psychology did not even recognize.

In Hall's first major book, *Adolescence*, he referred repeatedly and approvingly to the findings and the theories of Freud, especially Freud's emphasis upon early sexual development (e.g., Hall,

1904a, *1*, 233, 278-280, 284-285; and *2*, 120-122, 292-295). But he cited articles by Freud and Freud's book with Breuer on hysteria (Breuer & Freud, 1895) in these references. So the influence of Freud was, as above stated, present from the very start of psychoanalysis.

The present conjecture is, of course, just *that* since one cannot even be certain that by 1899 Hall knew Freud's exact date of birth. But, especially in view of Freud's own partiality for the psychic determinism of seemingly random numbers (cf. Freud's *Psychopathology of Everyday Life*, published in 1904, *Standard Edition, 6*, 240-250), the temptation to put forward this hypothesis is irresistible.

Moreover, precisely in 1899 Hall published a "Note on early memories" *(Pedagogical Seminary, 6)*. This lengthy article appeared in December 1899, three months after the publication of a similar article by Freud entitled "Screen Memories" (Freud, 1899a).

In Freud's contribution he described an innocent childhood recollection about a field with yellow flowers that turned out, by free association, to be connected with forbidden sexual play between the narrator and two childhood companions, a boy and a girl. By the free association process, the sexual connection that had been defensively omitted was recovered.

In Hall's 1899 article, reporting numerous recollections that he had collected by revisiting the farms in his native Ashfield, Massachusetts, where he had lived during his childhood and youth, one particular memory was extremely vivid. It derived from the place where he had resided from age two-and-one-half to eleven-and-one-half. Hall reported it in the following words: "The most striking experience of all was on coming suddenly upon a wild rose bush in a pasture near the house, which somehow affected me profoundly and actually evoked tears, and something almost like a sob for some reason utterly unaccountable. I could not possibly recall anything definite about it except that it somehow very closely suggested my mother and brought up later the image of her looking out from the front door up the rugged pasture hill, where it stood. I fancy that it was this very bush that my automatic imagery used to associate with her singing 'The Last Rose of Summer,' which always seemed to me very pathetic; but although I have racked my brain since, I can recall nothing else" (Hall, 1899, p. 489).

A dozen years later, now in an explicitly Freudian context, Hall referred again to this recollection. He did so at the end of a lengthy biographical contribution on Wilhelm Wundt (Hall, 1912), where, referring to the paucity of important results from Wundt's research by *conscious* introspection, he commended the more promising results from Freudian psychology: "They take us a most significant step nearer the underlying evolutionary nisus or push-up or will-to-live and will compel certain correlations with the Freudian psychology with its doctrines of wish and great *Einstellung* of sex love. For instance, a few years ago, revisiting a farm that I had not seen since I was thirteen or fourteen, and coming across a wild rose-bush, to my amazement I experienced something very like a sob in the throat and tears in the eyes. I could evoke at first no intellectual experience or even memory, but upon the heels of these challenging physiological phenomena came an image of my mother in the front door in the distance, as she used to stand many years ago, although even the house is gone. Then came an image of her singing 'The Last Rose of Summer,' and finally a suggestion that I had associated this, to me in childhood, very pathetic song with this particular rosebush" (ibid., p. 433).

The similarity between the yellow flowers in Freud's recollection and the rosebush in Hall's suggests the possibility that Hall had, indeed, read Freud earlier in 1899 and then "spontaneously" developed this first childhood memory.

This likelihood is, moreover, reinforced by a common contemporary event. Both psychologists were aware that in 1895 Victor Henri, the French investigator, had addressed a questionnaire to readers of several psychological journals soliciting from them their earliest childhood memories. In his paper on "Screen Memories," Freud explicitly referred to this research by Victor Henri as having started in 1895 (Freud, *Standard Edition, 3,* p. 304). He cited, in particular, the paper in which the findings of the survey were reported (Henri & Henri, 1897). The recollection about the field with yellow flowers recalled by a former patient in Freud's article was partly instigated, said Freud, by the knowledge which this patient had of the survey by Victor Henri. [15]

As for Hall, the questionnaire of V. Henri had been published in the *American Journal of Psychology* (owned and edited by Hall) in the January, 1896 issue (volume 7, pp. 303-305). (In fact, Hall had added to it a comment in which he pointed out three sources of possible error in the recall of such memories.)

Nearly a year earlier, Henri had published the same questionnaire in the French *Révue philosophique* (Henri, 1895a), and a month later it appeared in *Année psychologique* (Henri, 1895b). In that same month the questionnaire appeared in the (American) *Psychological Review* (Henri, 1895c). [16]

As mentioned above, Henri and Henri, on the basis of the replies received from various readers, published a digest of results (Henri & Henri, *op. cit.*). Freud definitely, and Hall, presumably, read this paper in addition to knowing about the original questionnaire of 1895. Were they thus stimulated to study their own childhood memories?

In fact, a case can be made for the hypothesis that Henri was a veritable midwife of psychoanalysis. His questionnaire appeared in the various periodicals in the early part of the same year as the earliest of Freud's dreams that he reported in *The Interpretation of Dreams*: the dream of Irma's injection, dated by Freud as occurring in July 1895.

This observation is highlighted by a fact disclosed by the writer's exhaustive examination of Freud's residual collection of books now housed at the Columbia University Health Sciences Library (formerly deposited at the New York Psychiatric Institute). It was thus discovered that the volume of *Année psychologique* for 1897, in which the report by Henri & Henri appeared, was in this Freud collection. Moreover, the article in question was marginally marked, presumably by Freud, in blue pencil (pages 190 and 192). From the thorough examination of the collection as a whole, it was reliably inferred that the blue pencil marking was a characteristic of Freud, who had similarly marked a number of other items in which the Freud signature appeared.

Hall's familiarity with the Henri questionnaire might likewise have stimulated him to start the search for his earliest memories soon after reading the 1897 report by the Henris. He states that in 1898 he returned to the several farms on which he had spent his childhood. That he did not publish a "Note on early memories" until December 1899 may also suggest that he had been stimulated not only by the Henri report but by Freud's article, published three months earlier (September), in a periodical that, it has been confirmed, was within Hall's ambience. This was the *Monatschrift für Psychiatrie und Neurologie,* a complete run of which, including the volume for 1899, is still on deposit at the Clark University Library.

It is evident from the above quotation (Hall, 1912, p. 433) that Hall was fully aware of the possible underlying erotic context of early, vivid recollections. In fact, after citing his recall of the wild rosebush vis-à-vis his mother, Hall commented (ibid., p. 434) on the relevance of Freud's monograph on Jensen's novel "Gradiva" (Freud, 1907) in which the repressed recollection of the moving foot of a girl was fetishistically associated with a sexual incident.

Hall's most recent biographer has speculated that he is a good candidate for Freud's theory of the Oedipus complex (Ross, 1972, pp. 9-12, 97-98). He exhibited a marked and persistent mother fixation and a pronounced father antagonism. One may question the validity of this interpretation, but in the context of the above conjecture about Hall's choice of May 6 as his putative birthday, it is arresting that both this alleged choice and his repeated recall of the early romantic memory of his mother reached publication in the same year—1899. Looking back with him from 1912, when he more fully developed the "unconscious" context of this early memory, one is inclined to believe that he was, indeed, applying to himself self-analytically the views of Freud as he became acquainted with them almost simultaneously with Freud's publications in the 1890s.

There is, however, a final qualification by Hall that detracts from his 1912 approbation. After alluding favorably to Freud's subtle analysis of "Gradiva," Hall goes on to reject the too zealous commitment to Freudian theory by disciples like Ernest Jones (ibid., p. 435). Jones had repudiated Morton Prince, who had a non-Freudian approach to personality dysfunction (multiple personality), a condition for which Freud, according to Hall, did not provide. Hall ruminates about the pitfalls of taking personal fantasy and free association too seriously without corroboration. This concern about error increases as one subjects the results of free association to critical scrutiny. There are, indeed, too many plausible alternative interpretations. One is here reminded of Hall's budding appreciation of Alfred Adler at precisely this time (1912-1913), with consequences that Freud later considered to represent "defection."

Instead of further speculating about Hall's alleged unconscious complexes, it seems more profitable to consider patent complexities of Hall's personality that, quite apart from Freud's innuendo, reveal unequivocal grounds for questioning Hall's constancy in interpersonal relationships.

Hall's Controversial Reputation

The complexity of G. Stanley Hall's character and the controversial nature of his place in American psychology was evident in his reputation even at the moment of his death in April 1924, when obituary articles began to appear. The earliest of these—the most candid and most illuminating—was that by E. C. Sanford (1924) which appeared in July, five months before the official memorial session at the American Psychological Association on December 30, 1924. Sanford earned his Ph.D. under Hall at Johns Hopkins in 1888 and was the first of Hall's colleagues in psychology appointed at Clark. He served amicably with Hall for the entire period of their joint service, including the crisis of 1892, from 1889 until Hall's death (which Sanford survived by only six months). Not only does Sanford ably characterize Hall's peculiar genius in positive terms, but he unabashedly describes the foibles of his mentor and chief. The latter included Hall's attraction to novel ideas, which he championed for a shorter period than required for the necessary testing because he became intrigued by other ideas and turned to them with enthusiasm. Sanford cites Ostwald (1909), who classified men of genius as either romantic or classic, and, on that basis, calls Hall a romantic. He frankly describes Hall's lack of precision, his impatience with detail, and his inconsistency in dealing with colleagues—all of which would detract from his enduring reputation but could not, he believed, eclipse his historic contribution to the opening up and first cultivation of the entire gamut of scientific and professional possibilities that psychology at the end of the 19th century had to offer. In view of the failure of fulfillment in Sanford's own career, the blame for which has been partly laid at Hall's door (cf. Titchener, 1925 and, in particular, Goodwin, 1987), this well-balanced appraisal is remarkable.

But even more revealing as regards the controversial quality of Hall's standing in the history of American psychology is the official obituary by Starbuck (1925). Starbuck earned his Ph.D. at Clark under Hall in 1897. Requested to take part in the memorial program, Starbuck explains: "I was reluctant to undergo the delicious ordeal. It did not seem to me humanly possible for anyone properly to evaluate Hall as a psychologist, for surely he is the most intricate, dominant, involved and self-contradictory personality that has come upon the psychological horizon" (Starbuck, 1925, p. 104). Starbuck finally consented only after hitting upon the idea that he would conduct a survey in which he queried all members of the American Psychological Association (at that time a rather small group). His contribution consisted of a tabular presentation of the results including Hall's overall rating as a psychologist, the value of his work as a pioneer, and the worth of his contributions to a whole gamut of topics ranging from studies of childhood through experimental psychology, history of psychology, eugenics and animal genetics. The findings were then appraised by the writer. In the present context the specific results are less important than the fact that Starbuck chose to perform his task in this unusual way—a demonstration of the broad variance in professional opinions of Hall even at the time of his death. Starbuck's final evaluation is highly positive but he introduced it by quoting the least as well as the most flattering opinions.

In passing, and at the price of a minor interruption in the sequence, attention should be called to a seldom cited obituary appreciation written by one of Hall's students, A. E. Hamilton (A.M. degree, Clark University, 1913), which appeared in a popular periodical and, unlike the professional obituaries, affords a picture of Hall, the teacher and friend at play as well as at work: "But, his work, of course, was his favorite play. People said that he overdid, that he attempted too much, that he never relaxed, that he burned his candle not only at both ends, but in the middle besides. Yet it was glorious to watch him at work . . ." (1924, p. 291). There follows a series of recollections in which the writer describes his association with Hall as student, research assistant and companion on frolics in the countryside. Even in his later years Hall is portrayed as a highly spontaneous and engaging friend. Despite his eminent position at the University, he needed and was able to relax with a congenial companion.

The one unqualified good for which Stanley Hall gets credit from nearly all American psychologists is the successful invitation he extended to Sigmund Freud in 1909. Even those who regard

Freud as an aberration in the history of psychology concede that his visit to America, increasing his visibility, was a landmark for which Hall deserves approbation. But this good deed stands out in the general opinion against ignorance of his other contributions or disapproval of them, e.g., his excessive use of questionnaires as his typical method of child study, an area that he significantly fostered. His place as a pioneer in the establishment of experimental psychology in the U.S.A., his founding of the first scientific journal in psychology, and of the American Psychological Association are not known to many professional psychologists. And some of those who are better informed are apt also to recall his dubious conduct in the 1892 crisis at Clark that entailed the exodus of the majority of the small but select faculty, and the departure of most of the University's graduate students. Since, in the last analysis, it is that 1892 crisis which continues to detract from Hall's reputation vis-à-vis the success of 1909, that crisis deserves at least a brief reexamination here.

One may begin by quoting the synoptic indictment of Hall by the esteemed historian of psychology Michael Sokal who, in turn, cites Dorothy Ross, Hall's most comprehensive biographer, and William Koelsch, the centennial historian of Clark University: ". . . in 1887, Jonas Clark began to implement a plan for an institution of higher education in Worcester. Soon thereafter, Clark and his trustees appointed Stanley Hall as founding president, and within a year Hall had recruited perhaps the strongest research faculty to ever grace an American university. By 1892, however, Hall's chronic secretiveness and dishonesty had alienated most of his colleagues, and by the end of the year most of them had left, primarily to go to the University of Chicago. (Characteristically, Hall displaced the cause of his difficulties on to Jonas Clark, and the depth of Hall's deception remained until the work of Ross and Koelsch was published." (Cf. Sokal, 1990, p. 114.)

Both Ross and Koelsch rely heavily on the conflict between Jonas Clark, the founder, and G. Stanley Hall, the first president, in their evaluation of Hall as guilty of duplicity with faculty members, particularly in the 1892 crisis. They repudiate his own account of that conflict (Hall, 1923, pp. 290-299), in which he ascribes his questionable conduct to the intentions and promises of the founder, which Hall took seriously and thus became a victim when he acted on these premises in making arrangements with faculty and staff. Hall assigned his assistant Amy Tanner the task of reviewing the history of the University from the standpoint of the will of Jonas Clark including the 1892 crisis. She wrote a documented account that was never published but is available in the Clark University Archives (Tanner, 1908). Not surprisingly, her conclusions are similar to those of her chief but one must add that she employed documentary evidence that Hall himself in his autobiography did not present. In the end it remains a question of preferential credibility whether one should rely upon the statements of Hall and Tanner or upon the various reports by Hall's colleagues that Ross and Koelsch quote or cite. But, even so, one must remember that these colleagues were rarely in a position to confront Jonas Clark, who was living in Europe or New York City during the time of the intense conflict in 1891-1892. And they were, of course, incensed by frustration which, in the first instance, was inflicted on them by Hall as President. He had entered into arrangements, largely oral, influenced by prior explicit or implicit intentions of Mr. Clark. To assume that Hall had been too sanguine agrees with his enthusiasm about the high ideals he tried to share with others for the new experimental university.

One early case is worth recalling in the context because it clearly reflects the direct involvement of Jonas Clark rather than of Hall. It is that of Arthur Michael who headed the Chemistry Department at the opening of the University in 1889 in the belief that his young wife, Helen, also a chemist, could assist in his laboratory work. Hall had given him this assurance, but when Mr. Clark happened to find Mrs. Michael working in the laboratory with her husband, he ordered Hall to disallow this collaboration. As was well known, Jonas Clark strongly opposed opening the laboratories or classrooms of the University to women, and Hall, in this instance, had disregarded Mr. Clark's stated policy. In the event, Hall had no choice but to carry out Clark's wishes and, in consequence, Michael resigned in November 1889 after less than two months of academic service (cf. Ross, 1972, pp. 218-219; Koelsch, 1987, p. 27). In this case it was not a conflict between Hall and Clark over financial matters that led to the unhappy outcome, but a disagreement over pedagogic principles in which Hall's more progressive views prevailed over the obedience that the founder expected of him. By the evidence of this instance one might well believe that Hall was similarly more optimistic—and more generous—than he had a right to be in making arrangements with future colleagues who were less committed than he was to the educational ideals Hall espoused. In the end they found themselves with less salary or staff than they thought they had been promised. Hence they accused Hall of duplicity and double-dealing. One conclusion that cannot be drawn is that Hall intended to acquire some strictly personal gain in these disagreements; in fact, he was himself a victim, and, in his own eyes, something of a martyr. He thus compared himself to the Swiss patriot Arnold von Winkelried who exposed himself to the spears of the enemy in order to obstruct the advance they were making in the field of battle (Hall, 1923, p. 294)—a comparison Hall makes in describing the difference between his own sanguine outlook about Clark's resources and the reality that eventually confronted the faculty: the latter then felt "that I had deceived them by great expectations" (ibid.).

The crisis of January 1892, to which Hall is here referring, has been described with unusual perspicacity by Dorothy Michelson Livingston (1973, pp. 163-170), in the biography of her father, Albert Michelson. He was, it appears, the most active of the rebellious professors during the crisis. In addition to the portrayal of the 1892 events, she recounts the tragedy of the accidental death of Hall's wife and daughter in 1890. Her uniquely thorough account arises, in part, from the fact that her father was professor of physics at Clark from 1889 onward and lived, with his family, opposite the Hall's. In consequence, and in the absence of Stanley Hall, he played the leading role at the scene of the tragedy.

Dorothy Livingston's account came too late by a matter of months for use in the book by Dorothy Ross (1972), yet it depended on independent archival research at Clark University, some of which does not appear to have been used by later biographers of Hall. I have been able to consult the archival notes and documents assembled by Dorothy Livingston, now deposited in the Special Collections of the Nimitz Library of the U. S. Naval Academy. Much of Livingston's testimony is also found in Ross and in Koelsch, but there is, at least, one line of her evidence not as clearly presented by them which it seems desirable to put on record here. It concerns the leading role played by Dr. Edward Cowles in the crucial negotiations of January 1892. [17]

After the failure of various preliminary efforts to persuade President Hall to remedy these complaints regarding administrative

arrangements involving salary and staff, a majority, consisting
of nine professors, on January 21, 1892 sent to the Board of
Trustees a joint resignation in which a lack of confidence in the
President was asserted. The document was signed, first, by Albert
Michelson, Professor of Physics, then by C. O. Whitman, Professor of Zoology, and these names were followed by the seven
others. This resignation was considered by the Board at a meeting
held on January 30. The Board regretfully accepted the resigna-
tions and, adverring full confidence in President Hall, recommended that the disaffected faculty members continue negotiation
with him because the Board was delegating to him the power to
resolve the disputes in whatever manner he deemed appropriate.

Even before the meeting of the Board on January 27, Dr.
Cowles was consulted by Professor Donaldson and by President
Hall individually. They travelled to Somerville to see him at
McLean Hospital, of which Dr. Cowles was the Superintendent.
After the Board meeting on January 31, Cowles called on
Donaldson to inform him of the action taken by the trustees the
day before. These and other contacts between faculty and president
began to bear fruit and for a short time there was a basis for
optimism.

As Livingston relates, an attempted reconciliation began
when Michelson and Whitman started to reconsider their earlier
decision, so that presently a truce was declared and the mass
resignation, withdrawn. How long this promising state of affairs
would have lasted, she remarks, and what it would finally have
led to, can only be conjectured "for into the fragile structure of
their unstable relationship swept a human hurricane in the shape
of William Rainey Harper. With John D. Rockefeller behind him,
Harper was scouting for talent to staff the new University of
Chicago. . . . Of the sixteen scientists at Clark, all but four
accepted Harper's offer." But when the bold recruiter tried to
entice Hall himself to a chair of psychology at double his present
salary, Hall, "shaking with indignation . . . invited his guest to
leave the office immediately" (Livingston, *op. cit.,* pp. 168-169). [18]

The Board of Trustees was not alone in its vote of confidence
in President Hall at this time of crisis. There was an incidental
but related event that has, at least, symbolic value. A community
drive to present an illuminated clock to Clark University was
conducted in the spring of 1892 and, as the *Boston Globe* reported

on May 10, the contributions were nearly double the required amount. The picture of the main building shown in Chapter I above is dominated by this emblematic clock in the tower.

In addition to the special contribution of Dorothy Livingston, one other witness, the eminent sociologist, Harry Elmer Barnes, who was professor at Clark in 1920-1923, published a memorable article about the institution the year after Hall's death (Barnes, 1925). His account of the relationship between Hall and Jonas Clark that entailed Hall's reputation for duplicity is noteworthy. In Barnes' view, "Hall himself never entirely recovered from the personality lesions caused by Clark's broken promises. The artistic mendacity which persistently characterized his administrative conduct had its pathogenesis in these troublesome days" (ibid., p. 274). How far Barnes was influenced in his judgment by Hall's own testimony in the 1923 autobiography and how much by other evidence is not easy to evaluate but he did have on site opportunity to acquire other testimony so that his judgment is not negligible. [19]

As already stated in Chapter V, the American Psychological Association was founded through an organization meeting of outstanding psychologists in Hall's study in Worcester on July 8, 1892. (See Editorial notice, *Science,* 1892. The centenary of the event was recently marked through the placing of a plaque by the membership of APA at the Goddard Library, Clark University.) It is evident from the foregoing discussion that the civil war between the Clark administration and faculty, which peaked in January 1892 and was temporarily resolved in April-May, just preceded this founding session. It is no wonder that there has been speculation about the role played by the Clark crisis in precipitating Hall's plan to arrange for this meeting. Was he partly inspired by the disorganization of his own immediate environment to move toward a national organization of psychologists which might compensate for his embarrassment on the local scene? Surely he had a need for solidarity. But the only sure facts are the proximity by date of the Clark disorganization in January-May; the national organization planned by Hall early in July of the same year, and the subsequent election of Hall as the first President of APA.

A final word regarding the 1892 crisis brings us back to 1909. Hall appears to have used the occasion for some reconciliation with the disaffected faculty at the twentieth anniversary celebration. Honorary degrees were conferred upon three leading participants of the 1890-1892 strife. From the University of Chicago Hall brought Albert Michelson, the physicist, and Charles Whitman, the biologist; and from Tufts College came Arthur Michael, the first to leave Clark in abashment. They now shared in the accolades with Freud, Jung and the 24 other distinguished scientists.

An earlier expression of Hall's conciliatory attitude occurred when President Harper of Chicago died unexpectedly at the age of fifty. Hall contributed a frank but unqualified tribute to this lost leader (Hall, 1906b). Mentioning the recruitment by Harper of three of Clark's professors who became chairmen of their departments at Chicago, Hall went on to say: "President Harper's name and fame will forever be a precious asset, not only for his University, but in the history of higher education throughout the world. The pathos of it all is in thinking what might have been, had he lived another fifteen years. The best possible memorial to him will be to maintain the University on the highest possible plane" (p. 234).

In 1920 Hall had an indirect contact with Freud. Hall was requested to prepare a Preface for an English translation of Freud's introductory lectures on psychoanalysis to be published in New York. [20] The manner in which this proposed translation came about has a special interest because it involved a nephew of Freud, Edward Bernays, the son of Eli Bernays and Freud's sister Anna who had lived in the United States since the 1890s. [21] Edward had been interested in his famous uncle for a long time and, knowing of the deprivations during the World War had sent a box of cigars to Freud in Vienna. In grateful acknowledgement Freud had sent Edward, who was serving in Paris as a consultant to the American mission at the peace conference, an inscribed copy of the *Introductory Lectures on Psychoanalysis* delivered at the University of Vienna in 1916-1917. On returning to the United States in 1919, Edward Bernays opened an office to begin a practice as public relations counsel. Among his clients was the publishing company of Boni and Liveright, of whom Edward knew personally Horace Liveright. He therefore proposed to him the possibility of publishing a translation of Freud's lectures. The publisher agreed so Bernays negotiated a contract on behalf of his uncle. He cabled

Freud for authorization to translate and publish the volume because correspondence at that time took eight weeks. By cable
Freud gave his authorization.

The aim of the new book was to provide the American
readership with an outline of psychoanalysis by Freud himself in
place of the popular and inaccurate accounts at secondhand by
others. To introduce the volume to the American public Edward
contacted G. Stanley Hall and invited him to write the above-
mentioned Preface. Hall agreed. As published, the Preface is
dated April 1920, and signed from Clark University.

Bernays has outlined in detail the vicissitudes of the book, and
its final great success, both financially and professionally. He was
able to provide Freud with considerable royalties over a period
of years at a time when his uncle experienced some financial
stringency as a result of the war. By 1926 the volume had been
reprinted 16 times. Freud was grateful.

From the account given by Edward Bernays it is evident that
the nephew had, without asking any financial return to himself,
undertaken to promote his uncle's cause as if he were serving a
client in public relations. Of the various developments from this
enterprise one is particularly interesting. Liveright arranged with
Edward to offer Freud a fee of $10,000 for giving lectures in the
United States over a period of six months. Freud declined, not
only because he considered the fee inadequate but also because he
was not feeling up to traveling and living abroad at that time.

A main theme of the Preface that Hall wrote for *A General
Introduction to Psychoanalysis* (1920) impinged on the king-maker
charge Freud would make later and provided an answer in advance. Hall's theme was almost identical with what he wrote to
Freud in the same vein in his final letter to him. [22] The occasion
was the prospective visit of Dr. E. J. Kempf, an American
psychiatrist who wanted to visit Freud in Europe. (See Letters
29 H and 30 F and the Notes.) Hall's difference with Freud
continued but he generalized the difference in 1913-1914. In
Hall's purview Freud should have been more tolerant of disciples
like Alfred Adler and Carl Jung. In this last exchange Hall, continuing to express his extraordinary indebtedness to Freud for ideas
that influenced his lifework, pled for Freud to move beyond the
role of the primal father in relation to his seemingly rebellious sons.
He compared Freud with Wundt who in his last years found it

hard to accept dissent in his former pupils. But Freud would not budge. To the end Freud defended his stance—a position that, as above explained, he considered to be essential to the survival of psychoanalysis as scientifically justified.

In this same context Freud tended to minimize the efforts of E. J. Kempf to tie in psychoanalysis with neuroanatomy, especially with the functions of the autonomic nervous system. Psychoanalysis for Freud had to focus on behavior, especially in the sexual domain, in its own terms without reduction or elevation to other conceptual levels or formulations. Why Freud was unable to escape the confines of his own observations is probably not only a matter of the logic of science but of Freud's peculiar genius—an expression of his unique strengths through his unique limitations. Only a detailed idiodynamic analysis of Freud's life and work may one day enable us better to appreciate this inner necessity.

Freud and America

One may begin with the moot question of Freud's conception of women, for on that issue he is on record as having brought back from America polemical ideas that he communicated to the Vienna Psychoanalytic Society (cf. Nunberg & Federn, 1974, III, p. 14, meeting of October 12, 1910). Referring to the opinion of G. Stanley Hall, Freud stated, with obvious concurrence, that co-education in America had not had good results: from that experience girls, developing more rapidly than boys, acquired feelings of superiority and lost esteem for males. To this opinion of Hall's, Freud added that in America the "father ideal appears to be down-graded, so that the American girl cannot muster the illusion that is necessary for marriage." Moreover, he believed that Americans escape a general neurosis because, despite their excessive repression of sexuality, in their educational system, family influence is played down with a resulting reduction in "the weight of the core [Oedipus] complex." (Ibid.)

These conservative opinions about the social role of women are, of course, those that present-day American feminists deplore in Freud's theory. And it is striking that in this informal, oral communication to his colleagues in Vienna soon after returning from the United States, Freud provided such direct evidence of his male chauvinism. That he attributed a similar attitude to Hall may partly have ensued from his own apperceptive expectation, but there are those who also read Hall's opinions of women as conservative—even reactionary—because, though he was one of the first educators to open the avenues of higher learning to women, he did display doubts about the mix of marriage with professional career and he tended to stress the function of women as mothers as too important to future generations to be subordinated to careerism. (See Diehl, 1986.)[23]

Despite the fact that Freud had benefited considerably from his American sojourn by the opportunity it afforded to give psychoanalysis its first truly international hearing and thus acquire new supporters, his opinion of the country, its people and its customs was, as just illustrated, largely negative.[24] This fact, widely recognized since then, has puzzled some of his biographers. For example, Ernest Jones, the authorized biographer, felt that certain irrational grounds not even recognized by Freud were here involved. To support his hunch Jones cited allusions to symptoms of indigestion that Freud attributed to the American diet though, Jones maintains, these did not actually start with the visit to the United States. Moreover, Freud's negative attitude was expressed before he saw America. At Bremen, for instance, while he waited to embark on the *George Washington*, he referred to the American worship of the "almighty dollar."[25]

Without attempting a solution of this problem or debating Freud's justification for his attitude, a circumstance that has rarely been noted may be mentioned. This was his intense dislike of his brother-in-law Eli Bernays, a dislike that Jones described in recounting Freud's early relationship to Eli. Soon after Eli married Sigmund's sister Anna, the couple emigrated to America in the 1890s. But even during the engagement period, Sigmund had experienced difficulties with Eli over money matters, and he was suspicious of Eli in the handling of finances. Moreover, Sigmund's hostility appeared during the 1909 visit itself, e.g., as above noted, in Freud's attempts to visit his sister Anna and her family in New York. When Freud finally did manage to see the Bernays family upon his return to New York after the sojourn in Keene Valley, Eli was away on business in Canada. Is it possible that part of Freud's anti-American attitude was a displaced sibling rivalry?

The surmise is supported by a letter Freud wrote to his nephew Edward Bernays at the time of the death of Edward's father Eli, in October 1923. Referring to this event, Freud said: ". . . You know it is hard for me to write more on this subject. Constellations [complexes] of many years cannot be changed by chance or sudden events" (Edward L. Bernays, *op. cit.,* pp. 268-269).

Though detailed speculation about Freud's hostility toward his brother-in-law may seem unwarranted, one familiar with Freud's writings and biography cannot but observe the closeness of Sigmund's relation to his sister Anna during childhood and up to the time of her marriage. Reciprocally, Anna's overweening pride in her brother is evident in an overlooked book-length auto-biography privately published by Anna in later life which dealt largely with her relationship to her famous sibling.[26] Was there a mutual "Oedipal" aspect to Freud's relationship with this sister and her husband? With Freud's own conceptualization about family romances, formulated just before the visit to America, the question is surely not irrelevant.

With this context in mind and with the above source (Edward L. Bernays, ibid., pp. 275-276), there is a sententious reply Freud wrote to his nephew, who, serving as agent for the publisher Liveright, offered Freud $5,000 as advance payment of royalties for a proposed autobiography. Freud pithily stated on August 10, 1929: "This proposal is of course an impossible one. An autobiography is justified only on two conditions. In the first place if the person in question has had a share in interesting events, important to all. Secondly, as a psychological study. Outwardly my life has transpired quietly and without content and can be dismissed with a few dates. A psychologically complete and sincere life recital would, however, demand so many indiscreet revelations about family, friends, adversaries (most of them still alive) with me as with everyone else, that it is precluded from the very outset. What makes all autobiography worthless is, in fact, its lying. Besides, it is really an example of your American editor's naïveté to believe that he could get a hitherto decent man to commit such an outrageous act for $5,000. Temptation would begin for me at a sum a hundred times as great and even then would be rejected after half an hour."

Among the matters that Freud implies he would have to discuss—and would be willing to do—was undoubtedly his early relationships to siblings, especially his young rival Julius who died in infancy and to Anna who was born eight months afterwards.

In contrast to Freud's anti-American complex, however constituted, there is the undoubted positive influence that his visit produced and which, with variations in valence and intensity, has persisted ever since. A special instance occurred in 1950 on the occasion of the sixtieth anniversary of Clark University. To celebrate it a Symposium on Genetic Psychology was organized and Anna Freud, daughter of Sigmund Freud, now a leader in child analysis, was invited as guest of honor. On April 20 she spoke on "The Contribution of Psychoanalysis to Genetic Psychology."[27] On April 22 she was awarded an honorary degree. In introducing her for this award, Heinz Werner, G. Stanley Hall Professor of Genetic Psychology, made this appropriate comment:

"On the occasion of Clark's Twentieth Anniversary in September, 1909, the work of Sigmund Freud, in the founding of Psychoanalysis, was recognized by this University by conferring upon him the honorary degree of Doctor of Laws. It is eminently fitting that on the occasion of the celebration of the Sixtieth Anniversary of Clark University, we should honour Anna Freud, eminent psychologist, who has creatively extended her father's work in psychoanalysis."[28]

By this generational marker the achievement of the 1909 American visit was reaffirmed; the quest, vindicated.

Coda

Did G. Stanley Hall succeed in satisfactorily introducing psychoanalysis to America by inviting Freud and Jung to active participation in the Clark University Conference? The answer is clearly affirmative. Not only did the lectures of Freud and Jung receive extensive coverage in the local Worcester newspapers but also in the prestigious *Boston Evening Transcript,* as has been above demonstrated in some detail. As a result, the visability of Freudian psychoanalysis was greatly enhanced. If, however, one asks whether psychoanalysis was more widely accepted by psychologists and other behavioral scientists as a consequence of the psychoanalytic participation, the answer has to be negative. As Freud had anticipated, there was considerable resistance to his sexual theory and his conception of the unconscious; it took years for these attitudes to change, and the change occurred only partially. These responses are surveyed for the period immediately following the Conference by Hale (1971b) in *Freud and the Americans: The beginnings of psychoanalysis in the United States, 1876-1917.* A more focused coverage of psychoanalytic influence with special reference to American medicine is found in the book by Burnham (1967), *Psychoanalysis and American medicine: 1894-1918.* An even more specialized and in-depth appraisal of the impact of psychoanalysis on psychology is found in the monograph by Shakow and Rapaport (1964) which considers the effects by topic as well as by particular psychologists and closes with a review of the penetration of psychoanalysis into histories of psychology and into various reference works.

A quite recent critical digest of the encounter between Freudian theory and scientific psychology is surveyed in *Freud and experimental psychology: The emergence of idiodynamics* by Rosenzweig (1985), a contribution to *A century of psychology as science,* edited by Koch and Leary. (A second, revised edition was published by Rosenzweig in 1986.) Here the focus is on the operational definition of psychoanalytic concepts provided by laboratory and other research methods, and considerable success is reported. From this digest the new orientation of idiodynamics emerges as an approach to the analysis of behavior which is, in part, a result of the experimental definition of psychoanalytic concepts. Indeed, one could tenably mention that Hall was a forerunner of the idiodynamic orientation which in his terms was the genetic-synthetic approach to individual human behavior and to the cultural expression of personality in the history of psychology. Without undertaking such argument, these words from Hall's *Founders of modern psychology* (1912, pp. 58-59) may be quoted: ". . . [a] higher standpoint is just emerging and that is that the old systems [of philosophy and psychology] one and all, are to us challenging data for further psycho-analysis, like myths, cults, religions and dreams and illusions. We do not really know the old systems till we understand their psychological motivation in both the age and the individual. How and why did these men in this age formulate the great questions of life and mind thus and give such answers. What was the *Zeitgeist,* environment, diathesis, the folk thought, aspiration, political and economic situation? What was their deeper meaning? What did the writers intend by what they said and what was left unsaid, and why? How have others sought to express the same thing in the same or other fields? How can we find or work out a way to the comparative standpoint and determine the canons of higher criticism for them all, and above all, how can we express all they meant in terms of our own age? Perhaps something like this is to be the culminating theme of the genetic psychology of the future. . . . We must not forget, however, that this is only a postulate, for this tendency is yet in its infancy."

In brief, it may be reliably stated that directly or indirectly, immediately or remotely, Hall's bold endeavor to make psychoanalysis a part of scientific psychology by inviting Freud and Jung to lecture among other nationally and internationally known leaders of science did notably succeed and it earned for him an unchallenged credit in the history of psychology.

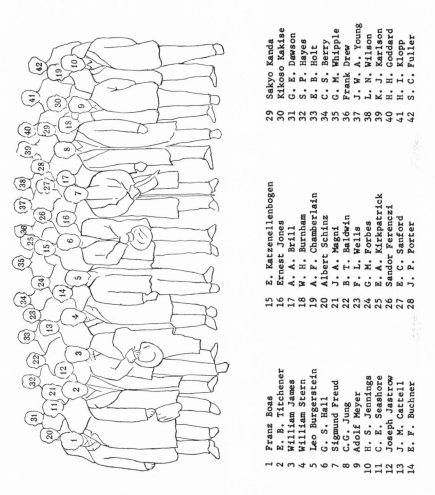

1 Franz Boas	15 E. Katzenellenbogen	29 Sakyo Kanda
2 E. B. Titchener	16 Ernest Jones	30 Kikoso Kakise
3 William James	17 A. A. Brill	31 G. E. Dawson
4 William Stern	18 W. H. Burnham	32 S. P. Hayes
5 Leo Burgerstein	19 A. F. Chamberlain	33 E. B. Holt
6 G. S. Hall	20 Albert Schinz	34 C. S. Berry
7 Sigmund Freud	21 J. A. Magni	35 G. M. Whipple
8 C.G. Jung	22 B. T. Baldwin	36 Frank Drew
9 Adolf Meyer	23 F. L. Wells	37 J. W. A. Young
10 H. S. Jennings	24 G. M. Forbes	38 L. N. Wilson
11 C. E. Seashore	25 E. A. Kirkpatrick	39 K. J. Karlson
12 Joseph Jastrow	26 Sandor Ferenczi	40 H. H. Goddard
13 J. M. Cattell	27 E. C. Sanford	41 H. I. Klopp
14 E. F. Buchner	28 J. P. Porter	42 S. C. Fuller

Participants in Psychology and Pedagogy Sessions, Friday, September 10, 1909

Chapter XIII

Synoptic Chronicle of Events

The following synoptic chronicle of germane events provides a good, though static, picture of the expedition to America in 1909. It supplements the dynamic portrayal of the preceding twelve chapters in which the interrelationships among the leading members of the cast have been depicted, and it describes the ramifications of the main event for the contemporary scene and for the future history of psychology. It includes the relevant occurrences before, during and after the Clark vigentennial. It is presented as a chapter to be perused in summary but may also serve for ready reference during the reading of Chapters I-XII. [1]

In connection with these multiple functions, it is instructive to take note of the essay by Samelson on recent historiography and to quote from it his summary characterization of the new dispensation. He has maintained that scholarly discipline in this field no longer views "its task as producing chronicles of scientific discoveries, or biographical accounts of its heroes, or the settling of priority claims. A new sensitivity for historical material has developed. It insists on respecting the integrity of the thought of past figures, on the need to understand them in their own terms, within their historical context, instead of mapping out straight lines of scientific progress or pointing to anticipations of the present" (Samelson, 1974, pp. 223-224). Similarly, Furumoto (1989) expresses the aims of the new history of psychology in these words: "Specifically, in contrast with traditional history, it [the new approach] is more contextual, more critical, more inclusive, more archival, and more past-minded" (p. 24). These conceptions well express the idiodynamic intent and method that have pervaded the writing of the present volume.

In the synoptic chronicle, specific month and day, when given, have been authenticated from original sources. Items for which the year only was determined have been listed at the beginning of the year unless there is evidence warranting a different relative position. The original dates of books published in German are given with the title translated into English for the convenience of the reader.

1842   William James born (Jan. 11).

1844   G. Stanley Hall born (Feb. 1).

1856   Sigmund Freud born (May 6).

1875   C. G. Jung born (July 26).

1880–   Breuer treats Bertha Pappenheim [Anna O.] for hysteria
1882   and cures her temporarily.

1885–   Freud studies in Paris with Charcot (Oct. 13–Feb. 28).
1886

1886   Freud starts private practice of psychiatry in Vienna (Apr. 15).

Clark University granted charter (March).

Freud participates in military maneuvers at Olmütz, Moravia (Aug. 11–Sept. 9).

Freud writes letter to Breuer mentioning that military exercises are good therapy for neurasthenia (Sept. 1).

Freud marries Martha Bernays immediately after the maneuvers (Sept. 13).

Freud presents controversial paper "On Male Hysteria" before the Vienna Society of Physicians (Oct. 15).

1887   Hall founds *American Journal of Psychology* and is its first editor (Oct.).

1888   Hall becomes first President of Clark University (Apr. 5).

1889   Clark University opens (Oct. 2).

1890   William James publishes *Principles of Psychology* (Oct.).

1891   Hall founds the *Pedagogical Seminary* (later *Journal of Genetic Psychology*).

1892   Hall assembles psychologists at Clark to discuss founding of National Psychological Association (July 8). (Hall, first President; again President in 1924.) William James in Europe on a sabbatical from May 1892 for about a year, hence not present at organizing session July 8.

1894   William James becomes third President of American Psychological Association.

1895   Breuer and Freud publish *Studies on Hysteria* (June).

         William James meets Pauline Goldmark (in the Adirondacks) for the first time (Sept.).

1898   Henry James publishes "The Turn of the Screw" (Feb. 5, Apr. 16).

         William James hikes and spends night at camp in Adirondacks with Pauline Goldmark. Overexertion by James brings on critical heart ailment (July 8–9).

1899   Decennial celebration of Clark University ("completion of the tenth academic year") (July 5–10).

         Freud publishes his masterpiece, *The Interpretation of Dreams* (English translation, 1913).

1904   Freud publishes first book edition of *The Psychopathology of Everyday Life.*

1904   Wertheimer (with Klein) publishes word-association ("complex") research from Prague, to verify truth in testimony (Apr. 7).

Jung publishes first researches on word association performed at Burghölzli Hospital, Zurich (Apr. 19).

Hall establishes *American Journal of Religious Psychology and Education* (May); published through 1915 (Dec.).

Hall publishes *Adolescence,* his most influential book, with numerous references to Freud's writings of the 1890s (June 4).

1905   Freud publishes *Three Essays on the Theory of Sex* and *Jokes and their Relation to the Unconscious.*

Morton Prince publishes *The Dissociation of a Personality* (Dec. 30).

1906   Pierre Janet lectures at Harvard Medical School in Boston.

Jung publishes first volume of word-association studies.

Jung publishes *The Psychology of Dementia Praecox.*

William James writes four letters to Pauline Goldmark just prior to a series of dissociative anxiety dreams published in 1910 (Jan. 4–Feb. 13).

Jung sends Freud copy of his book on word association and thus initiates their correspondence (1906–1913).

Morton Prince founds *Journal of Abnormal Psychology* (Apr.).

1907   Alfred Adler publishes *Organ Inferiority and its Psychical Compensation* (English translation, 1917).

1907   A. A. Brill, on the advice of Peterson, undertakes work at Burghölzli Hospital under Bleuler and Jung.

Visit of Dr. and Mrs. C. G. Jung to Freud in Vienna—first personal meeting (Mar. 3–7).

First International Congress of Psychiatry, Neurology and Psychology is held at Amsterdam; Jung, acting as Freud's surrogate, presents paper on Freud's theories and meets, for the first time, Ernest Jones, an adherent of these views (Sept. 2–7).

1908   "Freud Congress" (first International Psychoanalytic Congress) is held at Salzburg (Apr. 26–27).

Freud publishes second edition (1909) of *The Interpretation of Dreams* (Nov.).

Hall invites Freud to participate in Clark celebration planned for early July, 1909 (Dec. 15). Freud declines (Dec. 29).

1909   Hall invites Wundt (for same date); Wundt declines (Jan. 5, 1909).

Hall again invites Freud, with celebration time shifted to September (Feb. 16). Freud accepts (Feb. 28).

Freud invites Sandor Ferenczi to accompany him to America (Mar.).

First psychoanalytic journal *(Jahrbuch für psychoanalytische und psychopathologische Forschungen)* is published; Jung as Editor, Bleuler and Freud as the publishing directors.

Freud publishes case of "Little Hans" (Mar.).

Carl and (wife) Emma Jung again visit Freud in Vienna (Mar. 25–29).

1909   William James publishes *A Pluralistic Universe,* with conception of God as a cosmic multiple personality (Apr.).

Hall investigates the personality of the famous Boston medium Mrs. Leonore Piper who was "discovered" by William James (Apr.–May).

By this date Jung has received Hall's invitation to participate in the Clark celebration (June 12).

As first phase of 20th anniversary celebration, Conference on Child Welfare and Research is held at Clark University (July 6–10).

Bertha Pappenheim [Anna O.] visits U.S.A. and lectures on prostitution and white slavery (Aug.).

Sixth International Congress of Psychology is held at Geneva, Switzerland; E. Jones, H. S. Jennings, and Morton Prince present papers. Jung and Titchener were listed as participants but did not attend (Aug. 2–7).

Freud leaves Vienna for Bremen to embark for U.S.A. (Aug. 19).

Freud and Ferenczi are met by Jung in Bremen (Aug. 20).

The party of three board the North German Lloyd ship *George Washington* for the voyage to New York (Aug. 21).

Sixteenth International Congress of Medicine held at Budapest. Morton Prince and S. E. Jelliffe are listed as members (Aug. 29–Sept. 4).

Disembarkation interview (Aug. 29) with Freud, Jung and William Stern (also invited to Clark) published in German-language newspaper (Aug. 30).

1909   In early part of day Freud and Jung take a long walk
          in Central Park; they discuss one of Jung's dreams
          "concerning Jews and Aryans" (Aug. 30).

          In afternoon Freud attempts, without success, to visit
          Dr. Sigmund Lustgarten, erstwhile Vienna friend; then
          makes same effort, again unsuccessful, to visit sister
          Anna (Bernays) and family (Aug. 30).

          The three visitors dine at home of A. A. Brill, then (10-
          12 P.M.) tour Chinatown and ride through Jewish ghetto
          (Aug. 30).

          In the morning Jung visits Dr. Adolf Meyer at New York
          State Pathological Institute, Ward's Island; then to
          Metropolitan Museum of Art (Aug. 31).

          Freud visits Metropolitan Museum of Art in the afternoon
          (Aug. 31).

          In the evening the group visits Coney Island (Aug. 31).

          Jung mentions (in letter to wife) that prospective visit to
          Chicago is doubtful since time will be too short; return
          trip to Europe is planned for September 21 (Aug. 31).

          Jung mentions plans for trip to Niagara Falls, with
          possible tour of Canada. (Putnam Camp sojourn not yet
          in prospect.) (Aug. 31)

          All three visitors have digestive problems and "take turns
          fasting for a day" (Aug. 31–Sept. 2).

          Freud writes no letter home on this day. In his letter of
          September 2 to his wife he apologizes for his busy
          schedule. The group attend moving pictures (a new ex-
          perience) in the evening (Sept. 1).

          They book return passage for September 21 on the North
          German Lloyd *Kaiser Wilhelm der Grosse* (Sept. 2).

1909   They visit Columbia University. The Palisades, distantly visible from Riverside Drive, impress them. Freud has an attack of prostatitis (Sept. 2).

In the evening they attend Hammerstein's Victoria Theatre (vaudeville on "Paradise Roof") (Sept. 2).

In forenoon Freud visits the American Museum of Natural History; Freud lunches with Dr. Brill (Sept. 3).

It rains in New York City. All three visitors are afflicted with diarrhea (Sept. 4).

Jung visits paleontological collection of tertiary mammals at the American Museum of Natural History (Sept. 4).

Ernest Jones (just arrived from Europe) joins group (Sept. 4).

Enlarged party, consisting of Freud, Jung, Ferenczi, Brill and Jones, leave by night boat for Fall River, en route to Worcester (Sept. 4).

The party entrain to Fall River, Boston, Worcester. They check in at Standish Hotel. Next day Freud and Jung move to Hall's home as guests for the duration of celebration (Sept. 5).

Vigentennial celebration at Clark University opens (Sept. 6).

Freud presents first of his five lectures (in German) at 11 A.M. (Sept. 7). The four others given at same hour on each following day (through Saturday, Sept. 11).

Freud is interviewed at Hall's home by *Boston Evening Transcript* (Sept. 8; published Sept. 11).

Jung presents his first lecture (in German) at 9 A.M.; two others at same hour on Friday and Saturday (Sept. 9).

1909   William James arrives in Worcester to stay as guest at Hall's home until Friday evening. On Thursday evening he converses with Jung and other house guests (Sept. 9).

At 11 A.M. James attends Freud's fourth lecture which includes the topic of dreams (Sept. 10).

Psychology and Pedagogy group pose for photo on Clark Library steps (Sept. 10).

Late afternoon or early evening, Freud walks with James toward railway station (Sept. 10).

Honorary degrees conferred on Freud, Jung and six other behavioral scientists. Twenty-one other participants receive degrees on the 16th (Sept. 10).

Adolf Meyer squires Freud, Jung and Ferenczi by automobile around Lake Quinsigamond (Worcester and vicinity) (Sept. 11).

"Private clinic" on "the psychology of sex" is held with young medium at Hall's home (Sept. 11).

Jung takes train to Boston where he stays the night (Sept. 11).

In morning Jung goes by train to Gloucester to visit Mrs. (Frederick) Peterson; returns in afternoon to Worcester where Freud, Ferenczi and Brill come aboard, and the group continue to Albany and Buffalo on Sunday (Sept. 11–12).

The group tours Niagara Falls (Sept. 13).

Freud, Jung and Ferenczi take train from Buffalo via Utica to Lake Placid for the night (Sept. 14).

1909   In response to an invitation from Dr. James J. Putnam, Professor of Neurology at the Harvard Medical School, Freud, Jung and Ferenzci travel by horse-drawn carriage to Keene Valley (Sept. 15).

They arrive at Dr. Putnam's camp (in the Adirondacks) and stay three days. They occupy a three-room log cabin called The Chatterbox (Sept. 15).

Dr. Putnam arrives from Boston. During his sojourn at the camp, Freud suffers a mild attack of appendicitis (Sept. 16).

The visitors depart camp for New York City. They spend the night in Albany (Sept. 18).

They arrive in New York City (Sept. 19).

Freud visits his sister Anna (Bernays) and her children (Sept. 20).

The three visitors embark on *Kaiser Wilhelm der Grosse* for return to Europe (Sept. 21).

They reach Bremen. Jung departs for Zurich (Sept. 29).

Freud visits his mother in Hamburg (Sept. 30).

Freud meets his brother Emmanuel in Berlin (Oct. 1).

Freud arrives back in Vienna (Oct. 2).

Freud's case of the "Rat Man" is published; he sends offprint to Hall in December (Oct. 12).

Controversial session on Freud's theories held at 18th annual meeting of the American Psychological Association, Cambridge, Massachusetts (Dec. 29).

1910   Pauline Goldmark visits James in Cambridge (Jan. 15).

Freud's *Selected Papers on Hysteria and other Psycho-neuroses*, translated by Brill (first book by Freud in English), is published (Feb.).

Jung's *Psychology of Dementia Praecox*, translated by Frederick Peterson and A. A. Brill, is published (Feb.).

Pauline Goldmark to lunch at W. James's home (Mar. 25).

International Congress of Psychoanalysis is held at Nuremberg. International Psychoanalytic Association founded (Mar. 30–31).

Clark lectures by Freud and Jung published (in English translation) in *American Journal of Psychology* (Apr.).

American Psychopathological Association founded (May 2).

Jung publishes second volume of word-association studies (June).

William James dies (Aug. 26).

Amy Tanner (with Hall) publishes *Studies in Spiritism*, the report of the 1909 research on Mrs. Piper (Sept.).

1911   New York Psychoanalytic Society founded (Feb. 12).

Hall publishes *Educational Problems* (May 5).

American Psychoanalytic Association founded (May 9).

Adler resigns from the Vienna Psychoanalytic Society (Oct. 11).

1911–   Jung publishes *Transformations and Symbols of the Libido*
1912   (English translation, 1916–1917), which precipitates
        rupture with Freud.

1912   Adler publishes *The Neurotic Constitution* (Eng. trans.,
        1917).

        Hall publishes *Founders of Modern Psychology* (July).

        Stekel resigns from Vienna Psychoanalytic Society
        (Nov. 6).

1912–   Freud publishes *Totem and Taboo.*
1913

1913   Rupture of Freud/Jung relationship openly acknowl-
        edged.

1914   Freud writes *On the History of the Psychoanalytic
        Movement* (published later in same year) (Feb.).

        Jung resigns as President of International Psychoanalytic
        Association (Apr.).

1914–   World War I.
1918

1917   Hall founds *Journal of Applied Psychology.*

        Hall publishes *Jesus, the Christ, in the Light of Psy-
        chology.*

1917–   Hall serves as President of the American Psychoanalytic
1919   Association.

1918   Hall publishes "A Medium in the Bud," which refers to a
        1909 investigation with Freud and Jung as consultants
        during the Clark celebration.

1918   E. J. Kempf publishes *The Autonomic Functions of the Personality.*

1920   Freud publishes (in English) *A General Introduction to Psychoanalysis,* with Preface by Hall.

Hall retires as President of Clark University.

Kempf publishes his *Psychopathology.*

1922   Hall publishes *Senescence.*

1923   Hall publishes *Life and Confessions of a Psychologist* (July).

E. J. Kempf visits Freud, two days, at Lavarone in the South Tyrol (Aug. c. 20).

Hall publishes 2nd edition of *Jesus, the Christ, in the Light of Psychology* (Nov.).

1924   G. Stanley Hall dies (Apr. 24).

1925   Freud publishes autobiographical study, with allusion to Hall as "king-maker."

1939   Sigmund Freud dies (Sept. 23).

1950   Clark University celebrates its sixtieth anniversary; invites Anna Freud as its honored guest and confers an LL.D. on her (Apr. 20–22).

1961   C. G. Jung dies (June 6).

1962   Jung's autobiography is published.

1967   The Freud/Hall letters are recovered.

1974   *The Freud/Jung Letters* are published.

1992   Centenary of the founding of the American Psychological Association. APA places commemorative plaque, honoring Hall, in wall of Goddard Library, Clark University. (July 8).

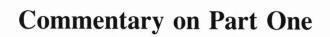

Commentary on Part One

Chapter I.   Cast in Context

1. This quotation is from Sigmund Freud, "An Autobiographical Study" (1925) in *The Standard Edition of the Complete Psychological Works of Sigmund Freud,* edited by James Strachey. London: Hogarth, 1959, *20,* pp. 51-52.

Unless otherwise stated, all future references to the writings of Freud will read *Standard Edition,* with volume number and page.

2. See Hall (1912). Hall's description of his postdoctoral sojourn in Europe is in his *Life and Confessions of a Psychologist,* 1923, 204-216. At the beginning of this account there is an error: 1876 should read 1878.

3. See Martin Trautscholdt, "Experimentelle Untersuchungen über die Association der Vorstellungen," *Philosophische Studien,* 1883, *1,* 213-250. The mention of Hall as one of the experimentees is on page 233. Hall also served more irregularly as an experimentee in the dissertation research of Wundt's first doctoral candidate, Max Friedrich (1883). In this context see the historical article by Peter J. Behrens (1980).

4. See Amy E. Tanner, *Studies in Spiritism,* with an Introduction by G. Stanley Hall. New York: Appleton, 1910 (pp. 23-25, 189f.).

5. See G. Stanley Hall, "The muscular perception of space," *Mind,* 1878, *3,* 433-450.

6. See Frederic W. H. Myers, *Human Personality and the Survival of Bodily Death.* London: Longmans, Green, 1903, 2 vols. Also W. James, "Frederic Myers's services to psychology," *Popular Science Monthly,* 1901, *59,* 380-389.

7. See *Standard Edition,* 1955, *2.*

8. For the first use of the term "psychoanalysis," see "Heredity and the aetiology of the neuroses" (1896a), *Standard Edition,* 1962, *3,* 151.

9. These various publications are available in the *Standard Edition.*

10. Letter dated March 23, 1965. See also Boring, 1965.

Chapter II. The Invitations

1. See W. A. Koelsch, *Clark University, 1887-1987: A narrative history.* Worcester, MA: Clark University Press, 1987.

1a. *Clark University 1889-1899: Decennial celebration.* Worcester, MA: Printed for the University, 1899.

2. An article by Boring (1965) on the subjectivity of historic dates in which he cited as an example the 1909 Clark conference convened by G. S. Hall impelled me to question this illustration for two reasons: the year 1909 was not arbitrarily selected as Boring surmised so that Hall could invite Freud who by then was sufficiently famous. Boring overlooked the precedent of 1899, when the Clark decennial was celebrated. Moreover, the conference in 1909 did not revolve around the presence of Freud even though for Hall that was the outstanding aspect. There were 28 other distinguished invited lecturers. But Boring's comment did usefully bring up the difference between the *founding* of Clark in 1887 and its *opening* in 1889 as occasions for celebration. For instance, at its 75th anniversary in 1937, the founding rather than the opening had been acknowledged. Prompted by our correspondence, Boring wrote to Clark President Howard Jefferson and received a reply (dated April 12, 1965) of which Boring sent me a copy. In it Jefferson took account of the several commemoratives at Clark— some that recalled the granting of the charter in 1887, others, the opening of the University for instruction in the fall of 1889. Neither Jefferson nor Boring noted that there had been three different times of the year involved in the various commemorations: spring, referring to the granting of the charter in March; summer, with sessions in July to mark the "completion of the academic year" (as in the first part of the 20th anniversary celebration devoted to the child research conference); and fall, marking the opening of the University for classes in September 1889 and remembered in 1909. In the publications from these celebrations the editors usually acknowledged the basis for the specific time of year, but no one has previously taken the trouble to assemble and compare the several occasions. To do so may clarify the situation and prevent future confusion by historians.

2a. From the Minutes of the Clark University Board of Trustees for the meeting of November 6, 1908 one learns that a motion was passed as follows: "President Hall is authorized to make arrangements for the commemoration of the twentieth anniversary of the University and to secure the attendance of such eminent scientists as he may deem advisable; also that he be authorized to incur an expenditure for such purposes not exceeding ten thousand dollars ($10,000)." At the meeting of January 6, 1909 it was voted that the main celebration occur in September 1909 (Clark University Archives).

2b. It is noteworthy that the connection with the 20th anniversary of Clark University was included as a subtitle of the *Proceedings*. An informative abstract was published by Amy Tanner (1909). For Hall these conferences were an aspect of his larger plan for the Children's Institute as he stated in his Introduction (p. xv). By the spring of 1910 he had gained financial support for it from the Clark Board of Trustees and, on that basis, had appointed a staff of nine under his directorship. Among them were William Burnham, Professor of Child Hygiene and Education; Dr. Theodate L. Smith, compiler of special literature on the history and survey of child welfare institutions; Dr. Amy Tanner, specialist in Experimental Pedagogy and Statistics, and Rudolph Acher, psychology, pedagogy and hygiene of sex. In this context, Hall's exposition in "A Children's Institute" in the March 1910 issue of *Harper's Magazine* is instructive. Not only did he refer to the child research conference at Clark in the previous summer, but early in the text Hall commended Meumann, whom he had originally invited to participate in the vigentennial, and Freud, without naming him: he surely had Freud in mind when he wrote pithily about the need to understand children's behavior not only in conscious terms but in those of the unconscious.

Hall picturesquely compared the unconscious to an iceberg, eight-ninths of which is submerged in the sea, and which can be "studied only objectively by natural history methods." By "objectively" he obviously meant to rule out inadequate *subjective* reports. Later, in his *Founders of Modern Psychology* (1912, p. 171), he would use the same figure of speech though then attributing the idea to Fechner, a forerunner of Freud without Freud's stress on dynamics or motivational forces. But investigation has established that Hall himself was the first to introduce the iceberg metaphor of the unconscious when he used it in 1908 (see Hall, 1908, p. 680). He employed it again a few months later (Hall, 1909a, pp. 265-266). He wrote: "The great newly discovered continent of the unconscious is still regarded by many members of our guild as mystical, perhaps superliminal, and its phenomena are used to cast auguries as to whether the soul is independent of or survives the body. The unconscious is really like the submerged eight-ninths of an iceberg, which is impelled by deeper currents in a denser medium, and which the glittering summits that emerge above the tide and are impelled by only atmospheric pressure have little control over."

It is remarkable that Hall here used the phrase "the great, newly discovered continent" at the time, in 1908-1909, of the fervid race between Frederick Cook and Robert Peary to discover the North Pole. This contest demanded public attention in newspaper headlines universally (see Wright, 1970). In these circumstances it is highly probable that Hall was influenced by the *Zeitgeist,* a conception that he invoked in the very first chapter of his *Founders* (Hall, 1912, p. 59), as essential to any historical inquiry. Thus the newly discovered continent of the unconscious and the impending discovery of the North Pole were linked by the emblem of the looming iceberg.

A more extensive publication that grew largely out of Hall's concern with child development and pedagogy is the two-volume *Educational Problems* (1911). For a careful review of Hall's earlier contributions to the field of child development see S. H. White (1990), "Child Study at Clark University: 1894-1904."

Though the Children's Institute failed of fulfillment, Hall's valiant effort shows how much it meant to him precisely at the time of the 20th anniversary celebration. It is described in some detail in the present context because Hall was significantly influenced by Freud's theories in the formulation of this enterprise. It has not previously been recognized that Hall's initial invitation to Freud was extended in this setting. On this basis one also better appreciates the large part played by Freud's case of Little Hans and Jung's Little Anna in their lectures at Clark University. (See Chapters VII-VIII.)

A free association arises here concerning the host's only son, Dr. Robert Hall (1881-1971). After receiving a Harvard M.D.,

Robert specialized in pediatrics and subsequently, for many years until his death, practiced this specialty in Portland, Oregon. From the extensive correspondence with me, it is evident that Robert was frustrated by the lack of appreciation extended at Clark to his father's work, despite the latter's generous bequest to the University for the endowment of a chair. Robert was greatly interested in the early plans for the present volume and made significant contributions to it. Incidentally, the G. Stanley Hall Professorship of Genetic Psychology did indeed exist at Clark. Its first incumbent was Walter S. Hunter, a moderate behaviorist, who assumed it in 1925 and occupied it for 11 years.

3. Letter of Freud to Abraham, December 26, 1908 in *A Psychoanalytic Dialogue: The Letters of Sigmund Freud and Karl Abraham.* New York: Basic Books, 1965, p. 63.

4. See E. Jones, *The Life and Work of Sigmund Freud.* New York: Basic Books, 1955, vol. 1, p. 40.

5. See *The Freud/Jung Letters: The Correspondence between Sigmund Freud and C. G. Jung.* Edited by William McGuire. Princeton, N.J.: Princeton University Press, 1974, p. 192.
Future citations to this volume will read *F/J Letters.*

6. *F/J Letters,* January 17, 1909, p. 196.

7. Jung's comment is in his letter to Freud dated January 19, 1909, p. 198. The slip is discussed in detail by William McGuire, the editor of the *F/J Letters,* in note 2, page 196, including a holograph of the relevant page. As perceived by Jung, Freud, in speaking of the Americans, had first written, "*your* prudishness," then changed it to "*their* prudishness." McGuire comments that Jung's discernment of a struck and modified word (in the German, actually only one letter) is "problematic." The important point is that Jung went out of his way to apply the slip as appropriate to himself personally.

8. *F/J Letters,* January 25, 1909, p. 203.

9. *F/J Letters,* July 19, 1909, pp. 242-243.

10. See "Twentieth Anniversary of Clark University" by G. S. Hall [unsigned]. *The Nation,* September 23, 1909, pp. 284-285.

11. Hall to Freud, December 15, 1908 (see Part Two).

12. The book by Pierre Janet was published as *The Major Symptoms of Hysteria.* New York: Macmillan, 1907.

13. The 1904 addresses of Pierre Janet and Morton Prince were included in a volume from the World's Fair as follows: *Congress of Arts and Science, Universal Exhibition, St. Louis, 1904.* Edited by H. J. Rogers, Vol. 5: Biology, Anthropology, Psychology, Sociology. Boston: Houghton, Mifflin, 1906.

14. See *F/J Letters,* Freud to Jung, April 16, 1909, pp. 218-220. On this date Freud began calling Jung "my successor and crown prince." The designation was apparently bestowed during Jung's second personal contact with Freud by a five-day visit to Vienna, March 25-29, 1907. The end of this visit is erroneously dated in Jones (Vol. II, p. 51) on which basis the same error is repeated in the *Freud/Jung Letters* (1974, p. 215). The correct date is available from Freud's letter to Pfister (1963, p. 22) dated March 30, 1909 where Freud states, "Jung left yesterday evening."

15. *F/J Letters,* Freud to Jung, March 9, 1909, p. 210.

16. The case of the Rat Man was published by Freud as "Notes upon a case of obsessional neurosis." In the German it appeared in the *Jahrbuch für psychoanalytische und psychopathologische Forschung,* 1909, *1,* No. 2, 357-421. It complemented his case of Little Hans—the five-year-old phobic boy (discussed at length later in this volume) which had been published in the previous (first) issue.

The English translation of the Rat Man case appeared in the *Standard Edition, 10,* 1955, 153-249. Quite exceptionally—the only time this happened—Freud's notes during the treatment of the case were included in this volume following the case history under the title, "Original record of the case," pages 253-318. Numerous disguised names were employed in the publication of the Original Record which appeared only in this English translation. A German version based on that of the *Standard Edition* was published in 1987.

The identity of the patient as Ernst Lanzer was first disclosed in *Freud and the Rat Man* by Patrick Mahony. New Haven: Yale

University Press, 1986. Mahony had access to the holograph of Freud's original record deposited at the Library of Congress and based his book on that source. It is, therefore, an important supplement to the above cited original record in the *Standard Edition*. It should be clear, however, that Mahony did not suggest or maintain (as is proposed here) that Freud himself was the prototype of the Rat Man case on the basis (in part) of his 1886 Olmütz experience. For a summary of Freud's military experience with special reference to 1886, see E. Jones, *Life and Work of Sigmund Freud*. New York: Basic Books, 1953, vol. 1, pp. 147-151.

A remarkably pertinent essay in the context of the present hypothesis—the relevance of the Rat Man case to Freud's personal neurosis—was published by Gottlieb (1989). He focused on the unique role of countertransference phenomena in Freud's analysis of this classic case and adduced a striking array of incidents from Freud's own life that found their way into the patient's fantasies and free associations. He did not, incidentally, include the comparison of the Original Record with the published account on the points singled out in the present text. Nor did he begin to consider the hypothesis, entertained here, that Freud himself experienced an emotional disorder during earlier army maneuvers before he treated the Rat Man for a similar experience. But this unconventional hypothesis would, it is submitted, go a long way toward resolving the anomalies of the countertransference exhibited in Freud's treatment of the Rat Man and, for that reason, it is proposed that the reader-scholar reconsider the evidence of Gottlieb's essay in the light of the present hypothesis.

17. Freud's sudden decision to write up the case of "the Salzburg rat man" was announced to Jung in the letter of June 3, 1909, *F/J Letters*, p. 227. The manuscript was sent to Jung on July 7, 1909, for publication (ibid., p. 239). It appeared in the *Jahrbuch*, 1909, *I* (2), released in October.

18. The three levels of communication were proposed in "Freud and experimental psychology: The emergence of idiodynamics," by Saul Rosenzweig, in *A Century of Psychology as Science*, edited by S. Koch and D. E. Leary. New York: McGraw-Hill, 1985. Pages 196-197 and note 31 reviews the historical background of these levels. (A second, revised edition of this contribution

appeared under the same title, published by Rana House, St. Louis, 1986.) A later version of the levels was described in the author's "Idiodynamics vis-à-vis psychology," *American Psychologist,* 1986, *41,* 241-245.

To repeat for clarification, the interweaving of the three levels constituted the essence of Freud's therapy and theory. It is submitted that Freud appears to have composed the classic case histories on a plan similar to that followed, deliberately or indeliberately, by many novelists. The narrative of the case as presented is actually a blend of the other two levels (or layers). The literal or presentational, the third level, is a combination of 1 and 2, with the qualification that these other levels are not used fully or completely every time, and that, in the blending process, modifications are made to disguise or otherwise accommodate derivation from the other levels. Level 1 is chiefly autobiographical; it provides the subjective ground for the apperception of level 2. Level 2 employs the opportunities of the environment to actualize what has been personally, often traumatically, experienced at level 1. The composing process thus is essentially the melding of 1 and 2 to produce 3.

To some extent Freud offered a similar formulation in his *Traumdeutung:* "dream work," as conceived by him, transformed the *latent* or unconscious content of the dream, consisting of repressed, often infantile, material into the *manifest* content. This transformation also absorbed the preconscious day-residues, attributed here to level 2. The manifest dream—the dream as recalled—was a blend of the preconscious and the unconscious.

What was Freud's justification for this alleged method of case history composition? Probably his conviction that there was a primordial type, a prototype, which any individual patient exhibits only partially or imperfectly. The truth lies in the prototype, which is more faithfully portrayed when the therapist (or writer) blends his own prior experience with that of the patient, especially if the therapist has some affinity with him or her. In psychoanalytic jargon, the process of therapy (and then of presentation) often similarly combines the *transference* with the *countertransference.*

Freud's case histories should therefore not be regarded as literal accounts of what the patient had related to Freud. The Freudian classic case history expressed what Freud experienced from his own depths as confirmed by the encounter with the patient. By combining these two levels (1 and 2) the case history emerged, less polished than a fine novel but strongly resembling such a product.

This formulation is not intended to repudiate the findings of Freudian psychoanalysis. The intent, rather, is to indicate the manner in which an idiodynamic reconstruction (by psychoarchaeology) makes it possible to determine the parameters and the limits of what Freud (and other gifted analysts) have had to say about the human condition.

A final word is necessary to discourage the inference that all Freud's case histories involved only himself at level 1. What is meant, instead, is that the treated patient was always complemented by knowledge of someone well known to Freud before the particular patient consulted him. For example, some of these other personally known individuals were his son Ernst, who probably complemented Herbert Graf, the contemporary Little Hans; and Freud's sister Rosa, who probably complemented the patient Ida Bauer in the Dora case. Moreover, in the latter case "Herr K" was, in all likelihood, Dr. Leopold Königstein, the ophthalmologist, who was a close friend and colleague of Freud and for whom Rosa at one time worked as a children's governess.

18a. In pursuing this hypothesis of Freud's identity further, one should recall the second revealing letter that Freud wrote to Jung dated April 16, 1909. It was actually the first he wrote Jung after the latter's second visit to Freud. Better to grasp its meaning one should recall that during the visit Freud "anointed" Jung as his son and successor. The elevation was the result of hours of heart-to-heart talk, probably including consultations with both Carl and Emma (who was also present) about their emotionally disturbed little daughter Agathli. Toward the end of the visit, Jung, perhaps emboldened by his new sense of authority, demonstrated to Freud the occult performance of a poltergeist that resided in a piece of Freud's office furniture; but Freud expressed scornful skepticism about the mysterious sounds. Thus Jung parted from Freud on a note of alienation. Jung's spiritualistic leanings, here first revealed, threatened the newly confirmed alliance. This was the background for Freud's letter in which he alluded to the demonstration of the poltergeist and then attempted to modulate his earlier skepticism. To that end he confessed to Jung that he, too, had moments of supernaturalistic belief. For example, in 1899 "two things happened." He had finished his *Interpretation of Dreams* and he had received a new telephone number: 14362. And the number seemed to him to be a portent of his date of death: 43 in the telephone number was his age at the time; the following 62, preceded by the initial 1, seemed to predict that he would die between 61 and 62. And, in fact, these numbers pursued Freud repeatedly, he stated, in his subsequent travels; for example, in 1904 when he visited Greece with his brother Emmanuel.

But while confessing this superstition, Freud had forgotten to mention a third such event of 1899: On August 27 the random number 2467 had occurred while writing a letter to his then dear friend and confidant Wilhelm Fliess. He had been telling Fliess that he had finished the dream book and was resolved to let it be published without delay even if it contained 2467 errors! Then in a postscript he tried to analyze the seemingly meaningless number in order to prove its unconscious determinism. (Cf. Freud, 1954, pp. 293-294 and note.) He recalled the circumstances in his thought at the time of writing. And he later decided to use this example of psychic determinism in his forthcoming book, *The Psychopathology of Everyday Life,* first published in 1901. Necessarily forgoing here all the other details of Freud's explanation, we mention the vital point that a certain General E. M., whom Freud had known well from 1880 onwards, was about to retire. Freud's own words were as follows: "In a letter to a friend I informed him I had just then finished correcting the proofs of *The Interpretation of Dreams* and did not intend to make any more changes in the work, 'even if it contains 2467 mistakes.' I at once tried to explain this number to myself and added the little analysis as a postscript to my letter. The best plan will be to quote it as I wrote it down at the time, just after I had caught myself in the act." (Cf. *Standard Edition, 6,* 242-243.)

The details of Freud's explanation will not be quoted here. However, it should be stated that from those details (and other idiodynamic data), I have been able to identify "General E. M." On that basis one can go well beyond what Freud was willing to reveal in 1899 and even fathom some of the "unconscious" meanings that the random number 2467 entailed in his idioverse.

Moreover, it was this "General E. M." who appears to have turned up at Olmütz in September 1886 as one of the team of officers assigned to evaluate the success of the maneuvers (Schieds-richter). His unexpected presence appears to have played a part in precipitating Freud's emotional disturbance at that time. A full explanation would stress the fact that this officer was a represen-tative of the established, aristocratic and anti-Semitic regime of the Austrian Court in 1880-1898.

Freud had not only forgotten to recall to Jung the number 2467 but also the prophetic age of 51—the age at which his friend Fliess, according to his theory of bisexual, biorhythmic cycles, had cal-culated the end of Freud's life at age 51 (in 1907). Freud had taken this prophecy quite seriously. In fact, he had followed Fliess in his speculative flights about the male and female cycles of 23 and 28 days and attempted to interpret events in his own clinical ex-periences in these terms, partly to encourage his friend. Only gradually was he developing his own theory of the unconscious with rival powers of interpreting behavior in terms of underlying psychic determinism, e.g., the random number 2467, and was be-ginning to reduce his dependence upon Fliess. The example of August 27 represented just such a thrust of independence—even as Jung's poltergeist incident represented for him a similar assertion of independence.

Why did Freud not also recall to Jung the earlier prediction of Fliess pertaining to 1899? Because (as "Rat Man") he needed an apotropaic. So instead of recalling 2467 and the Fliess prediction of age 51, he selectively remembered another number. He recalled the telephone number 14362 that he also associated with the com-pletion of *The Interpretation of Dreams*. From that number he had been able to predict a later death date, at age 61 or 62, i.e., in 1917 instead of 1907.

All this numerology is stated or implied in the letter of April 16, 1909 with the intent of placating Jung, the new son and "heir apparent," who fervently believed in occult phenomena. How could Freud justify this subversion of rationality? Grounds for doing so may reside in the terminal portion of the letter (p. 220). There he asserted that there is a "compliance of chance" by which the unconscious can express itself in thought comparable to the "somatic compliance" found in some hysterical condi-tions. Freud had explicitly formulated this concept in 1910, in a paper dedicated to his friend Leopold Königstein on the latter's 60th jubilee (*Standard Edition, 11*, 209-218).

At this point we enter a kind of interpretation based more upon what Freud implied by what he stated than what he spelled out. The justification lies in the events later in the year pertaining to the Rat Man case. When in 1907, the year predicted by Fliess was nearly over, the patient Ernst Lanzer turned up for analysis. Freud saw in this event a "compliance of chance" in that the patient's obsessional syndrome in large measure replicated his own in 1886. With the treatment of Lanzer completed, Freud, in early 1909, was beginning to think of writing up the case. Then Jung visited Freud, and after an exciting four days during which Freud bestowed upon Jung the role of "crown prince," Jung assertively announced his belief in a poltergeist. After having vigorously rejected this superstition, Freud, wishing to placate him, reverted to 1899 and his own superstitions—and set forth for his new confidant, the successor of Fliess, the prediction which counteracted the one made by Fliess. By introducing the number 14362, he provided an apotropaic. Not only did this alternative prediction counteract the other, but Ernst Lanzer now ratified Freud's self-analysis by the analysis Freud performed on Lanzer between October 1907 and September 1908.

The reasoning (or rationalization) in the foregoing may sound strange to conscious ratiocination but one cannot expect to understand the thinking of a Rat Man by sticking to conscious logic. In the world of the obsessional neurotic who has a particular history, one must exploit the "compliance of chance" to patch up discrepancies and repair failing friendship by exercising ingenuity. By composing the Rat Man case history in the following weeks, Freud would try to accomplish this feat and perhaps also give the feat a certain permanence. Hence his resolve, as we have seen, to perform the task before leaving for America in August. With that journey he would enter a new phase of his unconsciously determined life and appear on the lecture platform in Worcester as if by the "omnipotence" of his own thought and wishes he was fulfilling an "incredible daydream."

Though a full demonstration of Freud's identity as Rat Man is not to be given here, there are one or two further striking data that will be mentioned. The first consists of a letter Freud wrote from Olmütz toward the end of the maneuvers on September 1, 1886, to his patron and friend Dr. Josef Breuer. Jones, in his biography of Freud, reproduced this remarkable memoir of

Freud's contemporary experience with practically no comment. After greeting his "Esteemed Friend," Freud continued:

"Here I am tied fast in this filthy hole—I can't think how else to describe it—and am working on black and yellow. I have been giving lectures on field hygiene: the lectures were pretty well attended and have even been translated into Czech. I have not yet been 'confined to barracks.'

"The only remarkable thing about the town is that it doesn't look so far away as it actually is. It often means marching for three or four hours before one gets there, and there are times when I find myself ever so far from it at an hour when one is not usually awake to anything. Just as Paul Lindau once remarked in a review of a novel that took place in the Middle Ages, 'most of my readers would hardly remember that there had been such a time as the middle of the fourth century,' so I might ask if any decent citizen would think of being busy between three and half past in the early morning. We play at war all the time—once we even carried out the siege of a fortress—and I play at being an army doctor, dealing with chits on which ghastly wounds are noted. While my battalion is attacking I lie down on some stony field with my men. There is fake ammunition as well as fake leadership, but yesterday the General rode past and called out 'Reserves, where would you be if they had used live ammunition? Not one of you would have escaped.'

"The only bearable thing in Olmütz is a first-class café with ice, newspapers, and good confectionery. Like everything else the service there is affected by the military system. When two or three generals—I can't help it, but they always remind me of parakeets, for mammals don't usually dress in such colors except for the purple callosities of mandrills—sit down together, the whole troop of waiters surround them and nobody else exists for them. Once in despair I had to have recourse to swank. I grabbed one of them by the coattails and shouted, 'Look here, I might be a general sometime, so fetch me a glass of water.' That worked.

"An officer is a miserable creature. Each envies his colleagues, bullies his subordinates, and is afraid of his superiors; the higher up he is the more he fears them. I detest the idea of having inscribed on my collar how much I am worth, as if I were a sample of some goods. And nevertheless the system has its gaps. The Commanding Officer was here recently from Brünn and went into the swimming baths, when I was astonished to observe that his trunks carried no marks of distinction!

"But it would be ungrateful not to admit that military life with its inescapable 'must' is very good for neurasthenia. It all disappeared in the very first week.

"The whole business is coming to an end; in ten days I fly north and forget the crazy four weeks."

[The letter from Sigmund Freud to Josef Breuer, written from Olmütz and dated September 1, 1886, was published in Jones, *op. cit.,* vol. I, pp. 193-195. An error in the translation from the German has been corrected. The parenthetical phrase in the third quoted paragraph, "(save for the back part of Baboons)," has been here rendered: "except for the purple callosites of mandrills" ("von den rotblauen Schwielen des Mandrills abgesehen").

These German words are from *Das Leben und Werk von Sigmund Freud,* Band I, von Ernest Jones, übersetzt von Katherine Jones, Bern und Stuttgart: Hans Huber, 1960. This is the German edition (translation by Mrs. Ernest Jones) of Ernest Jones's biography of Freud, originally composed in English. It has been consulted for both this and other points on the assumption that for the German edition the holograph of Freud's letter to Breuer was available and used by the translator.

The entire metaphor is blatantly sexual. The officers are perceived as dressed in rampant colors (badges, etc.) like parakeets (love-birds), and then, turning more appropriately to mammals, Freud invokes the only mammal which exhibits such colors, the mandrill, a species of baboon, which displays such bright colors on its rump, especially during the mating period. Freud here stressed not only sex but dominance. He lampooned the assertion of authority by officers over subordinates in analogy with the relentless dominance of male over female baboons and within the male hierarchy.

The present gloss is, of course, a bridge for comparing the officers at Olmütz with the "cruel captain" of the Rat Man case. Freud's ironic metaphor is, in psychoanalytic exegesis, a reaction formation with not only heterosexual but (ambivalent) homosexual cathexis as well. The fact that at the letter's close (not quoted here) Freud literally "apologizes" for this "silly tittle-tattle" makes the present gloss not less but, perhaps, more apposite (by Freudian canons).

The first statement made by Freud regarding his having been "confined to barracks" is found in Freud (1954, note 1, pp. 293-294). It was included by Kris, et al. as a postscript to Freud's letter to Fliess dated August 27, 1899. A slightly modified version appeared in Freud's *Psychopathology of Everyday Life* (Standard Edition, *6*, 242-243). Freud used the postscript to the letter of August 27 to illustrate the determinism of the random number "2467." Freud had requested that Fliess return the postscript so that he might use it in the book (which appeared in a preliminary edition in 1901) as an illustration of the unconscious determinism of random numbers. His interpretation was based on the circumstances associated with the occurrence of the numbers as he recalled them. In the letter to Fliess he was flippantly supposing that there might be 2467 errors in *The Interpretation of Dreams* which he had just finished writing, but, he declared, even that many errors would not prevent his sending off the manuscript to the publisher. The version of 1901 varies slightly from that in the 1954 volume. The content in the versions of 1901 and 1954 is supplemented in a statement by Ernest Jones (1953, vol. I, p. 62) which states that Freud had been absent without leave from military duty eight times in succession before being sentenced. Jones cites an unpublished letter by Freud to his fiancée Martha Bernays, dated June 15, 1885, for this information. It is noteworthy that this letter has not been published, though countless others from the courtship period have been.

In the text of the letter to Breuer in 1886 the phrase "confined to barracks" is, as has been indicated, an allusion to the occurrence of just such an event in 1880. The important patient whom Freud had offended by his absence from duty on eight successive days was "the cruel captain," alleged in our text to have been (surprisingly) present at Olmütz on September 1, 1886. That patient had come for treatment to the military hospital in Vienna in 1880 and had presumptuously demanded that his treatment be finished within a week because he was engaged in some work for which the Emperor was waiting. Freud, a young medical officer-cadet at the time, was probably insulted by this patient, a general or colonel, perhaps when the young cadet told the pompous officer that the treatment could not be carried out in so brief a time, despite the alleged urgency. And in defiance of this officer, Freud apparently absented himself without permission for the very period (one week) during which the officer expected his treatment to occur and be finished. On this assumption one can begin to understand the confrontation when that very officer unexpectedly appeared at Olmütz in the capacity of referee—a judge of the maneuvers about to be completed. The pomposity of the officer-patient's demand agrees with Freud's description to Breuer of the high and mighty officers at Olmütz. He depicts them as essentially "miserable creatures" who rule with an iron hand over those under them but cower before superiors. However, the alleged presence of this officer as Freud's "cruel captain" rests only to a small degree on this similarity. Ascertainment of the identity of the officer determined from Freud's description of him in 1899 has made it possible for me to follow his career to the time of the Olmütz maneuvers. This evidence and the identity of the officer must be reserved for later publication.]

One of the most striking aspects of this communication is the allusion to the place and time as something out of "the middle of the fourth century"—a period that, as the critic Paul Lindau once remarked, most readers would hardly remember ever to have existed. Freud apparently was starting to experience a sense of regression to a repressed period of childhood (amnesia). The fact is that he was then in a locale only 40 miles from his birthplace (Freiberg, Moravia) which he left at the age of 2-3 years. One will recall that, in Freud's theory, every adult neurosis had its beginning in the earliest years of childhood which psychoanalysis attempts to reach by reconstruction.

There is also ground for believing, as indicated above, that at the end of August 1886 a military officer Freud had previously encountered in a humiliating situation in 1880 appeared unexpectedly at Olmütz and was present towards the end of the maneuvers as one of the designated umpires (Schiedsrichter) to judge the success of the maneuvers. This person was Freud's "cruel captain" (in parallel with the one in Lanzer's history)—a new edition of the "castrating father." By this coincidence another aspect of Freud's infantile neurosis was revived and helped produce the disturbance. (In the 1907 case, the Rat Man's encounter with a "cruel captain" at maneuvers in Galicia brought the patient to Freud for treatment in October.)

In idiodynamic terms it cannot be mere coincidence that when Freud began his letter to Breuer he jokingly quipped: "I have not

yet been confined to barracks." That remark was an allusion to
an actual previous experience of Freud, probably known to his
friend and confidant Dr. Breuer. Freud *had* been "confined to
barracks" for being absent from his military post without permission eight times, a humiliating occurrence Freud recalled to his
friend Fliess in the letter dated August 1899 above cited. By reconstructing the chance number "2467" adduced by Freud in this
same letter, I have established that this house arrest happened on
Freud's twenty-fourth birthday, on May 6, 1880, at the Josefinum,
the army hospital in Vienna, where Freud served out his compulsory year of military duty as a cadet in 1879-1880. The officer who
engineered the arrest, a later Master of Ordnance, was the same
officer alleged above to have appeared at Olmütz as an umpire
toward the end of the maneuvers 1886 and unwittingly played the
part of Freud's "cruel captain" in the emotional disturbance at
Olmütz.

The letter to Breuer thus apparently, without intent, described
the prodrome to Freud's personality disturbance during the final
days of the maneuvers (in parallel with the Rat Man case history
of 1909). This reading can be fully demonstrated only by the evidence of other letters which Freud doubtless wrote at the time but
all attempts to consult these surviving letters, particularly those
addressed to his fiancée in 1885-1886 and known to exist in the
closed portion of the Freud Collection at the Library of Congress,
have proved unavailing. Most of Freud's other letters to his fiancée
(Martha Bernays) have been published, but those of 1886 will not
be released until after the year 2000. On the strength of the present
hypothesis, it is a reasonable conjecture that the letters are being
withheld chiefly because they, indeed, supplement the letter to
Breuer in too revealing a way.

Shortly after the maneuvers at Olmütz, an article was published
about these fall military exercises by an army doctor who had
several recommendations to make on the basis of his recent experience. The paper appeared anonymously in a Vienna military
monthly. From internal evidence, including the style of the writing
and the nature of the recommendations, the anonymous writer was,
in all likelihood, Sigmund Freud. If this attribution is correct, the
paper would represent an indirect corroboration of the alleged personality disturbance described in the present text. For the suggested improvements in future maneuvers appear to represent a

manifest level for an underlying cathartic need—a need also for
confession—inferences that accord with and arise from Freud's
own psychodynamic criteria. At a later date the title of the article,
the periodical, exact date, etc. will be disclosed together with relevant exposition to justify the attribution. It will then also be
indicated that on the basis of this article, at least one of Freud's
dreams reported in *The Interpretation of Dreams* would acquire a
new and illuminating latent level of meaning.

19. *F/J Letters*, Jung to Freud, June 12, 1909 and note 2,
p. 233.

20. See *Psychoanalysis and Faith: The Letters of Sigmund
Freud and Oskar Pfister.* New York: Basic Books, 1963, p. 25.

21. See *A Psycho-Analytic Dialogue: The Letters of Sigmund
Freud and Karl Abraham 1907-1926.* New York: Basic Books,
1965. Letters for June-July 1909 omitted from the published
collection here cited were kindly supplied by Dr. Abraham's son,
Grant Allan.

22. C. G. Jung. *Memories, Dreams, Reflections.* New York:
Pantheon, 1963, p. 120.

23. The possibility exists that the prominent and wealthy
Harold McCormick, who with his wife Edith, came on March 7,
1909 to consult Jung, facilitated his invitation to the Clark
conference. They were millionaires and philanthropic benefactors
of the University of Chicago and other cultural enterprises. It is
conceivable that they volunteered to help Jung in his long-cherished
hope for an American trip. The scanty and indirect evidence for
this speculation is present in the Freud/Jung letters between March
1909 and the time of the American visit. There is also a cryptic
allusion to Harold McCormick as an "American patient" whom
Jung describes in his autobiography in paragraphs immediately
following his mention of his invitation to Clark University. At
present the evidence to support this speculation is too scanty and
is hence not further explored here. (But see Chapter III, p. 82 and
Note 2.) A very informative discussion of the McCormicks in relation to Jung is available in Paul Stern's fine book *C. J. Jung:
The Haunted Prophet* (New York: Braziller, 1976, pp. 147-153).
Stern states that the Jung Psychology Club, which came into

existence in 1916, was a brainchild of Edith McCormick who endowed it handsomely. As Stern and others have shown, Edith Rockefeller McCormick was the first of a series of wealthy American women patients who supported Jung's cause financially and by favorable publicity. The series culminated with Mary Mellon who was the first president of the Bollingen Foundation when it was incorporated in 1942. The foundation was named for Jung's tower at Bollingen, Switzerland. (Cf. Stern, *op. cit.*, p. 227; McGuire, 1982).

24. The dream in question is in the original German edition of *The Psychology of Dementia Praecox* published in the latter half of 1906. (It is now available in English in Jung's *Collected Works*, 1967, vol. 3, pp. 57-62). Jung sent it to Freud as indicated in his letter to Freud dated October 5, 1906 (*F/J Letters*, 1974, p. 5). Freud acknowledged the book and offered further interpretations of dreams that Jung himself had there analyzed without identifying the dreamer. The editor in a note (ibid., p. 13) states that this letter from Freud is missing. In Jung's reply of December 29, 1906, p. 14, Jung confesses that he, indeed, was the dreamer, and in Freud's response (January 1, 1907, ibid., p. 17) Freud avows that he had guessed the identity but diplomatically did not state that conclusion. In the same letter (p. 19) Freud alludes to Jung's fantasy, revealed in these dreams, about a greatly desired journey to America, and Freud jestingly suggests that before making that trip Jung should come to Vienna—"it's nearer."

25. *F/J Letters*, Freud to Jung, January 17, 1909, pp. 196-197.

26. See *F/J Letters*, Freud to Jung, April 14, 1907, pp. 32-33 in which Freud approves of Jung's taking his place at the Amsterdam meeting. From the hotel in Amsterdam Jung reported at length the exciting results of the session in which Jung defended Freud's theories against an attack by Freud's archenemy of the time, Dr. Gustav Aschaffenburg. Incidentally, it was at the meeting in Amsterdam that Ernest Jones first met Jung, whom he soon visited for a week in November at the Burghölzli.

27. This meeting, often referred to as the First International Congress of Psychoanalysis, had been suggested to Jung by Jones during the latter's visit to Zurich in November 1907. But it was

Jung who picked up the idea and actually organized it. Jones later described the event, including the names of the approximately 40 individuals from five countries who attended, together with a list of the papers presented, cf. *The Life and Work of Sigmund Freud.* New York: Basic Books, 1955, 39-44. For a contemporary account of the planning and the results of this Congress, cf. *F/J Letters,* pp. 101-146, especially the summary description of the meeting by the editor of the *F/J Letters,* p. 143.

28. *A Psycho-Analytic Dialogue: The Letters of Sigmund Freud and Karl Abraham.* New York: Basic Books, 1965, Freud to Abraham, May 3, 1908, p. 34. This letter was a sequel to the Salzburg Congress which Abraham had attended. Future references in the present text to the correspondence of Freud and Abraham regarding Jung's leadership role will usually be sufficiently identified by the date given in the discussion.

29. Ibid., pp. 44-45.

30. Ibid., p. 46.

31. Ibid., Freud to Abraham, December 26, 1908, p. 64.

32. Ibid.

33. Ibid., Freud to Abraham, July 20, 1908, p. 46.

34. Wittels, F. *Sigmund Freud: His Personality, His Teaching, and His School.* London: Allen and Unwin, 1924, p. 140.

35. Some of the Freud/Ferenczi unpublished correspondence for the period 1908-1909 has been made available to me by the Manuscript Division of the Library of Congress. The role of Sandor Ferenczi during Freud's stay in Worcester is discussed in connection with Freud's lectures at Clark.

36. The account of Ernst Meumann is based primarily on Boring (1950, pp. 429 and 581), the recent vita in the *Biographical Dictionary of Psychology* (1984, p. 292), and two necrologies. The first of these was by Wilhelm Wundt (1916), the master with whom Meumann performed important and original post-doctoral research. Wundt (1910) had expressed skepticism about the experimental pedagogy that Meumann had pioneered. Hall in his *Founders of Modern Psychology* (1912, pp. 315, 424

and especially 437) rejected this evaluation of Meumann's contribution. In the obituary, Wundt moderated his earlier appraisal. In 1923, Stoerring, professor at the University of Bonn, published an appreciative account of Meumann's life and work at the request of the Editor of the *American Journal of Psychology* (who at that time was E. B. Titchener). Why the request was made at that date is unknown but, again, Hall, who published his autobiography that year, may have had a part in the decision. In any event, the article is a thoughtful appreciation of the work of a promising psychologist who died so prematurely, at age 52, and it reflects the writer's close personal and professional friendship with the subject.

The best known book in English by Meumann is cited in the Bibliography. It represents his landmark contribution to educational psychology through the experimental investigation of learning and memory. This translation, published in 1913, was made from the third German edition. The translator, J. W. Baird, was the director of the Clark University psychology laboratory. The interest of President Hall, head of the psychology department, may, again, have influenced Baird. Hall's continuing esteem for Meumann is evident, and the appearance of the Baird translation, in a sense, made up for Meumann's inability to participate at Clark in 1909.

37. The information about these distinguished, invited participants who declined Hall's invitation was gleaned from surviving copies of Hall's correspondence with them discovered by retiring President Jefferson; from the Preliminary Announcement of the celebration (dated May 15, 1909), and from minutes of the Clark University faculty and of the Board of Trustees (Clark University Archives).

38. The information concerning the 1899 invitation to Wundt is documented by letters of Wundt to Hall dated February 23, 1899 and July 2, 1899 in the Clark University Archives.

39. Sanford's ambassadorial mission to Leipzig is described in the biographical sketch of Edmund Sanford by Martha Sanford (Clark University, 1925, p. 8).

40. See Wundt, 1909, p. 119.

41. This surprising conclusion was reached by Bringmann and Bringmann (1980) after reviewing the evidence of Hall's relationship to Wundt in Leipzig during Hall's stay in 1879-1880 and in his correspondence with Wundt and the publications of them both. The authors focus on the statement by Hall in his *Founders of Modern Psychology* (1912), in particular, his long chapter on Wundt in which he states, at the outset, that Wundt for a time had been an assistant of Helmholtz "who later, desiring a helper more accomplished in mathematics and physics, sought another in his place" (p. 311). When Wundt encountered this remark in a German translation of Hall's account (Hall, 1914d), he repudiated it as "slander," first in an especially written article entitled "Correction" (Wundt, 1915) and, again, in his autobiography (Wundt, 1920). In the latter he included a footnote (p. 155) that characterized Hall's entire biography of him as "contrived" and "fictitious," then ridiculed Hall's statement that Helmholtz had engaged him as an assistant "in his mathematical work, but when his mathematical skill proved inadequate, he was dismissed" ("entlassen"). Taking up Wundt's cause, Bringmann and Bringmann submit that not only had Hall committed this slander but that Hall characteristically "invented and distorted while giving the impression that he possessed inside information" (*loc. cit.,* 1980, p. 191). They contend that this mischief by Hall was only one of a "long litany of falsehoods, half-truths and poisonous invective (which) makes his otherwise very dull account of Wundt's work readable" (ibid. 187). They conclude with the above-stated inference that Hall was deeply frustrated by Wundt's declination of the invitation to the Clark celebrations of 1899 and 1909 and, after the second one, "Hall finally released all his stored up resentment in a venomous manner" (p. 190).

This indictment of Hall is noteworthy not only because of its relevance to the topic of this volume and, in particular, the declined invitations, but because the characterization of Hall's personality and writing accords with other detractions, usually less clearly partisan in the motivation. (This aspect of Hall's reputation will be further considered in Chapter XII. The argument by Bringmann and Bringmann is also arresting because in a paper by Benjamin, et al., (1992) this analysis of the Wundt/Hall relationship has not only been accepted but carried to the further conclusion that Hall's "contact with Wundt was so minimal that he cannot seriously be considered one of Wundt's students, first or otherwise" (p. 134).

Both the 1980 and 1992 indictments of Hall lack persuasiveness because they overlook Wundt's hypersensitivity regarding his entire relationship to Helmholtz, not merely Hall's "slander" about the end of the assistantship. Hall's remark on this latter point is much exaggerated in Wundt's re-telling of it and by his characterization of it as slanderous. But it is in the thrust of Hall's biography of Wundt as a whole, dismissed by Wundt as "fictitious from beginning to end," that one discovers the real stimulus to which Wundt responded: Hall repeatedly compares Wundt with Helmholtz to Wundt's disadvantage, e.g., in the comment that Wundt "is not a . . . great scientific genius like Helmholtz" (Hall, 1912, p. 316). (Incidentally, these comparisons by Hall are strikingly brought out in the Foreword by Max Brahn to the German translation of Hall's biography of Wundt [Hall, 1914d, pp. iv-viii]. Wundt must have seen this appraisal, so favorable to Hall's portrayal, since it is this translation that he cited in his article of Correction [Wundt, 1915]).

Moreover, Hall's portrayal of Wundt as the acknowledged founder of modern experimental psychology is made grudgingly. For Hall, Wundt lacked the spontaneity, the charisma of Helmholtz and other contemporaries (e.g., Carl Ludwig) from whom Wundt gained the knowledge for his lengthy books without making equally inspired contributions.

These opinions of Hall are, of course, personal—even subjective—but they can hardly be dismissed as "fiction." And these opinions about Wundt, freely expressed by Hall in his *Founders,* could not have escaped Wundt; indeed, that pervasive message must have determined his apperception of the specific, much-refuted "slander" concerning his early relationship to Helmholtz.

There is, finally, an aspect of Wundt's assistantship to Helmholtz and its termination that must have been known to Hall as relevant, but which has been overlooked by recent critics. Hall doubtless knew that Julius Bernstein was Wundt's successor, and, if so, this fact might have entered into his readiness to accept the termination "rumor"—as Hall (1921b, p. 154) more cautiously called it. Julius Bernstein (1839-1917) was a truly gifted physicist and mathematician who made landmark contributions to electrophysiology and thus won a place in history (cf. Brazier, 1988, pp. 88-91). Whether Helmholtz had this particular successor in mind when Wundt resigned is not particularly material; that Hall knew who the successor was can, however, hardly be doubted and that fact is materially important. The contrast between Bernstein and Wundt in the knowledge of mathematics and physics would surely have influenced Hall's readiness to credit what he learned about the Wundt/Helmholtz early relationship during Hall's period of study in Leipzig and Berlin in 1879-1880.

The rumor about Helmholtz's willing acceptance of Wundt's resignation would have had a special appeal to Hall not only because of his awareness of Wundt's successor but because Hall had a general dislike for Wundt's retiring aloofness and an unfavorable opinion of his uninspiring (to Hall) and dull general conception of psychology. But to conclude from this preference that Hall had never been a student of Wundt is, indeed, extravagant. Had Hall not been a student of Wundt how could he have acquired the necessary evidence for his markedly negative appraisal? The three ways in which Stanley Hall served as a postdoctoral student of Wundt during 1879-1880 are indicated in Chapter I.

It has just come to my attention that Bringmann & Bringmann (1980) presumably retracted their indictment of Hall in a paper presented at the March 1991 meeting of the Southern Society for Philosophy and Psychology authored in collaboration with R. La Guardia under the title "Hall and Wundt: A Reassessment." This paper is cited in an article by Bringmann, Bringmann & Early (1992) that favorably reviews "G. Stanley Hall and the History of Psychology." In that article (p. 254) one reads: "Hall was a post-graduate student at Leipzig University from the winter term of 1879 through the following summer term (Bringmann & Bringmann, 1980). During this time Hall 'participated . . . [in the] psychophysical laboratory' of Wilhelm Wundt (1832-1920) with 'great industry and success' (Bringmann, Bringmann & La Guardia, 1991)." The operative word is "reassessment."

That Hall was not, however, Wundt's favorite American student is surely true. That honor belonged to James McKeen Cattell who became, by his own volition, an assistant of Wundt in 1885-1886. Wundt himself acknowledged this designation when, in composing a history of his Institute, he called Cattell his "Volontäre-Assistent" (Wundt, 1909, p. 119). On the same page he coupled Hall's name with that of Cattell as his two earliest American adherents. But unlike Hall, Cattell was a past master at constructive aggression. He set out to cope with both the limitations and the needs of his mentor. Thus he took the initiative against Wundt's controlling reticence and gradually Wundt accepted his advances. Observing his mentor's failing eyesight and compelling literary output, Cattell made him a gift of an American typewriter— a rarity in the Germany of 1886. Cattell was later told that "Avenarius said it was an evil gift for with it Wundt wrote twice as many books as would otherwise have been possible" (Cattell, 1921, pp. 156-158).

Chapter III.   Lunch in Bremen and the Ocean Voyage

1. Most of the information in this chapter is derived from four sources: (1) Freud's unpublished 1909 travel journal (referred to as Travel Diary in this text), which exists in holograph in the restricted portion of the Freud Collection at the Library of Congress. A photocopy was made available through permission granted me by the late Anna Freud to use this material for the present purpose. I am responsible for the English translation quoted here. Freud kept this Diary only for the early days of the journey. (2) Freud's unpublished letters to his family sent me by the Library of Congress with the travel journal. (3) The Freud/Jung Letters (referred to as F/J Letters), edited by William McGuire. Princeton, NJ: Princeton University Press, 1974. (4) The Life and Work of Sigmund Freud (referred to as Jones) by Ernest Jones, vols. 1 and 2. New York: Basic Books, 1953, 1955.

2. To supplement Note 23 in Chapter II concerning the possibility that a wealthy patient from Chicago, Harold McCormick, and his wife Edith Rockefeller McCormick may have facilitated Jung's journey to America, the following is of interest. Jung had told Freud on July 10, 1909 that the McCormicks had booked passage for August 21 on the George Washington, and he expressed misgivings that they would be on the ship along with Freud and himself. Freud responded to this concern on July 19. With or without relevance to this concern, the McCormicks modified their plans. An article in the August 16 issue of the (Chicago) Record-Herald described a dinner party that the McCormicks hosted on August 14, a week before the psychoanalytic trio left Bremen.

3. Jones, vol. 1, 316-317. In Jones, vol. 2, 146-147, there is further discussion of Freud's fainting attacks, both in Bremen and in Munich. The relation of this behavior to death wishes (by Jung against Freud) and by Freud, unconsciously wishing his own death as restitution for guilt about the death of his younger brother Julius, are considered in some detail.

4. See S. Rosenzweig, "The day of Freud's death," *Journal of Psychology,* 1970, *74,* 101-103. The critical relevance of Freud's "Three Fates" dream is indicated in this publication which—not brought out there—deals almost centrally with *biting:* by association with the image of the shark, etc. A portion of the self-analytic evidence for Freud's having bitten his brother Julius, who then died, is contained in the material of that dream. Hence the emphasis there on "owing a death to Nature"—in expiation or restitution for the primal sin.

5. Leo Burgerstein (1853-1928), Professor of Education and School Hygiene, University of Vienna.

6. William Stern (1871-1938), Professor of Philosophy, University of Breslau. His lectures at the Clark celebration will be discussed in Chapter VI.

7. William Stern reviewed Freud's *Traumdeutung* in *Zeitschrift für Psychologie und Physiologie der Sinnesorgane,* 1901, *26,* 133.

8. See Max Wertheimer and Julius Klein, "Psychologische Tatbestands diagnostik," *Archiv für Kriminal-Anthropologie und Kriminalistik,* 1904, *15,* 72-113. This monograph has the historic distinction of being the first published study that employed Galton's method of word association as a diagnostic device. While Wertheimer and Klein, students of the famous criminologist Hans Gross, had used the technique to detect falsification or bias in the testimony of court witnesses, Jung had employed the same method to detect "complexes" in neurotic patients. In both instances some form of deception was involved. A controversy regarding priority in the use of the word-association technique as a diagnostic tool developed when Jung in his 1906 monograph on word association (*Diagnostische Assoziationsstudien.* Leipzig: J. A. Barth) went out of his way to state that Wertheimer and

Klein had based their work on the model of the research by Jung and his associates with mental patients. Wertheimer responded in the *Archiv für die gesamte Psychologie,* 1906, *7,* 139-140 that he and Klein had used the technique independently of the publication by Jung (and Riklin) which appeared on April 19, 1904. His work with Klein, he showed, appeared originally on April 7, 1904. Jung reluctantly conceded priority to Wertheimer and Klein in a note published in the *Zeitschrift für angewandte Psychologie,* 1908, *1,* 163.

The priority issue is, of course, trivial but it turned a spotlight on the essential simultaneity of applying Galton's method in the two disparate fields of criminology and psychiatry and for quite similar purposes. From the dynamic standpoint the two approaches overlap if the repressed complexes of the neurotic are seen to involve *self-deception,* just as a biased or false witness in a court of law employs *deception* to influence a judge or jury. In both instances the assumption is that a reality "true to the facts" has been distorted and requires a corrective or cure once the fact of distortion has been detected.

9. The legendary foreboding of Napoleon's mother and her often quoted phrase of warning are discussed in Emil Ludwig's *Napoleon* (New York: Boni and Liveright, 1926, p. 199) and in *The Golden Bees: The Story of the Bonapartes* by Theo Aronson (Greenwich, CT: New York Graphic Society, 1964, p. 40).

10. The interview appeared in the German-language newspaper *New Yorker Staats-Zeitung,* Monday, August 30, 1909, page 8. It was part of a more general article concerning the arrival of two German ships with more than 3300 passengers but the "German honored guests" were described in a portion of the article that mentioned the forthcoming 20-year anniversary of Clark University in Worcester, Mass. for which three of the speakers had just arrived on the *George Washington.* Stern was indeed mentioned at greater length than Freud and Jung and Freud's name was misspelled "Freund," as he had remarked.

11. The book translated by A. A. Brill was entitled *Selected Papers on Hysteria and Other Psychoneuroses* by Sigmund Freud. It was published as No. 4 in the *Nervous and Mental Disease Monograph Series,* New York: Journal of Nervous and

Mental Disease Publishing Co., 1909. Though Freud and Brill expected it to appear in two weeks, it was not actually published until September 30, 1909, about two weeks after the Clark Conference.

12. Bronislav Onuf, M.D. (1863-1929) was active in New York psychiatric circles since his arrival there around 1895. He knew as colleagues not only Dr. Brill, but Dr. Adolf Meyer and the neurologist Bernard Sachs. (Sachs published an obituary of him in the *Journal of Nervous and Mental Disease,* December 1929, vol. 70, pp. 661-662.) A brief biography and bibliography appeared in the *Semi-Centennial Anniversary Volume of the American Neurological Association, 1875-1924,* pp. 217, 575-576. A timely publication by Onuf in which he surveyed the situation in psychotherapy, including the contributions of Freud, appeared in the *New Yorker Medizinische Monatschrift,* 1908, *19,* 291-301. Even more directly relevant is a paper entitled "Dreams and their interpretation as diagnostic and therapeutic aids in psychopathology," *Journal of Abnormal Psychology,* 1910, *4,* 339-350, based on an address before the American Neurological Association, May 29, 1909.

13. Freud wrote (at least) three letters home from New York dated August 30, August 31 and September 2 (available to me from the restricted Freud Collection). In addition there was the cable sent on arrival, dated August 29, 1909, with only the two words, "Splendid, Love." A post card of greeting from Brill's house, dated August 30, was addressed to Frau Martha Freud and signed by A. A. Brill, Rose Owen Brill [his wife], S. Ferenczi and C. G. Jung. Quotations in the text dealing with the arrival and first days in New York are from these items.

Chapter IV.   A Walk in Central Park

1. See *C. G. Jung: Word and Image,* edited by Aniela Jaffé. Princeton, NJ: Princeton University Press, 1979, p. 47. Letter of Jung to his wife Emma, August 31, 1909. This early statement by Jung on ethnic differences, Jews and Aryans, has generally been overlooked even in controversial discussions about his Aryan sympathies during the Hitler regime. That this difference was

highlighted in a current dream makes it psychoanalytically very significant—the "unconscious" was involved. But day-residues were provided by the conspicuous ethnic diversity in the suddenly new environment of New York's Central Park.

2. Both Freud and Jung in writing to their wives described Brill's wife, particularly about her being "an American." Mrs. Rose Brill, née Owen, was not Jewish. She was a Methodist of English descent. After marriage she did not practice her Protestant religion and Dr. Brill was not religiously a Jew either. According to their son Edmund, from whom these facts derive, both parents practiced a kind of "ethical culture" in bringing up their children, and were influenced by the Mental Hygiene movement and by psychoanalysis in their educational practices. K. Rose Owen was an M.D. (Letter to the writer from Edmund R. Brill, January 27, 1983.)

3. My interview with Jung occurred at his home in Küsnacht on July 6, 1951 at 5 P.M. It lasted for 70 minutes during which time Jung, as I naturally desired, did most of the talking. Immediately after the interview I walked to a small restaurant a couple of blocks in the direction of the railway station and there, at a table in the restaurant garden, wrote out the interview in detail. I then boarded the train that took me back to my hotel in Zurich.

At the time, Jung's allusion to the Palisades was puzzling. It was only later that I was able to identify the locale and recognize that while the visitors made no excursion to that region, the New Jersey Palisades were quite visible from Riverside Drive at Columbia University. The definition of "Palisades" in the *Random House Dictionary of the English Language,* 2nd ed., 1987, p. 1397, reads as follows: "The line of cliffs in NE New Jersey and SE New York extending along the W bank of the lower Hudson River ab. 15 mi. (24 km.) long; 300-500 ft. (91-152 m.) high."

4. The allusion to the "Palisades" in the interview as the locale of Freud's mishap was at first puzzling because Jung merely said "the Palisades" with no location indicated. When I later realized the importance of the incident and tried to place the Palisades, the only conjecture that made sense was the visit to the Psychiatric Clinic at Columbia University on September 2 about which I knew from a letter sent by Freud to his family. The form of Jung's statement apparently meant that the mishap did not occur in the

Clinic itself but as a distinct episode while the group were looking at the Palisades. But I needed to confirm this interpretation. To that end I communicated with Jung's son Franz who was in possession of his father's 1909 letters from America. The response, the essential part of which will be quoted here by-permission, places beyond any doubt that my conjecture had been correct. Dr. Jung wrote to his wife on September 3, 1909: ". . .Yesterday we saw Columbia University with its magnificent library. Everything is very beautiful and impressive. From nearby Riverside Drive (broad promenade) one sees the Palisades on the other side of the West River. These are very far away and quite outside the city limits. New York is simply enormous." (An excerpt from Jung's unpublished letter translated by this writer.)

By "West River" Jung must have meant the Hudson which, in its location in the northwest, corresponds to the "East River" at the south and east of the city.

From this letter of Jung as related to the interview, it is clear that Freud's mishap occurred on the occasion of the group's visit to Columbia University, not on a separate excursion. The group were on Riverside Drive (a "broad promenade") while visiting the Clinic and could see the distant Palisades on the other side of the Hudson River. This particular becomes important, as will presently be seen, when this Hudson River seascape is considered in juxtaposition to that of the Austrian Danube River.

5. In this connection one should recall Freud's later paper (*Standard Edition, 22,* 185-193) on the discovery of fire in the myth regarding Prometheus. The ability to control the primitive impulse to extinguish fire by urination was here introduced by Freud as the key to the monumental discovery of fire by Prometheus. As in several of Freud's original writings, the source may have been his own enuresis in childhood, plainly confessed in the "Count Thun" dream in association to which two incidents of incontinence, punished by his father, are recalled. These were used to explain the impulse to urinate underlying the dream, immediately after which he had to relieve himself. In 1910, J. Sadger formulated the concept of a urethral erotic stage which highlighted excessive ambitiousness as one of its repressed derivatives. The reference is: "Über Urethralerotik," *Jahrbuch für psychoanalytische Forschungen,* 1910, *2,* 409-450.

6. Jones in his account of the American visit alludes obliquely to this incident. He mentions Freud's "prostatic discomfort," painful and embarrassing, caused by American arrangements for public rest rooms. He then quotes Freud's own words: "They escort you along miles of corridors and ultimately you are taken to the very basement where a marble palace awaits you, only just in time." (Jones, 1955, vol. 2, p. 60.)

7. Freud's dream of Count Thun is discussed repeatedly in *The Interpretation of Dreams* but primarily in *Standard Edition, 4,* 208-218.

8. Strong support for recognizing the various elements in Freud's dream of Count Thun—both the manifest dream and the latent content revealed by the free associations—is afforded in the book *The Socialism of Fools* by Andrew Whiteside (1975). Here on an historical basis the plight of Count Thun in June 1898 precisely fits the occasion of Freud's dream. Moreover, the various other facts about the drive in Austria toward Pan-Germanism in the previous 20 years—the role of the symbolic cornflower and of the white carnation, the student societies of the '70s which militantly espoused the Germanic myth, with debates, demonstrations, etc.—pervades Freud's dream. In his associations to it he confessed his naive, if brief, participation in this movement due to his excessive ambition, neurotically linked to his childhood enuresis and his father's dire prophecy about his future. Freud now saw how misguided he was in denying his Jewishness by joining the German majority with the cultural heritage it represented, e.g., Goethe and Schiller. Behind the figure of Count Thun was an official far more personally significant to Freud, for whom he was an arch representative of the anti-Semitism prevalent in Austria. This person, whose effect on Freud runs like a black thread through the entire dream, is the "Cruel Captain" alluded to in the account of Freud's fainting spell at Bremen.

9. Freud's allusion to the Wachau and the short trip he had made to that region on the Danube River shortly before the Count Thun dream are described in *Standard Edition, 4,* 211. The high bluffs occupied by old castles are described by John Lehmann, *Down River: A Danubian Study.* London: Cresset Press, 1939, pp. 154-155.

10. Hitler, A. *Mein Kampf* (1925-1927). English trans. by R. Manheim, 1943. Cf. p. 22 in Chap. II, "Years of study and suffering in Vienna." Boston: Houghton Mifflin, 1943.

11. Kubizek, A. *The Young Hitler I Knew.* Translated from the German by E. V. Anderson. Boston: Houghton Mifflin, 1955, p. 182.

12. Hitler, *op. cit.*, 59.

13. Kubizek, *op. cit.*, 251.

14. Cf. W. A. Jenks, *Vienna and the Young Hitler.* New York: Columbia University Press, 1960; Jones, J. S. *Hitler in Vienna 1907-1913.* New York: Stein & Day, 1983; Waite, R. G. *The Psychopathic God: Adolf Hitler.* New York: Basic Books, 1977.

15. Hitler, *op. cit.*, 308-329 and *passim*.

16. See Hitler, *op. cit.*, Chap. II, *passim*.

17. Cf. G. Cocks, *Psychotherapy in the Third Reich: The Göring Institute.* New York: Oxford, 1985, pp. 127-135. Cocks does not mention that Ernst Kretschmer, whom Jung replaced as head of the International Medical Society, was a Jew who resigned for political reasons. This point and much else of interest in the cultural context is covered in the paper by R. Haymond, "On Carl Gustave Jung: Psycho-social basis of morality during the Nazi era," *Journal of Psychology and Judaism,* 1982, *6*, 81-112. A commentary on Haymond's essay by a Jewish Jungian analyst, James Kirsch, presented incidents and considerations favorable to Jung. (Cf. *Journal of Psychology and Judaism, op. cit.*, 113ff.) Yet Jung himself in "A rejoinder to Dr. Bally," (1934) (*Collected Works, 10,* 543 and *passim*) boldly avowed that he had called attention to the subjective, racial basis of psychological conceptions as early as 1913. In a subsequent letter, written to the editor of the journal in which his rejoinder had appeared, Jung cited other avowals concerning race made by him in 1918 and 1926. (See *Collected Works, ibid.*, 544n.) Jung did not, of course, allude to his even earlier Aryan/Jewish dream communicated to Freud in Central Park in 1909.

18. *Oxford companion to German literature.* Oxford: Clarendon Press, 1976, p. 380.

19. Jung, C. G. "The state of psychotherapy today," *Collected Works, 10,* 165-166.

20. Hitler, *op. cit.,* vol. 1, pp. 302-305.

21. This article, published at the end of World War II, is included in *Collected Works, 10,* 194-217. See pp. 203-204 for the diagnosis cited here.

22. Stern, P. J. *C. G. Jung: The Haunted Prophet.* New York: Braziller, 1976, pp. 220-221.

23. Jaffé, A. *From the Life and Work of C. G. Jung.* New York: Harper & Row, 1968. Chap. III, "C. G. Jung and National Socialism."

Chapter V.   At the Home of the Host

1. For these letters see the Appendix of C. G. Jung, *Memories, Dreams, Reflections.* New York: Pantheon, 1963, pp. 365-368.

2. The letters between Hall and James are among the Hall Papers, Clark University Archives, or in the James Papers at Houghton Library, Harvard University.

3. Letters of William James to his wife, James Papers, Houghton Library, Harvard University.

4. C. G. Jung. *Letters.* Princeton, NJ: Princeton University Press, 1973, vol. 1, pp. 530-532. (Letter dated July 23, 1949.)

5. James, William. Report on Mrs. Piper's Hodgson control, *Proceedings of the American Society for Psychical Research,* 1909 (June), *3.*

6. G. S. Hall. The muscular perception of space, *Mind,* 1878 (October), *3,* 433-450.

7. Quoted in *G. Stanley Hall: A Sketch* by Louis N. Wilson. New York: G. E. Stechert, 1914, p. 47. Wundt's letter was dated November 5, 1913.

8. The open letter from Wundt appeared under the title, "Spiritualism as a scientific question," *Popular Science Monthly*, 1879 (September), *15*, 577-593.

9. James, W. *Essays in Psychical Research*, vol. 16 in *The Works of William James*. Cambridge: Harvard University Press, 1986, p. 80. This edition of William James's writings is the best currently available collection. The four essays involved in the present discussion appear in the collection as follows: A Record of Observations of Certain Phenomena of Trance (1890), No. 12, pp. 79-88; Address of the President before the Society for Psychical Research (1896), No. 19, pp. 127-137; Report on Mrs. Piper's Hodgson-Control (1909), No. 37, pp. 253-360; The Confidences of a "Psychical Researcher" (1909), No. 38, pp. 361-375. An earlier collection of James's papers on this topic was compiled and enlarged with letters of James and editorial comments in *William James on Psychical Research*, edited by Gardner Murphy and Robert O. Ballou. New York: Viking, 1960.

10. See *The Literary Remains of the Late Henry James,* edited with an Introduction by William James. Boston: James R. Osgood & Co., 1885.

11. See James, W. *Principles of Psychology*. New York: Holt, 1890, 2 vols. and *Varieties of Religious Experience: A Study in Human Nature*. New York: Longmans, Green, 1902.

12. See Morton Prince, *The Dissociation of a Personality: A Biographical Study in Abnormal Psychology*. New York: Longmans, Green, 1906 (actually copyright and published December 1905). A scholarly reconstruction of this classic case of Sally Beauchamp by Saul Rosenzweig appeared under the title, "Sally Beauchamp's Career: A psychoarchaeological key to Morton Prince's classic case of multiple personality," *Genetic, Social and General Psychology Monographs*, 1987, *113*, 5-60. The collaboration of Dr. Hodgson in Prince's treatment of this case was disclosed and discussed in this monograph.

13. See *Studies in Spiritism* by Amy E. Tanner, with an Introduction by G. Stanley Hall. New York: Appleton, 1910. This book, based upon the investigation of Mrs. Piper's mediumship in the spring of 1909, appeared in October of the following year. It

was therefore not known to James as such during his visit in Worcester in 1909 but he surely knew about the arrangements Hall had made with Mr. George Dorr for the work done by Amy Tanner under the guidance of Stanley Hall.

A recent study (Coon, 1992), which involved the use of archival material at Clark University, has shown that three years before the meeting of Hall and James at the 20th anniversary conference in September, Hall was involved in the reception of a grant of $5,000 for the conduct of psychical research at the University. He attempted to get the conditions of the grant modified so that the funds would not be restricted to the limited field of parapsychology and was able to effect a compromise that broadened the objectives. It is evident that at this time a number of universities were awarded funds for psychical research and the temptation in this direction was thus increased and engendered conflict between more conventional psychological research and work with mediums, etc.

14. G. S. Hall, "Spooks and telepathy," *Appleton's Magazine*, 1908 (December), *12*, 677-683. See also Dorothy Ross, *G. Stanley Hall: The Psychologist as Prophet*. Chicago: University of Chicago Press, 1972, pp. 163-164. Ross well summarizes Hall's attitude toward psychical research as chiefly created by deception, conscious or unconscious. For a detailed, revealing account of Hall's interest in and mastery of magicians' tricks as an important key to the understanding of mediumistic phenomena, see *G. Stanley Hall: A Sketch* by Louis N. Wilson. New York: Stechert, 1914, pp. 109-113.

14a. See Tanner (1910), pp. 23-25, 189f.

15. Ibid., p. 208.

16. Somewhat exceptional in this regard is the standard biography *Richard Hodgson: The Story of a Psychical Researcher and His Times* by A. T. Baird. London: Psychic Press, Ltd., 1949. The author does not take very seriously the allegation of Mrs. Piper's daughter (Alta Piper, *Life and Work of Mrs. Piper*. London: Kegan Paul, 1929, p. 190) that Tanner and Hall in their investigation caused injury to Mrs. Piper's tongue and right arm in making tests for anesthesia. Baird states that the tests were justified and that the findings of Tanner and Hall—that the trance states were not very convincing—brought no surprise to the Society

for Psychical Research because Mrs. Piper by 1909 had begun to give poor sittings in contrast to her earlier first-class performances. Baird recommends the Tanner/Hall book to those interested in evidence on the negative side of spiritism.

17. I was able to learn, presumably for the first time, some of the obscure facts about the blind medium consulted by Mrs. Piper. He was James R. Cocke (1862-1900), born in Knoxville, Tenn., who became a resident of Boston during the period of his training that began March 1, 1889. Despite his profound handicap he obtained an M.D. degree from Boston University School of Medicine. He was therefore not an M.D. when Mrs. Piper first consulted him in 1884 and was, in fact, only 22 years old. He published a number of medical papers on the uses of hypnotism in the 1890s and a book of over 350 pages entitled *Hypnotism: How It is Done, Its Uses and Dangers.* Boston: Lee and Shepard, 1894. Two years later, four years before his death, he published a long novel entitled *Blind Leaders of the Blind: The Romance of a Blind Lawyer.* Boston: Lee and Shepard, 1896.

The record of Mrs. Piper's surgery, described by Dr. Tanner as having occurred 1893-1896, was verified from the Records Department of the Massachusetts General Hospital. Under the name Mrs. Leonora Piper (her actual given name which she modified in usage to Leonore), residing in Arlington, she is described as having had an operation in 1896 for "ventral hernia" which resulted from surgery three years earlier, at which time she had a "laparotomy for removal of both tubes and ovaries." The evidence for the accident while sledding at age 16 was apparently obtained orally by Doctors Hall and Tanner from Mrs. Piper herself. It is probably in this same manner that the investigators learned about her gynecological surgery. It is striking that these data were used by the investigators as an almost literal demonstration of the medium's "hysteria" as a physical basis for her nervous shock with a resultant splitting of the personality. The literalness here mentioned refers to the ancient Egyptian and Greek theory of the wandering "hystéra" (womb or uterus) that causes the mental symptoms of the hysterical woman; but the modern theories of Janet and, particularly, Breuer and Freud, in which psychosexual trauma takes the place of the gynecological etiology, have been superimposed on the traditional theory reaching back to ancient times classically formulated in Plato's *Timaeus*. A fascinating and well documented history of this disease will be found in *Hysteria: The History of a Disease* by Ilza Veith. Chicago: University of Chicago Press, 1965.

18. Tanner, *op. cit.,* p. 34f.

19. Ibid., p. xxxii.

20. See G. S. Hall, *Jesus, the Christ, in the Light of Psychology.* Garden City, NY: Doubleday, Page, 1917. 2 vols. 2nd ed., 1923.

20a. Though Hall's contributions to education are not much discussed in the present volume, attention is here called to a masterly survey of them in a book by Partridge entitled *The Genetic Philosophy of Education* with an Introductory Note by Hall (Partridge, 1912).

21. See G. S. Hall, "A reminiscence," *American Journal of Psychology,* 1917, *28,* 297-300. For the second account, cf. G. S. Hall, "The American Journal of Psychology," *American Journal of Psychology,* 1921, *32,* 1-30. In his autobiography Hall also referred to the beginnings of the *American Journal of Psychology* and spoke of "my patron, Pearsall Smith, whose chief interest was in psychic research and who gave up even his subscription when the *Journal* criticized this movement. . . ." *Life and Confessions of a Psychologist.* New York: Appleton, 1923, pp. 227-228. William James must have been informed by Smith of this misunderstanding for he took Hall to task for "running the greatest confidence game in N. America." (James to Hall, August 1 [1888], Clark University Archives).

A little-known but very interesting account of the new journal was published by the psychiatrist Dr. E. Cowles in the *American Journal of Insanity,* 1887-1888, *44,* 544-546. It is noteworthy that Hall also founded the *Journal of Genetic Psychology* (originally called *Pedagogical Seminary*) in 1891 and the *Journal of Applied Psychology* in 1917.

21a. The information about the beginning of Mary Calkins's career is from Furumoto (1979). In particular, see page 350, which includes the quotation from the letter of William James to Miss Calkins. The letter itself was dated May 24, 1890. The original is in the Archives of Wellesley College. It is probably more than coincidence that in April 1890 Joseph Jastrow assembled and published in the *American Journal of Psychology* accounts of instructional programs in psychology offered at American colleges and universities, including, of course, Harvard and Clark (Jastrow, 1890). The description for Clark was written by E. C. Sanford; that for Harvard, by William James. The former is three times as long as the latter, and tends to support James's appraisal of the Clark program—unless one considers the even more detailed and impressive description written by J. McK. Cattell for the University of Pennsylvania.

A later and fuller discussion of Mary Calkins's quest for graduate education is available in Scarborough and Furumoto (1987, Chap. 1).

Not to leave Miss Calkins stranded, we add that she did obtain permission later in the year to attend the seminars by James and Royce in the fall of 1890. She was not, however, permitted to register as a regular student or to take the courses toward a degree. And that same fall she began work with Professor E. C. Sanford at Clark. With him she conducted the study of dreams described in Chapter IX, note 4.

22. "The founding of the APA," Wayne Dennis and Edwin G. Boring, *American Psychologist*, 1952, *7*, 95-97. In this context it is appropriate to recall Hall's influence on the profession of psychology as judged by the number of Ph.D.s granted at Clark University from its beginning during its first twenty years (through 1908) as compared to the other 14 universities granting such degrees. The number from Clark was 60 while the total from the other 14 was 129 (i.e., Clark granted 32% of the total). The nearest competitors were Harvard, with 28, and Columbia, with 27. (See R. S. Harper, "Tables of American doctorates in psychology," *American Journal of Psychology*, 1949, *62*, 579-587.)

22a. The information about the first annual meeting of the American Psychological Association which, incidentally, is accompanied by some details about the Preliminary Meeting at Clark University, Worcester, July 8, 1892, is to be found in the reprint of the Proceedings in the *American Psychologist*, 1973 under the title "APA's First Publication: Proceedings of the American Psychological Association, 1892-1893," edited by Michael M. Sokal.

The citation of Hall's contribution appears on page 3 of the Proceedings. The Proceedings included only a brief abstract of Hall's presentation, and it appears that he did not publish the entire paper. With the given title it is not unlikely that in the presentation Hall anticipated the editorial in the *American Journal of Psychology* in 1895 that aroused James's ire. Lacking the paper—which, incidentally, was an uncommon omission, for Hall characteristically published his addresses—this conjecture cannot be verified.

23. Cf. *Science*, 1895, n.s. *2*, 626-628. Hall replied in *Science*, 1895, n.s. *2*, 734-735. See letter of James to Hall, Oct. 12, 1895, Hall Papers, Clark University Archives. Also D. Ross, *op. cit.*, p. 244, n. 48. The controversy was provoked by Hall's lengthy editorial in the October 1895 issue of the *American Journal of Psychology*, *7*, 3-8. It said more to James than Hall intended regarding the beginnings of experimental psychology in America and Hall made an explanation that probably failed to satisfy his rivals.

24. Hall's review of James's *Principles of Psychology* appeared in the *American Journal of Psychology*, 1891, *3*, 585-591. Another review of the *Principles* is noteworthy because it was written by the originator of "pragmatism" 20 years before James revived and gave currency to the term under a revised definition. The philosopher Charles Sanders Peirce was neglected in his lifetime but has been rediscovered and is "enjoying" a posthumous fame. His advanced gifts as a logician are better appreciated today—a point that bears on the present review because it is largely in logical terms that Peirce faults James's work though otherwise praising it. A characteristic quotation is warranted: "Prof. James's thought is highly original, or at least novel; but it is originality of the destructive kind. To prove that we do not know what it has been generally supposed that we did know, that given premises do not justify the conclusions which all other thinkers hold they do justify, is his peculiar function. For this reason the book should have been preceded by an introduction discussing the strange positions in logic upon which all its arguments turn. Even when new theories are proposed, they are based on similar negative or skeptical considerations, and the one thing upon which Prof. James seems to pin his faith is the general incomprehensibility of things. He clings as passionately to that as the old lady of the anecdote did to her total

depravity. Of course, he is materialistic to the core—that is to say, in a methodical sense, but not religiously, since he does not deny a separable soul nor a future life; for materialism is that form of philosophy which may safely be relied upon to leave the universe as incomprehensible as it finds it. It is possible that Prof. James would protest against this characterization of his cast of mind. Brought up under the guidance of an eloquent apostle of a form of Swedenborgianism, which is materialism driven deep and clinched on the inside, and educated to the materialistic profession, it can only be by great natural breadth of mind that he can know what materialism is, by having experienced some thoughts that are not materialistic. He inclines towards Cartesian dualism, which is of the true strain of the incomprehensibles and modern material-ism's own mother. There is no form of idealism with which he will condescend to argue. Even evolutionism, which has idealistic affinities, seems to be held for suspect. It is his *métier* to subject to severe investigation any doctrine whatever which smells of intelligibility" (Peirce, 1891, p. 15).

25. Quoted in Arthur L. Blumenthal, *Language and Psychology: Historical Aspects of Psycholinguistics.* New York: Wiley, 1970, p. 238.

26. The excerpt from the letter of James to Hugo Münsterberg, August 11, 1892, is quoted from G. W. Allen, *William James, op. cit.,* p. 363.

27. William James to Alice Gibbens James, July 15, 1880 (James Papers).

28. E. G. Boring's appraisal of Hall's contribution, partly in a comparison with William James, is available in *A History of Experimental Psychology.* New York: Appleton, 1950, 2nd ed., pages 517-524. This account is both comprehensive and fair and is, in many respects, superior to the longer book-length biographies for the picture it conveys of Hall's achievements as well as his limitations.

29. See W. James, "The confidences of a 'psychical re-searcher'," *American Magazine,* October, 1909, 580-589. Re-printed in *Essays in Psychical Research, op. cit.* The page references in the text are to this reprinting.

30. William James's confession of his own justified cheating during Prof. Martin's popular lecture at Sanders Theatre recalls Robert Browning's "Mr. Sludge, 'The Medium'." In Browning's dramatic monologue the poet let Sludge make his confession of one fraudulent incident so that he could then pour out his claims to credibility in a manner not unlike James's lively account in his valedictory paper first entitled "Confidences of a 'Psychical Researcher'." Browning, who had ample direct experience with mediums, allowed the reader to draw his own conclusions though the poet's own are plainly conveyed by the mood he created.

31. Hall's article, "A Medium in the Bud," with a full report of the case of the 20-year-old girl, was published in the *American Journal of Psychology*, 1918, *29*, 144-158. It had been more briefly reported by him and A. E. Tanner in their book *Studies in Spiritism, op. cit.*, Chapter 17, with a passing reference to Dr. Freud's opinion that the girl was slightly paranoid: she felt persecuted by the failure of others to recognize her powers. Her unrequited love was considered by Hall to be the beginning of the mediumship which, by its power, in fantasy, she believed would make her attractive to the man she desired. Hall had discussed the importance of sex and sexual fantasies as related to spiritism in his book *Educational Problems*, 1911, Chapter 6. Earlier, in his work *Adolescence, its Psychology and its Relation to Physiology, Anthropology, Sociology, Sex, Crime, Religion and Education* (New York: Appleton, 1904, 2 vols.), he had discussed in detail what he called the erotic "effervescence of the ephebic girl" (vol. I, p. 308; vol. II, p. 409f.).

32. See C. G. Jung, *Memories, Dreams, Reflections, op. cit.*, p. 367. (This letter, from Jung to his wife, is erroneously dated September 14 instead of September 11.)

33. Hall's presidential address to the New England Watch and Ward Society was included in its Thirty-first Annual Report (for the year 1908-1909). Further evidence of Hall's interest in this organization is shown by a memorandum about it, dated February 24, 1910, which is on deposit in the Clark University Archives. In this three-page typescript he briefly commented on its history and current functions and made recommendations for improving its future effectiveness. In passing, Hall alluded to Judge Rowe [sic] who was combating white slavery. The Hon. Clifford G. Roe

published a volume in 1911, *The Great War on White Slavery*, a work of 400 pages which (in Chapter XXII) included comments by various civic leaders. Among these was G. Stanley Hall—a part of whose statement (p. 380) read: "The white slave traffic is one of the most tragic and barbarous aspects of our civilization which it has long besmirched. I am in hearty sympathy with every righteous and judicious mode of suppressing it, and such a campaign cannot be carried on without work that is not only hard but in its details very repulsive to decent people. The suspicions that attach to pure young men and even the few earnest Christian women graduates who lately sought to investigate with a view to suppression of the social evil is a sad commentary on the state of things and one of the chief obstacles in really getting at the facts. I have no sympathy with the kid glove method of handling these questions." The difference between Hall's forthrightness and the reserved attitude of others that he deprecated is highlighted in *The "Proper" Bostonians* by Cleveland Amory. New York: Dutton, 1947. Mentions of the Watch and Ward Society are included there (pp. 30-31; 328-330). A further specimen of Hall's involvement in contemporary sexual reform is found in a speech he gave in New York City on February 13, 1908 entitled "Education in Sexual Hygiene" (published in *Eugenics Review*, 1910, *1*, 242-253). A few months later he would be inviting Freud to participate in the Clark celebration.

34. See G. S. Hall, *Life and Confessions of a Psychologist*. New York: Appleton, 1923, pp. 406-414.

35. See vol. 2, Chap. 11 in G. S. Hall, *Adolescence, op. cit.* The 1896 paper by Freud that Hall quotes from, in his own English translation on page 121, and very briefly cites in a footnote, is "The aetiology of hysteria," now available in *Standard Edition, 3*, 191-221. Hall's quotation, including the phrase "*caput Nili* of neuropathology," occurs on p. 203.

36. Hall, G. S., *op. cit.*, vol. II, Chap. 14, entitled "The adolescent psychology of conversion." The long footnote in which he criticizes William James is on pp. 292-293. I am indebted to David Shakow (personal correspondence, February-March 1972, November-December 1980) for verifying the cut and uncut portions of William James's presentation copy of Hall's *Adolescence* which

Shakow acquired at a sale of James's books in 1921, held ten years after the death of William and shortly after the death of his wife Alice. My knowledge of Shakow's acquisition of this book came from Dorothy Ross's *G. Stanley Hall (op. cit.,* p. 299, note 66), where she observed that Shakow had said to her in 1965, "James did not cut the pages of *Adolescence* that Hall gave him." In trying to verify this comment by Shakow, I wrote to him and he carefully reviewed the two volumes of *Adolescence* and revised his casual remark to her. Shakow also informed me that he was giving *Adolescence* and several other books acquired at the same sale to the Harvard University rare book collection.

37. See E. G. Boring (1950), *op. cit.,* p. 523.

38. See E. L. Thorndike, "Review of *Adolescence* by G. S. Hall," *Science,* July 29, 1904, p. 143.

39. G. S. Hall. *Educational Problems.* New York: Appleton, 1911. 2 vols. See, in particular, vol. I, Chap. 7, 388-539.

40. For the identity of Anna O. as Bertha Pappenheim, see Jones, *op. cit.,* I, p. 223, note b; for a synopsis of her real-life career, pp. 223-227. For an authoritative account of Bertha Pappenheim's work as a leader of the feminist movement in Germany, see M. Kaplan, *The Jewish Feminist Movement in Germany,* 1979, Chap. 2, 118-119 and *passim.* Her visit to America in 1909 is documented in *Israelitisches Familienblatt, 11,* no. 31 (5 Aug. 1909), p. 11.

41. *William James: A Biography,* by G. W. Allen. New York: Viking, 1967, 211-212.

42. The letter of William James to Robertson James, dated November 14, 1869, is quoted by permission of James's descendant Henry J. Vaux.

43. See Jean Strouse, *Alice James: A Biography.* Boston: Houghton, Mifflin, 1980, pp. 125-128. Strouse not only uses the letters of William to his brother Bob but pointedly discusses William's own serious mental ills around 1870, including a description of the crisis that he disguised as an experience of a French correspondent. See also in this context S. Rosenzweig, "The Ghost of Henry James," *Character and Personality,* 1943,

12, 79-100, which, though referring primarily to William's brother Henry, considers also the relationship of both to their father, Henry, Sr.

44. See S. Rosenzweig, ibid., note 43. See also his, "The James's stream of consciousness," *Contemporary Psychology,* 1958, *3,* 250-257.

45. *The Letters of William James and Théodore Flournoy,* edited by R. C. LeClair, Madison, WI: University of Wisconsin Press, 1966. See pp. 35, 200-217 for the Brown-Séquard and Roberts-Hawley lymph compounds. For a reproduction of James's notes from a lecture by Brown-Séquard at the Harvard Medical School while James was in attendance, see D. W. Bjork, *William James: The Center of His Vision.* New York: Columbia University Press, 1988, p. 55. Bjork discusses James's recourse to the lymph compound remedy and the exchange of correspondence about it with Flournoy. For an informative account of Brown-Séquard's lectures at the Harvard Medical School during the period 1865-1868 see *Charles-Édouard Brown-Séquard: A Nineteenth Century Neurologist and Endocrinologist* by J. M. D. Olmsted, Baltimore: Johns Hopkins Press, 1946. A contemporary account of the Roberts-Hawley therapy will be found in *The New Animal Cellular Therapy* by J. R. Hawley. Chicago: Clinic Publishing Co., 1901.

46. See W. James, *Principles of Psychology, op. cit.,* vol. II, p. 438.

Chapter VI.   The Behavioral Scientists at Clark

1. All these lectures by the behavioral scientists were published in the *American Journal of Psychology,* April, 1910, and in the *Lectures and Addresses before the Departments of Psychology and Pedagogy,* edited by G. S. Hall (1910).

2. Titchener's appreciation of the literary ability of Ebbinghaus is matched by his own similar reputation. It was because of that reputation that he alone among the 29 lecturers at the Clark celebration received the degree of Doctor of Letters.

3. The question of Titchener's definition of psychology is considered in detail in the recent book *Defining American Psychology: The Correspondence Between Adolf Meyer and Edward Bradford Titchener,* edited by Ruth Leys and R. B. Evans. Baltimore: Johns Hopkins University Press, 1990.

Chapter VII.   Freud Introduces Psychoanalysis

1. Cf. Hall, 1922, p. x.

2. An anecdote connected with Freud's lecturing at the Library is worth recalling for what it reveals about his personality. While teaching at Clark, I used to browse at the Library in search of materials related to the 1909 visit. In that context, a veteran librarian who had acted as an usher when Freud lectured in the Art Room remembered a picturesque incident. When Freud entered the building for the first lecture given there, he was smoking a small cigar [cigarello]. As he started up the stairway to the third floor she pointed to a nearby "No Smoking" sign. Freud nodded politely but did not remove the cigar. When he returned the next day, she again designated the sign and he responded as before; on the third day the ritual was repeated. The lady concluded that the famous Professor was a polite nonconformist in more than one respect. But there was another conclusion: in 1939 Freud died as a result of oral cancer contracted through his nicotine addiction. He had suffered for sixteen years from its pain, a long series of surgical interventions, and a tormenting prosthesis. This ending was a natural part of his uniquely complicated journey through life, fighting quietly and stubbornly all the way on his own terms.

3. Freud's obituary of Sandor Ferenczi, who died in 1933, shortly before his 60th birthday, appears in translation in *Standard Edition, 22,* 227-229. It was a supplement to a tribute by Freud in a letter written on the 50th birthday of Ferenczi (*Standard Edition, 19,* 267-269).

4. See *Freud/Jung Letters,* June 3-4, 1909, pp. 228-229 and E. Jones, *Life and Work of Sigmund Freud,* New York: Basic Books, 1955, vol. II, p. 56.

5. The evidence for Freud's "unconscious" interest in political anarchism has not been previously noted because to have done so would have required the comprehension of association in two of his dreams of 1898 that have not heretofore been fathomed. In both the "Three Fates" dream (which occurred around September 16, 1898) and the dream of "riding a horse" (which occurred two weeks later), Freud alluded to the assassination of Empress Elizabeth of Austria-Hungary which occurred on September 10, 1898. Moreover, he seems to have identified with the assassin Luccheni, an anarchist, who committed the murder in Switzerland during a journey of the Empress on which he had secretly followed her. The most telling evidence of Freud's unconscious identification is found in the second of the just-mentioned dreams where, in the manifest content, he is accosted by a hotel bellboy as he approaches the building and is shown a note, presumably written by the dreamer, on which had been stated "no work, no food." This aphorism was Luccheni's own justification for his act of assassination—a protest against the luxury in which royalty lived at the expense of the poor. The phrase appeared in a contemporary newspaper account of the assassination with Luccheni's own statement as to his motivation. One is, of course, not to conclude from this inference that Freud entertained anarchistic intent at the conscious level, but there can be little doubt about his unconscious sympathies, not only from this intrusion of the assassin's words into Freud's dream associations but from the latent content of both dreams. They occurred at the peak of Freud's self-analysis when the sense of rejection by the anti-Semitic establishment of Vienna was pivotal. (Cf. Freud, *The Interpretation of Dreams, Standard Edition*, 1953, *4-5*, 204-208, 229-232; also the Count Thun or "revolutionary" dream of mid-June 1898, pp. 208-218, in which anti-Semitism is pervasive.)

Chapter VIII.   Jung Supports Freud

1. See Lecture Three, *American Journal of Psychology*, 1910, *21*, 251-269.

2. Ibid., pp. 251-252.

3. Ibid., p. 262.

4. Ibid., pp. 267-268.

5. See Freud, *Standard Edition, 10,* p. 19, n. 1.

6. Freud's characterization of this other mother as "a neu-rotic, who was unwilling to believe in infantile masturbation" serves to explain his delight at the surprising report of her little daughter's "attempt at seduction." Thus Freud started his letter to Jung on October 15, 1908 with the words: "Please tell your wife that one passage in her letter gave me particular pleasure." This message tends to identify the mother in the passage which was preserved by Freud in the footnote to Little Hans. Cf. also the published letter of Agathe's mother, written about two years later (24. No-vember, 1911), found in the *Freud/Jung Letters,* p. 467. In it Emma Jung thanks Freud for helping her in her relations with her complex, and very popular, husband with whom "the women are all in love" so that she is left to her own devices even when they are in the midst of a company of friends. In that context she states: "What with my strong tendency to autoerotism it is very difficult, but also objectively it is difficult because I can never compete with Carl." How to interpret the term "autoerotism" here is not alto-gether clear, but as used by an educated woman living in the shadow of Freud and Jung for five years in the heyday of the theory of infantile sexuality and the new libido theory, and used in a letter that was undoubtedly part of an exchange of correspondence with Freud with something in the nature of a therapeutic purpose, it is reasonable to assume that the term was not idly used.

7. See *The Inner World of Childhood* by Frances G. Wickes. New York: Appleton, 1927.

8. See *A Secret Symmetry: Sabina Spielrein between Jung and Freud* by Aldo Carotenuto. New York: Pantheon, 1982, p. 92.

9. Ibid., pp. 93-94.

10. *American Journal of Psychology, op. cit.,* p. 265; *Jahr-buch,* 1910, pp. 51f.; Jung, *Collected Works, 17,* pp. 26f.

11. The fact that this striking phase of Agathe's mistrust of her father is prominently present in the Clark lecture, in the *Jahr-buch* version and in the final *Collected Works* but is not found in the Freud/Jung correspondence must mean that Jung's reports of

his observations of Agathli as made to Freud contemporaneously before the Clark conference were not published in full. It is quite possible that the reason for the omission of these particular observations lies in their proximity to the revelations about Sabina Spielrein made by Jung to Freud. To have included these observations could have too readily suggested to the reader the very interpretation that has been broached in the present discussion.

12. Jung's letter to Freud, June 2, 1910, went to the heart of his dissatisfaction with Freud's infantile sex theory and its view of incest. The religious impetus is evident: "My mythology swirls about inside me, and now and then various significant bits and pieces are thrown up." He continues by citing "the inexhaustible depths of Christian symbolism, whose counterpart seems to have been found in the Mithraic mysteries." Then comes the new interpretation of Freud's Oedipus or "nuclear complex." Jung calls it a "profound disturbance—caused by the incest prohibition—between libidinal gratification and propagation. The astral myth can be solved in accordance with the rules of dream interpretation: Just as the sun mounts higher and higher after the winter, so will you attain to fruitfulness in spite of the incest barrier (and its odious effects on your libido)." He then alludes to the *Zend-Avesta*. He concludes with the sentence: "You will soon get the material where all this is described." (William McGuire, the editor of the *Letters*, here added in a footnote a cross-reference to volume 5, paragraph 395, of Jung's *Collected Works*.)

Since Jung must just have completed his German edition of the Agathe case, which appeared in the August 1910 issue of the *Jahrbuch*, he may be cryptically alluding here to his revision of the "incest barrier" implied in that case. Is he, a year in advance of its publication, announcing his repudiation of the Freudian theory of infantile sexuality with its literal (biological) view of (father-daughter) incest?

13. See Jung's *Memories, Dreams, Reflections.* New York: Pantheon, 1963, p. 167.

14. See C. G. Jung, *Symbols of Transformation, Collected Works*, vol. 5.

15. Ibid., pp. 417-418.

16. Ibid., p. 419.

17. Ibid., p. 420.

18. Jung, *op. cit.,* 1963, p. 168.

Chapter IX.   James's Day at the Conference

1. In James's Diary he describes seven sittings for his portrait (April 16-22, 1909) and calls the painter by the familiar name "Bay Emmet." From this indication and from the name Emmet (which I recognized as perhaps significant in the James genealogy), the relationship of Ellen Emmet to James was followed up. It turned out that she was, indeed, a blood relative. The fact is well attested in the biography of her in the *National Cyclopedia of American Biography* (1955).

The portrait was commissioned by friends and former pupils of James and was presented to Harvard University on January 10, 1910. It was hung in the Faculty Room of University Hall.

The artist was only 33 years old when she painted James. At the early age of 28, she won a silver medal at the St. Louis World Exposition, 1904. She painted not only William James but the American sculptor Augustus Saint-Gaudens and President Franklin Delano Roosevelt.

1a. S. Freud, An autobiographical study (1925), *Standard Edition, 20,* p. 52.

2. See C. G. Jung, *Letters.* Princeton, NJ: Princeton University Press, 1973, vol. I, p. 531.

3. S. Freud, *Gesammelte Werke,* 1948, *14,* p. 78.

4. See R. B. Perry, *The Thought and Character of William James.* Boston: Little, Brown, 1935, vol. 2, p. 123. The recipient of this letter, Mary Whiton Calkins, had been a student of William James at Harvard University in 1890 and in 1892-1895. She simultaneously (in 1890) began studies at Clark University with Edmund C. Sanford in collaboration with whom she carried out a "minor" study on recalled dreams which she published in the *American Journal of Psychology,* 1893. Professor Calkins occupies a memorable place in American psychology by virtue

of her having been refused the Ph.D. by the Harvard Corporation because of her sex though she had fulfilled all the academic requirements. (Harvard's charter excluded women.) She began teaching psychology at Wellesley early in 1890 while pursuing her graduate studies and she remained there for the rest of her professional life. She attained the rank of Professor of Philosophy and Psychology and retired in 1929. It is remarkable that even without the Ph.D., she was elected President of the American Psychological Association in 1905—the first woman president. During her mature professional life she expounded and defended a "self-psychology" which she called "personalistic." Most of her autobiography was devoted to the exposition of this point of view (Calkins, 1930). (See also Furumoto, 1979.)

A brief comment on the above-mentioned study is appropriate here because this work was carefully read and several times cited by Freud in his now famous book, *The Interpretation of Dreams,* published six years later (Freud, 1899, pp. 19, 21, 43, 221). Professor Sanford (1859-1924) not only supervised the work but collaborated in it by recording and analyzing his dreams just as Miss Calkins did hers. The dreams were collected during a period of approximately seven weeks. During the first part of the research the observers set alarm clocks to wake them at various times during the night, and they immediately noted down what they had been dreaming. The method was abandoned for the later part of the study because the excitement caused by the alarm was found to interfere more than it helped. (It is relevant that an arousal method has been recently employed in research on sleep and dreaming.) One of the results obtained was noted by Calkins (1930, p. 32) as confirming Freud's assertion that dreaming is almost continuous for nearly everyone though a contrary opinion is prevalent because the dreams are forgotten. Other similarities and differences between the views of Freud and the findings of the study are briefly mentioned in the above cited autobiography (Calkins, ibid.).

It is noteworthy that the collaborator in the dream study, E. C. Sanford, was not a joint author. Characteristically for him, he allowed the student to publish the article exclusively. She was duly grateful for his supervision and subsequent guidance in the establishment of a laboratory of psychology at Wellesley. In her autobiography she described him as "a teacher unrivaled for the richness and precision of his knowledge of experimental procedure and for the prodigality with which he lavished time and interest upon his students." (*Loc. cit.*, 32; see also p. 35.)

Though Mary Calkins was present at the Clark conference, as shown by the letter from James to her, she does not appear in the photograph taken on Friday, February 10; but neither did other individuals who attended many of the sessions.

5. See *The Letters of William James and Théodore Flournoy*, edited by R. C. LeClair. Madison, WI: University of Wisconsin Press, p. 224.

6. The newspaper article with Freud's condemnation of American religious therapy as "dangerous" and "unscientific" had appeared in the *Boston Evening Transcript*, Saturday, September 11, 1909 (Part III, p. 3, col. 1-2). This then current form of pastoral counseling was the Emmanuel Movement, conducted from an Episcopal church in Boston. James was actively supportive of such nonmedical applications of psychotherapy. He had, for example, signed a petition opposing a pending bill in the Massachusetts legislature to limit the practice of medicine to individuals with medical degrees, and to explain his opposition he published a long letter in the *Boston Transcript*, March 24, 1894. He had expressed similar views as late as 1908, two years before his death, and he had repeatedly undergone treatment by nonmedical mental healers (cf. *William James* by G. W. Allen, 1967, pp. 371-373).

The interview in the *Transcript* was conducted by Adelbert Albrecht who apparently saw Freud at Hall's house on Wednesday, September 8 (as indicated in a letter of that date by Jung to his wife). Freud's comment about the Emmanuel Movement was in response to a question put by the interviewer. It occupied a prominent place, the first section, of the article. The movement, which combined religion and counseling in matters of mental health, was formally started in November 1906 at the Emmanuel Church in Boston where Dr. Elwood Worcester had been rector since July 1904. The formal launching began with a group of lectures on the relation of religion to medicine by prominent speakers including Dr. James Jackson Putnam, Professor of Neurology at the Harvard Medical School, and Dr. Richard C. Cabot, an eminent internist and pioneer in the social aspects of medicine. By 1909 the movement had become conspicuously controversial in its relation to Christian Science, and this fact probably accounted for the question put to Freud by the interviewer. A contemporary book with an excellent chapter on the Emmanuel Movement was entitled *Mind and Health: with an Examination of Some Systems of Divine Healing,* authored by Edward E. Weaver (New York: Macmillan, 1913, 500 pp.). Weaver had obtained his Ph.D. in psychology at Clark University in 1910 under G. Stanley Hall, who contributed an Introduction to the volume.

7. See William James, *Essays in Philosophy.* Cambridge, MA: Harvard University Press, 1978, pp. 157-165, "A suggestion about mysticism." This essay was originally published in the *Journal of Philosophy, Psychology and Scientific Method,* 1910, *7,* 85-92 (no. 4, Feb. 17). An earlier discussion of this paper concerning William James's dreams was published by me in the *Journal of the History of the Behavioral Sciences,* 1970, *6,* 258-260.

8. See Frederick Hall, "An ether 'vision'," *Open Court* (December), 1909, *23,* 736-737. James was consistent in his interest in this topic. A few months after responding to Frederick Hall he wrote what was to be the last manuscript before his death in August, 1910. It appeared under the title "A pluralistic mystic," *Hibbert Journal,* 1910, *8,* 739-759, and concerned an amateur philosopher who, likewise, had inhaled ether as an anesthetic. He, however, had his mystical experience while regaining consciousness. This philosopher, Benjamin Blood, experienced a spiritual universe consisting of "a numberless many," and James therefore claimed him as a "pluralistic mystic," like himself.

9. James, 1978, *op. cit.,* p. 161.

Chapter X. A Reinterpretation of Dreams

1. William James to Mrs. Alice James, September 5, 1895. This first letter about Pauline Goldmark is, like the majority of James's letters *to* Pauline Goldmark, in the unpublished James Papers in the Houghton Library, Harvard University.

2. The quotation from William James's letter to his brother Henry is reproduced from page 242 of the annotated edition of W. James's *Talks to Teachers on Psychology.* Cambridge, MA:

Harvard University Press, 1983. The book in question was originally published in 1899.

3. See *The Letters of William James,* edited by his son Henry James. Boston: Little, Brown, 1920, vol. 2, pp. 75-77.

4. "An Adirondack Friendship: Letters of William James" by Josephine Goldmark, sister of Pauline, appeared in the *Atlantic Monthly,* 1934, *154,* September, pp. 265-272 and October, pp. 440-447.

5. Was it sheer coincidence that James referred to what was in his time the famous *Walpurgisnacht,* celebrated in Goethe's *Faust?* When Faust was being prepared by Mephistopheles to seduce the lovely Gretchen, Mephisto brought him to the Witches Kitchen. There he was fed a love potion that rejuvenated him. Had James any such free associations when, in 1894, unsuccessfully, and, then, beginning 1900, successfully, he injected himself for eight years regularly with the rejuvenating Roberts-Hawley compound? It was administered for his general well-being and also in the desperate hope that it might arrest his heart ailment. In *Faust,* a few scenes after the love potion, Mephisto's victim consorted with the demons in the revelries of *Walpurgisnacht.* Three years before July 1898 James had shown a persistent interest in demonic possession. He favorably reviewed a book on this topic by John Nevius in *The Nation* (1895). He thought the subject sufficiently relevant for modern psychopathology to use it as the topic for one of his eight Lowell lectures in 1896. That same year, in his address as President of the Society for Psychical Research (James, 1896a), he cited a series of ten cases of ghosts and haunted houses to stress this subject as worthy of serious psychical research (cf. *Essays in Psychical Research,* 1986, *op. cit.,* p. 135). In 1897 he lectured on demonic possession in New York at the Academy of Medicine before the Neurological Society. But in none of these presentations did James mention any kinship between demonic possession and sexual motivation. The omission—if such it was—was corrected by his brother Henry, the novelist, who in the February and April issues of *Collier's Magazine,* 1898 (a few months before William's experience of "Walpurgisnacht") published the now classic "The Turn of the Screw." This tale may psychodynamically have reflected the author's childhood

family: the boy Miles as the writer Henry, Flora as his younger sister Alice, and their elder brother William as the villain Peter Quint. It is their "unconscious" affinities that make the story so effective. That, at the denouement, Miles is demonically possessed and dies of an apparent "heart attack" (the demon being Peter Quint), is prophetic of the pseudo-coronary ailment from which Henry James suffered in 1908-1909 on the model of his brother William's organic heart condition. (Cf. Edel, 1972, 434f.) The tale abounds in "Freudian" symbolism: for example, the name Peter Quint probably alludes not only to "Peter" as *penis* but may, through "Quint," point to the fact that William James was the first of the *five* children of Henry James, Sr., and, by his dominance, was the *quintessence* of the progeny. Quintessence was defined in Pythagorean and other ancient philosophies as a fifth essence, a spiritual or ethereal one that pervades or presides over the mundane four—air, earth, fire and water—and sometimes possesses a demonic quality.

"The Turn of the Screw" is by no means unique in portraying a James family provenance at level one. A long series of similar stories by the younger brother Henry have been identified, for example, "Professor Fargo" (James, 1874) in which the seductive relationship of a spiritualistic Professor to a young deaf-mute named Miss Gifford appears to reflect William's involvement with his younger sister Alice. William at the time of the tale had entered into his second appointment to the Harvard faculty. Alice, in 1868, at age 19, had begun her prolonged hysterical invalidism (see Strouse, 1980, p. 117). Colonel Gifford, father of the victimized girl, resembles the gifted paterfamilias Henry James, Sr. That, at the end, he goes mad as a result of having lost his daughter to the villainous mesmerist is an exaggeration that fits the family melodrama of Henry's invention, and reflects the ambivalence of William's relation to his father.

An almost incredible example of the inveterate rivalry between the elder and the younger brother is found in an event of 1905 of which Edel gives a documented account. When the American Academy of Arts and Letters began selecting its distinguished membership, Henry James was elected in the second ballot, February 1905. William was elected during the fourth ballot, in May, and was notified. William brooded over the matter for a month, then in a letter dated June 17, informed the Academy secretary that he could not accept the honor. He formulated one of his chief reasons in these astonishing terms: "I am the more encouraged to this course by the fact that my younger and shallower and vainer brother is already in the Academy and that if I were there too, the other families represented might think the James influence too rank and strong." (Edel, 1972, p. 298.)

There is good ground for viewing G. Stanley Hall as a surrogate for Henry James, Jr., the younger brother of William, in the later relationship of James and Hall. Henry was born in 1843, Hall in 1844, so both were a year or more younger than the elder William. While in the beginning of Hall's apprenticeship relationship to James, there was a positive friendliness such as usually prevailed between William and Henry, Jr., in 1895, the other pole of the ambivalence in William's orientation to his younger brother came to the fore. There was, of course, a seemingly appropriate provocation by Hall. This analogy is well worth further consideration—more than is here possible.

From the ambivalent relationship of the eldest son, William, and his father, it is only a short step to the anomaly of Henry James, Sr.'s will in 1882. In it not William, the eldest son, but Henry, the younger—a settled resident of England!—was surprisingly named as the executor. That decision must surely have reflected something of the mistrust, by both parents, of William's impartiality. (Cf. Strouse, *op. cit.*, 211.)

5a. The review by William James of the Nevius book appeared in *The Nation*, 1895 (August 22), *61*, 139. The lecture on demoniacal possession is No. V in *William James on Exceptional Mental States: The 1896 Lowell Lectures*, Reconstructed by Eugene Taylor. New York: Scribner, 1983, pp. 95-114. For James's Presidential address, see *Essays in Psychical Research* by William James. Cambridge, MA: Harvard University Press, 1986, pp. 127-137. The lecture before the Neurological Society in New York is mentioned by James in a letter to Henry W. Rankin, dated February 1, 1897. See *The Letters of William James*, edited by his son Henry James. Boston: Little, Brown, 1920, p. 56.

It is arresting, and not previously noted, that Henry James's 1898 tale, "The Turn of the Screw," which clearly included the theme of demonic possession, appeared soon after William James's repeated expressions of favorable interest in that subject-matter (during the period 1895-1897).

6. The two quotations—the omitted portion of James's letter to Alice and the appended comment by his son Henry—are from the holograph of the letter of July 9, 1898 in the James Papers at Houghton Library, Harvard University.

7. The book mentioned by James to Pauline Goldmark was *Talks to Teachers on Psychology*, published in April 1899.

8. The essay, "On a certain blindness in human beings," was included in *Talks to Teachers on Psychology*. The quoted portions appear on pp. 138-139 in the 1983 (reprint) edition, *op. cit.*

9. This revealing letter about Pauline Goldmark to James's friend F. C. S. Schiller at Oxford was published only recently in *William James: Selected Unpublished Correspondence 1885-1910*, edited by F. J. D. Scott. Columbus: Ohio State University Press, 1986. The letter appears on pages 186-188 and is dated May 19, 1899.

10. William James to Pauline Goldmark, Bad-Nauheim, August 12, 1899 (*The Letters of William James*, edited by his son Henry James, *op. cit.*, vol. II, pp. 95-96.) James also described his misadventure in an (unpublished) letter to his brother Henry in early August 1899, in which he said that this experience resulted in "a very much worse condition of the cardiac organ, with entirely new symptoms." (Cf. James Papers.)

11. These letters for the period January 4-February 13, 1906 are from the unpublished William James Papers at Houghton Library, Harvard University. James's Diary is among these same papers.

12. See *Essays in Philosophy, op. cit.* It is to this 1978 edition that the page citations in the text refer.

13. Though, as mentioned, James does not describe the content of the dreams in any detail or offer a narrative account of them, he does mention, in passing, a few particulars, two of which suggest possible sources. He says of the first dream that it was an elaborate one dealing with "lions, and tragic." Was W. J. remembering the 1894 tale of his brother Henry called "The Death of the Lion"

which dealt with the death of a literary lion—a lionized writer who was terminally ill? Later in the paragraph W. J. stated that another of the dreams concerned "trying on a coat" and, again, there is a possible relevant source: a published dream of Freud in which just such an action occurs in the middle of it when the dreamer tries on a long coat that seems not to fit. This is the "Three Fates" dream in Freud's *The Interpretation of Dreams,* published in 1900 [1899]. Latently, as Freud revealed in his associations, this dream touched on the theme of death—via the Three Fates—and recalled to him the thought of "owing a death to Nature." These words are a variant by Lawrence Sterne in *Tristram Shandy* of a remark in Shakespeare's *Henry IV.*

14. The suggestion that there was a connection with his heart ailment when James suffered from serious gout at Stanford for almost two weeks is supported by a statement in the James biography by G. W. Allen. Describing James's return from Europe shortly before his death in 1910, Allen wrote: "By the time the motor reached Chocorua William's feet were badly swollen—the first evidence that his 'heart failure' had become so acute that the fluids were now accumulating in his body." See G. W. Allen, *William James,* 1967, *op. cit.,* p. 490.

15. See Freud, *Standard Edition,* 1957, *11,* 37.

16. See M. Prince, *The Dissociation of a Personality.* New York: Longmans, Green, 1905. Also S. Rosenzweig, "Sally Beauchamp's career: a psychoarchaeological key to Morton Prince's classic case of multiple personality," *Social and General Psychology Monographs,* 1987, *113,* 5-60.

17. Letter of Alice James to Pauline Goldmark, September 14, 1910. James Papers, Houghton Library, Harvard University.

18. A careful and illuminating discussion of the relationship between William James and his wife Alice from the courtship in 1876 to the end of William's life in 1910 is available in Chapter 7, "Tragical Marriage," of *William James: The Center of His Vision* by D. W. Bjork, New York: Columbia University Press, 1988. (See especially pp. 96-101.) That biographer is the first who had access and made detailed critical use of the over 1400 letters James wrote to Alice over the 34 years of their association. As Bjork

explains in his Preface, James's "intellectual-emotional dependence on his wife has been underplayed" by biographers, partly through lack of access to their correspondence until 1980. As he indicates, these letters shed light on many aspects of W. J.'s life and thought, especially on his continuous health problems, particularly those associated with his heart condition in the period 1898-1910.

19. See *The Varieties of Religious Experience: A Study in Human Nature,* first published in New York by Longmans, Green in 1902; and *Pragmatism: A New Name for Some Old Ways of Thinking,* first published by Longmans, Green in 1907.

20. See Chapter V, notes 42 and 43 and the accompanying text discussion.

21. W. J.'s 10 or 11 visits to Lydia E. Pinkham, "The Venus of Medicine," are colorfully described to his sister on February 5, 1887 (see G. W. Allen, *op. cit.,* 1967, 287-288). The Roberts-Hawley testicular-lymph compound, which James shared with his Swiss friend Théodore Flournoy, is described in detail in *The Letters of William James and Théodore Flournoy, op. cit.,* pp. 206-207. The treatments by Dr. James Ralph Taylor and by L. C. Strang are mentioned continuously in James's Diary of 1908-1909.

Chapter XI.   Aftermath (First Part)

1. *Boston Evening Transcript,* Saturday, September 11, 1909, Part III, p. 3, col. 1-2.

2. Letter of James to Flournoy in *The Letters of William James and Théodore Flournoy,* R. C. LeClair (Ed.). Madison, WI: University of Wisconsin Press, 1966, p. 224. See also Note 6, Chap. IX.

3. *Worcester Telegram,* Saturday, September 11, 1909, p. 4, col. 3-4.

4. The importance to Jung of his honorary degree, received at the early age of 34, was displayed in a new printing of his letterhead. He used it in writing to Freud on June 2, 1910. (See facsimile included in the *Freud/Jung Letters,* opposite p. 325.)

Jung underlined the LL.D. printed after his name and added an exclamation point.

5. *Worcester Telegram, op. cit.,* col. 1.

6. Ibid.

7. All the lectures in psychology, with some of those in pedagogy, appeared in the *American Journal of Psychology,* 1910, *21,* 181-282. The English translation of Jung's three lectures was by A. A. Brill. In quoting from Jung's third lecture, in the text the translation by Brill has been followed with occasional stylistic revisions. These lectures in psychology and pedagogy were issued in a separate brochure entitled *Lectures and Addresses Delivered before the Departments of Psychology and Pedagogy in Celebration of the Twentieth Anniversary of the Opening of Clark University, September 1909,* edited by G. Stanley Hall and published by Clark University, Worcester, Mass., 1910. It opened with an Introduction by Hall followed by a list of the 29 lecturers and the honorary degrees awarded them by all the concerned departments. Hall also published lectures on pedagogy in the current *Pedagogical Seminary,* 1910, *17.*

At least three other collections of lectures resulted from the celebration: *Chemical Addresses Delivered at the Celebration of the Twentieth Anniversary of Clark, in September 1909,* by Theodore W. Richards, et. al. Published jointly by Clark University, Worcester, Mass. and the American Chemical Society, 1911; *Lectures Delivered at the Celebration of the Twentieth Anniversary of Clark University under the Auspices of the Department of Physics* by V. Volterra, et al. Published by Clark University, Worcester, Mass., 1912; and from the lectures on history a book appeared: *China and the Far East,* George E. Blakeslee, Editor. New York: Crowell, 1910.

8. Chase's subsequent distinguished career in higher education, including the presidency of several leading universities, is described in a biography by Louis R. Wilson, the Librarian of Clark University, who had earlier served as Hall's first biographer. Cf. *Harry Woodburn Chase.* Chapel Hill: University of North Carolina Press, 1960.

9. See N. G. Hale, Jr. (Ed.) *James Jackson Putnam and Psychoanalysis.* Cambridge, MA: Harvard University Press, 1971.

10. A recent historical account of "Putnam Camp" was published by Nancy Lee in *Adirondack Life,* 1980, Nov.-Dec., 42-46. It traces the origin of the camp (the Beede family) through various vicissitudes up to the time of writing when it still existed with the same folksy "flavor and community life" it always had. Among other interesting details there is mention of the fact (p. 44) that "Dr. William James, one of the original owners, returned for many summers to the delights of Putnam Camp even after he had sold his share to James Putnam in 1880." It would therefore appear that when Freud and his confreres visited there in 1909 James was no longer one of the owners, but it is also evident that he had been visiting it and its vicinity continuously for 30 years.

11. See "Freud and the porcupine" by G. E. Gifford. *Harvard Medical Alumni Bulletin,* March-April, 1972, 28-31. This account of Freud's sojourn at the Putnam Camp in 1909 not only describes the cabins, including The Chatterbox, at which the European party lodged, but sheds light on Freud's jest about coming to America to see a porcupine. This wish was fulfilled when, on a hike, he found a dead one. Gifford traces the jest to a footnote in one of Freud's works citing a parable of Schopenhauer about the porcupines' dilemma: because of their quills, they were prevented from crowding together beyond a certain mean distance as a protection against the cold.

12. See pp. 23-24 in N. G. Hale, Jr. (Ed.), *James Jackson Putnam and Psychoanalysis.* Cambridge, MA: Harvard University Press, 1971. Not only is Freud's letter to his family reproduced there but, as the Introduction by Hale explains, the many-sided relationships of Putnam with contemporary figures in psychoanalysis and psychopathology are illuminated by this volume.

13. *Addresses on Psycho-Analysis* by J. J. Putnam, with a Preface by Sigmund Freud. London: International Psychoanalytical Press, 1921. This volume not only includes nearly all Putnam's contributions to the topic but is concluded with an extensive obituary (and bibliography by Ernest Jones). Significantly, it omits Putnam's first paper on Freud's psychoanalysis, an

unfavorable evaluation included in the first volume of the newly founded *Journal of Abnormal Psychology,* 1906, of which Morton Prince was owner and editor.

14. At first glance it may appear that Freud is overreaching when (p. 111) he calls Putnam the first American to interest himself in psychoanalysis. However, he may have had in mind the very early contribution in which Putnam refers, without giving a specific reference, to the work on hysteria by Breuer and Freud. Putnam's paper, though published in 1895, clearly reflects a knowledge of the preliminary communication on hysteria published in 1893 because the paper was presented at a meeting in Boston on March 4, 1895 before the book *Studies on Hysteria* by Breuer and Freud had been published. Putnam's presentation appeared under the title "Remarks on the psychical treatment of neuresthenia," *Boston Medical and Surgical Journal,* 1895, *132,* No. 21, 505-511.

15. The first English translation of Freud's essays on sex appeared as No. 7 in the *Nervous and Mental Disease Monograph Series* as follows: *Three Contributions to the Theory of Sex* by Prof. Sigmund Freud, LL.D. [sic], translated by A. A. Brill, M.D. with Introduction by James J. Putnam, M.D. New York and Washington: Nervous and Mental Disease Publishing Co., 1910. This citation specifically reflects Freud's participation at the Clark conference by indicating his honorary degree. The only earlier book by Freud published in English, *Selected Papers on Hysteria and Other Psychoneuroses,* was also translated by A. A. Brill and appeared on September 30, 1909. It constituted No. 4 in the same series.

16. See Hale, *James Jackson Putnam and Psychoanalysis, op. cit.,* pp. 39, 125-132.

17. See "Proceedings of the Eighteenth Annual Meeting of the American Psychological Association, Boston, December 29, 30 and 31, 1909," in *Psychological Bulletin,* 1910, *7,* 37f. See especially, re Freud, pp. 44-46. Cf. also Part Two, in Letters 23 H and 24 F.

18. The paper by Sidis also appeared in the *Journal of Abnormal Psychology,* owned and edited by Morton Prince. It was published in vol. 5, the December-January 1910-1911 issue.

19. See E. Jones, *The Life and Work of Sigmund Freud.* New York: Basic Books, 1955, vol. 2, Chapter 3.

20. An English translation (abridged) of the German original is available in *Final Contributions to the Problems and Methods of Psychoanalysis* by S. Ferenczi. New York: Basic Books, 1955, 299-307.

21. Ferenczi, ibid., p. 307.

22. See J. C. Burnham, *Psychoanalysis and American Medicine: 1894-1918.* Also *American Psychoanalysis: Origins and Development,* edited by J. M. Quen and E. T. Carlson. New York: Brunner/Mazel, 1978.

23. Some of the essential information regarding Hall's activity in this connection was derived from correspondence with Dr. Arcangelo R. T. D'Amore, Chairman, Committee on History and Archives of the American Psychoanalytic Association. A survey of the formation of "American Psycho-analytic Organizations, 1910-1917" is available in *Freud and the Americans* by N. G. Hale, Jr. New York: Oxford, 1971, 313-331.

24. An illuminating article in this context is by Samuel W. Hamilton, "Notes on the History of the American Psychopathological Association," *Journal of Nervous and Mental Disease,* 1945, *102,* 30-53.

Chapter XII.   Aftermath (Second Part)

1. *F/J Letters,* Jung to Freud, October 14, 1909, p. 250.

2. S. Freud, Great is Diana of the Ephesians, *Standard Edition,* 1956, *12,* 342-344.

3. Goethe's poem is available in *Goethe's Werke.* Herausgegeben im Auftrage des Grossherzogin Sophie von Sachsen. 2. Band. Weimar: Herman Böhlau, 1888, pp. 195-196. Notes fully elucidating the relationship of the poem to the Goethe/Jacobi relationship may be found in *Goethe's Gedichte.* Zweiter Theil. Mit Einleitung und Anmerkungen von G. von Loeper. Berlin: Verlag von Gustav Hempel, 1883, pp. 428-430. An English

translation of this poem, not otherwise readily available, together with an excellent discussion of its significance will be found in Paul Carus, *Goethe: Special Consideration of his Philosophy.* Chicago: Open Court Publishing Co., 1915, pp. 208-211. From that discussion it becomes clear that Goethe wrote the poem by early 1812 and referred to it in correspondence with Jacobi on March 10 of that year.

4. See *Freud/Jung Letters,* Jung to Freud, December 18, 1912, p. 535. Freud's response, January 3, 1913, ibid., pp. 538-539.

5. The earliest detailed discussion of the Freud/Jung break is found in the biography of Freud by E. Jones, *op. cit.,* vol. 2, 137-151. The crucial importance of Jung's treatise on the concept of libido is there stressed, and it makes clear that this doctrinal difference eventually led Freud to sever his relationship with Jung. Jones also traces the various stages of the dissension that followed, including the events of the 1913 International Congress of Psychoanalysis and, finally, Jung's resignation in 1914 as president of the International Association. A shorter, more recent discussion is available in *Freud: The Man and the Cause* by R. W. Clark. New York: Random House, 1980, pp. 316-338. Clark gives a detailed chronology of the history of the Freud/Jung relationship. Among other matters he brings out the role of Emma Jung, "the perceptive wife," who recognized signs of the coming storm in letters that she wrote to Freud in the fall of 1911 (see *Freud/Jung Letters*). He dwells on the part played by Jung's reception in America on trips after the Clark conference. Freud's account in his *The History of the Psychoanalytic Movement,* a draft of which he had completed in March 1914, is described. He carries his account to the summer of 1914 when the break was completed. Biographers of Jung, particularly those that have appeared since the *Freud/Jung Letters* were published, have added significantly to the picture of the dissension and eventual outcome. Notable here for its forthrightness is *C. G. Jung: The Haunted Prophet* by P. J. Stern. New York: Braziller, 1976, chapter 7, "The Break with Freud." A more recent work is: *Freud and Jung: Years of Friendship, Years of Loss* by Linda Donn. New York: Scribner, 1989. From research in several archival sources and from conversations of the author with Carl Jung's son Franz, she includes many previously unknown details,

e.g., the revelation that after the break Dr. Jung was so emotionally disturbed that he slept with a gun by his bed (p. 174). She also quotes Freud's letter to Putnam (July 8, 1915) in which Freud referred to Jung's "religious-ethical crisis" accompanied at the very same time by "lies, brutality and anti-Semitic condescension toward me" (ibid.). Also significant is *Intimate Friends, Dangerous Rivals: The Turbulent Relationship between Freud and Jung* by D. Schultz. Los Angeles: Jeremy Tarcher, 1990.

6. See Freud/Abraham, *A Psycho-Analytic Dialogue, op. cit.,* p. 186.

7. N. G. Hale, Jr. *James, Jackson Putnam and Psychoanalysis, op. cit.,* p. 189.

8. See S. Freud, "From the history of an infantile neurosis" (1918), *Standard Edition,* 1955, *17,* 112-113n. It is remarkable that, though Hall was cited in this long note and the argument regarding castration anxiety was rejected, Freud suppressed the name of Adler as the source of Hall's preference!

9. A detailed documentary survey of the relationship between G. Stanley Hall and Alfred Adler was published by Ansbacher in 1971. (Ansbacher, H. L., "Alfred Adler and G. Stanley Hall: Correspondence and General Relationship," *Journal of the History of the Behavioral Sciences,* 1971, 7, 337-352.) In this article not only the relevant publications by Hall, in particular those on fear and anger, were discussed, but an exchange of correspondence between Adler and Hall from April 1914 to November 1921 was reproduced. Moreover, according to a letter from Freud to Ferenczi (May 10, 1914), Hall intended to invite Adler to give some lectures in the United States. (Cf. Jones, *op. cit.,* vol. 2, 134, 471.) This fact is confirmed by Hall's letter to Freud (31 H, Part Two, September 24, 1923) in which Hall mentions that some years ago he had thought of bringing Adler to the United States "to give a few lectures." The plan was apparently abandoned because of the outbreak of World War I. As Ansbacher stated, Freud was sensitive to this development because by the invitation to Adler, Hall appeared to be abandoning Freud. And Adler did, indeed interpret Hall's interest along these lines. In an article published in 1930, Adler wrote, "This was also the time [1914] when our great Stanley Hall turned away from Freud and ranged himself with the

supporters of Individual Psychology. . ." (Cf. Adler, A., "Individual psychology," in *Psychologies of 1930,* edited by Carl Murchison. Worcester: Clark University Press, 1930, p. 398.) It is obvious that Adler, like Freud, thought in exclusionary terms. Neither of them appreciated what Hall in his "synthetic psychology" was attempting to accomplish. Later, in writing to Freud in 1923, Hall clearly expressed his eclectic orientation and made it clear that he did not think of his interest in Adler or others as in any way diminishing the revolutionary contribution that Freud had made to psychology. An illuminating instance of Hall's synthetic approach is found in his short article on anger (*op. cit.,* letter 26 H, note 6). When Hall there applied the unconscious mechanisms of defense to anger, as Freud had done for sex, and stated that the same could be done for other drives such as gregariousness, he intended only to broaden the scope of the Freudian methods and mechanisms, not to deny the role of sexuality. But this position was opposed to Freud's dogma that psychoanalytic theory demanded the unqualified recognition of biological sexuality as all-pervasive. At least at this stage of Freud's thinking (around 1914), the *equal* importance of egoistic or aggression drives was seen as *resistance* that would in the end defeat the fundamental aims of psychoanalysis. The sublimation of sexual impulses was permissible but Jung's recourse to a "germinal spiritual disposition," discussed in Chapter VIII, was to Freud a repudiation of the full intent of "infantile sexuality."

10. Hall, G. S. *American Journal of Psychology,* 1915, *26,* 550-613.

11. Freud, S. (1919). *Beyond the Pleasure Principle. Standard Edition,* 1955, *18,* 7-64. Freud's involvement in superstitious predictions about his own death. His guilt about his brother Julius's death in 1858 was confessed by Freud to more than one of his confidants, particularly to Ernest Jones. He stated that his fainting attacks, two in the presence of Jung, had some roots in the early experience of his infant brother's death. In a paper by me (Rosenzweig, 1970a) this question has been considered in terms of Freud's day of death—the Day of Atonement in 1939. That Freud requested his physician, Dr. Schur, to administer the fatal doses of morphine was confirmed to me by the physician in a personal conversation (Rosenzweig, 1986, p. 55 and n. 23). Here

it is being further suggested that Freud's concept of the "death instinct" may have grown out of the same complex of guilt. He, of course, offered an impersonal, psychobiological basis to justify the concept, deriving it from various predecessors and tied it to the Hindu belief in Nirvana. But in Freud's case a diathesis seems to have resided in his own prior idioverse.

Elsewhere (Rosenzweig, 1956, p.792, n.4, p.795) the castration complex has been redefined as follows: "In its original sense the concept referred to the child's conscious or unconscious fear of the loss of the male sex organ, as a punishment for any sexual offense; in later reformulations, this complex was broadened to include loss of life in general. As employed in the present discussion the term should be construed to mean fear or anxiety—primarily unconscious—of personal extinction. The sexual context is still strongly implied since 'extinction' of sexual potency, especially in youth, is readily equated in the unconscious with loss of life generally. When the 'castration compulsion' is introduced in the latter portion of the present paper, a departure from Freudian theory is made. This novel concept, to be developed in another communication, is a recognition that the fear of castration is sometimes found neurotically interlocked with the wish for such a fate—the wish proceeding from the femininity of the male in whom such a compulsion exists. Thus conceived the castration compulsion is an aspect of human bisexuality; and it may well be asked whether it is even possible for there to be a castration complex in the negative, Freudian sense of fear, without the simultaneously existing, complementary and positive wish." Earlier, in depicting typical reactions to frustration (Rosenzweig, 1935, p. 397 n.2; p. 588 & n.1), it was postulated that there appears to be in some cases of obsessional neurosis a profound need for punishment, designated as "Nemesism." Nemesism was conceived as a counterpart or complement to Narcissism. It was construed as sometimes evoked from guilt in having caused (even accidentally) the death of others, particularly a close relative like a parent or sibling rival. In these instances an unconscious wish for the death may have been fulfilled by the death with an entailed need for condign punishment. In Greco-Roman mythology, the Erinyes or Furies similarly pursued the victim as an expression of divine justice.

A modern classical case, over and above the dramatic instances in Greek tragedy, is that of Captain Ahab, the anti-hero of Melville's *Moby Dick*. Research on the biographical model used by Melville for this character (reserved for presentation elsewhere) demonstrates that the author was depicting Ahab from this biographical source at the intermediate level of communication.

For Freud, the fear and fatal attraction of death seems to have resided in an obsessional neurosis that had roots in his infancy and was reinforced by later experiences. From that orientation of intropunitive aggression he distilled the "castration complex." This complex was, according to his formulation, a part of the Oedipus complex which he extensively employed to account for neurosis, especially in males. It is now suggested that in the latter part of Freud's life the "death instinct" had evolved as a psycho-philosophic myth. In his actual death on the Day of Atonement he acted out the conceptualization, thus verifying it.

12. Freud, S. *An Autobiographical Study. Standard Edition,* 1959, *20,* 51-52. The term "king-maker" derives from Shakespeare (*King Henry VI,* Part III, Act III, sc. 3: 157) in which the Earl of Warwick is addressed as an "impotent and shameless . . . proud setter up and puller down of Kings." This 15th-century Earl was sometimes called "the last of the Barons" and was regarded as the ultimate representative of the old Norman, self-enhancing chivalry.

13. Freud published "On the History of the Psycho-Analytic Movement" in 1914; it is available in translation in *Standard Edition,* 1957, *14.* See, in particular, page 31.

14. For Boring's appraisal, see *A History of Experimental Psychology, op. cit.,* note 28 for Chap. V, above.

15. This "former patient" was demonstrated by Siegfried Bernfeld (1946) to have been Freud himself. The protocol was disguised to conceal private details not only about himself, but about other still living persons. There is, however, a more historically pertinent aspect of this disclosure. Since Freud states that the recollection involving the field of yellow flowers was instigated by the patient's knowledge of the Henri research, is Freud not saying that he himself was thus stimulated in 1895-1897? In a sense, then, Freud's "Screen Memories" is not only a confession

of childhood sexual play but of the impetus given to Freud by the Henri inquiry of 1895.

As noted above, one of the journals in which Henri published his questionnaire was the *Révue philosophique* for 1895. That periodical was apparently read by Freud habitually—it was one of the early "psychological" journals. At any rate, several articles published in that journal were cited by Freud in his *The Interpretation of Dreams* (1899). These appeared in the years 1894 and 1896, and one may thus infer the probability that Freud saw also the volume of 1895 in which the Henri questionnaire was published.

16. The fact that the Henri questionnaire did not appear in the *American Journal of Psychology* until January, 1896—nearly a year after it had been published in the other journals—invites the speculation that Hall may have solicited the item from Henri after seeing the questionnaire in one of the other periodicals. Hall's desire to have the questionnaire published in his journal could well have been based on his keen interest in the topic, demonstrated in his paper, a "Note on Early Memories."

17. Dr. Edward Cowles was an eminent psychiatrist, Superintendent of McLean Hospital as well as a member of the Clark Board of Trustees. He stood Hall in good stead in the crisis of 1892. It was through Hall's recommendation that Dr. Cowles had been appointed to the Board in 1889 after the untimely death of Dr. Joseph Sargent of Worcester. Sargent was a friend and business partner of Jonas Clark and was the only trustee with scientific training and experience. When Sargent died just before the opening of the University, it was natural to replace him by another physician scientist. Hall, in his recommendation was doubtless influenced by the fact that Cowles had attended Johns Hopkins University in a preceding summer to study with Hall while he was Professor of Psychology there. In later years Dr. Cowles served Clark University in various other capacities, often in collaboration with Hall. Dr. Adolf Meyer, pathologist at the Worcester State Hospital, had assisted Hall in the teaching of psychopathology at Clark by demonstrating patients at the Hospital. When Meyer left Worcester in 1902, Dr. Cowles took his place in the teaching. (For biography of Cowles, cf. Abbot, 1919, and American Neurological Association, 1924.)

18. The foregoing information is from the archival papers of Dorothy Livingston obtained from the Naval Academy, as previously mentioned. In her book, Livingston mistakenly described Dr. Cowles as Chairman of the Board of Trustees but her notes, quite rightly, do not so designate him. However, they plainly establish his leadership role in the negotiations.

19. The cited article by Barnes (1925) was largely motivated by the author's participation in a second faculty rebellion at Clark University (*op. cit.,* pp. 286-288). That conflict occurred in 1921-1922 and came to a head at a lecture given at Clark by the radical socialist Scott Nearing, on March 14, 1922. An invitation had been extended by students of the Liberal Club; the topic was "The Making of Public Opinion."

Like the conflict in 1892, a clash between the new President Wallace Atwood, Hall's successor, and several members of the faculty, was involved. Atwood had been having problems with them since his appointment in 1920, allegedly on the grounds that, representing the interests of the business and industrial elite at the expense of the average citizen, he had regimented and deprived the faculty, especially in the social sciences. Barnes maintained that Atwood had acted thus, in part, so as to expand his own department of geography.

At the culmination of the conflict, Atwood, in person, interrupted Nearing's lecture. He did so when the speaker began to criticize higher education in America as being controlled by university administrations and trustees who furthered the goals of the leisure class. The professors were expected to mold the opinion of the students accordingly. The President loudly demanded that the lecture be stopped and, when opposed by the students, had the janitor put out the lights in the hall.

The psychologist, E. G. Boring, serving in his first academic post, was then also a member of the Clark faculty, and was drawn into the conflict. As a result of his involvement, Boring left Clark for a professorship at Harvard. (Cf. Boring, 1961, pp. 35-38.) In his autobiography, Scott Nearing eloquently describes the episode (1972, pp. 79-82). Saltmarsh, Nearing's biographer, provides a detailed and graphic account including the ironic bit that among the audience of 300 students and faculty the ex-president of Clark

University, G. Stanley Hall, was present (1991, pp. 169-171). The Nearing episode occupied a prominent place in Upton Sinclair's bold critique of American higher education, *The Goose Step*, (1922).

20. A *General Introduction to Psychoanalysis* by Sigmund Freud, with a Preface by G. Stanley Hall. New York: Boni & Liveright, 1920. This volume was the first English translation of Freud's 1916-1917 Vienna University lectures on psychoanalysis. These are now available in final form in *Standard Edition*, 1963, volumes 15-16.

21. Edward L. Bernays, *Biography of an Idea: Memoirs of Public Relations Counselor Edward L. Bernays*. New York: Simon & Schuster, 1965. See Chap. 18 "Correspondence with Freud," pp. 252-276.

22. The final letter from Hall to Freud in 31 H in Part Two of this volume, dated September 24, 1923.

23. In connection with Freud's report on Hall, the cited article by Lesley Diehl (1986) is remarkably relevant. She examines the paradox between Hall's opposition to coeducation and his support of higher education for women. Her resolution of the paradox is too complex for brief restatement here, but it is clear on any basis that Hall, champion of motherhood, was, nevertheless, one of the first among leaders of education to encourage and abet the higher education of women. In that context it has often been overlooked that the Clark Board of Trustees at its meeting of November 14, 1900, less than six months after the death of the founder Jonas Clark, "voted that the University will admit candidates for the Degree of Doctor of Philosophy, and will confer that degree without regard to the distinction of sex." It should be recalled that the founder had adamantly opposed the use of his money for the education of women. This progressive action so soon after the death must therefore have reflected the initiative of G. Stanley Hall. Koelsch, the historian of Clark University, in discussing the education of women at Clark was aware of this early progressive action (see Koelsch, 1987, pp. 72-73) but he failed to recognize Hall's part in it since he states, to the contrary, that Hall "In his autobiog-

raphy . . . would have us believe that Clark University had always been open to women students and he [Hall] had been their champion against the trustees," (ibid., p. 74).

Another relevant point which concerns not Hall vis-à-vis Jonas Clark, but Hall vis-à-vis Freud, in respect to women is Freud's stress on female "penis envy," a view that Hall nowhere appears to have shared. While Freud regarded the girl's wish for a child as a compensation for the missing penis, Hall more positively stressed the maternal drive. But they did share a common stress on motherhood as one basis for the future of the race. The issue is still moot among feminists and their critics.

24. See Nathan G. Hale, Jr. *Freud and the Americans, op. cit.*

25. Ernest Jones, who was with Freud for a considerable part of the American visit, has discussed Freud's largely negative attitude toward America resulting from this visit, in the biography *The Life and Work of Sigmund Freud, Years of Maturity 1901-1919,* vol. 2, 59-62. A later and wide-ranging discussion of Freud's anti-American sentiments is found in *Freud: A Life for Our Time* by Peter Gay. New York: Doubleday, 1988, 562-570. In particular, Gay stresses Freud's view that America was "governed by the dollar." He does not, however, confine himself to this point and cites numerous remarks by Freud about America, mostly unfavorable.

26. Anna Freud-Bernays, *Erlebtes.* Vienna: Kommissionsverlag der Buchhandlung Heller, n.d., pp. 176. Mrs. Anna Bernays also published a brief article, "My Brother, Sigmund Freud" in the *American Mercury,* 1940 (November), *51,* 335-342.

27. See "Symposium on Genetic Psychology," *American Journal of Orthopsychiatry,* 1951, *21,* 471-522. Anna Freud not only participated in the symposium but gave a popular lecture, Saturday, April 22, on the topic, "Early Sleeping and Feeding Problems." On Friday afternoon she held a press conference for reporters of leading Worcester, Boston and New York newspapers.

28. The award of the degree of Doctor of Laws *(honoris causa)* to Anna Freud on April 22, including the introductory remarks of

Dr. Werner, is described in the *International Journal of Psycho-analysis,* 1950, *31,* 297.

Chapter XIII.   Synoptic Chronicle of Events

1. The sources of many of the items in this Chronicle are indicated in the Introduction, "In the Beginning . . . ."

PART TWO

The Freud/Hall Letters

Introductory Note on Provenance and Translation of the Letters

The 31 following letters, dated from 1908 to 1923, are numbered consecutively, with H or F following the numeral to identify the author of the letter by his surname initial.

Of the 17 letters by Hall, all typewritten, the earliest 13 were sent to the writer by the late Ernst Freud (Sigmund Freud Copyrights Ltd.) who made them from originals in his possession. Copies of these same letters, augmented by the letter of September 26, 1913 (26 H) and January 31, 1917 (28 H), were also received from Clark University. A copy of Hall's letter, dated June 19, 1923 (29 H), was fortunately recovered from Dr. Kempf the year before the latter's death. The final letter, dated September 24, 1923 (31 H), became available from a copy of the holograph in the Clark Archives. All Hall's letters are printed as written.

Of the 14 items by Freud, all are handwritten, 12 in German (Gothic) script and 2 in English. The first 12 of these letters came to the writer from Clark University in photocopies of the holographs together with transliterations and working translations which were apparently prepared for the use of President Hall. Of the two last letters (27 F and 30 F), the first (23 November 1913) was published in Freud's *Briefe 1873-1939* (Frankfurt am Main: Fischer Verlag, 1960) and translated as No. 166 in the English edition (*Letters of Sigmund Freud,* edited by E. L. Freud. London: Hogarth, 1961). The second (28 August 1923) derived from the collection of Robert G. Hall, the son of G. Stanley Hall. It was first published, with transliteration and translation, in an article annotated by John C. Burnham (*Psychoanalytic Quarterly,* 1960, *29,* 307-316). Copies of the holographs of these two letters came to the writer from photocopies in the collection of Ernst Freud. The peculiarities of the two English items have been retained. Transliterations of the 12 German letters have been carefully collated with the script holographs, and all translations have been made anew by the writer. The translations are as faithful as possible to the original. The punctuation of the German has naturally been altered as part of the translation, but the conventions of punctuation in the salutations and polite endings have been reproduced without change. Where underlining of words occurs in the letters of either correspondent, this indication has been translated into italics.

A concerted attempt has been made to obtain all the extant letters of Hall to Freud and of Freud to Hall. Those printed here represent the total yield. It is, of course, possible that others were written but have not survived.

The historical notes are intended to identify persons and events alluded to by the authors, to clarify contexts, and to unify the letters so that they can be read as a continuous series.

S. R.

1 H

Clark University
Worcester Massachusetts

PRESIDENT'S OFFICE   December 15, 1908.

Professor Siegmund Freud[1]
Vienna, Austria

My dear Sir:

Although I have not the honor of your personal acquaintance, I have for many years been profoundly interested in your work which I have studied with diligence, and also in that of your followers. I venture herewith to send one or two documents that may serve to identify myself.[2]

The purpose of this letter is to ask if you can come to this country and to this University the first week in next July, and give perhaps four or six lectures, either in German or English, setting forth your own views, either the substance of those already printed or something new—whatever shall seem best to you.[3]

The occasion is the twentieth Anniversary of the founding of this institution, and we hope to attract a select audience of the best American professors and students of psychology and psychiatry.[4]

Janet, who has visited this country and given a similar course of public lectures, has had a profound influence in turning the attention of our leading and especially our younger students of abnormal psychology from the exclusively somatic and neurological to a more psychological basis.[5] We believe that a concise statement of your own results and point of view would now be exceedingly opportune, and perhaps in some sense mark an epoch in the history of these studies in this country.

We are able to attach to this proposition an honorarium of four hundred dollars, or sixteen hundred Marks, to cover expenses. You will, of course, be free, after the week's engagement here, to make any others in this country.

Hoping that you may be so situated as to give us a favorable response, I am, with great respect,

Sincerely yours,
G. Stanley Hall
President.

1. This variant of Freud's given name, which persisted through the first four of Hall's letters, is intriguing. On the birth record in Freud's native Freiberg, Moravia, the name is "Sigismund," but he changed this to "Sigmund" by 1875, during his Gymnasium (high school) days. His publications from 1876 to 1908 were almost invariably signed "Sigm. Freud"—an abbreviation which perhaps made it easier for Hall to spell out the name incorrectly.

2. When, some years ago, the writer made a survey of the portion of Freud's professional library then housed as a special collection at the New York State Psychiatric Institute, he came upon three reprints of articles by G. Stanley Hall: The Jesus of history and of the Passion versus the Jesus of the Resurrection, *American Journal of Religious Psychology*, 1904, *1*, 30-64; Mental science, *Science*, 1904, n.s. *20*, 481-490; and The affiliation of psychology with philosophy and with the natural sciences, *Science*, 1906, n.s. *23*, 297-301. The second paper is a speech given by Hall at the St. Louis World's Fair. In the third, an invited address at Harvard, Freud has marginally marked three passages, and one of these stresses the dominance of unconscious over conscious processes. These pre-1908 reprints are, in all probability, the identifying "documents" referred to by Hall.

3. In view of the "postponement" (3 H) which finally brought Freud to Worcester in September, it is noteworthy that sessions were, indeed, held in July 1909. These were published under the title *Proceedings of the Child Conference for Research and Welfare, 1, 1909, Held at Clark University in Connection with the Celebration of the Twentieth Anniversary*, Worcester, Mass., July 6-10, 1909. Volume 2 of the *Proceedings* was dated June 28-July 2, 1910. (Both volumes were issued by G. E. Stechert and Co., New York City.) It thus appears that Hall's first intention was for Freud to present his lectures during that part of the anniversary celebration that did occur in July, 1909. When Freud declined, as did others who were invited for the same month, the decision was made to hold a second, major portion of

the celebration in September not connected with the Child Conference. Did Hall think of Freud's pioneer contribution as primarily concerned with the development of personality in childhood, a field of study that Hall had singled out for special investigation early in his Clark career?

4. The word "founding" is not strictly accurate; it should be "opening." Hall was writing casually and did not want to bother his correspondent with a technical distinction that had little bearing on the invitation being extended. The distinction is, however, historically significant. Clark University was founded in 1887 when its charter of incorporation was received. But it did not *open* for classes until the fall of 1889, and it is that event which was celebrated at the 10th Anniversary in 1899 and, again, at the 20th, in 1909.

5. Pierre Janet (1859-1947), the eminent French psychopathologist who was Freud's rival from almost the beginning of their respective careers.

2 F

Prof. Dr. Freud
Wien, IX. Berggasse 19.

29. Dec. 08

My esteemed Colleague

Your invitation to offer a series of lectures at your University in the first week of July is a great honor for me, but I do not know how the following difficulty can be overcome. I am a practicing physician and because of the summer habits of my countrymen, I am obliged to discontinue work from July 15 to the end of September.[1] If I were to lecture in America in the first week of July, I should have to suspend my medical work three weeks earlier than usual, which would mean a significant and irretrievable loss for me.[2] This consideration makes it impossible for me to accept your proposal.

With many thanks for the items you sent and which arrived earlier

Faithfully yours
Freud

1. This description of the Viennese summer customs and of Freud's vacation habits is confirmed, with interesting added details, in E. Jones, *Life and work of Sigmund Freud.* New York: Basic Books, 1953, vol. 1, 331f.; 1955, vol. 2, 392f.

2. Freud stresses the financial consideration exclusively. Other inducements, e.g., the subsequently offered honorary degree, were not yet in evidence. In the event, a higher honorarium was offered, but not to compensate for a loss of income from patients. The shift of the celebration to September avoided that problem. (See 3 H.)

3 H

Clark University
Worcester Massachusetts

February 16, 1909.

My dear Sir:

On December 15th I had the honor of conveying an invitation of our Board to you to be present at the celebration which we are planning for next June which, to our regret, you were obliged to decline December 29th. [1]

Our situation has changed here in two important respects. First, we have received an addition to our financial budget which enables us to increase our financial proposition to $750 (3000 Marks); and, secondly, the date of our celebration has been changed from June to the week beginning September 6th.

In view of these two modifications of our programme, I venture to write you once more in the hope that you may be induced to spend a few days that week with us and give us a few informal lectures, and to allow us to bestow upon you an honorary degree.

I am, with great respect,

Very truly yours,
G. Stanley Hall
President.

1. The inconsistencies of this letter as compared to 1 H (regarding the proposed time of the celebration and the so-called "postponement") are explained in 1 H, note 3.

4 F

Prof. Dr. Freud
Wien, IX. Berggasse 19.

28. 2. 09

Most esteemed Colleague

Your letter of the 16th brought me a very happy surprise. The postponement of the celebration to the second week in September makes it possible for me to accept your invitation without substantial sacrifice to me and after I have been able to recuperate for several weeks from the year's work. [1] I shall therefore come and I also gratefully accept the increase for my travel expenses as well as the honor which you intend to confer upon me. [2]

The annual report of Clark University has reached me. In the next few days the just published Second Series of my Shorter Papers on the Theory of the Neuroses will be sent to you. [3]

With great esteem
Faithfully yours
Freud

1. The "postponement" of the Conference to the second week of September was occasioned not only by Freud's declination but by that of at least two other invited participants, Wilhelm Wundt (1832-1920) and August Weismann (1834-1914), who had declined without conditions.

2. The degree actually conferred was that of Doctor of Laws. Freud had never before received an honorary degree nor did he, in fact, ever receive another.

3. This monograph was: *Sammlung kleiner Schriften zur Neurosenlehre. Zweite Folge.* Leipzig und Wien: F. Deuticke, 1909. It was the second volume of Freud's collected papers in German; the first group had appeared in 1906. The earlier volume included his papers from 1893 to 1906, with some omissions; the second brought together articles published between 1905 and 1909. Freud sent Hall the volume which had just come off the press.

5 F

Prof. Dr. Freud
Wien, IX. Berggasse 19.

4. 4. 09

Dear Colleague

Forgive me for troubling you about an uncertainty connected with your invitation to Clark University in September. The question concerns the coordination of schedules. I could travel on the 21st of August by the Austro-American Line from Trieste, which would be very convenient for me from my summer location, and it would also have the advantage of the beautiful tour through the Mediterranean.[1] It has been confirmed that this route requires only fourteen days so that I could arrive in New York on the 4th of September. However, an additional day or two on any such journey cannot be ruled out. I should naturally not like to arrive late. Do you think, in the light of the program for the University celebration, which is not yet known to me, that I can risk embarking on a route with such a schedule? May I request that you kindly advise me soon since I must make a reservation before the end of this month.

Respectfully and faithfully yours
Freud

1. Freud had hoped to extend his summer vacation by the route here outlined. A Mediterranean tour always appealed to him. He apparently tried for a reservation on a ship leaving from Trieste and calling at Palermo (E. Jones, *Life and work of Sigmund Freud*. New York: Basic Books, 1955, vol. 2, p. 54). This route, requiring 14 days, would have brought him to New York by about September 4, only a day or two before the beginning of the Conference (see 7 H). For good reasons, reinforced by his "travel phobia" (Jones, ibid., vol. 1, pp. 13, 181, 305) which, in its residual form, impelled him to arrive at railway stations long before the scheduled departure time, Freud chose a safer, alternative route. It took only one week but it left Europe on the very same date (August 21; see 7 H, note 1). The Mediterranean portion of his vacation was replaced by a pre-Worcester week of sightseeing in New York and vicinity.

CLARK UNIVERSITY
WORCESTER MASSACHUSETTS

PRESIDENT'S OFFICE

April 13, 1909.

Professor Siegmund Freud,
    K. K. University,
        Vienna, Austria.

My dear Professor Freud:

I need not tell you that we received your acceptance
of our invitation for next September with great pleasure,
and we are pushing our plans ahead as rapidly as possible,
and will inform you from time to time of their progress.
We have given out no notices as yet; nevertheless, in some
way the news of your coming has reached a number of
people in this country who have been profoundly interested
in your work and have written us expressing their pleasure
and their desire to hear whatever you may have to say to
us.

I am sending you a printed report of our Decennial
Celebration, ten years ago; also our latest register.

I am, with great respect,

Very truly yours,

G Stanley Hall
President.

Facsimile of letter from Hall to Freud, April 13, 1909,
regarding Freud's acceptance

6 H

Clark University
Worcester Massachusetts

April 13, 1909.

My dear Professor Freud:

I need not tell you that we received your acceptance of our invitation for next September with great pleasure, and we are pushing our plans ahead as rapidly as possible, and will inform you from time to time of their progress. We have given out no notices as yet; nevertheless, in some way the news of your coming has reached a number of people in this country who have been profoundly interested in your work and have written us expressing their pleasure and their desire to hear whatever you may have to say to us. [1]

I am sending you a printed report of our Decennial Celebration, ten years ago; also our latest register.

I am, with great respect,

Very truly yours,
G. Stanley Hall
President.

1. Two instances have survived. Letters from and to Dr. Isador Coriat (1875-1943), a pioneer Boston psychoanalyst, and a similar exchange between Ernest Jones (1879-1958) and Hall, all dated April 1909, are in *Hall Papers 1909.* Coriat left a posthumously published memoir of reminiscences, including the impact of Freud's 1909 American visit (*Psychoanalytic Review,* 1945, *32,* 1-8). His continuing relationship with Hall in the cause of psychoanalysis in America is shown in his obituary of GSH in the *Internationale Zeitschrift für Psychoanalyse,* 1924, *10,* 201-203. Jones, at that time located in Toronto, was prominently present at the Clark Conference. He later became Freud's official biographer.

7 H

Clark University
Worcester Massachusetts

April 15, 1909.

My dear Professor Freud:

I wrote you two days before your favor of April 4th was received. In response thereto would say that our exercises begin Monday, September 6th, and continue several days. If your steamer from Trieste is not delayed, you would of course have ample time. Doubtless the Steamship Company would furnish you with a list of the time occupied during the past year by their vessels in making the voyage; and if they would do so, you would of course be able to estimate the chance of great delay. [1]

We are hoping, as I intimated, that you will be here in time to give us a few addresses before our session closes, which will probably be Friday night, September 10th, after which nothing could be done. Of course, we should rather like to have you begin early in the week; but if you were one or even two days late, it would not be very vital.

I am,

Very truly yours,
G. Stanley Hall

1. Freud took the tactful hint and changed his route. He and his traveling companions, Ferenczi and Jung, reached New York from Bremen, Sunday evening, August 29 on the vessel *George Washington,* North German Lloyd Line. The group arrived in Worcester, after several days of sightseeing in and about New York, on Sunday, September 5, the day before the Conference began.

8 F

Prof. Dr. Freud
Wien, IX. Berggasse 19.

2 May 09

Dear Colleague

I am gratefully indebted to you for the two letters of the 13th and 15th of April and for the information contained in the latter. I hope to arrive in good time for the beginning of the week of festivities.

That my visit in Worcester has aroused the interest of many individuals is, on the one hand, very gratifying to me, but on the other it increases my concern as to whether I can succeed in offering something that will come up to these expectations.

I am most warmly and faithfully
Yours
Freud

9 F

POSTAL CARD

WIEN 25. 5. 09

Freud acknowledges with thanks the receipt of the Report of your founding celebration ten years ago, 1899,[1] and is eagerly looking forward to his own visit.[2]

1. *Clark University 1889-1899. Decennial Celebration.* Worcester, Mass. Printed for the University, 1899. This earlier celebration served, in part, as a model for the vigentennial of 1909.

2. It is noteworthy that after this postal card, dated May 25, 1909, there is no correspondence between Freud and Hall until August 9, 1909 (10 H). This interval of over two months seems surprisingly long in view of the fact that during this very time Jung's participation in the Clark Conference was being arranged. In the meantime Freud had changed from Trieste (Austro-American Line) to Bremen (North

German Lloyd) for his departure on August 21, and Jung, after being invited to Clark early in June, booked passage on the same ship *(George Washington)*. Another reason for inferring that one or more letters are missing around this time concerns Freud's change in travel plans. On May 23 he wrote to Karl Abraham about this change (Freud & Abraham, 1965, p. 80). Though Hall was quite reassuring and extraordinarily accommodating about the earlier plan, Freud knew that he was running a serious risk by planning to reach New York only two days before the Conference was scheduled to begin in Worcester on September 6. He would naturally have informed Hall about the change, but there is no such letter extant. (See Letter 5 F, note 1.)

10 H

Clark University
Worcester Massachusetts

August 9, 1909. [1]

My dear Professor Freud,

I am writing you now merely to say that I hope you will be my guest as long as you can stay in this city. It would be well to take a carriage from the Worcester station to my house, 94 Woodland Street, where you will find your rooms in readiness. Should Madame Freud accompany you, it would give Mrs. Hall and myself great additional pleasure. We not long since entertained M. and Madame Raymond Cajal of Madrid. [2]

Some guests prefer the liberty of a hotel to being entertained at a private house. Should that be your choice, we will provide the best rooms we are able at the Hotel Standish on Main Street, which is the best in the neighborhood of the University.

If you have already determined on what the general or the special topics of your lectures are to be or how many lectures, or anything else you desire to send concerning them in advance, we can use it to advantage in our announcements. There is a wide and deep interest in your coming to this country, and you will have the very best experts within a wide radius.

I am

Very respectfully yours,
G. Stanley Hall

1. This letter failed to reach Freud before he left Europe and was forwarded to his hotel in New York, and there he answered it (13 F).

2. Mrs. Freud did not accompany her husband. Santiago Ramón y Cajal (1852-1934) was the distinguished neurophysiologist who was one of the five honored lecturers at the previous celebration in 1899. The Cajals were not guests of Dr. and Mrs. Hall but of the Stephen Salisburys.

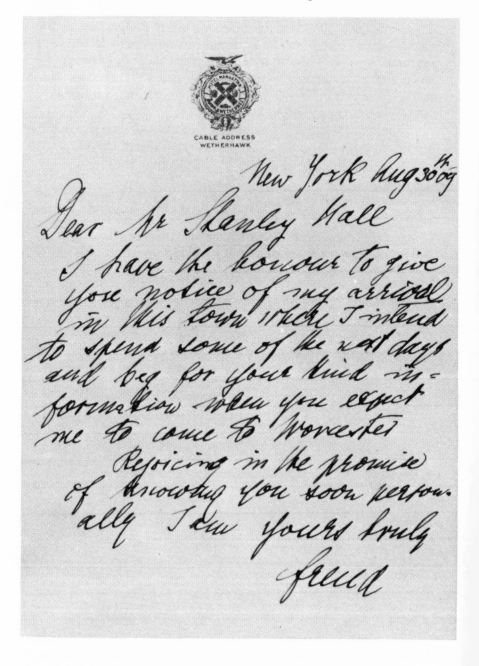

Facsimile of letter (in English) from Freud to Hall on arrival in
USA, August 30, 1909

11 F

HOTEL MANHATTAN
Cable Address
Wetherhawk

New York, Aug 30th 09

Dear Mr. Stanley Hall[1]

I have the honour to give you notice of my arrival in this town where I intend to spend some of the next days and beg for your kind information when you expect me to come to Worcester.

Rejoicing in the promise of knowing you soon personally

I am yours truly
Freud

1. Written in English, perhaps an expression of Freud's ebullience on reaching America. After arriving in New York on Sunday, August 29, the three visitors registered at the Hotel Manhattan where they stayed until September 4.

12 H

Clark University
Worcester Massachusetts

August 31, 1909.

Professor Sigmund Freud,
Hotel Manhattan,
New York City.

My dear Professor Freud,

I am very glad to learn of your arrival in New York. Our exercises here open Monday, September 6th. If you take the 9 a.m. train from New York, you will arrive in Worcester just about in season. On reaching Worcester will you kindly take a carriage for yourself and your luggage to my house, 94 Woodland Street, where I hope to have the pleasure of entertaining you during your stay here. I enclose herewith a copy of a letter which I sent sometime ago which probably has not yet reached you. If you can favor us by sending the topics of your lectures and stating whether you will speak in German or in English and how many lectures you wish to give so that we can have it a day or two in advance, it will be very agreeable to us.

Very sincerely yours,
G. Stanley Hall

13 F

HOTEL MANHATTAN
Cable Address
Wetherhawk

New York Sept 1st 09

Dear Sir[1],

Your kind letter of Aug. 9th missed me in Europe and sent back to this continent it did not become perception [sic] to me until yesterday to be revived soon after by your copy of this morning.

I heartily accept the invitation to live in your house during my stay at Worcester coming alone, and I trust I will not prove a troublesome guest.

Please present my best thanks to Mrs. Hall for her share in the invitation.

Owing to the missing of the latter [sic] aforesaid I am very sorry I could not give you information about the topics of my lectures at the time you wanted them. I hasten to tell you that I intend calling the lectures:

> "On the origin and development (growth)? of psycho-
> analysis" (Über die Entstehung ŭ Entwicklung der
> Psychoanalyse)

My English is but poor as you will have found out at this moment, so I am obliged to transfer the difficulty to the side of the hearers and talk in my native tongue. I will try to treat the subject in 5 hours.

I thank you very much for your will [sic] about the arrival. I am travelling in company with my friend Dr. Jung[2] of Zürich and two followers more (Dr. Ferenczi[3]—Budapest and Dr. Brill[4]—New York) and we might reach Worcester Sonday [sic] evening or Monday morning.

Yours truly
Freud

1. Again written in English. This time, however, Freud is also demonstrating that "my English is but poor" to explain, perhaps, why he will lecture in his "native tongue." In fact, Freud knew many languages, not only Latin and Greek, learned in high school, but French and Italian, some Spanish and far more English than he modestly asserts here. But it was characteristic of him to speak to groups spontaneously—a practice which he insisted upon for all contributors to the sessions of the Vienna Psychoanalytic Society. This fact may help explain why he did not write out his lectures, either in English or in German, in advance of the Conference.

2. This is the first mention of C. G. Jung (1875-1961) in the correspondence with Hall. The circumstances of his invitation to participate in the Clark Conference are enigmatic. No correspondence between Hall and Jung regarding the Conference survives. Freud welcomed the news from Jung about the latter's invitation but, surprisingly, no mention of this occurrence is found in any of the extant Freud/Hall letters.

That the arrangement was made late, as compared with Freud's, is clear; the first and only mention of Jung in the Minutes of the Clark Faculty meetings is under the date June 15, 1909. Yet in his auto-biography (*Memories, dreams, reflections*. New York: Pantheon Books, 1963, p. 120), Jung insists that he was invited "simultaneously" with Freud.

3. Dr. Sandor Ferenczi (1873-1933) was a Hungarian psychoanalyst who apparently first met Freud in 1908 and almost at once became one of his closest associates. Though not an invited participant (lecturer), he voluntarily accompanied Freud and played a part in the informal rehearsal of each of Freud's lectures at Clark. (See also 19 F.)

4. Dr. A. A. Brill (1874-1948), the New York psychoanalyst, Freud's earliest English translator whose first such effort appeared only a few weeks after the Clark Conference: Sigmund Freud, *Selected Papers on Hysteria and Other Psychoneuroses*. New York: Nervous and Mental Disease Publishing Company, 1909.

14 H

Clark University
Worcester Massachusetts

September 2, 1909.

My dear Professor Freud:

I have yours of September 1st. We shall welcome you to my house any time that is convenient for you to arrive, whether Sunday evening or Monday morning. [1]

I think all the questions in my note of two days ago are answered in your letter. I am forwarding you some mail.

I am,

Very respectfully yours,
G. Stanley Hall

1. From the surviving letters written home by Freud and Jung, it is possible to reconstruct how the travelers spent their first week in America. They remained in New York City. On August 30 (Monday) Freud and Jung took a long walk in Central Park and discussed, among other things, some of Jung's ideas about the differences between Aryans and Jews. Freud then attempted to visit his sister Anna (Bernays) and

her family but they were away on vacation. Freud, Jung and Ferenczi dined at the home of Dr. A. A. Brill, then explored Chinatown. The next day was partly spent at the Metropolitan Museum of Art, with the evening at Coney Island. Beginning on August 31, all three men had digestive problems for several days. On September 2 they booked reservations for the return trip to Europe (September 21). That same day they visited the hospitals and library of Columbia University, where Brill had studied medicine. From Riverside Drive they had an impressive view of the Palisades. In the evening they attended Hammerstein's famous Victoria Theatre (vaudeville). On the 3rd and 4th they spent some time at the American Museum of Natural History. Ernest Jones joined them on the 4th. That evening the group, now consisting of Freud, Jung, Ferenczi, Brill and Jones, took the night boat for Fall River (Massachusetts), then went by train on Sunday to Worcester. They checked in at the Standish Hotel and, after resting, visited Hall at his home in the evening. Freud and Jung moved to Hall's home the next morning as guests for the Conference week. The ceremonies of the celebration began on Monday, the 6th, but Freud's first lecture was on Tuesday, the 7th, and Jung's first, on Thursday, the 9th. Freud gave five lectures, the last on Saturday; Jung, three. On the 10th, honorary degrees were conferred on Freud and Jung (among others). Accompanied by Ferenczi and Brill, they left Worcester on Sunday afternoon, heading for Buffalo.

15 F

POSTAL CARD

21 Sept 09[1]

Three who are homeward bound bid you farewell with warmest thanks.

> [Signatures of]
> Freud
> Jung
> Ferenczi

1. Before returning to New York, the place from which this farewell card was mailed to their host Stanley Hall, the three travelers had toured

Niagara Falls, then spent three days in the Adirondacks at the camp of Dr. James J. Putnam (1846-1918), Professor of Neurology at the Harvard Medical School. He had invited them there after meeting them in Worcester. They appear to have enjoyed the primitive but hearty camp life despite a mild attack of appendicitis which Freud suffered (yet did not mention) during that sojourn. On leaving Putnam Camp on Saturday the 18th for New York City, Freud was presented with a metal porcupine to commemorate his facetiously announced objective in coming to America ("to see a wild porcupine"). They traveled via Albany and arrived in New York on the 19th. On Monday, the 20th, Freud visited with his sister Anna and her children. The next day the three analysts embarked for the return journey to Europe and reached Bremen on the 29th. After spending time with his mother in Hamburg and with his brother Emmanuel in Berlin, Freud arrived back in Vienna on October 2.

16 H

Clark University
Worcester Massachusetts

October 7, 1909.

My dear Professor Freud:

You will remember that while you were here I spoke to you with regard to the possibility of your giving us your admirable lectures in a form in which we could print them; and you thought it could be done in some way.

The circumstances are these:— No request was made for a copy in our invitation, nor did you make any promises, so that there is no obligation whatever to do anything on your part; and we shall accept your decision in the matter, even if adverse, in good part and with perfect equanimity.

On the other hand, your lectures here seemed to the best men who heard them: e.g. Putnam, Meyer,[1] etc. so admirably calculated to introduce American physicians and psychologists to your system; and your lectures were such masterpieces of simplification, directness, and comprehensiveness that we all think that for us to print them here, giving you reprints of course, would greatly extend your views at a psychological moment here and would do very much toward developing in future years a strong American school.

In view of these facts, if you can write or dictate the substance of your lectures, with any modifications you see fit to make, so that we can translate and print them here, it seems to me it would be a good thing to do.

With the most pleasing memories of your visit here and with all good wishes, I am,

Very respectfully yours,
Stanley Hall

1. Dr. Adolf Meyer (1866-1950) was a pioneer Swiss-American psychiatrist, formerly associated with both the Worcester State Hospital and Clark University.

17 F

Prof. Dr. Freud
Wien, IX. Berggasse 19.

21 Oct. 09

Mr Dear Mr. President

If my memory has not betrayed me, I gave you my firm promise while still in Worcester to send you for translation and publication the manuscript of the lectures which I delivered there. I recollect from that conversation the further details that you would send me the English translation for my approval and that you would remember to distribute a number of reprints to interested Americans. I therefore interpret your letter as a very gracious way of reminding me of an obligation to which I am already committed.

But even if that were not the case and I had not already promised, the expression of your wish would be sufficient to move me to do the work which you consider appropriate. I should like to take this opportunity to show you with what grateful feelings I recall the invitation to Clark University and the fascinating week spent in your home. In Vienna I found so much taxing medical work that I must despair of quickly completing any other tasks. I would therefore consider it as a useful incentive to know by what deadline you expect the manuscript of the five lectures.

With warmest wishes to you and Mrs. Hall for your well being,
Gratefully and faithfully yours
Freud

P.S. I hope the Schriften zur Angewandte Seelenkunde have already reached you. [1]

1. The content of these brochures on applied psychoanalysis, edited by Freud and published by Deuticke in Vienna 1908-1909, can be identified from the review of the series by Hall (unsigned) which he printed in the next issue of his *American Journal of Psychology* (January 1910, *21*, 168-170). The contributors were Freud himself and five of his leading followers of that period: Abraham, Jung, Rank, Riklin and Sadger. The significance of this review in reflecting the immediate impact of Freud's visit is self-evident.

18 H

Clark University
Worcester Massachusetts

November 4, 1909.

My dear Dr. Freud:

I have your favor of October 21st and in reply would state that we wish to go to press not later than January first; and if we could have your manuscript before Christmas it would much facilitate matters.

I have received since writing you last the pamphlets in your *Seelenkunde* series and have already read them with great interest. I am a very unworthy exponent of your views and of course have too little clinical experience to be an authority in that field; but it seems to me that, whereas hitherto many, if not most, psycho-pathologists have leaned upon the stock psychologists like Wundt, your own interpretations reverse the situation and make us normal psychologists look to this work in the abnormal or borderline field for our chief light. [1,2]

I am, with cordial greetings,

Very truly yours,
G. Stanley Hall

1. The theme of this paragraph is elaborated in the above-cited review by Hall (cf. 17 F, note 1).

2. This letter so impressed Freud that he quoted a substantial portion of it to Jung on 21 November 1909. (See *The Freud/Jung Letters,* edited by William McGuire. Princeton, NJ: Princeton University Press, 1974, p. 265.) He started with the words "I am a very unworthy exponent" but in transcribing further, he wrote "pathologists" for "psychopathologists."

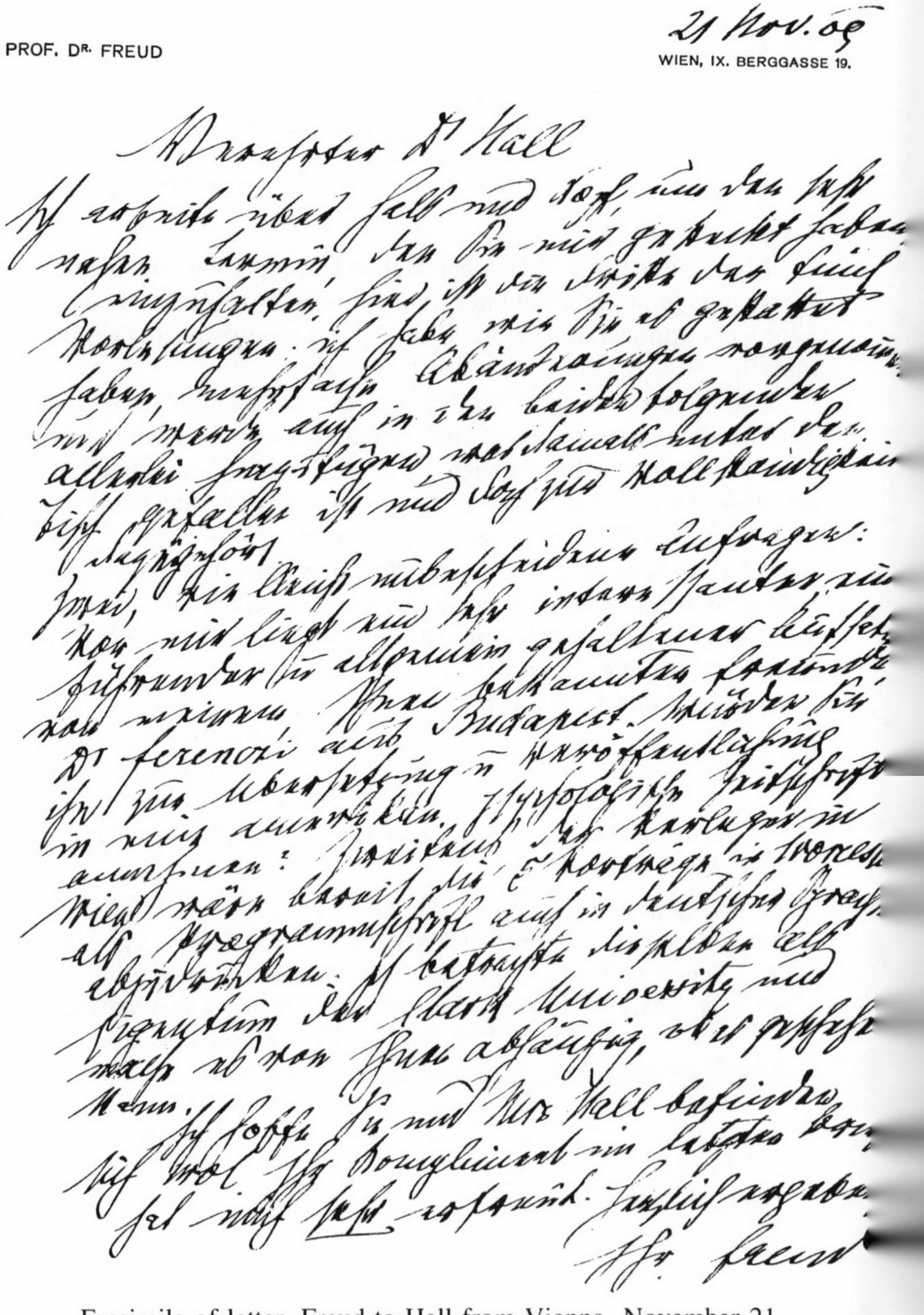
PROF. Dr. FREUD
21 Nov. 09
WIEN, IX. BERGGASSE 19.
Verehrter Dr Hall
Ihr Freud

Facsimile of letter, Freud to Hall from Vienna, November 21, 1909, regarding the publication of Freud's five lectures

19 F

Prof. Dr. Freud
Wien, IX. Berggasse 19.

21 Nov. 09

My dear Dr. Hall

I am working head over heels to meet the imminent deadline which you have set for me. Here is the third of the five lectures: with your permission I have made several changes and shall in the two following ones also add various details which were previously overlooked but which are needed for the sake of completeness. [1]

Two, perhaps presumptuous questions: there is before me a very interesting introductory and generally sound article by my friend, whom you know, Dr. Ferenczi of Budapest. [2] Would you accept it for translation and publication in an American psychological periodical? Secondly, my publisher in Vienna would be willing to print in the German version the five lectures which I gave in outline in Worcester. I consider them to be the property of Clark University and will let you decide whether that can be done.

I hope that you and Mrs. Hall are well. The compliment in your last letter made me *very* happy.

Cordially and faithfully
Yours
Freud

1. The changes made by Freud can be partially inferred by collation with the contemporary newspaper reports but are too detailed for discussion here.

2. This is the first of six letters in which Freud persuaded Hall to accept an article by Ferenczi for publication (S. Ferenczi, The psychological analysis of dreams, *American Journal of Psychology*, 1910, *21*, 309-328). Freud's persistence is an instructive example of his efforts in behalf of his disciples and his cause. The parallel with Jung, whom Freud favored at this time even more than Ferenczi and upon whom he looked as his successor ("the Crown Prince"), is noteworthy. This repeated mention of Ferenczi contrasts strikingly with the absence of any mention of Jung's invitation in Freud's earlier correspondence with Hall (see 13 F, note 2).

20 H

Clark University
Worcester Massachusetts

December 3, 1909.

My dear Professor Freud:

I have received the first three lectures of the five, and am glad that you have made changes. This is entirely proper and, so far as I know, also very customary here.

As to your questions—We should have no objection to a German publisher bringing out your lectures in German, provided he would observe the following two conditions, which our Board have suggested in similar cases: a. that he should state that they are lectures given at Clark University; and b. that he would not publish them until after we had published them here. These are the conditions that have been observed in other cases here and I sincerely trust you will find them entirely agreeable and convenient.

As to publishing Dr. Ferenczi's article—I do not find that we have the article here, and therefore I do not know how long it is. I will see if I can find it here and, if I can, will do what I am able toward getting it translated.

The three lectures you have sent have to be transcribed into English script and then translated. I hope you will find the translation satisfactory, although of course there is difficulty about technical terms.

I am,

Very truly yours,
G. Stanley Hall

21 H

Clark University
Worcester Massachusetts

December 8, 1909.

My dear Professor Freud:

I enclose herewith the original text and our translation of your first lecture. [1]

May I ask if you will kindly revise it promptly, as we wish to rush it to press as soon as possible.

I am, with great respect.

Very truly yours,
G. Stanley Hall

1. This earliest translation of Freud's five lectures at Clark was made, under Hall's supervision, by one of his Ph.D. students, Harry Woodburn Chase (1883-1955). He received his Ph.D. degree in 1910 and in that same year published "Psychoanalysis and the unconscious," *Pedagogical Seminary* [presently the *Journal of Genetic Psychology*], 1910, *17,* 281-327. This was his doctoral dissertation. It was obviously written in the light of Freud's Clark lectures and is in a sense a gloss on his translation of them. Chase was a close associate of Hall in his plans for a Children's Institute. He later became eminent in university administration and successively served as President of the University of North Carolina, the University of Illinois, and New York University.

22 F

Prof. Dr. Freud
Wien, IX. Berggasse 19.

14. Dec. 09

My dear Dr. Hall

I am very sorry that my lectures are giving you so much trouble. I am grateful for the permission to have these published in the German language as well, and I consider the conditions connected therewith self-evident and easy to fulfill. I therefore await the return of the manuscript so that it may be employed for this secondary purpose. [1]

As for Ferenczi's paper, you write that you are searching for it and that you are willing to accept it if it is not too long. But I had not yet sent it off to you because I wanted to await your reply as to whether you were in principle inclined to accept it. You will receive it very soon and can then kindly let me know your decision. In the meantime I have learned that the author is planning to publish this paper with other lectures which he delivered in Budapest as an independent volume in the Hungarian language. [2]

Simultaneously there will be sent you a reprint of my article on the case of compulsion neurosis published in the Jahrbuch, I, 2. [3]

With many thanks for the help which you have given me.

Cordially and faithfully yours
Freud

1. See Part Three (below) for a new translation of this German edition. The Introductory Note describes the editions and translations of the lectures. See also *Standard edition of the complete psychological works of Sigmund Freud,* London: Hogarth, 1957, *11,* 3-5.

2. See 19 F, note 2 for the reference to this article, which was eventually published under Hall's editorship in a translation by Harry W. Chase. It was originally delivered as a lecture before the Royal Society of Physicians, Budapest, October 16, 1909 and published in *Psychiatrisch-Neurologischen Wochenschrift,* 1910, *12,* Nr. 11, 101-107; Nr. 12, 114-117; Nr. 13, 125-127.

3. The work referred to is Freud's famous case history of the "Rat Man" which he wrote before leaving for America. It appeared as

"Bemerkungen über einen Fall von Zwangsneurose," *Jahrbuch für psychoanalytische Forschungen*, 1909, *1* (No. 2), 357-421. The English translation is in the *Standard Edition, 10,* 153-249, under the title "Notes upon a case of obsessional neurosis." (Cf. Chap. II.)

23 H

Clark University
Worcester Massachusetts

December 30, 1909.

My dear Professor Freud:

In answer to your favor of December 14th would state that I shall be greatly interested to receive and read Ferenczi's article. I hope the volume of his papers may be translated from Hungarian into German.

You will be interested to know that an entire afternoon session of the American Association of Psychologists (which embraces some three hundred teachers of Psychology throughout the country and which met at Harvard) was devoted to the discussion of Freud and his theories. [1]

Dr. Putnam, whom you will remember here, led off with a paper entitled "A Comparison of Bergson's and Freud's Theories of the Unconscious Mental Life." It was not very clear and I doubt if anyone understood that there was anything in common. I certainly did not. Morton Prince [2] reported an interesting case of dreams and subscribed in part to your theories of their explanation, dissenting from some points of the mechanisms. Dr. Jones [3] read a brief paper expounding your dream theory, which was very lucid and just what was needed; while Boris Sidis [4] deprecated the present prospect of a Freud cult in this country and said it seemed likely to be a passing craze but that people would get over it. To this, Putnam replied that it ill became him to criticize a method which he himself had appropriated with only petty variations and a too scant acknowledgment so long. He, Sidis, gave an account of three psychoneurotic cases in which the patients ascribed their condition to fear, and said this could not at all be explained by either wish fulfillment or sex. To this I ventured to object that the time had now passed for the mere narration of patients' own ideas of themselves, with no attempt at psychoanalysis.

On the whole, the meeting which lasted three hours cannot fail to interest a larger circle of psychologists in your work.

I am hoping to receive at your early convenience your revisions of Dr. Chase's translation.

Dr. Brill[5] is translating Jung's lectures and if Ferenczi's Aufsatz is not too long and if I can also print the condensed little paper of Jones read yesterday, we shall have a Freud number of our Journal, which I hope will do good.[6]

I am,

Very truly yours,
G. Stanley Hall

1. The reference is to the 18th annual meeting of the American Psychological Association, Cambridge, Massachusetts, December 29-31, 1909. The afternoon of December 29 was given over to abnormal psychology and psychoanalysis. (See Part One, Chapter XI.)

2. Morton Prince (1854-1929) was the distinguished Boston psychiatrist who founded (and edited) the *Journal of Abnormal Psychology* in 1906, one of the first professional periodicals to include psychoanalytic papers. Later he became increasingly hostile to Freud's theories.

3. For Ernest Jones, see 6 H, note 1.

4. Boris Sidis (1867-1923), a psychologist-psychiatrist, trained at Harvard University under William James and Hugo Münsterberg, later at the Harvard Medical School (Harvard A.B. 1894, A.M. 1895, Ph.D. 1897; M.D. 1908). His Ph.D. dissertation was the basis of his first book, *The psychology of suggestion* (New York: Appleton, 1898), with an appreciative Introduction by William James. In that volume and in later writings he reported ingenious experimental investigations of multiple personality and dissociated states, including the hypnoidal condition which he employed and investigated in his psychotherapeutic practice. From the first he was an adherent of the French psychopathological school, epitomized in Janet, and a critic of psychoanalysis, as was Münsterberg, the chief of the Harvard Psychological Laboratory since 1892. By 1909 his opposition to Freud had crystallized and combined with the growing opposition of Morton Prince who had already included him as an Associate Editor of the *Journal of Abnormal Psychology*. The paper Sidis presented at the meeting of the American Psychological Association in 1909 was published after some delay in

the February-March 1911 (anti-Freudian) number of Prince's *Journal* and was entitled "Fundamental states in psychoneurosis" (vol. 5, 320-327). On page 322 a footnote was added which clearly reflects the tone of the discussion provoked by Sidis's original presentation. It starts by quoting a passage from the second edition of *Traumdeutung* (p. 376) in which Freud asserted that at the root of every psychoneurosis there lies the fulfillment of a repressed infantile wish. Sidis ridicules this unconfirmed assertion and, in the main text of his paper, argues instead for the "fear instinct and the sense of the mysterious . . . accompanied by deeply rooted superstitions and prejudices of a religious and moral character" as giving rise to "the phobias or the anxieties of psychoneurosis." He adhered to and elaborated this position in his later writings and in his practice at the Psychotherapeutic Institute, Portsmouth, N.H., which he founded in 1909, the year of Freud's U.S. visit. Sidis corresponded with Pavlov, whose ideas he incorporated, and he developed a behavioral approach to therapy not unlike the contemporary position of Joseph Wolpe (*Psychotherapy by reciprocal inhibition*. Stanford, CA: Stanford University Press, 1958). It is highly probable that Freud knew the work of Sidis as early as 1898 and therefore responded to the attack upon him at the APA meeting in 1909 as an overdue redress of wrong done to "the cause" by this offender.

5. For Brill, see 13 F, note 4. He was an obvious choice as translator of Jung's lectures since he had worked with Jung at the Burghölzli in Zurich 1907-1908. He had already translated (with Peterson) Jung's *Psychology of dementia praecox* (New York: Nervous and Mental Disease Publishing Co., 1910). Brill late in life published a brief account of "The introduction and development of Freud's work in the United States," *American Journal of Sociology*, 1939, *45*, 318-325.

6. Just such a "Freud number" of the *American Journal of Psychology*, founded and edited by Hall, appeared in April 1910. It contained the lectures of Freud and of Jung as well as papers by Ferenczi and Jones.

24 F

Prof. Dr. Freud
Wien, IX. Berggasse 19.

11 Jan. 1910

My Dear Dr. Hall

The great satisfaction I got from your letter of Dec. 30, '09, which I received today, and your comment about the article by my friend Dr. Ferenczi induce me to reply by return post.

The article about the interpretation of dreams by Ferenczi, prepared in German, was *assuredly* sent to your address *before* my last lectures and should have been in your hands long ago. If it has been lost, it will be easy for the author to send along a second copy. (Address: Budapest VII. Erzsebet-Körset 54) He will be proud that, through your kindness, he can be introduced to American readers, and I can assure you that both as a man and as an investigator he is a person of the greatest promise.

Accept my warmest thanks for the information you conveyed about the American Association of Psychologists. I cannot suppress a certain quite unchristian satisfaction that you and Dr. Putnam so fittingly repulsed Boris Sidis who is neither very honorable nor very wise. I think he deserved no better. [1]

The revision of the last two Worcester lectures is already on the way to you. I am not unaware of the extraordinary difficulties which the material and probably also my style have made for the translator; and I think the translation is good and that it will serve its purpose. At certain points the meaning was obscure because of the vagueness of the German text, so I took the liberty of trying my hand as translator.

The German edition (which will conscientiously keep to the stipulated conditions) is going to have the following title which I submit for your approval:

Five Lectures
ON PSYCHOANALYSIS [2]
Delivered at the 20th anniversary of the founding
of Clark University in Worcester, Mass.
by
Prof. Dr. Sigm Freud LL.D.

May I ask your permission to have the second page arranged as follows:

To Dr. Stanley HALL
President of Clark University and
Professor of Psychology and Pedagogics
gratefully dedicated. [3]

I hope that it does not sound presumptuous.

Very sincerely and faithfully yours
Freud

1. Freud's elation about the proposed "Freud number" was repeated by him in a letter to his friend and fellow analyst Karl Abraham (1877-1925) to whom he also imparted the happy news about the dressing down of Boris Sidis. (Cf. *A Psycho-analytic Dialogue. The Letters of Sigmund Freud and Karl Abraham 1907-1926*, edited by Hilda C. Abraham and Ernst L. Freud. New York: Basic Books, 1965, pp. 84-85.)

2. In the subsequent German edition, the title was *On Psychoanalysis.* In the earlier English translation by Chase, the wording suggested by Freud to Hall in 13 F was adopted. The new translation in Part Three, below, conforms to the German edition.

3. This dedication, approved by Hall in the next letter, appeared in the first and subsequent editions of the book.

25 H

Clark University
Worcester Massachusetts

January 26, 1910.

My dear Professor Freud:

I acknowledge hereby with thanks your kind letter of January 11th. Dr. Ferenczi's article was received here some time since, and is now translated by Mr. Chase, the same gentleman who translated your own papers. I think it goes to press to-day.

We have now received copy of all five of your lectures and the printer has them nearly set up. We have all put our heads together in regard to the two or three uncertain matters of translation and I hope you will find them all right.

I assure you that I shall feel very greatly honored by allowing my name to be so pleasantly associated with yours in having the German text of your lectures here inscribed to me on the second page, as you propose.

We now have all three of Jung's lectures. I have taken the liberty of asking Dr. Brill, whom I saw the other day in New York, if he would be disposed to undertake an article which should do for your work on the actions of daily life what Ferenczi attempts to do for the Traumdeutung. He seems very favorably inclined thereto. [1]

I am,

Very truly yours,
G. Stanley Hall

1. The occasion for the meeting between Brill and Hall was the presentation by the latter of two lectures on pedagogy at New York University in January 1910. (See correspondence between Brill and Hall, December 27 and 30, 1909 in *Hall Papers 1909*.) The plan for Brill to write the article was changed the following month (Jones and Hall, February 8 and 26; Hall and Brill, February 12 and 18, 1910, ibid.). Brill consented to the substitution of an article by Ernest Jones which, in the event, proved to be an address on "The psychopathology of everyday life" delivered before the Detroit Academy of Medicine, May 16, 1911, subsequently published in the *American Journal of Psychology*, 1911 (Oct.), *22*, 477-527.

26 H

Clark University
Worcester, Massachusetts

September 26, 1913

Professor Sigmund Freud,
University of Vienna,
Vienna, Austria.

My dear Professor Freud:

Will you kindly permit me to express the very great satisfaction which I have had in receiving several very kind cards of greeting from you since your visit here?[1]

Though I have had little or nothing to say or write about your own work, it has been a great inspiration to me as a student and teacher of psychology. Indeed I think I have read about everything that I have been able to get of your own writings, together with nearly all contained in "Imago", the "Zeitschrift" and the "Jahrbuch", and last year I ventured with a great deal of trepidation upon a course of one hour a week of Freudian Psychology, or perhaps it should better have been entitled "The lessons of Freudian psychology for students of normal psychology," which are those I have to teach.[2]

The three points that impress me are the following: 1. the immense genetic significance of it all. You of course are very careful not to lay great stress upon prenatal influence in the sense of Ferenczi's *Allmacht* theory.[3] We long-time students of childhood certainly have to modify our opinions essentially in view of the "polymorphic perversities." I cannot but feel that sooner or later psychologists must break into the big open field of phylogeny and postulate many rather specific influences of the development of the race upon that of the individual, as Stekel seems to have gone far in doing in some respects.[4]

2. I have been trying in a very crude way to apply your mechanisms to the study of children's fears and anger, which seem to me to have plenty of *Verdrängung, Verschiebung,*[5] and most of the rest.[6]

The thing I stick on is what seems to me the rather wild use of sex symbolism, e.g. that dreams of money means spermatozoa, that every curve is feminine and every straight line masculine. It seems to me there is much danger of repeating the extravagancies of the old students of phallicism, Westorp [sic.], Jennings, [7] etc., or of Max Müller and Cox, [8] who regarded the spear of Ithuriel, the darts of Apollo and everything straight as a ray of sun, and everything curved as its disk.

However, I am only a novice, and only a student of normal psychology, so that I am debarred from the vaster and richer field of abnormal psychology.

May I say in closing, however, that no one in the last twenty years has been a source of so much inspiration as you and your associates.

I am, with great respect,

Very sincerely yours,
G. Stanley Hall

1. These "cards of greeting" have not survived but they are, in any event, only a pretext for the (presumed) actual stimulus for this letter, the first which Hall wrote to Freud after a lapse of over three and one-half years. That stimulus may have been provided by the meeting of the American Psychopathological Association in Washington, D.C. on May 8, 1913 and, more specifically, the publication of its Proceedings in the Association's official *Journal of Abnormal Psychology* which began with the Presidential address by Dr. J. J. Putnam in the August-September issue. At this meeting Hall contributed a provocative paper on "Sex-symbolism in the psychology of Freud" which figured prominently in the Discussion by several of the participants, notably, Jelliffe, Jones and Prince, as published in the subsequent December-January issue of the *Journal*. But while all the other papers presented at the meeting seem to have appeared in full in one or another number of the *Journal*, Hall's was, a footnote states, "reserved for publication." It never was published—a striking exception in view of the marked attention accorded it in the Discussion. There may have been other reasons for the present letter but its structure, which leads up to an emphatic criticism of sex symbolism, appears to stamp it as a substitute for the suppressed paper. Was Hall afraid of offending Freud? Did he instead write this letter which alternately flatters and criticizes Freud and ends with an apology ("I am only a novice") and a renewed avowal of extraordinary indebtedness to Freud?

A new stimulus for Hall's present letter has been discovered in the form of an abstract to a paper given by Hall at the meeting of the American Psychological Association at the end of December 1913 (cf.

Hall, 1914a). It is discussed at some length in Part One, Chapter XII, but is noted here for its clear reflection of Hall's having read the new book by Alfred Adler, *The Neurotic Constitution,* published in 1912. It is, again, noteworthy that Hall did not publish the full paper, perhaps having been inhibited by the "ambivalence" toward Freud noted in the title of the paper itself!

2. These are the three earliest journals devoted exclusively to Freudian psychoanalysis (excepting the *Zentralblatt für Psychoanalyse,* 1910-1914, which was absorbed into the *Internationale Zeitschrift*). The first, started in 1908, was the *Jahrbuch für psychoanalytische und psychopathologische Forschungen.* It was edited by Jung. *Imago,* directed by Freud and edited by Otto Rank (1886-1939) and Hanns Sachs (1881-1947), began in 1912 and was devoted to the application of psychoanalysis to the humanities (literature, art, religion). The *Internationale Zeitschrift für ärztliche Psychoanalyse* (volume 1, 1913) was the new journal of the International Psychoanalytic Association, founded in 1910.

3. "Allmacht der Gedanken" or "omnipotence of thoughts," presumed to be common in the child and in primitive cultures, was first mentioned by Freud in his monograph on the Rat Man case, published in 1909 (cf. 22 F, note 3). Ferenczi's elaboration was entitled: "Entwicklungsstufen der Wirklichkeitssinnes," *Internationale Zeitschrift für ärztliche Psychoanalyse,* 1913, *1,* 124-138 (now available in English as "Stages in the development of the sense of reality," Chapter 8 of Ferenczi's *Contributions to psychoanalysis.* Boston: Richard G. Badger, 1916). The appeal of this concept for Hall lay partly in Ferenczi's anchoring it in the phylogenesis of man—an emphasis which was carried to the extreme in Hall's application of the recapitulation principle (ontogeny repeats phylogeny), derived from Haeckel. Hall is here subtly recommending this orientation to Freud who, as a matter of fact, had already begun to share it (cf. Animismus, Magie und Allmacht der Gedanken, *Imago,* 1913, *2,* 1-21, which became Chapter 3 of *Totem and Taboo,* published in book form later that year. See *Standard Edition of the Complete Psychological Works of Sigmund Freud.* London: Hogarth, 1955, *13,* 75-99). Three years later, in his Introductory Lectures, Freud went further and spoke of "primal fantasies" out of which such strange notions as the castration complex appear to emerge ready-made "from a phylogenetic endowment" (*Standard Edition, 16,* 371).

4. Wilhelm Stekel (1868-1940). Hall is probably referring to Stekel's *Die Sprache des Träumes* published in 1911 (Wiesbaden: Verlag von

Bergmann; translated into English, in part, as *Sex and Dreams; the Language of Dreams.* Boston: Richard G. Badger, 1922) in which dream symbols are extensively treated as universal and hence, in a certain sense, phylogenetic. It is noteworthy that in the first two editions of *The Interpretation of Dreams* (1899 and 1909) Freud had not stressed universal symbolism but depended for interpretation primarily upon the particulars of the free associations of the individual dreamer. The change from this idiodynamic practice—a shift which has ever since led to so much criticism—began playing a prominent part in the third edition of *The Interpretation of Dreams* (1911) and the second edition of his briefer *On Dreams* (1911). As Freud himself avowed (*Standard Edition, 5,* 350), it was largely under the influence of Stekel that this change occurred. While Freud deplored the heuristic irresponsibility of Stekel in other respects, he does not appear to have recognized the damage done to the scientific objectivity of dream interpretations by his heavy emphasis on universal symbols. (See *Standard Edition, 4,* pp. xii-xiii, and *5,* 350f., 685.) It is not improbable that Jung exerted a similar influence for, again in 1911, he published the first part of his book *Symbols of Transformation (Wandlungen und Symbole der Libido,* 1911-1912). (See the discussion in *The Freud/Jung letters,* 1974, Letter No. 268F.) By the end of this present letter Hall is rejecting the "wild use of sex symbolism" which he compares to some earlier anthropological extravagances. But it is questionable that, with his phylogenetic bias, he fully appreciated the deterioration in Freud's use of symbols which the above history reveals to the student of idiodynamics (cf. Rosenzweig, 1985, pp. 145-147).

5. Repression, displacement, two of the Freudian mechanisms for interpreting the dynamics of behavior.

6. Hall's papers on fear and on anger appeared as follows: A synthetic genetic study of fear, *American Journal of Psychology,* 1914, *25,* 149-200, 321-392; The Freudian methods applied to anger, *American Journal of Psychology,* 1915, *26,* 438-443. In both contributions he gives recognition to Adler's work, especially in the long article on fear (p. 165) and he rejects (p. 167) Freud's interpretation of the "more generic form of fear as rooted in sex" [i.e., castration anxiety]. It is evident that at the time of this letter Hall was starting to pit Freud against Adler, and his above-cited criticism of sex symbolism in Freud's psychology probably derived in part from that orientation.

7. Hodder M. Westropp (1820-1884) and Hargrave Jennings (1817?-1890) were social historians who interpreted early customs and religious practices as forms of sympathetic magic which reflected the worship of

sexual activity and fertility in nature. The difficulty in these studies, to which Hall alludes, lies in the interpretation of archeological remains. These artifacts, like the manifest content of dreams, are open to diverse readings.

8. Max Müller (1823-1900) and George W. Cox (1827-1902) avoided the extravagances of phallicism but, as Hall points out, tended to offer equally overgeneralized, though asexual, interpretations of folklore, myth and religion as reflecting the adoration of the sun, moon, etc.

27 F

Prof. Dr. Freud
Wien, IX. Berggasse 19.

21 Nov. 1913

Dear Sir [1]

The few years that have elapsed since my visit in your home and at your University have not diminished my sense of gratitude for your hospitality. A letter from you is a most welcome reminder of that significant time.

I am happy that your interest in our work has not lessened. You must realize even at a distance how distinctly everything is caught up here in change and ferment, and yet, despite all digressions from the path, the direction of progress has, on the whole, been maintained. I shall also in the future make it my business to send you everything that is published in our cause.

That it is the particular question of sexual symbolism which disturbs you causes me no concern. You will surely have noticed that psychoanalysis creates very little that is new in this regard but rather makes use of what has long been known, turns it to good account, and supports it with a wealth of observations. The occasional excesses will be eliminated but most of it will, I believe, stand up to verification.

The only inauspicious changes in the psychoanalytic movement concern personal relationships. Jung, with whom I shared my visit with you, is no longer my friend, and our collaboration is approaching complete dissolution. Such changes are regrettable but inevitable.

I hope that you and Mrs. Hall are enjoying uninterrupted good health, and remain

> Gratefully and faithfully yours
> Freud

1. Two things are notable. It took Freud two months to answer Hall's letter and the salutation is "Dear Sir" (Verehrter Herr), with no title or surname. A Freudian would surmise "resistance" in the letter-writer. Though Freud mentions Jung by name, he may, more importantly, have sensed or even known that Hall was beginning to admire Alfred Adler (see 26 H) who had quit the Vienna Psychoanalytic Society in 1911. Freud's explicit chagrin about Hall's "defection" to Adler was avowed a little later, in a letter to Jones, May 1914 (Ernest Jones, *The Life and Work of Sigmund Freud*. New York: Basic Books, 1955, vol. 2, p. 105). In that same year he also took Hall to task in a footnote to his case history of the "Wolf Man." The context was a criticism of Adler in which Freud compared the Freudian with the alternative Adlerian interpretation of the patient's behavior. In the course of the argument he unfavorably cited Hall's study of fear (see 26 H, note 6). Though written in 1914, this paper was not published until 1918. (See *Standard Edition, 17, 112-113.*)

28 H

Clark University
Worcester Massachusetts

January 31, 1917 [1,2]

Professor Sigismund Freud,
University of Vienna,
Vienna, Austria.

My dear Professor Freud:

Among the results of this awful war is the fact that this university has not received your Jahrbuch since the end of Vol. 6, 1914, nor the Zeitschrift since the end of Vol. 4, nor Imago since Vol. 4, No. 3, nor Stekel's Centralblatt for about a year and a half. [3] I suppose that these and other books and journals from Germany are held up by the English, but there have been reports that one or more of the above four publications have suspended during the war. I cannot express to you how much we miss these publications, and after writing and inquiring through our government at Washington and the Congressional Library, and being able to hear nothing, I venture as a last resort to take the forlorn hope of trying to reach you, the source of it all, for information. Is there any possible way by which if these missing journals were sent personally to me instead of to the university they would have a better chance of getting through?

Please accept renewed assurance of my greatest respect and sincere good wishes.

Very sincerely yours,
G. Stanley Hall

1. This letter is reproduced from a carbon copy at the Clark University Archives. The original is not in the London collection of Hall's letters to Freud. It is probable that, because of wartime conditions, Freud never received the letter—an inference strengthened by the fact that no answer from Freud to Hall has been discovered.

2. The stimulus for this letter, indicating much concern about the official psychoanalytic journals, may have been Hall's pending election as President of the American Psychoanalytic Association, an office which he held from May 1917 to May 1919. Hall was for years the only non-M.D. President of the Association. However, he appears not to have attended the meetings in 1917-1919.

3. For the identification of these periodicals, see 26 H, note 2. Not only were the mails disrupted by the War of 1914-1918 but several of the psychoanalytic journals suspended publication or changed format at that time because of internal conflicts among the psychoanalysts (the defections of Adler, Jung and Stekel). For example, the *Jahrbuch*, formerly edited by Jung, suspended publication after 1914, and the *Zentralblatt für Psychoanalyse* merged into the *Internationale Zeitschrift für Ärztliche Psychoanalyse und Imago* in 1913-1914.

29 H

G. Stanley Hall
156 Woodland Street
Worcester, Mass.

June 19, 1923 [1,2]

Professor Sigmund Freud,
Vienna

My dear Dr. Freud,

May I introduce to you the bearer, my friend, Dr. Edward J. Kempf, in the hope that you will not only establish a personal entente cordiale with him, but will facilitate his purpose of getting acquainted with your circle in Vienna. [3]

Dr. Kempf has, as you doubtless know, done most noble work in promoting the spread of your great and epoch-making ideas among neurologists and psychiatrists. He has done, I think, far more than any one else in this country toward interesting the members of the American Association of Psychologists—who have stood so strangely aloof in psychoanalytic conceptions—especially in his work on the autonomic system, and his monumental "Psychopathology."

May I take this occasion to add that your own work still continues to be to me, as it has ever since you were here and before, the most important formative influence that has ever come into my thinking and my life.

I have thought of you a great deal during the war, and wondered how you fared personally amidst the awful trials which you must have gone through. With all my heart I wish for you many, many years of life, health and continued activity.

Most sincerely yours,
G. Stanley Hall

1. This letter of introduction was written by Hall for Dr. Kempf when the latter was planning to visit and discuss his work with Freud in 1923. The original has not survived but, stimulated by an appeal from the writer in 1970, Dr. Kempf was "unexpectedly" able to find a copy which he had made and filed with other correspondence from Hall. Kempf's visit was thus the occasion for the resumption of the correspondence after an interval of six years.

2. As the address 156 Woodland Street indicates, Hall was no longer writing as President of Clark University. He had retired in 1920. His home "94 Woodland Street" (in 10 H and 12 H) was changed to 156 in a general re-numbering of Worcester streets.

3. Edward J. Kempf (1885-1971), a psychiatrist who, though clearly influenced by Freud, attempted systematically to ground the concepts of psychodynamics in autonomic physiology. (See, for example, *The Autonomic Functions of the Personality*. New York: Nervous and Mental Disease Publishing Co., 1918.)

30 F

Prof. Dr. Freud
Wien, IX. Berggasse 19.

Lavarone Trentino
28 Aug. 1923 [1]

My dear Mr. President

Dr. Kempf, whom you recommended to me, has visited me in my solitude on this presently Italian plateau and has left me with a very favorable impression of his personality. [2] My evaluation of his scientific work is disturbed by the circumstance that he is not really an analyst but instead has adopted an anatomical byway which, in my opinion, will lead him nowhere. As for introducing him to my Viennese circle, I could do nothing on that score since by the middle of August they had all left Vienna.

I was very happy to hear that you are enjoying excellent health and that you have quite recently given evidence of your intellectual vigor through a significant publication. [3] I had been informed previously that you complained about never receiving answers from me and mine to your letters. But I can assure you that since the War not a line from you has reached me.

I learned from your letter with great satisfaction that your evaluation of my contribution to psychopathology has remained unaltered. I had not expected this for you have demonstrated in a most decided manner your partiality for Alfred Adler, and yet it cannot have escaped you that the complete repudiation of psychoanalysis is involved in the message of his doctrine. [4] Even today

I am at a loss to reconcile the two aspects of your avowals. Had the actual events been better known to you, you would probably not have concluded that here again is a case of a father who will not permit his sons to come into their own. Instead you would have seen that the sons wanted to depose their father—exactly as in primal times. [5]

    With sincere greetings and very best wishes for your welfare

Yours
Freud

1. Dr. Kempf visited Freud at his summer vacation address in Italy.

2. Freud at the time of Kempf's visit was obviously not sympathetic to his effort, which strongly resembled one he had himself made and abandoned as long ago as 1895 during the birth throes of psychoanalysis. After that ambitious project, Freud pursued the problems of abnormal and normal behavior in purely psychological terms. It is perhaps on the basis of this portion of his past personal history that in this letter he vigorously condemns Kempf's aims. Freud's abandoned early effort was indeed *anatomical:* the first sentence of his Project (p. 355) reads, in part: "its aim . . . is to represent psychical processes as quantitatively determined states of specifiable material particles [neurones] . . ." (S. Freud, "Project for a scientific psychology," posthumously published in *The origins of psychoanalysis.* New York: Basic Books, 1954). In contrast to Freud, Hall thought so highly of Kempf's work that he singled it out for commendation in his autobiography, published the same year as Kempf's visit to Freud. It was, in fact, Hall who proposed to Kempf that he visit Freud to discuss his improvements on psychoanalytic theory.

3. *Senescence.* New York: Appleton, 1922.

4. Concerning Adler, see 27 F, note 1.

5. Freud is referring here to Charles Darwin's concept of the "primal horde" (*The descent of man.* London: J. Murray, 1871, p. 346) and his own elaboration of that hypothesis in *Totem and taboo,* 1913. (See *Standard Edition, 13,* p. 125, where the page reference to Darwin is incorrectly given as 362f.) This allusion by Freud subtly indicates another stimulus for the present letter in addition to Kempf's visit. In 1920 Hall, responding to an invitation, had contributed a Preface to the English translation of Freud's *A general introduction to psychoanalysis* (New York: Boni and Liveright). In it he compared Freud with Wundt (see 31 H, note 6) who, after rendering "inestimable

services" to psychology, became too aware of his limitations and, in his later years, got embroiled in bitter contentions with his more advanced students. Hall's pleas for a more wholesome outcome in psychoanalysis was defensively rejected by Freud in the present letter.

31 H

156, Woodland Street[1]
Worcester, Mass.
September 24th, 1923.

My dear Professor Freud,

I am very glad you made sympathetic personal touch with Kempf.[2] Although he is not so exactly a follower of your views as Brill, he has been profoundly influenced by them, more I think than he knows, and has influenced others in that direction.

As to your kind and frank comments about me, it is quite true that I have found real help in my own thinking from Adler's ideas of compensation and *Minderwertigkeit,* and that I had a brief correspondence with him some years ago and would have liked to have brought him to this country to give a few lectures.[3]

I have also found much that helped in Jung, mystical and unintelligible as much of his writing is to me.[4]

I think the world knows that both these men owe their entire impulsion to you, and I also think that both illustrate the revolt against the father which you have so well explained. I do not know that psychoanalysis tells us what is the instinctive, or what ought to be, the attitude of the father toward his revolting sons.[5] Wundt had the same feelings against his own pupils who developed methods of introspection.[6] In my own small sphere I, too, have had painful experiences with those whose model seemed to be *periunt illi qui nostra ante nos dixerunt.*[7] I think the impulse to wish the death of those who said our things before we did is pretty strong, and it is most exasperating to those who suffer from it.

But your own achievements are far and away beyond those of any psychologist of modern times; in fact history will show that you have done for us a service which you are not at all extravagant in comparing with that of Darwin for biology.[8] It seems to me you can well afford to be magnanimous toward these revolting children.

I know far too little of clinical or pathological psychology, and have had far too little clinical experience, to judge the severer scientific aspects of psychoanalysis, although I realize that it is just here where lies the crux of everything; but I am amazed to see how many members of our American Psychological Association who (before in their publications slighted or condemned psycho-analysis, and on the program of the meetings of which it very rarely occurred), are now being subtly and profoundly influenced by it,[9] and also to see how very often its themes are the leading motives in dramas, historical studies and novels (e.g. Elsa Barker's "Fielding Sargent" which I have just finished.)[10]

For me, your work has been the chief inspiration of most that I have done for the last fifteen years. It has given me a totally new view of psychic life, and I owe to you more than to anyone else living or dead.[11] I think I am the only American Psychologist of the normal who has given through all these years a special course upon this subject.[12] To my mind the psychology of the normal in this country lives in a pre-evolutionary age. Until you came genetic considerations of things psychic were unknown or taboo. I think I have read about everything you have ever written, although in my limitations, there is much that I did not understand, and a little which, if I did understand it aright I have to question. Nevertheless, I owe to you almost a new birth of intellectual interest in psychology, as is perhaps best shown in my Jesus book, which, without this, would not have been written.[13]

Please pardon the length of this letter, and accept my most heart-felt wish that you may continue for many, many years the great work you have already established in the world.[14]

Most sincerely yours,
G. Stanley Hall.

1. In his retirement, at age 79, Hall boldly took the liberty of applying some of Freud's psychoanalytic concepts to the master himself. It is significant that, as Hall told Dr. Kempf in a letter dated October 1, 1923, he had resigned two or three years earlier from the American Psychoanalytic Association "because I thought they were too narrow."

Previously he had been proud of his charter membership as an exceptional, non-medical person.

2. For Kempf, see 29 H, note 3.

3. The surviving correspondence between Alfred Adler and Hall is reproduced and discussed in the informative paper by Heinz L. Ansbacher, *Journal of the History of the Behavioral Sciences,* 1971, *7,* 337-352. See also 26 H, note 6 and 27 F, note 1.

4. A brief exchange of letters between Hall and Jung occurred in 1917. (Hall Papers, Clark University Archives.)

5. In writing thus, Hall by this time probably knew Freud's *On the History of the Psychoanalytic Movement,* published in 1914 (Zur Geschichte der psychoanalytischen Bewegung, *Jahrbuch für psychoanalytische Forschungen,* 1914, *6,* 207-260. See *Standard Edition, 14,* 7-66) in which Freud takes to task his two former disciples, Adler and Jung, in the manner of the irate father. See also 30 F, note 5.

6. Wilhelm Wundt (1832-1920) was the founder of experimental psychology. Hall had been his first American student. He went to study with Wundt at the University of Leipzig in 1879, the year usually assigned to the founding of Wundt's now famous laboratory. On the same day, December 15, 1908, that Freud was first invited by Hall, Wundt was sent a similar letter (Hall Papers, 1909). But while Freud was offered $400, Wundt's honorarium was to be $750. After Wundt declined, Freud was offered $750! The differential fees say something about Hall's comparative evaluation of the two men in their initial importance to him for the celebration.

7. The correct wording of the aphorism is: "Pereant qui ante nos nostra dixerunt," i.e., "May those perish who said what we are saying before we did." The saying is attributed to Aelius Donatus, the fourth-century Roman grammarian, by his pupil St. Jerome in the latter's Commentary on *Ecclesiastes (Corpus Christianorum,* 1959, LXII, pp. 256-257). Jerome quotes it as a comment on the well-known *Ecclesiastes* 1:9, ". . . there is no new thing under the sun."

8. Hall is alluding to Freud's bold comparison of himself with Copernicus and Darwin in a 1917 paper describing the three blows delivered to man's narcissism in the history of science: Copernicus diminished man by demonstrating that the earth is only one of several planets revolving around the sun; Darwin, by his theory of evolution, destroyed the idea of man's special creation as the image of God; and

Freud, as he saw it, delivered the final blow by proving the power of the unconscious over man's feeble ego. (A difficulty in the path of psychoanalysis, *Standard Edition, 17,* 135-144. First published 1917.)

9. The acceptance of Freudian psychoanalysis by American psychologists proved less generally favorable than Hall depicts here.

10. The popular book singled out here is the psychoanalytical novel *Fielding Sargent* by Elsa Barker (New York: Dutton, 1922). Though not the first novel of this sort, it attracted favorable attention by portraying the progress of its central character in his psychoanalytic therapy with Dr. Sigurd Aubrey.

11. Hall had at this very time completed his autobiography (*Life and Confessions of a Psychologist.* New York: Appleton, 1923) in which he publicly portrayed the influence of Freud on his life and work in very nearly the same terms (pp. 409-414). Moreover, he reveals there (p. 449) that he had attempted to psychoanalyze himself but "finding the task too hard, called in an expert to finish the work, with results which nothing would ever tempt me to tell." This comment is made by Hall in the context of a discussion (pp. 447-451) of the various tests and methods to which he had, through the years, submitted himself for self-knowledge.

12. For a synopsis of Hall's courses at Clark University from 1908 onwards which involved psychoanalysis, see J. C. Burnham, "Sigmund Freud and G. Stanley Hall," *Psychoanalytic Quarterly,* 1960, *29,* 314-315. However, Hall was teaching similar subject matter before 1908.

13. *Jesus, the Christ, in the Light of Psychology.* (New York: Appleton, 1923.) Originally published in 1917, this book was reissued, nearly unchanged except for a very much longer Introduction, in November 1923. Hence the mention of it to Freud at this time. It is significant that Hall here explicitly avows Freud's influence in the writing of this personally special book which he republished simultaneously with his autobiography. However, the text itself shows only occasional applications of psychoanalytic theory, and it was in large measure finished by 1900. (See Dorothy Ross, *G. Stanley Hall.* Chicago: University of Chicago Press, 1972, p. 418.) The book is clearly significant in linking Hall's earlier theological vocation—he was first trained as a minister—to his later commitment to psychology.

14. Seven months after writing this letter Hall died of pneumonia on April 24, 1924 at the age of 80. In the spring of 1923, four months before writing his last letter to Hall, Freud developed an oral cancer of which he died, after sixteen years of suffering, on September 23, 1939, at the age of 83.

Coda

Freud did not answer this letter at the time but in the year after Hall's death in 1924, he contributed a short autobiography to a medical series *(Standard Edition, 20,* 3-74), in which he gave his answer in a word. Freud expressed gratitude for the 1909 recognition in Worcester and paid tribute to Hall "justly esteemed as a psychologist and educator [who] had introduced psychoanalysis into his courses several years earlier"; but he then added: "there was a touch of the 'king-maker' about him, a pleasure in setting up authorities and then deposing them." Hall's recognition of Adler and Jung still irritated Freud by thus detracting from his own eminence. Freud's need exceeded even the supreme tribute which Hall had paid him in his last letter. (See Part One, Chapter XII, "Hall the King-Maker.")

PART THREE

Freud's Clark Lectures

Introductory Note on Editions and
Translations of the Lectures

The five lectures which Freud delivered at Clark University, Tuesday, September 7, through Saturday, September 11, 1909 are here reproduced in a new translation by Saul Rosenzweig. These are presented not only for the orientation of the reader who may wish to enlarge his knowledge of the occasion but also because they still represent the best available outline by Freud of his theory in its essence. The anticipation of these lectures was, of course, the reason for the beginning of the Freud/Hall correspondence.

Freud delivered his lectures in German extemporaneously. He wrote them out after his return to Vienna, largely at the instigation of Hall who was arranging to have them translated for publication in a "Freud number" of the *American Journal of Psychology*, founded and edited by him. They corresponded about the translation from October 1909 through January 1910 and in that interval Freud sent the manuscript, in parts, to Hall for the use of the translator.

The contemporary translation, by Harry W. Chase, a Fellow in Psychology at Clark University under Hall, appeared in the April 1910 issue of the *Journal,* volume 21, pages 181-218, with the title "The Origin and Development of Psychoanalysis." This translation was often inaccurate and generally inept, partly perhaps because it was done under time pressure. (Hall in his letters to Freud about the pending translation, and to Brill, who made the translation of Jung's three lectures, repeatedly stressed the publication deadline.)

The later translation by James Strachey in the *Standard edition of the complete psychological works of Sigmund Freud* (1957, volume 11, pages 1-57) is based upon Freud's minimally revised version of the lectures prepared for his *Gesammelte Schriften* (volume 4, pages 349-406), published 1924. It is for some reason far less felicitous and fluent than the translations of other works in the *Standard Edition.*

Moreover, as Patrick J. Mahony has recently observed (*Freud and the Rat Man,* New Haven, Yale University Press, 1986, *passim*), Strachey's translations of Freud's writings often inadequately reflect Freud's message and unique rhetorical style. Mahony has tellingly cited many such shortcomings. His remarks are particularly pertinent in relation to the somewhat informal lectures at Clark in which Freud was attempting to convey a history of the origin and development of psychoanalytic theory in a manner that would carry conviction to a mixed audience, very few of whom were trained in psychoanalysis. Though the present new translation may not entirely satisfy Mahony's criteria, it was for just such reasons that the translation was undertaken years before his critique appeared. My intention was to make the translation both more accurate and more faithful to Freud's style than was the translation by Strachey. The effort appeared to be more or less uniquely justified because these lectures represented a turning point in the history of psychoanalysis—a watershed at which Freud paused, as it were, to provide a pithy and eloquent synopsis of the preceding pioneer decade of his work.

With Hall's assent, the German version of the lectures appeared during the week of May 26, 1910. The title was *Über Psychoanalyse. Fünf Vorlesungen gehalten zur 20jährigen Gründungsfeier der Clark University in Worcester, Mass., September, 1909.* Leipzig und Wien: Deuticke, 1910. Freud dedicated the volume to G. Stanley Hall. For historical authenticity that edition was employed in the present entirely new translation. To Freud's original footnotes has been added the only new one he prepared for the 1924 edition—the first footnote, in which he retracted the statement of his indebtedness to Breuer. It is noteworthy that this footnote constitutes the only difference in substance between the 1910 and 1924 German editions.

In the present translation all the footnotes have been collected and are printed in one continuous section at the end of the lectures.

Finally, it should be observed that in his publication of the lectures Freud took the liberty of not adhering strictly to the delivered content. He also significantly modified the order of the topics discussed. These differences, reconstructed by collating the published lectures with the contemporary newspaper reports, have been described in detail in Part One, Chapter VII.

S. R.

Lectures by Topic

Freud, Jung, and Hall the King-Maker

The psychoanalytic group with G. Stanley Hall

On Psychoanalysis

Five Lectures Delivered at the
Twentieth Anniversary Celebration of
the Founding of Clark University
in Worcester, Massachusetts
September 1909

By
PROF. DR. SIGM. FREUD, LL.D.

To
G. Stanley Hall, Ph.D., LL.D.

President of Clark University
Professor Psychology and Pedagogy

in gratitude

First Lecture

Ladies and Gentlemen: It is a novel and confusing experience for me to appear as lecturer before an eager audience in the New World. I assume that I owe this honor only to the connection of my name with the topic of psychoanalysis and, consequently, it is of psychoanalysis that I intend to speak. I shall attempt to give you in very brief compass a historical survey of the origin and further development of this new method of investigation and treatment.

If merit is due to the originator of psychoanalysis, the merit is not mine.[1] I did not participate in its earliest beginnings. I was a student, occupied with the preparation for my final examinations, when another Viennese physician, Dr. Josef Breuer,[2] applied this method for the first time in the case of a hysterical girl (1880-82). We shall start by examining the history of this case and its treatment. You can find it described in detail in *Studies on Hysteria*[3] later published by Dr. Breuer and myself.

First, however, an incidental remark. I have discovered with satisfaction that the majority of my audience are not of the medical profession. Now have no concern that a medical education is necessary to follow my discourse. We shall at the outset accompany the physicians for a short time, but soon we shall separate from them and go with Dr. Breuer along a unique path.

Dr. Breuer's patient was a highly intelligent girl of 21. She had developed, in the course of her more than two years of illness, a series of physical and mental disturbances which well deserve to be taken seriously. She had a severe paralysis of both right extremities, with anaesthesia, and at times she had the same disturbance in the limbs of her left side; she had disordered eye-movements, and many visual restrictions; difficulty in keeping her head in an upright position, an intense *Tussis nervosa* (uncontrollable cough); nausea when attempting to take nourishment, and, at one time, during a period of several weeks, an inability to drink despite tormenting thirst. There was a reduction in her capacity for language which progressed to the point of her being unable either to speak or to understand her mother tongue; and, finally, she was subject to states of "absence," of confusion, delirium— alterations of her whole personality—which we shall later have to consider separately.

When one hears of such a syndrome one does not need to be a physician to incline to the opinion that one is here concerned with a serious illness, probably of the brain, for which there is little hope of recovery and which will probably lead to the early death of the patient. However, physicians inform us that in a certain type of case with such severe symptoms a different and quite favorable prognosis is justified. When such a syndrome appears in a young female whose vital internal organs (heart, kidneys) are shown by objective investigations to be normal but who has experienced intense *emotional* agitations, and if the individual symptoms are exceptional in certain of their minute characteristics, then physicians do not regard such a case too gravely. They maintain that an organic lesion of the brain is not present but, rather, an enigmatic condition, known since the time of Greek medicine as *hysteria,* which can simulate a large number of syndromes of serious illness. They then judge that the life of the patient is not threatened and that even a complete restoration to health is probable. The differentiation of such a case of hysteria from one of severe organic illness is not always easy to make. But we do not need to know how a differential diagnosis of this kind is made; it is sufficient for us to be assured that Breuer's patient was just such a case in which no competent physician would fail to make a diagnosis of hysteria. We can also at this point add from the case report that her illness arose while she was nursing her dearly loved father, during his serious and fatal illness, and that she had to withdraw from this duty as a consequence of falling ill herself.

Thus far it has been an advantage to go along with the doctors, but we shall soon take leave of them. You should not, indeed, expect that the prospects of a patient to receive medical aid are, in fact, increased by a diagnosis of hysteria instead of serious brain disease. Medical skill is powerless in most cases involving serious brain disease, but the physician is likewise helpless in combating hysterical illness. He is obliged to rely upon benign Nature as to when and how the hopeful prognosis is to be realized. [4]

Hence, with the diagnosis of hysteria little is changed for the patient, though for the physician a great deal is thereby altered. We can observe that he orients himself quite differently toward a hysterical patient as compared to one with an organic illness. He will not take the same interest in the former as in the latter because, though his suffering is much less intense, the patient yet seems to demand that he be taken just as seriously. But there is still another element involved here. The physician who, through his studies, has learned so many things that are hidden from the layman, is able to visualize the causes of disease and the changes brought about by it (e.g., in the brain of a patient suffering from apoplexy or neoplasm). This must, up to a certain point, meet the situation since it suffices to give him an understanding of the disease picture. However, in the presence of the particulars of hysteria, all his knowledge, all his anatomic-physiological and pathological conceptualizations leave him in the lurch. He cannot comprehend hysteria; in its presence he is himself like a layman. And this situation is, of course, not agreeable for anyone who usually sets such great store by his knowledge. Hysterical patients are, accordingly, deprived of his sympathy. He regards them as persons who overstep the laws of his science—just as the orthodox believer regards the heretic. He attributes all possible evil to them, blames them for exaggeration and intentional deception, for malingering; and he punishes them by withholding his interest.

But Dr. Breuer in his relation to his patient does not merit this reproach. He offered her sympathy and interest although he did not at first understand how to help her. She apparently lightened his task through the distinguished characteristics of mind and character to which he bears witness in his graphic case history. His solicitous mode of observation also soon found the method by which the first effective relief became possible.

It had been noticed that the patient in her states of absence— alterations of consciousness with confusion—used to mutter a few words to herself which appeared to derive from some connection with the thoughts preoccupying her. The doctor, after recovering these words, put her into a kind of hypnosis and reiterated these words in order to encourage her associations to them. The patient complied and reproduced for the physician the mental images which controlled her mind during her states of absence and had betrayed themselves in the mentioned fragmentary utterances. These were deeply tragic, often poetically beautiful fantasies—we might call them daydreams—which usually took as their starting point the situation of a girl at the sickbed of her father. Once she had narrated a number of such fantasies, she seemed to be set free and restored to her normal mental condition. The state of ensuing wellbeing, which continued for several hours, yielded on the next day to a new state of absence which would be removed in the same manner through the narration of other fantasies. One could not escape the impression that the mental alterations which expressed themselves in the states of absence were a consequence of stimuli derived from these highly emotional fantasy formations. The patient herself, who at this stage of her illness, rather remarkably spoke and understood only English, named this novel method of treatment "talking cure" or, as a joke, designated it as "chimney sweeping."

It was soon realized that by such purging of the mind more could be accomplished than a temporary removal of the constantly recurring mental turbulence. Symptoms of the illness could be brought to disappear when during hypnosis the patient recalled on what occasion and in which connections the symptoms had first appeared if at the same time she gave vent to her feelings. "During the summer there had been a time of intense heat and the patient was suffering very severely from thirst; for, without being able to assign any reason, it had suddenly become impossible for her to drink. She reached for a desired glass of water but as soon as it touched her lips she pushed it away from her like a hydropobiac. As she did so, she was for a few seconds clearly in a state of absence. She took only fruit, melons and the like, in order to assuage her tormenting thirst. After this condition had lasted for about six weeks, she was once ruminating, under hypnosis, about her English lady companion, whom she did not like. She related with every sign of disgust how she had come into that lady's room and had seen her little dog, a nauseating creature, drinking out of a glass. She had said nothing for she wanted to be polite. After she had given energetic expression to her stifled anger, she asked for water, drank a large quantity of it uninhibitedly, and woke from hypnosis with the glass at her lips. Thereupon the disturbance disappeared forever." [5]

Permit me to dwell on this experience for a moment. No one had ever previously cured a hysterical symptom by such means or had, by doing so, entered so deeply into the understanding of its causation. It would have to be a discovery of great consequence if one were able to confirm the expectation that still other symptoms, perhaps the majority of them, arose in the patient in such a manner and could be removed in this way. Breuer spared no pains to convince himself of this assertion and he methodically investigated the pathogenesis of the other and more serious symptoms. Such was actually the case; almost all the symptoms had arisen in this way, as residues, as precipitates—if you will—of affect-laden events which we later labeled "psychic traumas," the peculiarity of which was explained through their relationship to the causative injurious situations. They were, to use the technical term, *determined* by the scenes, the memory traces of which they embodied, and need not any longer be described as capricious or enigmatic aspects of neurosis. Only one qualification must be noted: it was not always a single event which left the symptom behind. Most symptoms, instead, arose through the effective convergence of numerous, often very many similar, repeated traumas. This entire chain of pathogenic memories would then have to be reproduced in chronological order, but, in fact, reversed, the last ones first, and the first ones last. It was quite impossible to push through to the earliest, and often most cogent trauma, by skipping those which came later.

You will certainly now want to hear about other examples of the origin of her hysterical symptoms in addition to the one concerning the drinking inhibition which resulted from her disgust at seeing the dog drink from a glass. However, if I am to adhere to my program, I must limit myself to very few instances. Breuer relates that her visual disturbances could be traced to occasions "such as when the patient, sitting at her father's sickbed with tears in her eyes, was suddenly asked by him what the time was, whereupon trying to look but seeing only indistinctly, she brought the watch up so close to her face that the dial appeared much enlarged (compare the later macropsia and convergent squint). Again, she exerted herself to suppress her tears so that the sick man would not see them." [6] In like manner, all the pathogenic impressions stemmed from the period when she shared in the care of her sick father. "Once, at night, she was very anxiously attending the sick man, who had a high fever, and she was in suspense because a surgeon was expected from Vienna to perform an operation. Her mother had gone out for a while and Anna was sitting by the sickbed with her right arm over the back of the chair. She fell into a state of daydreaming in which she saw a black snake approaching the sick man as if to bite him. (It is very probable that in the meadow behind the house there actually were some snakes which had previously frightened the girl and thus furnished the material for the hallucination.) She wanted to drive away the animal but seemed paralyzed. Her right arm, hanging over the back of the chair, had 'fallen asleep.' It had become anaesthetic and paretic, and when she looked at it, the fingers were transformed into little snakes with death-heads (fingernails). She probably made an attempt to drive off the snake with her paralyzed right hand and in this way the anaesthesia and the paralysis became associated with the snake hallucination. When this image vanished, she tried in her anxiety to pray, but all speech failed her. She could not talk in any language until at last an *English* children's verse occurred to her and thereafter she continued to think and to pray in that language." [7] With the recall of this scene under hypnosis, the paralysis of the right arm which had existed since the start of the illness, was eliminated, and the treatment came to an end.

When, a number of years later, I began to employ Breuer's method of investigation and treatment with my own patients, I discovered that my experience agreed completely with his. A woman about 40 years of age had a tic, a peculiar smacking sound which she uttered without appropriate cause whenever she became excited. It had its origin in two events during both of which she had determined to make no sound and both times, by a kind of counter-will, this sound came from her mouth to break the stillness. The first time she had, after much effort, finally managed to get her child, who was ill, to fall asleep, and she told herself that she must now remain absolutely quiet in order not to awaken it. On the second occasion, during a carriage ride with her two children, a thunderstorm arose, the horses bolted, and she carefully avoided making any sound in order not to frighten the animals still more. [8] I give you these examples from among many others which are cited in the *Studies on Hysteria*. [9]

Ladies and Gentlemen, if you will permit me a generalization, which is inescapable in so abbreviated a presentation, we can summarize our findings up to this point in the formula: *Our hysterical patients suffer from reminiscences.* Their symptoms are residues and memory symbols for certain (traumatic) events. A comparison with other memory symbols in other areas will perhaps lead us to a deeper understanding of this symbolism. The memorials and monuments with which we decorate our large cities are just such symbols. If you take a walk through London, you find in front of one of the largest railway stations of the city an elaborately

decorated gothic pillar—*Charing Cross.* One of the old Planta-
genet kings in the XIIIth century, who had the body of his beloved
Queen Eleanor carried to Westminster, erected gothic crosses at
each of the stations where the coffin was set down, and *Charing
Cross* is the last of the monuments preserving the memory of the
sad procession. [10] At another place in the city, not far from London
Bridge, one sees a more modern, lofty pillar which is merely called
"The Monument." It commemorates the great fire which broke
out in that neighborhood in the year 1666 and destroyed a great
part of the city. These monuments are therefore memory symbols
similar to the symptoms of hysteria, and up to this point the comparison seems justified. But what would you say to a Londoner
who today stood in sorrow before the monument to the funeral of
Queen Eleanor instead of going about his business, with the haste
demanded by modern industrial conditions while rejoicing in the
youthful queen of his own heart? Or to another who, standing
before the "Monument," bemoaned the burning down of his beloved
native city which has long since been restored in more splendor
than before? Hysterical patients, indeed all neurotics, behave like
these two impractical Londoners, not only in that they remember
the painful experiences of the distant past but because they are still
strongly affected by them. They cannot free themselves from the
past; by dwelling on it they neglect the reality of the present. This
fixation of the mental life on pathogenic traumas is one of the most
important and practically significant characteristics of neurosis.

I am willing to yield to an objection which you are probably
framing as you think over the case history of Breuer's patient. All
traumas stemmed from the time when she was nursing her sick
father, and her symptoms can be regarded as memory traces of his
illness and death. They therefore express a state of mourning, and
fixation on memories of the dead person such a short time after
his decease signify nothing pathological. Instead, such conduct is
a normal expression of feeling. I concede this point; the fixation
on such traumas in the case of Breuer's patient is not at all
surprising. But in other cases, as in the one treated for tic, the
precipitations of which were distant by ten or fifteen years, the
mark of an abnormal adherence to the past is very clear, and
Breuer's patient would probably also have developed it had she not
benefited from the *cathartic* treatment so soon after experiencing
the traumas and developing the symptoms.

We have thus far discussed only the relationship of the hysterical symptoms to the life history of the patient. By considering two further aspects which Breuer observed, we can gain a clue as to how to conceptualize the process of falling ill and of recovering. With regard to the first, it is especially to be noted that in almost all pathogenic situations Breuer's patient had suppressed any strong excitement instead of permitting its discharge by appropriate emotion, by word and deed. In the minor episode of the lady-companion's dog, the patient suppressed, out of deference, every manifestation of her very intense disgust. While she was sitting by the bed of her father she was continually careful not to let the sick man observe any sign of her anxiety or of her sorrowful mood. When she later reproduced the same scene for the physician, the emotion which she had previously inhibited burst forth with special intensity as though it had been long pent up. In fact, the symptom which had been left over from that scene achieved its highest intensity when the doctor got close to the cause of it, and it vanished after the cause had been fully aired. On the other hand, experience shows that the recollection of a scene in the presence of the physician remained without effect if, for any reason whatever, it occurred without emotional expression. The fate of these affects, which can hence be conceived as displaceable quantities, were thus the decisive basis for the development of the illness as well as for the recovery. One is impelled to the assumption that the illness came into existence because the emotions developed in the pathological situations were denied a normal outlet; the essence of the illness consisted in an abnormal use of this underlying "strangulated" affect. In part they remained as a persisting burden on the psychic life and constituted a source of constant excitement for it; in part they underwent a transformation into unusual physical *innovations* and *inhibitions* which manifested themselves as the somatic symptoms of the case. We have coined the term "hysterical conversion" for this latter process. A certain portion of our own psychical excitement is, apart from this special process, led into the path of somatic innovation and yields what we know as "the expression of emotions." Now, hysterical conversion exaggerates that portion of the discharge of an affectively cathected mental process; it bespeaks a much more intensive expression of the emotions directed into new paths. If the bed of a stream flows in two channels, there will be an overflow of one of them as soon as the stream meets with an obstruction of the other.

You will note that we have arrived in our thinking at a purely psychological theory of hysteria in which we assign the affective processes the chief place. But now a second observation of Breuer obliges us to assign a role of great significance to the condition of consciousness in characterizing the pathological proceedings. Breuer's patient displayed numerous peculiar mental states—conditions of absence, confusion, and character alterations along with her normal condition. In the normal state she knew nothing of the pathogenic scenes and of their relation to her symptoms; she had forgotten these events or, at any rate, had split away the pathogenic connection. When she was hypnotized, it became possible, but only after considerable exertion, to recall these scenes to her memory, and by this process of recall the symptoms were removed. One would have encountered great difficulty in finding a way to interpret this situation had not previous experiences and experiments in hypnotism pointed the way. Through the investigation of hypnotic phenomena the conception had become familiar, though it seemed at first preposterous, that in one and the same individual mind several mental groupings are possible and that these can remain quite independent of one another, "know nothing" of one another, and can, by splitting, alternate in consciousness. Cases of this kind, known as "double conscience" [French for dual personality], occasionally come under observation as spontaneous occurrences. When in such splitting of the personality consciousness remains persistently attached to one of these two states, it is called the *conscious* mental condition, and the split-off portion is termed *unconscious*. In the well-known phenomenon of posthypnotic suggestion, in which a command given in hypnosis is involuntarily carried out in the later normal state, one has an excellent prototype of the influence which can be exerted upon consciousness by what is unconscious. Moreover, on this model one can interpret the phenomena of hysteria. Breuer arrived at the postulate that hysterical symptoms originate in such special mental states, which he called *hypnoidal*. Affective stimulation which occurs in such hypnoidal states readily becomes pathogenic because such states do not provide the conditions for a normal discharge of aroused emotion. There ensues, after the emotional arousal, an unusual product, namely, the symptom, which intrudes itself like a foreign body into the normal state of consciousness and the latter lacks any knowledge of the hypnoidal, pathogenic situation. When a symptom arises one thus finds an amnesia, a memory gap, and the closing of the gap is accomplished by the removal of the originating conditions of the symptom.

I am afraid that this part of my exposition may not have seemed very clear. However, you must bear in mind that we are dealing here with new and difficult views which can perhaps not be made much clearer. This circumstance proves that we have not yet advanced very far in our knowledge. Breuer's concept of the *hypnoidal* states has, moreover, proved to be a handicap, and to be superfluous, and it has been dropped from contemporary psychoanalysis. Presently you will learn at least something of the influences and processes discovered behind the dubious construct of hypnoidal states advanced by Breuer. You may also quite rightly have received the impression that Breuer's formulation was able to give only a very incomplete and unsatisfying explanation of the observed phenomena. But complete theories do not fall from heaven, and you would be even more justified to be skeptical if anyone at the beginning of his observations offered you a well-rounded theory without any gaps. Such a theory could certainly be only a child of speculation, not the product of an unprejudiced and objective investigation.

Second Lecture

Ladies and Gentlemen: At about the same time that Breuer was employing his "talking cure" with his patient, the renowned Charcot in Paris had begun those researches with his hysterical patients at the Salpêtrière which would lead to a new understanding of the disease. These results could not, however, have been known in Vienna at the time. But when, about a decade later, Breuer and I published our preliminary communication on the psychical mechanism of hysterical phenomena, which involved the cathartic treatment of Breuer's first patient, we were both of us completely under the influence of Charcot's investigations. We regarded the pathogenic experiences of our patients as psychical traumas equivalent to the physical ones the influence of which Charcot had invoked for hysterical paralyses; Breuer's hypothesis of hypnoidal states is nothing but a reflection of the fact that Charcot had artificially produced traumatic paralyses under hypnosis.

This great French observer, whose student I was in 1885-1886, was not himself inclined toward psychological conceptualizations. It was his student P. Janet who first attempted a deeper penetration into the distinctive psychical processes in hysteria, and we followed his example when we placed mental splitting and the dissociation of personality at the center of our conceptualization. In Janet, one encounters a theory of hysteria which accommodates itself to the prevailing doctrine in France concerning the role of heredity and degeneration. According to him, hysteria is a form of degenerative alteration of the nervous system which manifests itself through a congenital weakness of the capacity for psychic synthesis. The hysterical patient is, from the outset, incapable of bringing mental processes together into a unity, and thus arises the tendency toward mental dissociation. If you will allow me a banal but graphic analogy, Janet's hysterical patient resembles a frail woman who has gone out to shop and is now returning, laden with packages and boxes. She cannot manage the entire lot with her two arms and ten fingers, so she soon drops one. When she bends over to pick it up, she drops another, and so it continues. It is not consistent with this assumed mental weakness of hysterical patients that one can observe in them, in addition to the phenomena of diminished capacity, other instances of a partial increase in efficiency which may represent a compensation. At the time when

Breuer's patient had forgotten her mother tongue and every other language save English, her command of it was so great that if a German book was placed before her, she was able to give a faultless and fluent translation at sight.

When I later set about on my own account to continue the investigations begun by Breuer, I soon reached a different view of the origin of hysterical dissociation (or splitting of consciousness). Such a wide divergence of opinion was inevitable, and it was decisive for everything that followed; for my point of departure was not, like Janet's, that of laboratory research but, rather, a result of therapeutic intervention.

Above all else I was actuated by practical need. The cathartic treatment, as it had been practiced by Breuer, presupposed that the patient be put into deep hypnosis, for only in the hypnotic condition did the patient gain the knowledge of those pathogenic associations which eluded him in the normal state. But hypnosis soon became disagreeable to me as a capricious and, so to speak, a mystical treatment device, and when I discovered that in spite of all my efforts, I could not hypnotize more than a fraction of my patients, I decided to abandon hypnosis and to make the cathartic procedure independent of it. Since I could not successfully alter the conscious state of most of my patients at will, I directed my efforts to working with them in the normal state. At first this maneuver really seemed to be a senseless and hopeless undertaking. I had set myself the task of learning from the patient something that I did not know and which he himself did not know. How could one hope to acquire this knowledge in this way? But then there came to my aid a recollection of a very noteworthy and instructive experiment which I had personally observed under Bernheim at Nancy. Bernheim at that time demonstrated to us that individuals whom he brought into hypnotic somnambulism, and in that state had been put through all sorts of experiences, had only apparently lost the memory of these events, and that it was possible to revive these memories in the normal state. When he interrogated them about the somnambulistic events, they, indeed, at first asserted that they knew nothing, but if he did not yield, if he urged and assured them that they really did know, then the forgotten memories came back to them every time.

Accordingly, I did the same with my patients. When I had reached a point with them at which they asserted that they knew nothing more, I would assure them that they did know, that they should just continue to speak, and I ventured to assert that the memory which would emerge at the moment when I placed my hand on the patient's forehead would be the correct one. In this manner I succeeded in learning from the patients without employing hypnosis that which was required to reconstruct the connection between the forgotten pathogenic scenes and the symptoms which these had left behind. But this was a laborious procedure and, in the long haul, an exhausting one which was not suited to be a definitive technique.

But I did not give it up without drawing definite conclusions from the observations I had made. I had thus confirmed that the forgotten memories were not lost. They were in the possession of the patient, ready to become conscious and form associations with his other mental content, but were prevented from becoming conscious and obliged to become unconscious because of some hindering force. One could with assurance assume the existence of this force since one detected its operative strength when one tried, in opposition to it, to bring the unconscious memories into the patient's consciousness. One could recognize this force, which maintained the pathological condition, as *resistance* on the part of the patient.

It was on this idea of resistance that I based my conception of the mental processes in hysteria. It proved necessary to remove this resistance in order to effect a recovery. Starting with the mechanism of the recovery, one could now formulate some very definite ideas about the genesis of the illness. The same forces, which now, as resistance, stood in the way of the appearance of the forgotten ideas in consciousness, must themselves have caused the forgetting by repressing the pathogenic experiences in question from awareness. I named this hypothetical process *repression* and considered it as proved by the undeniable existence of *resistance.*

One could now examine the problem as to what these forces were and what were the conditions of repression in which the pathogenic mechanism of hysteria could be recognized. A comparative investigation of the pathogenic situations which we had learned to know through the cathartic treatment made possible an answer to this question. It appeared that in all these experiences a wish had been aroused which stood in sharp opposition to the individual's other wishes and which could not be reconciled with the ethical and esthetic standards of his personality. There had been a brief conflict, and at the end of this inner struggle the idea which presented itself to consciousness as the representative of this irreconcilable wish met with repression. The idea with all its associated memories was forced out of consciousness and forgotten. The incompatibility of the idea in question with the ego of the patient was thus the motive of the repression; the ethical and other demands of the individual were the repressing forces. The acceptance of the unbearable wish or the continuation of the conflict would have involved a high degree of unpleasantness; and this unpleasantness was avoided by the repression which was thus shown to be a device for the protection of the personality.

Instead of giving you many examples, I shall describe a single one of my cases in which the conditions and the advantages of repression can be clearly enough recognized. For the present purpose I shall, of course, have to abridge the case history and omit important theoretical points. A young girl had recently lost her beloved father in whose care she had participated—a situation analogous to that of Breuer's patient. When her older sister married, the patient came to have a peculiar feeling of sympathy for her new brother-in-law which she was readily able to disguise as a form of family affection. This sister soon fell ill and died while the patient was away with her mother. The absent ones were hastily recalled without being given definite information about the painful event. When the girl stood by the bed of her dead sister there arose in her mind for one brief moment an idea which might be expressed in these words: Now he is free and can marry me. We may safely assume that this idea, betraying to her the intense love which she felt for her brother-in-law but not previously conscious to her, was consigned the next moment to repression by her revolted feelings. The girl fell ill with severe hysterical symptoms. When I undertook her treatment it appeared that she had completely forgotten the scene at the bed of her sister and the hatefully egotistic impulse that had arisen in her. During the treatment she remembered and reproduced the pathogenic moment with every indication of intense emotional excitement, and by this treatment she recovered her health.

Perhaps I can make the process of repression and its essential relation to resistance more vivid for you through a rough analogy drawn from our own situation at the present instant. Let us assume

that in this hall and among this audience, whose exemplary quiet-
ness and attentiveness I cannot sufficiently commend, there is
nevertheless present one individual who is creating a disturbance
and, by his ill-bred laughter, chatter and foot-shuffling, distracts
my attention from my task. I declare that I cannot continue with
my lecture under these circumstances, whereupon some of the
strong men among you get up and, after a short struggle, eject the
disturber of the peace from the hall. He is thus now "repressed"
and I can continue my lecture. However, in order to prevent a
repetition of the disturbance in case the ejected man should again
attempt to enter the hall, the gentlemen who have acted in my
behalf take their chairs to the door and establish themselves there
as a "resistance" to maintain the repression. If you now translate
the two localities in this example psychologically as "conscious"
and "unconscious," you will have a rather good facsimile of the
process of repression.

We now see wherein the difference between our theory and that
of Janet lies. We do not derive the mental splitting from a congenital incapacity in the mental apparatus to synthesize experiences; rather, we explain it dynamically by the conflict of opposing
mental forces and recognize in it the result of an active striving of
two psychical groupings against each other. Unseen by us there
now arise a large number of new questions. The situation of psychic
conflict exists very frequently, and an effort of the ego to protect
itself against painful memories can be regularly observed without
finding it to result in a mental splitting. We cannot avoid the
conclusion that there must be still further conditions before conflict
will result in dissociation. I thus gladly grant you that with the
hypothesis of repression, we stand not at the end but only at the
beginning of a psychological theory. But we can advance only one
step at a time, and the completion of our knowledge must await
further and more thorough work.

Let us refrain from trying to interpret the case of Breuer from
the standpoint of repression. This case history does not lend itself
to such a formulation for it was achieved by the help of hypnosis.
Only when you exclude hypnosis can you observe the resistances
and repressions and get an adequate idea of the pathogenic
processes. Hypnosis conceals the resistance and makes a certain
portion of the mental field accessible, but it at the same time heaps

up the resistances at the frontiers of this area into a rampart beyond which everything is inaccessible.

The most valuable result which we have learned from Breuer's observations concerns the findings about the connection between the symptoms and the psychogenic, traumatic experiences, and we must not now neglect to evaluate these insights from the standpoint of the repression theory. It is not at first evident how we can move from repression to the formation of symptoms. Instead of giving you a complicated theoretical formulation, I shall at this point return to the illustration previously used to clarify the repression process. Recall that with the expulsion of the rowdy and the establishment of the guards at the door, the affair was not concluded. It can quite readily happen that the ejected person, now embittered and quite reckless, gives us further trouble. He is indeed no longer among us; we have been freed from his presence, his scornful laughter, and his half-audible remarks. But in a certain sense the repression has still miscarried, for he now makes a terrible exhibition of himself on the outside, and by his outcries and by hammering on the door with his fists interferes with my lecture even more than he did by his previous bad behavior. Under these circumstances we would be delighted if our honored President, Dr. Stanley Hall, were willing to undertake the role of mediator and peacemaker. He would speak with the rowdy on the outside and then come to us with the recommendation to let the fellow return with Dr. Hall's guarantee that the offender would henceforth behave himself properly. On Dr. Hall's authority we resolve to accept this suggestion, and so lift the repression, and now quiet and peace reign again. The analogy is a quite good description of the task which falls to the physician in the psychoanalytic therapy of the neuroses.

To state the matter more directly: Through the investigation of hysterical patients and other neurotics we reached the conviction that their repression of the idea to which the intolerable wish is attached has *failed*. They have indeed driven it out of consciousness and out of memory and appear to have thereby spared themselves a great deal of pain. *But in the unconscious the repressed wish continues to exist,* just waiting for the opportunity to become activated, and when this happens, to send into consciousness a distorted and unrecognizable *substitute* for the repressed idea. To this substitute is attached the same unpleasantness which the repression had been intended to prevent. But this surrogate of the repressed—the *symptom*—is secure against further attacks on the part of the defending ego: instead of a short conflict, there now begins a state of illness which time does not bring to an end. One can discern in the symptom, alongside the signs of distortion, a remnant of indirect similarity to the originally repressed idea. The route along which the substitute formation was produced can be discovered during the psychoanalytic treament of the patient; and for his recovery it is necessary that the symptom be traced back over the same route to the repressed idea. If the repressed material is once more made part of the conscious mental activity—a procedure which presupposes the overcoming of considerable resistance—the ensuing psychic conflict, which the patient had wanted to avoid, can achieve, under the guidance of the physician, a better outcome than repression had afforded. There are several such effective solutions for bringing conflict and neurosis to a happy termination, and in certain cases these may be combined with one another. Either the person may become convinced that he had been wrong to reject the pathogenic wish, and he then is induced to accept it in whole or in part; or this wish may itself be directed to a higher and hence unobjectionable goal (a process called *sublimation*); or, again, the rejection of the wish may be recognized as rightly motivated, and then the automatic, and therefore ineffective, mechanism of repression is replaced by a judgment made under the auspices of the highest mental functions of the person, i.e., a conscious control of the impulse is achieved.

Forgive me if I have not succeeded in giving you a more readily intelligible conception of the main points of the treatment method now known as *psychoanalysis*. The difficulties lie not merely in the novelty of the subject. My continuing remarks will therefore elucidate the manner in which intolerable wishes, despite repression, are able to make their appearance outside the unconscious; and we shall also consider what subjective or constitutional conditions must be present in a person to account for the failure of repression and permit the formation of surrogates or symptoms.

Third Lecture

Ladies and Gentlemen: It is not always easy to tell the truth, especially when one has to be concise; hence I am today obliged to correct an error which I made in my last lecture. I told you then that after abandoning hypnosis I, nevertheless, pressed my patients to tell me whatever entered their minds in relation to the problem under discussion. I urged that they, indeed, knew everything that was apparently forgotten, and that the thought to emerge would certainly be what we were seeking. I did indeed then find that the next idea of the patient did produce the right clue and could be shown to be the forgotten continuation of the memory. Now that statement is not, by and large, correct; I made it sound as simple as that out of the need for brevity. In reality, it usually happened only the first few times that the forgotten material emerged through mere pressure on my part. If the procedure was continued, ideas kept on coming that could not be the right ones since they were not to the purpose and were rejected by the patients themselves as incorrect. Pressure was of no further service here and it seemed regrettable that hypnosis had been given up.

In this state of perplexity I clung to a prejudice for which the scientific justification was produced years later by my friend C. G. Jung and his students in Zurich. I must admit that it is often of great advantage to have prejudices. Mine was a strong belief in the rigorous determination of mental processes and I therefore could not believe that any thought occurring to the patient under concentrated attention could be entirely arbitrary or entirely unrelated to the forgotten idea we were seeking. That the two ideas were not identical could be explained satisfactorily through the hypothetical psychological situation. In the patient under treatment, two forces were working against each other: on the one hand, the conscious endeavor to bring up into consciousness the forgotten experience present in the unconscious; on the other, the resistance about which we already know and which would set itself against the emergence of the repressed material or its associates. If this resistance was absent or very weak, the forgotten material would become conscious without distortion. So it was plausible to assume that the disguise of the material being sought would be the greater, the greater the resistance to the emergence of it. The idea which occurred to the patient in place of the one being sought had therefore itself been produced like a symptom; it was a new artificial and transitory substitute for the repressed and differed from the repressed just in proportion to the completeness of the disguise created by the resistance. However, the substitute must still exhibit a certain similarity to what was being sought by virture of its character as a symptom, and if the resistance was not too intense, one should be able to detect from the idea which had occurred the hidden object of the search. The idea which had occurred would have to stand in relation to the repressed element like an allusion, like a statement of the same thing in *indirect* terms.

We know instances in the field of normal mental life in which situations analogous to that which we have assumed yield similar results. One such case is that of wit. The problems of psychoanalytic technique obliged me to consider the technique of making jokes. I shall offer one such example, which, incidentally, originally appeared in English.

The anecdote runs: Two not overly scrupulous businessmen had succeeded in accumulating a large capital through a series of very dubious deals, and they then began trying to force their way into high society. It seemed to them that, among other effective means, it would be well to have their portraits painted by the most famous and expensive artist in the city—one whose finished paintings were considered to be special events. At a large soirée the expensive portraits were exhibited for the first time and the two hosts personally led the most influential connoisseur and art critic up to the wall of the salon on which both portraits had been hung, side by side, in order to elicit his admiring judgment. The critic gazed at the pictures for a long time, shook his head as though something was missing, then pointed to the empty space between the portraits, and quietly asked: "And where is the Saviour?" [11] I see that you are all laughing at this excellent joke which we shall now attempt to elucidate. We infer that the connoisseur means to say: You are a couple of thieves, like those between whom the Saviour was nailed on the cross. But this he does not say; instead he expresses himself in a manner that at first seems peculiarly inappropriate and unrelated to the matter in hand, but which at the next moment is recognizable as an *allusion* to the insult he intends and serves as a perfect substitute for it. Now, we cannot expect to find in jokes all those characteristics which we presume to be involved in the source of the associations that occur to our patients, but I want to stress the identity of the motivation in jokes and in patients' associations. Why does our critic not say directly to the two rascals what he would like to say? Because, in addition to his desire to say it to their faces, there is active in him a very definite counter-motive. It is not without danger to insult people whose guests we are and who can call to their aid numerous servants with powerful fists. One might readily suffer the same fate which, in my previous lecture, I brought forward in the analogy to "repression." Hence the critic does not express the intended insult directly but instead puts it in a disguised form as an "allusion with omission"; and the same pattern is involved, according to our view, when our patients produce some more or less distorted substitute for the forgotten idea which is being sought.

Ladies and Gentlemen, it is very convenient to designate a group of interdependent ideas which possess a common affect a *"complex,"* in accordance with the practice of the Zurich school (Bleuler, Jung, and others). In that context we see that if we set out from the last memories of a patient in order to seek a repressed complex, we shall have every prospect of discovering it if the patient will communicate to us a sufficient number of his freely occurring associations. So we let the patient talk along as he will and hold firmly to the hypothesis that nothing can occur to him unless it depends in some indirect way on the complex we are seeking. If this method of discovering the repressed material appears to be too circumstantial, I can at least assure you that it is the only practicable one.

If this technique is adopted we are, however, disturbed by the fact that the patient will often pause, come to a standstill, and assert that he finds nothing to say—nothing whatever occurs to him. If this were really the case and the patient correct in his assertion, then our procedure would again be proved ineffectual. But closer observation shows that such an absence of ideas never actually happens. This phenomenon is only present when the patient holds back or rejects an idea he has become aware of under the influence of resistances which disguise themselves as various critical judgments about the value of the idea. One can protect oneself in advance against this difficulty by warning the patient of this circumstance and instructing him to renounce such criticism. He must say whatever comes into his mind with complete disregard of such critical selection, even if he may think it incorrect, irrelevant, nonsensical and, above all, if it is unpleasant for him to dwell on the thought that has occurred to him. By following this prescription we are sure to obtain the material which puts us on the track of the repressed complex.

This associative material upon which the patient places little value when he is under the influence of the resistance instead of relying on the physician, is comparable, for the psychoanalyst, to ore from which, by the aid of simple interpretive methods, one can extract a yield of valuable metal. If one desires to obtain a rapid and preliminary knowledge of a patient's repressed complexes without going into their organization and interconnection, one can usefully employ the method of the *association experiment* as developed by Jung and his students. [12] This procedure is for the psychoanalyst what qualitative analysis is for the chemist. It can be dispensed with in the therapy of neurotic patients but it is indispensible for the objective demonstration of complexes and in the research on the psychoses which the Zurich school has undertaken with such fruitful results.

Working over the ideas which enter the mind of the patient when he submits to the chief condition of the psychoanalytic method is not the only technical means for the exploration of the unconscious. The same object is served by two other procedures: the interpretation of dreams and the evaluation of bungled and haphazard acts.

I confess, my esteemed listeners, that for a long time I hesitated whether, instead of offering you a condensed survey of the whole field of psychoanalysis, I should rather offer you a thorough consideration of the *interpretation of dreams.* A purely subjective and seemingly secondary motive dissuaded me from that choice. It seemed almost scandalous that in a country so devoted to practical goals I should present myself to you as a "dream interpreter" before you had a chance to know what significance this ancient and despised art can claim. The interpretation of dreams is, in fact, the *via regia* to the knowledge of the unconscious—the most secure foundation of psychoanalysis and the field in which every worker must acquire his convictions and gain his education. If I am asked how one can become a psychoanalyst, I therefore answer: through a study of one's own dreams. With fine discretion all opponents of psychoanalysis up to now have either evaded any evaluation of *The Interpretation of Dreams* or have attempted to pass over it with the most superficial objections. [13] If, on the contrary, you are able to accept the solution of the problems of dream life, the innovations which psychoanalysis presents to your thought will no longer involve difficulties.

Do not forget that our nightly dreams show, on the one hand, the greatest external similarity and internal relationship to mental illness but, on the other hand, they are compatible with complete health in waking life. It does not sound at all absurd to say that anyone who regards these "normal" sensory illusions, delusions, and alterations of character with amazement, instead of attempting to understand them, has very little prospect of comprehending diseased mental states except in the lay sense. You may confidently count all of today's psychiatrists among such laymen. Follow me now on a rapid expedition through the domain of dream problems.

When we are awake, we are accustomed to treat our dreams with as little consideration as the patient does the association of ideas which the psychoanalyst requires of him. We also dismiss them from our minds since, as a rule, we quickly and completely forget them. Our low estimate of dreams is founded on the alien character even of those which are not confused and nonsensical, and upon the obvious absurdity and senselessness of other dreams. Our rejection derives from the uninhibited shamelessness and immoral longings which come to the fore in many dreams. Antiquity, as is well known, did not share this low opinion of dreams. Even today the lower strata of our society do not make the mistake of underestimating dreams; like the ancients, they expect dreams to reveal the future.

I confess that I feel no need to adopt mystical hypotheses in order to fill the gaps in our present knowledge and, therefore, I have never been able to find any support for the prophetic nature of dreams. But there remain many other things, quite wonderful enough, to be said about dreams.

In the first place, not all dreams are to the dreamer alien, incomprehensible and confused. If you undertake to examine the dreams of very young children, from ages one-and-a-half onward, you find it quite simple and easy to explain them. The little child always dreams the fulfillment of wishes which were aroused in him the day before and were not satisfied. You need no interpretive skill to arrive at this simple solution; you only need information about the experiences of the child on the previous day (the "dream day"). Now it would certainly be the most satisfying solution of the dream riddle if the dreams of adults were, like those of children, the fulfillment of wishes which had been aroused in them on the dream day. Such is, in fact, the case; the difficulties that stand in the way of this solution can be removed step by step through a systematic analysis of the dreams.

There is, first of all, the most weighty objection that the dreams of adults ordinarily have an incomprehensible content which is not readily traceable to wish fulfillment. The answer runs thus: these dreams have undergone a process of distortion; the psychic process which underlies them would have originally found a quite different verbal expression. You must distinguish the *manifest dream content,* which in the morning you recall confusedly and laboriously, clothed in words rather arbitrarily, from the *latent dream thoughts* which, you must assume, were present in the unconscious. This dream distortion is the same process which you have learned to know from the investigation of hysterical symptom formation. Investigation shows that the same interplay of psychical forces enters into the formation of dreams as into the formation of symptoms. The manifest dream content is the distorted surrogate for the unconscious dream thoughts, and the distortion is the work of the defensive forces of the ego, of resistances. These generally prevent the repressed wishes of the unconscious any access to consciousness during waking life, but even in the more relaxed condition of sleep, they are still at least strong enough to necessitate that they be cloaked in a sort of masquerade. The dreamer therefore knows as little about the meaning of his dreams as the hysterical patient does about the organization and significance of his symptoms.

You can convince yourself that there are latent dream thoughts and that between them and the manifest dream content there exists, in fact, the relationship I have described by undertaking an analysis of dreams by a technique consistent with that of psychoanalysis. You lay aside entirely the apparent connections of the elements in the manifest dream and look for the spontaneous thoughts which are yielded by free association according to the psychoanalytic rule of procedure for every single dream element. From this material the latent dream thoughts may be discovered exactly as one discovers from spontaneous thoughts of the patient the relation of his symptoms and memories to his concealed complexes. From the latent dream thoughts found in this way you will at once see how well justified one is in comparing the dreams of adults with those of children. What is now substituted for the manifest dream content is the true sense of the dream, something which is always clearly understandable, is related to the life experiences of the dream day, and which proves to be the fulfillment of unsatisfied wishes. The manifest dream which one recalls on waking can then be described as a *disguised* fulfillment of *repressed* wishes.

You can also now, by a kind of synthetic work, gain insight into the process of disguise by which the unconscious dream thoughts have become the manifest dream content. We call this process the "dream work." It merits our fullest theoretical interest because in it, as nowhere else, we can study what unsuspected psychical processes are possible in the unconscious or, expressed more exactly, *between* two separate psychical systems like the conscious and the unconscious. Among these newly discovered psychical processes those of *condensation* and *displacement* stand out most prominently. Dream work is a special case of the interaction of different mental groupings upon one another, hence it is a consequence of mental splitting; and it appears in all essentials to be identical with that distortion which transforms the repressed complexes into symptoms in the event of unsuccessful repression.

You will furthermore discover with astonishment by the analysis of dreams, most convincingly of your own, the unsuspected importance which the impressions and experiences of the early years of childhood have for the development of human beings. In dream life the child continues his existence in the man and retains all his peculiarities and wishes, including those which have become useless in later life. With irresistible power it will be impressed upon you by what processes of development, transformation, sublimation, and reaction formation there arises out of the child, who is by endowment quite different, the so-called normal man, the bearer and, in part, the victim of our painfully acquired civilization.

I would also call your attention to the fact found through the analysis of dreams that the unconscious makes use of certain special symbolism for the representation of sexual complexes—symbolism which is, in part, variable with the individual, but, for the rest, is typical in form and seems to make use of the symbolism suspected to underlie myths and fairy tales. It is not impossible that these creations of the folk mind may find their explanation through the study of dreams.

Finally, I must warn you not to be led astray by the objection that the occurrence of anxiety dreams contradicts our view of the dream as a wish fulfillment. Apart from the fact that these anxiety dreams require interpretation before one can pass judgment on them, one must quite generally say that the anxiety does not depend on the content of the dream quite so simply as one might suppose without further knowledge and attention paid to the conditions of neurotic anxiety. Anxiety is one of the ways in which the ego reacts against wishes which have become strongly repressed and, therefore, anxiety in the dream can also be quite well explained by assuming that the dream has gone too far in the representation of these repressed wishes in the service of fulfilling them.

You see that the investigation of dreams would be justified for its own sake by the conclusions it has yielded concerning matters otherwise difficult to understand. But we came to it in connection with the psychoanalytic treatment of neurotics. From what has been said up to now you can easily understand how the interpretation of dreams, if it has not become excessively difficult through the resistances of the patient, leads to a knowledge of the hidden and repressed complexes which he is harboring. Now I can pass on to the third group of mental phenomena, the study of which has become one of the technical aids of psychoanalysis.

These phenomena are the small bungled acts of normal, as well as of neurotic, individuals to which no significance is ordinarily attached. They include the forgetting of things which one is expected to know and at other times actually does know (for example, the temporary forgetting of proper names); slips of the tongue, which so frequently occur; the analogous slips in writing and in reading, faults in performance, and the losing or breaking of objects, etc. For all these matters a psychological determination is not, as a rule, expected and they have been allowed to pass unexplained as chance events, as the consequences of distraction, inattention and similar conditions. Here, too, are found the acts and gestures which individuals carry out without noticing them at all, to say nothing of the fact that they attribute no psychological importance to them: acts such as playing or trifling with objects, humming melodies, manipulating parts of one's body and one's clothing, and other such behavior. [14] These small matters, the *faulty performance* of *symptomatic* and *accidental acts,* are not quite as meaningless as people are ready to suppose by a sort of tacit agreement. They invariably have a meaning which can be easily and surely ascertained from the situations in which they occur. It can be demonstrated that they, again, give expression to impulses and intentions which are meant to be held back and hidden from the consciousness of the person, or that they derive from exactly the same repressed wishes and complexes that we have already learned to recognize as the makers of symptoms and the fashioners of dreams. These also, therefore, deserve to be regarded as symptoms, and examination of them, like the study of dreams, can lead to the disclosure of what is hidden in the life of the mind. By their aid a person usually betrays the most intimate of his secrets. If they come to light so very easily and frequently even in healthy individuals with whom repression has, on the whole, been quite successful, this fact is attributable to their triviality and inconspicuousness. But they can lay claim to a high theoretical value because they demonstrate the existence of repression and of substitute formation even under conditions of health.

You already see that the psychoanalyst is committed to a very strong belief in the determination of mental life. For him there is nothing trifling, nothing arbitrary or accidental in mental activity. He expects always to find sufficient motivation where one ordinarily does not make such claims. Indeed, he is prepared to find *several motives* for the same mental effect while our presumably innate need for casual explanation declares itself satisfied with a single psychical cause.

If you will now bring together the means that we possess for discovering the hidden, the forgotten, and the repressed in mental life—the study of the ideas produced in patients by free association, their dreams, and their accidental and symptomatic acts—and if you will add to these the evaluation of other phenomena that occur during psychoanalytic treatment and on which I shall later make some remarks under the heading of "transference," then you will come with me to the conclusion that our technique is already efficacious enough for the solution of the problem of how to introduce the pathogenic psychical material into consciousness and so to do away with the suffering produced by the formation of substitute symptoms. It is certainly to be regarded as a special advantage and merit of this work that during our therapeutic endeavors we enrich and deepen the knowledge of the mental life of both normal and sick human beings.

I do not know whether you have received the impression that the technique of which I have shown you the resources is peculiarly difficult. In my view it is, on the contrary, entirely practicable for one who has mastered it. But it is quite certain that it is not self-explanatory, that it has to be learned just as the techniques of histology and surgery need to be. You will perhaps be surprised to hear that in Europe we have encountered a spate of judgments on psychoanalysis from individuals who know nothing about this technique and do not employ it and then scornfully demand of us that we must demonstrate to them the correctness of our results. Among these adversaries there are certain individuals who are not unfamiliar with the scientific mode of thought, for example, those who would not reject the result of a microscopic investigation because it cannot be confirmed in an anatomical preparation with the naked eye, and would judge the matter only after they themselves had made use of the microscope. But in the psychoanalytic area the prospects of recognition are, indeed, less favorable. Psychoanalysis tries to bring that which is repressed in the mind to conscious recognition, and everyone who passes judgment is himself a human being who shares such repressions which are perhaps kept under control only with difficulty. It must, therefore, arouse in him the same resistance which it awakens in patients, and this resistance finds it easy to cloak itself as an intellectual rejection and to advance arguments similar to those against which we protect our patients by the basic psychoanalytic rule. We can often observe in our opponents, just as we can in our patients, a very marked affective influence upon their judgmental capacity which tends to diminish it. The presumptuousness of the conscious mind, which, for example, dismisses the dream so disdainfully, constitutes one of the strongest protective devices that universally prevails in us to prevent the breaking through of unconscious complexes, and for that reason it is very difficult to convince people of the reality of the unconscious and to teach them new facts that stand in contradiction to their conscious knowledge.

Fourth Lecture

Ladies and Gentlemen: You will at this point be wanting to know what the availability of the technical methods I have described has taught us about the pathogenic complexes and repressed wishes of neurotics.

This one thing above all others: psychoanalytic research with quite surprising regularity traces back the symptoms of our patients to impressions from their sexual life and shows us that the pathogenic wishes derive essentially from erotic impulse components— a result which obliges us to assume that, equally in both sexes, the greatest significance must be attributed to erotic disturbances in the etiological factors of the illness.

I know that this assertion will not readily be believed. Even those investigators who are quite ready to follow along in my psychological endeavors are inclined to believe that I overrate the etiological contribution of sexual factors and ask me why other mental excitations should not also lead to the phenomena of repression and substitute formation that I have described. My answer is: I do not know why they should not, and I have no objection to their doing so, but experience demonstrates that they do not have such significance and that at most they lend support to the effect of sexual factors but cannot replace them. This position was not postulated by me on theoretical grounds; even in the *Studies on Hysteria,* published in 1895 with Dr. J. Breuer, I did not adopt this standpoint. I had to adopt it when my experiences became more numerous and led me more deeply into the nature of the matter. Gentlemen, there are present among you here some of my closest friends and adherents who have traveled with me to Worcester. Inquire of them and you will learn that they were all at first completely skeptical of the assertion concerning the decisive significance of the sexual etiology until through their own analytic efforts they were obliged to concur in it.

The behavior of patients does not make it easier to acquire conviction about the correctness of the view here in question. Instead of quite willingly imparting to us information about their sexual life, they seek by every possible means to conceal it. People are not generally candid in sexual matters. They do not freely discuss their sexuality; instead they wear a heavy overcoat, to conceal it with a fabric of lies, as though bad weather prevailed in the world of sexuality. And they are not wrong in so behaving. Sun and cool wind are not really favorable to sexual activity in our civilized world; in fact, none of us can freely disclose his sexual life to others. But when your patients have come to realize that in your treatment of them they can be comfortable in making such disclosures, they lay aside this veil of lies and then only are you in a position to form an opinion on this controversial subject. Unfortunately even physicians are not favored above the other children of men in their personal orientation to the question of the sex life, and many of them are under the ban of that mixture of prudery and prurience which dominates the attitude of most "civilized men" in matters of sexuality.

Let me now proceed to share our findings with you. In one series of cases, psychoanalytic investigation, it is true, traces back the symptoms not to sexual but to commonplace traumatic experiences. But this distinction becomes meaningless on further consideration. A thorough explanation and complete cure of a patient require that the analytic work not cease in any instance with the experiences current at the time of the illness onset; in all cases it finds its way back to the time of puberty and early childhood. Only there does one come upon the impressions and events which determined the later ailment. Only the childhood experiences can provide the explanation for the susceptibility to later traumas, and only by disclosing and making conscious these memory traces, almost regularly forgotten, do we achieve the capacity to remove the symptoms. We arrive here at the same conclusion as in the investigation of dreams—that it is the enduring, repressed wishes of childhood which provide the power for the formation of symptoms, and without them the reaction to later traumas would have taken a normal course. But these powerful childhood wishes are almost invariably of a sexual nature.

Now, at any rate, I can be certain that I have provoked you to astonishment. Is there a sexuality of infancy? you will ask. On the contrary, is not the time of childhood just the period of life which is characterized by a lack of sexual drive? No, Gentlemen, it is not true that the sexual drive enters into children at puberty as, in the Gospel, the Devil entered into the swine. The child has sexual drives and sexual behavior from the outset; he enters the world with them, and the so-called normal sexuality of adults emerges in stages from that source through an intelligible and rich development. It is not really difficult to observe these sexual activities of children; rather, it requires a certain ingenuity to overlook them or deprive them of significance.

Through a lucky chance, I am in a position to call a witness for my assertion from your own midst. I hold in my hand the work of a Dr. Sanford Bell which was published in 1902 in the *American Journal of Psychology* [vol. 13, 325-354]. The author is a Fellow of Clark University, the very institution in the precincts of which we are now meeting. In this work, entitled "A preliminary study of the emotion of love between the sexes," which appeared three years before my *Three Essays on the Theory of Sexuality,* the author says exactly what I have been telling you: "The emotion of sex-love . . . does not make its appearance for the first time at the period of adolescence, as has been thought." [p. 328] He carried out his work in what we in Europe call the American manner, i.e., by making no less than 2500 empirical observations, gathered in the course of 15 years, and including 800 made by him personally. About the indications through which the condition of being in love manifests itself, he states: "The unprejudiced mind in observing these manifestations in hundreds of couples of children cannot escape referring them to sex origin. The most exacting mind is satisfied when to these observations are added the confessions of those who have, as children, experienced the emotion to a marked degree of intensity, and whose memories of childhood are relatively distinct." [p. 330] However, those of you who are not inclined to believe in infantile sexuality will be mainly surprised to learn that, among those children who fell in love so early, not a few are found at the tender ages of three, four and five years.

It would not surprise me if you were more inclined to believe the observations of a fellow countryman rather than mine. I myself was fortunate enough to enjoy such an experience a short time ago. I acquired a rather complete picture of the physical and mental activity present at an early stage of childhood sexual life through the analysis of a five-year-old boy, who was suffering from anxiety, and which was skillfully conducted by his own father. [15] And I may remind you that in this same hall a few hours ago my friend Dr. C. G. Jung delivered a lecture on his observation of a quite young girl who, from a similar precipitating condition as that in my patient—the birth of a sibling—disclosed and confirmed almost the identical sensual impulses, wishes and complexes. [16] I therefore am not without hope that you will be reconciled to the idea of infantile sexuality which at first seemed so strange. And I should like to cite the commendable example of the Zurich psychiatrist E. Bleuler who asserted publicly a few years ago that he "could not comprehend my sexual theories" but since then has confirmed infantile sexuality in its entire scope through his own observations. [17]

It is only too easy to explain why most individuals, medical observers and others, are inclined to know nothing concerning the sexual life of the child. Under the pressure of civilizing education they have forgotten their own infantile sexual behavior and they do not want to be reminded of what has been repressed. They would acquire a different conviction if they were to begin their inquiries by a self-analysis—a revision and intepretation of their own childhood memories.

Lay aside your doubts and join me in an evaluation of infantile sexuality from the earliest years onward. [18] The child's sexual drive manifests itself as highly composite. It can be resolved into many components that derive from different sources. It is still distinctly independent of the function of reproduction in the service of which it will later be engaged. It permits the individual to obtain various kinds of pleasurable sensation which we comprehend, by its analogies and connections, as sexual. The chief source of infantile sexual pleasure is the auto-excitation of specific, particularly sensitive parts of the body: in addition to the genitals, the orifices of the mouth, anus, and urethra, as well as the skin and other sensory [mucous] surfaces. Since in this first phase of the child's sexual life satisfaction is derived from the individual's own body and is perceived apart from any external source, this phase is called *autoerotism,* according to the term coined by Havelock Ellis. Those parts of the body significant for yielding sexual pleasure are called *erogenous zones.* The thumb-sucking or other compulsive sucking of the very young child is a good example of such autoerotic satisfaction derived from an erogenous zone. The first scientific observer of this phenomenon, a pediatrician in Budapest named Lindner, quite rightly interpreted it as sexual satisfaction and exhaustively described its transition to other and higher forms of sexual activity. [19] Another sexual satisfaction of this period of life is the excitation of the genitals by masturbation which preserves such a great significance for later life and is, moreover, never

completely overcome by many individuals. Along with these and
other autoerotic activities there are found, very early in the child's
life, those instinctual components of sexual pleasure, or of libido
(as we like to designate it), which assume some other person as an
object. These impulses appear in pairs of opposites, as active and
passive: among the most important representatives of this group
may be noted the pleasure in actively inflicting pain (sadism) and
its passive counterpart (masochism); and the state of looking or
being looked at, from the former of which the curiosity for other
knowledge later branches off, while from the latter is derived the
tendency toward artistic and theatrical representation. Other sexual activities of the child quite early come under the rubric of *object-
choice* according to which a chief role is played by some extraneous
person, someone who originally owed his significance to the child's
instinct of self-preservation. But in this childhood period the distinction between the sexes as yet plays no decisive role; hence one
can, without injustice, attribute to every child some degree of homosexual disposition.

The confused, rich, but disorganized sexual life of the child,
in which separate components pursue their satisfaction independently of each other, are brought together and organized in two
dominant directions so that by the close of puberty the definitive
sexual character of each individual is usually fully formed. On the
one hand, the separate instinctual components subordinate themselves to the dominance of the genital zone whereby the entire sexual
life enters into the service of reproduction and the satisfaction of
the separate components retains its significance only as a preparation for, and encouragement of, the intrinsic sexual act. On the
other hand, object-choice prevails over autoerotism so that now
in the person's erotic life all the components of the sexual drive
will be satisfied through the beloved person. However, not all the
original sexual components will be given a share in this final establishment of the sexual life. Even before the advent of puberty
certain components have undergone extremely energetic repression
under the influence of education, and mental forces like shame,
disgust, and morality have been instituted which, like sentinels,
watch over these repressions. Thus when the high tide of sexual
needfulness arises at the period of puberty it arises in these
particular forms of reaction and resistance, dams that prescribe its
flow into the so-called normal channels and make it impossible to

revive the impulses which have undergone repression. It is, especially, the *coprophilic,* i.e., the excremental, pleasure impulses of childhood which will have undergone the most rigorous repression, and the same fate awaits the fixation of the child on persons of primary object-choice.

Gentlemen, there is a proposition in general pathology which states that every process of development brings with it the seed of a pathological disposition in so far as the process gets inhibited, delayed or incompletely carried out. This statement is true of the very complicated development of the sexual function. It is not accomplished smoothly in all individuals and hence may leave behind it either abnormality or the predisposition for later illness by way of retrogressive movement (regression). It may happen that not all the partial drives surrender to the dominance of the genital zone. A drive of this kind which remains independent establishes what we call a *perversion* which may supplant the normal sexual goal with one of its own. As has already been mentioned, it very frequently happens that autoerotism is not fully overcome, a condition which brings in its train a multiplicity of observable disturbances. The originally equal valence of both sexes as sexual objects may persist and result in a tendency toward homosexual activity in adult life and, under certain conditions, this may intensify to the level of exclusive homosexuality. This series of disturbances is a direct result of any developmental inhibition of the sexual function. These include the *perversions* and the general *infantilism* of the sexual life which is not infrequently encountered.

A predisposition to neurosis is derived in a different way from damage in sexual development. The neuroses are related to the perversions as a negative to a positive. In the neuroses are found the same drive components that appear in the perversions, but they operate from the unconscious as vehicles of complexes and architects of symptoms. They have undergone a repression, yet, in spite of it, assert themselves out of the unconscious. Psychoanalysis permits us to recognize that excessive expression of these drives in very early years leads to a kind of partial *fixation* which then constitutes a weak spot in the pattern of the sexual function. If the exercise of the normal sexual function encounters hindrances at maturity, the repressions at the time of development will break through at those very places where the infantile fixations took root.

You will perhaps now make an objection: But all this is not sexuality. I have used the word in a much broader sense than you are accustomed to. This much I willingly concede. But the question is whether you are accustomed to use the word in a much too narrow sense when you limit it to the domain of reproduction. You thereby sacrifice an understanding of the perversions and of the connection between perversion, neurosis and normal sexual life. You deny yourselves a recognition of the readily observed beginnings of the physical and mental sex life of the child in their true significance. However, you may opt to decide the verbal usage, keep well in mind that the psychoanalyst comprehends sexuality in that complete sense to which he is led by an appreciation of infantile sexuality.

Let us return now to the sexual development of the child. We have much to catch up on here since we have paid more attention to the physical than to the mental sexual life. The primary object-choice of the child, which derives from his need to be cared for, demands our further interest. It first attaches itself to all those individuals who look after him, but these soon are replaced by the parents. The relation of the child to its parents is, according to the direct observation of the child and its later corroboration by the analytic study of adults, by no means free from elements involving sexual arousal. The child involves both parents but usually with a preference for one as the object of his erotic wishes. Ordinarily such attachment results from some incitement by the parents themselves whose tenderness quite distinctly resembles sexual activity even though it is inhibited in its aim. As a rule, the father prefers the daughter, the mother, the son; the child, as son, reacts by wishing to take the place of the father; as daughter, the place of the mother. The feelings awakened in these relationships between parents and children and in the subsequent ones between siblings to each other are not only of a positive and tender, but also of a negative and hostile kind. The complex thus built up is destined to early repression but it still exerts a great and lasting effect from the unconscious. We hold the view that, together with its ramifications, this pattern constitutes the *nuclear complex* of every neurosis, and we are thus prepared to encounter it with no less influence in other areas of mental life. The myth of King Oedipus, who slew his father and won his mother in marriage, is an only slightly modified revelation of this infantile wish, which is later rejected by the opposing incest barrier. Shakespeare's play *Hamlet* rests on a similar basis but with a better concealed incest complex.

At the time when the child is dominated by the as yet unrepressed nuclear complex a significant part of his intellectual activity is in the service of his sexual interests. He begins to investigate where babies come from and, on the basis of the signs available to him, deduces more about the actual situation than adults are apt to suspect. Usually his investigative interest is aroused by the real threat of a newly arrived child in whom at first he sees only a rival. Under the influence of the component drives active in himself he reaches a number of "infantile sexual theories," e.g., that both sexes possess the same male genitals; that babies are conceived by eating and are born through the end of the digestive tract; or that intercourse between the sexes consists of a hostile act, a kind of conquest. But the essential immaturity of his sexual constitution and the gaps in his knowledge, which result from the invisibility of the female vagina, obliges the young investigator to discontinue his work as a failure. The fact of his childhood research itself, as well as the particular infantile sexual theories brought to light by it, remains of definite significance in the character formation of the child and in the content of his later neurotic illness.

It is inevitable and quite normal for the child to choose his parents as the objects of his first love. But his libido should not remain fixed on these first objects; instead, they should later merely be taken as prototypes and from them it should transfer to unrelated persons at the time of definitive object-choice. The *disengagement* of the child from his parents will thus be an inescapable task if the social effectiveness of the young individual is not to be jeopardized. During the time when repression is making a choice from among the partial sexual drives and, later, when the influence of the parents, which has contributed the main investment for these repressions, is to be loosened, substantial problems fall to the process of education which, at present, is certainly not always performed in intelligent and unobjectionable ways.

Gentlemen, please do not conclude that with these discussions about the sexual life and the psychosexual development of the child we have departed too far from psychoanalysis and the task of overcoming nervous disorders. You can, if you choose, consider psychoanalytic treatment as just a continuing education for the conquest of childhood's residues.

Fifth Lecture

Ladies and Gentlemen: With the discovery of infantile sexuality and the derivation of neurotic symptoms from erotic drive components we have arrived at some unexpected formulations about the nature and goals of neurotic illness. We see that individuals become ill when, as a result of external obstacles or internal lack of adaptive capacity, the satisfaction of their neurotic needs is denied in the world of *reality*. We see that they then *take flight into illness* in order to find by its aid a substitute satisfaction for what has been denied them. We recognize that the symptoms of illness contain a fraction of the individual's sexual activity, or even the whole of his sexual life, and we find in the withdrawal from reality the chief aim, and also the chief damage, of the illness. We infer that the resistance of our patients to recovery is not a simple matter but is a compound of several motives. Not only does the ego of the patient struggle against the surrender of the repressions by which it has tried to rise above its original lack but it is also disinclined to renounce its substitute satisfaction as long as there is no assurance that reality will provide something better.

The flight from unsatisfying reality into what, on account of its biological harmfulness, we call illness—illness which is, however, never without some immediate pleasure gain for the patient—takes place by the route of retrogressive movement (regression), the return to earlier phases of sexual life when satisfaction was not then lacking. This regression is apparently twofold: a *temporal* one, insofar as the libido, the erotic need, reaches back to an earlier stage of development, and a *formal* one, in which the original and primitive means of mental expression are utilized in demonstrating this need. But both kinds of regression focus upon childhood and coincide in producing an infantile status of the sexual life.

The deeper you probe into the pathogenesis of nervous illness, the more will the connection of neurosis with other productions of the human mind, even the most valuable, be revealed to you. You will then be reminded that we humans, with the high demands of our civilization and under the pressure of our inner repressions, find reality to be quite generally unsatisfying and thus entertain a life of fantasy in which we like to compensate for what is lacking in reality by products of wish fulfillment. These fantasies often contain a great deal of the intrinsic constitutional nature of the personality as well as those impulses of it which are repressed in real life. The energetic and successful man is he who succeeds by his work in transforming his wishful fantasies into reality. Where this effort is not successful, in consequence of obstacles in the outer world and the weakness of the individual, withdrawal from reality ensues; the individual retreats into his satisfying fantasy world the content of which is transformed into symptoms if he should become ill. Under certain favorable conditions it still remains possible for him to find a route from these fantasies back into reality instead of alienating himself from it permanently through regression to the infantile. If a person who is at odds with reality possesses an *artistic aptitude*—something which is still for us a psychological riddle— he can transform his fantasies into artistic productions instead of symptoms. Thus he escapes the fate of neurosis and by this round-about course regains his relation to reality. [20] Where there is a persistent opposition to the real world and this precious aptitude is lacking or inadequate, it is practically unavoidable that the libido, following the tendency of fantasy, succeeds by way of regression in reviving infantile wishes and thereby creates neurosis. In our time, neurosis takes the place of the cloister in which all those who had been disillusioned by life or who felt themselves too weak to cope with it used to take refuge.

Let me at this point insert the chief result at which we have arrived through the psychoanalytic investigation of neurotics: the neuroses have no psychic content peculiar to them that may not also be found in healthy persons; or, as C. G. Jung has expressed it, they suffer from the same complexes with which we healthy individuals also struggle. It depends upon the quantitative considerations concerning the relationships of the conflicting forces whether the struggle leads to health, to neurosis, or to compensatory high achievement.

Ladies and Gentlemen, I have as yet withheld from you the most important experience which corroborates an assumption concerning the power of the sexual drive in neurosis. Whenever we treat a neurotic psychoanalytically, there occurs in him the strange phenomenon of the so-called *transference*, i.e., he directs to the physician a measure of tender feeling, not infrequently mixed with hostility, which is grounded in no real relationship between them and, according to all the indications of its appearance, must be derived from the old wishful fantasies of the patient which have become unconscious. Every aspect of the patient's emotional life, including what he can no longer consciously recall, is reexperienced in his relationship to the physician. It is only through this reliving in the "transference" that the patient becomes convinced of the existence, as well as of the power, of the unconscious sexual impulses. The symptoms—to use an analogy from chemistry—are precipitates of earlier erotic experiences (in the broadest sense of the term) and can be resolved only in the elevated temperature of the transference experience and translated then into other psychic products. The physician plays the role of a *catalytic ferment* in this reaction—according to the excellent term employed by S. Ferenczi[21]—which temporarily attracts to itself the feelings which have been released in the process. The study of the transference can also give us the key to the understanding of hypnotic suggestion of which we had at first made use as a technical means for investigating the unconscious of our patients. Hypnosis proved itself to be a therapeutic aid at that time but it was a hindrance to a scientific grasp of the situation since it removed the psychic resistances from a certain region only to pile them up into an unscalable wall at its boundaries. You must not conclude that the phenomenon of transference, about which I can unfortunately tell you too little at this time, is created under the influence of psychoanalytic treatment. Transference arises spontaneously in all human relationships, just as it does in that between the patient and the doctor. It is at all times the special vehicle of therapeutic influence, and it works all the more effectively, the less one suspects its involvement. Psychoanalysis does not, therefore, create it, but merely discloses it to consciousness and masters it in order to steer it to the desired goal. But I cannot abandon the topic of the transference without emphasizing the fact that this phenomenon is of decisive importance in bringing conviction not only to the patient but to the physician. I know that all my adherents became convinced about the correctness of my views on the pathogenesis of the neuroses through their experiences with the phenomenon of transference; and I can quite readily understand that one does not acquire such assurance as long as one himself has not carried out psychoanalyses and has not therefore himself observed the effectiveness of transference.

Ladies and Gentlemen, I believe that there are, from the intellectual standpoint, two special obstacles to the acknowledgment of the psychoanalytic way of thinking which must be recognized. In the first place, there is the unusualness of accounting for mental events with a strict and unexceptional determinism; and, in the second place, the unfamiliarity of the characteristics that distinguish unconscious mental processes from those conscious ones upon which we usually rely. One of the most widespread resistances against psychoanalytic work, among the sick as well as the healthy, derives from the latter of these two factors. There is a fear of doing harm through psychoanalysis—the anxiety of calling the patient's repressed sexual impulses into consciousness and the related danger of thus overwhelming his higher ethical strivings and robbing him of his cultural accomplishments. It is observed that the patient has sore places in his mental life but one then shies away from touching them lest his suffering be thus increased. We can accept this analogy. It is, indeed, prudent not to disturb diseased spots if by so doing one can produce nothing put pain. But the surgeon, as is well known, does not refrain from investigating and probing a focus of infection if he does so with the goal of thus being able to bring about lasting relief. No one thinks of blaming him for the unavoidable discomfort involved in the exploration or the side effects of the operation if this action accomplishes its purpose of bringing about a lasting cure though the price is a temporary worsening of the patient's condition. The situation is similar in psychoanalysis: it may plead the same justification as does surgery. The increase in suffering caused the patient during the treatment is, with the proper technique, incomparably less severe than that which the surgeon produces, and it is altogether negligible in comparison with the price of a serious illness. Moreover, the dreaded consequence of destroying the patient's cultural character by the release of his repressed impulses is quite untenable; this concern fails to consider what our experience has surely taught us—that the mental and physical power of a wish impulse, once the repression has failed, produces incomparably worse effects if it is unconscious than if it is conscious, and by making it conscious one can only weaken it. An unconscious wish cannot be influenced and is independent of all opposing tendencies, whereas a conscious one can be inhibited by everything that is similarly conscious and stands in opposition to it. Psychoanalytic work, therefore, provides a better substitute for unsuccessful repression precisely by serving the interests of the highest and most valuable cultural endeavors.

What, now, is the fate of the unconscious wishes which have become freed by psychoanalysis? By what methods can we bring it about that they are made harmless to the life of the individual? There are several routes. The most frequent is that these wishes are consumed during the analytical work by the appropriate mental activity of those better adapted tendencies which are opposed to them. The *repression* is supplanted by a *condemnation* carried through by the best means at the person's disposal. This is possible since, for the most part, it is necessary only to remove the sequelae of the earlier developmental stages of the ego. The individual at that earlier time instituted the repression of unadaptable impulses because he was then still incompletely organized and weak; in his present maturity and strength, he can probably render harmless those impulses which are opposed to his interest. A second outcome of the work of psychoanalysis may be that the disclosed unconscious impulses can now be put to those useful applications which, in the event of undisturbed development, they would have found earlier. The extirpation of the infantile wishes is not at all the ideal goal of development. The neurotic has by his repressions lost many sources of mental energy the influences of which would have been very valuable for his character development and his life adjustment. We know a far more adaptive process of development, so-called *sublimation,* by which the energy of infantile wishes is not excluded but remains available when these particular demands, instead of becoming useless, achieve a higher, and eventually no longer sexual, goal. The components of the sexual instinct are peculiarly distinguished by the capacity for such sublimation and the exchange of the sexual goal for one that is more remote but socially more valuable. To the energy contributed in such a way to the functioning of our mental life we probably owe our highest cultural accomplishments. Prematurely instituted repression excludes the sublimation of the repressed impulses; after the removal of repression the way to sublimation is again open.

We must especially stress the third of the possible outcomes of psychoanalytic work. A certain portion of the suppressed libido has a right to direct satisfaction and ought to obtain it in the course of living. The standards of our civilization make life too hard for most human beings and thus encourage a turning away from reality and an outbreak of neurosis without producing any increase in cultural accomplishments by this excessive sexual repression. We ought not aim so high that we completely neglect the original animality of our nature, nor must we forget that the happiness of the individual cannot be overlooked among the goals of civilization. The plasticity of the partial sexual impulses, demonstrated by their capacity for sublimation, may beget a strong temptation to achieve greater cultural accomplishments by an ever increasing sublimation. But just as in the use of our machines we scarcely expect to transform more than a certain fraction of the heat employed into effective mechanical work, so we should scarcely expect to direct the sexual drive in the entire extent of its power away from its intrinsic aim. Such an effort cannot succeed, and if the restriction upon sexuality were to be pushed too far, the same evil effects would result as those which occur in excessive exploitation of farm land.

It would not surprise me if you regarded my closing exhortation as presumptuous. I shall risk only an indirect statement of my conviction by relating to you an old tale of which you may make such use as you choose. In German literature there is a town called Schilda to whose inhabitants every sort of clever prank used to be attributed. The citizens of Schilda, as the story goes, owned a horse with whose capacity for work they were well satisfied, and about whom they had only one complaint—that he consumed such a large amount of expensive oats. They decided that they would carefully break him of this bad habit: they would cut down his rations by several stocks daily until he had grown accustomed to complete abstinence. For a time things went very well; the horse was weaned to just one stock a day and on the next he would finally be working with no oats at all. But the morning of that day the malicious beast was found dead. The citizens of Schilda could not fathom why it had died.

We are inclined to believe that the horse had died of starvation and that without a certain ration of oats, no work can indeed be expected from an animal.

I thank you for your invitation and for the attention which you have granted me.

Notes and References for the Lectures

The following notes are those supplied by Freud himself in the two published editions of his Clark lectures. However, Freud's often abbreviated reference citations have been verified and completed. For the convenience of the English reader, the German titles in the text have been translated and, if available, later translations of the cited works have been added in the references. Passages from other authors quoted by Freud in the text of the lectures have been verified and fully cited. All emendations by the editor are given in square brackets.

1. However, in this context compare my statement [in 1914] in which I acknowledge my unrestricted responsibility for psychoanalysis. (Zur Geschichte der psychoanalytischen Bewegung, contained in *Gesammelte Werke, X*). [On the history of the psycho-analytic movement. *Standard Edition*, 1957, *14*, 7-66]

2. Dr. Josef Breuer, born 1842, Corresponding Member of the Kaiserliche Akademie der Wissenschaften [Vienna], is known by publications on respiration and on the physiology of the sense of equilibrium.

3. *Studien über Hysterie.* Wien: Deuticke, 1895. 2nd ed., 1909. [Josef Breuer and Sigmund Freud. *Studies on hysteria. Standard Edition*, 1955, vol. 2. Case of Anna O., pp. 21-47.] Sections of my contribution to this book have been translated into English by Dr. A. A. Brill of New York. (*Selected papers on hysteria and other psychoneuroses*, by S. Freud. *Nervous and Mental Disease Monograph Series*, No. 4, New York.)

4. I know that this assertion is no longer true today, but in the lecture I take myself and my audience back to the time before 1880. If things have become different since then, the effects of the history which I am sketching are in large part responsible.

5. *Studien über Hysterie,* 2nd ed., p. 26. [*Standard Edition, 2,* pp. 34-35.]

6. Ibid., p. 31. [Ibid., pp. 39-40.]

7. Ibid., p. 30. [Ibid., p. 38.]

8. Ibid., pp. 43 and 46. [Ibid., pp. 54 and 57, case of Emmy von N.]

9. A selection from this book, augmented by several later essays on hysteria, lies before me in an English translation by Dr. A. A. Brill of New York [published September 30, 1909]. [*Loc. cit.*, note 2, supra.]

10. Rather, the later copy of such a monument. The name *Charing* is itself derived, as Dr. E. Jones has told me, from the words *chère reine* [dear queen].

11. *Der Witz und seine Beziehung zum Unbewussten.* Wien: Deuticke, 1905, p. 59. [*Jokes and their relation to the unconscious. Standard Edition, 8,* 74.]

12. C. G. Jung. *Diagnostische Assoziationsstudien.* [Leipzig: Barth, 1906-1909. 2 vols. *Studies in word-association.* London: Heinemann, 1918.]

13. *Die Traumdeutung.* Wien: Deuticke, 1909, 2nd ed. [*The interpretation of dreams. Standard Edition, 4* and *5.*]

14. *Zur Psychopathologie des Alltagslebens.* Berlin: S. Karger, 1910, 3rd ed. [*The psychopathology of everyday life. Standard Edition, 6.*]

15. Analyse der Phobie eines 5-jährigen Knaben. *Jahrbuch für psychoanalytische und psychopathologische Forschungen,* 1909, 1, [1-109]. [Analysis of a phobia in a five-year-old boy. *Standard Edition, 10,* 5-147.]

16. [An error here requires comment. Jung's lecture, his third, which included the case of the "quite young girl," was not delivered "a few hours ago" if Freud's fourth (published) lecture is the point of reference. As *delivered,* the lecture by Freud that included the topic of infantile sexuality came on Saturday, September 11, at 11:00 A.M. and Jung's third was given at 9:00 A.M. But when, months later, Freud came to write out his lectures for *publication,* he forgot to allow for a change in the sequence he had introduced. As indicated in

letters 19 F and 20 H, Freud took the liberty of making changes in the published, as compared to the informally delivered, version of the lectures. The most important difference was a change in the order of topics treated in the fourth and fifth lectures. As *delivered,* the subjects of free association and dream interpretation were discussed not in the third but in the fourth lecture (Friday, September 10); infantile sexuality, including the case of Little Hans, was discussed not in the fourth but in the fifth lecture (Saturday). Cf. Part One, Chapter VII.]

17. E. Bleuler. Sexuelle Abnormitäten der Kinder. *Jahrbuch der schweizer Gesellschaft für Schulgesundheitspflege,* 1908, *9,* [623f.].

18. *Drei Abhandlungen zur Sexualtheorie.* Wien: Deuticke, 1905; 2nd ed., 1910. [*Three essays on the theory of sexuality. Standard Edition, 7,* 135-243.]

19. *Jahrbuch für Kinderheilkunde,* 1879. [Lindner, S. Das Saugen an den Fingern, Lippen etc. bei den Kindern. (Ludeln). Bd. 14 (N.F.), 68-91.]

20. Cf. O. Rank. *Der Künstler. [Ansätze zu einer Sexual-psychologie.]* Wien: Heller, 1907. [Included in *Art and artist.* New York: Knopf, 1932.]

21. S. Ferenczi. Introjektion und Übertragung. *Jahrbuch für psychoanalytische und psychopathologische Forschungen,* 1909, *1,* [422-457]. [Introjection and transference. Chapter 2 of Ferenczi's *Contributions to psychoanalysis.* Boston: Richard G. Badger, 1916.]

Bibliography of Cited Books
and Articles

This bibliography includes only published books and articles. Unpublished sources such as archival papers, letters and diaries, as well as contemporary printed items in newspapers, are described in the Introduction, "In the Beginning . . . ," the Commentary on Part One (notes and references) for the individual chapters, and in the Introductory Notes for Parts Two and Three. The date in parentheses following an author's name is the date of *first* publication in the original language. Frequently Cited Manuscript Sources are listed on a supplementary page following this Bibliography.

Abbot, E. S. (1919). Dr. Edward Cowles (Obituary). *Journal of Nervous and Mental Disease, 50,* 504-510.

Adler, A. (1907). *Study of organ inferiority and its psychical compensation.* New York: Nervous & Mental Disease Publishing Co., 1917.

Adler, A. (1912). *The neurotic constitution.* English translation. New York: Moffatt, Yard, 1917.

Adler, A. (1930). Individual psychology. In C. Murchison (Ed.), *Psychologies of 1930.* Worcester, MA: Clark University Press.

Allen, G. W. (1967). *William James: A biography.* New York: Viking.

American Psychological Association. (1910). Proceedings of the eighteenth annual meeting. *Psychological Bulletin, 7,* 37f.

Amory, C. (1947). *The "proper" Bostonians.* New York: Dutton.

Ansbacher, H. L. (1971). Alfred Adler and G. Stanley Hall: Correspondence and general relationship. *Journal of the History of the Behavioral Sciences, 7,* 337-352.

Aronson, T. (1964). *The golden bees: The story of the Bonapartes.* Greenwich, CT: New York Graphic Society.

Baird, A. T. (1949). *Richard Hodgson: The story of a psychical researcher and his times.* London: Psychic Press.

Barker, E. (1922). *Fielding Sargent.* New York: Dutton.

Barnes, H. E. (1925). Clark University: An adventure in American educational history. *American Review, 3,* 271-288.

Behrens, P. J. (1980). The first dissertation in experimental psychology: Max Friedrich's study of apperception. Pp. 193-209 in *Wundt Studies*. W. G. Bringmann & R. D. Tweney (Eds.). Toronto: C. J. Hogrefe.

Bell, S. (1902). A preliminary study of the emotion of love between the sexes. *American Journal of Psychology, 13*, 325-354.

Benjamin, L. T., Jr., Durkin, M., Lind, M., Vestal, M., & Acord, J. (1992). Wundt's American doctoral students. *American Psychologist, 47*, 123-131.

Bergson, H. (1907). *Creative evolution*. English translation. New York: Holt, 1911.

Bernays, A. F. (1940). My brother, Sigmund Freud. *American Mercury, 51* (November), 335-342.

Bernays, A. F. (n.d.). *Erlebtes*. Vienna: Kommissionsverlag der Buchhandlung Heller.

Bernays, E. L. (1965). *Biography of an idea: Memoirs of public relations counselor Edward L. Bernays*. New York: Simon & Schuster.

Bernfeld, S. (1946). An unknown autobiographical fragment by Freud. *American Imago, 4*, 3-19.

Bjork, D. W. (1988). *William James: The center of his vision*. New York: Columbia University Press.

Blakeslee, G. E. (Ed.). (1910). *China and the Far East*. New York: Crowell.

Bleuler, E. (1908). Sexuelle Abnormalitäten der Kinder. *Jahrbuch der schweizer Gesellschaft für Schulgesundheitspflege, 9*, 623f.

Blumenthal, A. L. (1970). *Language and psychology: Historical aspects of psycholinguistics*. New York: Wiley.

Boas, F. (1910). Psychological problems in anthropology. *American Journal of Psychology, 21*, 371-384.

Boas, F. (1928). *Anthropology and modern life*. New York: W. W. Norton.

Boring, E. G. (1950). *A history of experimental psychology*. 2nd ed. New York: Appleton.

Boring, E. G. (1961). *Psychologist at large: An autobiography and selected essays*. New York: Basic Books.

Boring, E. G. (1965). On the subjectivity of important historical dates: Leipzig, 1879. *Journal of the History of the Behavioral Sciences, 1*, 5-9.

Brazier, M. A. B. (1988). *A history of neurophysiology in the 19th century*. New York: Raven Press.

Breuer, J., & Freud, S. (1895). *Studies on hysteria. Standard Edition of the Complete Psychological Works of Sigmund Freud, 2.*

Brill, A. A. (1939). The introduction and development of Freud's work in the United States. *American Journal of Sociology, 45,* 318-325.

Bringmann, N. J., & Bringmann, W. G. (1980). Wilhelm Wundt and his first American student. In *Wundt Studies,* W. G. Bringmann & R. D. Tweney (Eds.). Toronto: C. J. Hogrefe.

Bringmann, W. G., Bringmann, M. W., & Early, C. E. (1992). G. Stanley Hall and the history of psychology. *American Psychologist, 47,* 281-289.

Bringmann, W. G., Bringmann, M. W., & La Guardia, I. (1991, March). Hall and Wundt: A reassessment. Paper presented at the meeting of the Southern Society of Philosophy and Psychology, Atlanta, GA.

Brome, V. (1978). *Jung.* New York: Atheneum.

Burgerstein, L. (1910). Co-education and hygiene with special reference to European experience and views. *Pedagogical Seminary, 17,* 1-15.

Burnham, J. C. (1960). Sigmund Freud and G. Stanley Hall. *Psychoanalytic Quarterly, 29,* 307-316.

Burnham, J. C. (1967). *Psychoanalysis and American medicine: 1894-1918.* New York: International Universities Press.

Cadwallader, T. C. (1992). The historical roots of the American Psychological Association. Chapter 1 in *The American Psychological Association: A historical perspective.* R. B. Evans, V. S. Sexton & T. C. Cadawallader (Eds.). Washington, D.C.: American Psychological Association.

Calkins, M. W. (1893). Statistics of dreams. *American Journal of Psychology, 5,* 334-352.

Calkins, M. W. (1910). *A first book in psychology.* New York: Macmillan.

Calkins, M. W. (1930). In *History of psychology in autobiography,* C. Murchison (Ed.), vol. 1, 31-62. Worcester, MA: Clark University Press.

Calkins, M. W. (1971). In *Notable American women, 1607-1950,* vol. 1, 278-280. Cambridge, MA: Harvard University Press.

Carotenuto, A. (1982). *A secret symmetry: Sabina Spielrein between Jung and Freud.* New York: Pantheon.

Carus, P. (1915). *Goethe: Special consideration of his philosophy.* Chicago: Open Court Publishing Co.

Cattell, J. McK. (1921). In memory of Wilhelm Wundt. *Psychological Review, 28,* 155-159.

Chase, H. W. (1910). Psychoanalysis and the unconscious. *Pedagogical Seminary* [presently the *Journal of Genetic Psychology*], *17*, 281-327.

Clark, R. W. (1980). *Freud: The man and the cause.* New York: Random House.

Clark University. (1899). *Decennial celebration 1889-1899.* Worcester, MA. Printed for the University.

Clark University. (1909). Preliminary Announcement, The second decennial celebration of the opening of Clark University. Worcester, MA: Clark University (proof copy).

Clark University. (1910). *Proceedings of the child conference for research and welfare held at Clark University in connection with the celebration of its twentieth anniversary, Worcester, Massachusetts.* Vol. 1, July 6-10, 1909; vol. 2, June 28-July 2, 1910. New York: G. E. Stechert.

Clark University. (1911). *Chemical addresses delivered at the celebration of the twentieth anniversary of Clark, in September 1909.* Worcester, MA: Clark University and American Chemical Society.

Clark University. (1912). *Lectures delivered at the celebration of the twentieth anniversary of Clark University under the auspices of the department of physics.* Worcester, MA: Clark University.

Clark University. (1925). *Edmund Clark Sanford, In Memoriam.* Vol. 8, No. 1. Worcester, MA: Clark University Library.

Cocke, J. R. (1894). *Hypnotism: How it is done, its uses and dangers.* Boston: Lee & Shepard.

Cocke, J. R. (1896). *Blind leaders of the blind: The romance of a blind lawyer.* Boston: Lee & Shepard.

Cocks, G. (1985). *Psychotherapy in the Third Reich: The Göring Institute.* New York: Oxford University Press.

Coon, D. J. (1992). Testing the limits of sense and science: American experimental psychologists combat spiritualism 1880-1920. *American Psychologist, 47,* 143-151.

Coriat, I. (1924). Nachruf: G. Stanley Hall. *Internationale Zeitschrift für Psychoanalyse, 10,* 201-203.

Coriat, I. (1945). Some personal reminiscences of psychoanalysis in Boston: An autobiographical note. *Psychoanalytic Review, 32,* 1-8.

Corrie, J. (1927). *A B C of Jung's psychology.* New York: Frank-Maurice, Inc.

Cowles, E. (1887-1888). The American Journal of Psychology, edited by G. Stanley Hall. *American Journal of Insanity, 44,* 544-546.

Cowles, E. (1906). The problem of psychiatry in the functional psychoses. *Congress of Arts and Sciences.* H. J. Rogers (Ed.), vol. 6, 262-304.

Cowles, E. (1924). Biographical sketch. In *Semi-centennial anniversary volume of the American Neurological Association, 1875-1924,* pp. 162-164. Privately printed.

Darwin, C. (1871). *The descent of man.* London: J. Murray.

Dennis, W., & Boring, E. G. (1952). The founding of the APA. *American Psychologist, 7,* 95-97.

Diehl, L. A. (1986). The paradox of G. Stanley Hall: Foe of coeducation and educator of women. *American Psychologist, 41,* 868-878.

Donn, L. (1989). *Freud and Jung: Years of friendship, years of loss.* New York: Scribner.

Douglas, C. (1989). Christiana Morgan's visions reconsidered: A look behind *The Visions Seminars. The San Francisco Library Journal, 8,* 5-27.

Ebbinghaus, E. (1911-1913). *Grundzüge der Psychologie.* 2 vols. Leipzig: Veit.

Edel, L. (1972). *Henry James, the master: 1901-1916.* Philadelphia: Lippincott.

Editorial notice. (1892). The American Psychological Association. *Science* (August 19), *20,* 104.

Ferenczi, S. (1909). Introjection and transference. Chapter 2 in Ferenczi's *Contributions to psychoanalysis.* Boston: Richard G. Badger, 1916.

Ferenczi, S. (1910). The psychological analysis of dreams. *American Journal of Psychology, 21,* 309-328.

Ferenczi, S. (1913). Stages in the development of the sense of reality. Chapter 8 in his *Contributions to psychoanalysis.* Boston: Richard G. Badger, 1916.

Ferenczi, S. (1955). *Final contributions to the problems and methods of psychoanalysis.* New York: Basic Books.

Fischer, S. C. (1925). The psychological and educational work of Granville Stanley Hall. *American Journal of Psychology, 36,* 1-52.

Freud, A. (1951). The contribution of psychoanalysis to genetic psychology. *American Journal of Orthopsychiatry, 21,* 476-497.

Freud, S. (1896a). The aetiology of hysteria. *Standard Edition, 3,* 191-221.

Freud, S. (1896b). Heredity and the aetiology of the neuroses. *Standard Edition, 3,* 141-156.

Freud, S. (1899a). Screen memories. *Standard Edition, 3*, 301-322. Originally published in *Monatschrift für Psychiatrie und Neurologie, 6*, 215-230 (September issue).

Freud, S. (1899b). *The interpretation of dreams. Standard Edition, 4-5.* 2nd ed., 1909.

Freud, S. (1900). *On dreams. Standard Edition, 5*, 633-686.

Freud, S. (1904). *The psychopathology of everyday life. Standard Edition, 6.*

Freud, S. (1905a). *Three essays on the theory of sexuality. Standard Edition, 7*, 135-243. First English translation by A. A. Brill, 1910. *Nervous and Mental Disease Monograph Series*, No. 7. New York & Washington: Nervous and Mental Disease Publishing Co. This edition had an Introduction by J. J. Putnam.

Freud, S. (1905b). *Jokes and their relation to the unconscious. Standard Edition, 8.*

Freud, S. (1907). *Delusions and dreams in Jensen's "Gradiva." Standard Edition, 9*, 1-95.

Freud, S. (1909a). Analysis of a phobia in a five-year-old boy. *Standard Edition, 10*, 5-147.

Freud, S. (1909b). Notes upon a case of obsessional neurosis. *Standard Edition, 10*, 153-249.

Freud, S. (1909c). *Selected papers on hysteria and other psychoneuroses.* Translated by A. A. Brill. *Nervous and Mental Disease Monograph Series*, No. 4. New York: Nervous and Mental Disease Publishing Co.

Freud, S. (1910a). Leonardo da Vinci and a memory of his childhood. *Standard Edition, 11*, 59-137.

Freud, S. (1910b). The origin and development of psychoanalysis. Translated by H. W. Chase. *American Journal of Psychology, 21*, 181-218. Also, *Standard Edition, 11*, 1-57.

Freud, S. (1910c). The psycho-analytic view of psychogenic disturbances of vision. *Standard Edition, 11*, 209-218.

Freud, S. (1911). Great is Diana of the Ephesians. *Standard Edition, 12*, 342-344.

Freud, S. (1912-1913). *Totem and taboo. Standard Edition, 13*, 1-161.

Freud, S. (1914). On the history of the psycho-analytic movement. *Standard Edition, 14*, 7-66.

Freud, S. (1915-1916). *Introductory lectures on psychoanalysis. Standard Edition, 15-16.*

Freud, S. (1917). A difficulty in the path of psychoanalysis. *Standard Edition, 17,* 135-144.

Freud, S. (1918). From the history of an infantile neurosis. *Standard Edition, 17,* 7-122.

Freud, S. (1919). *Beyond the pleasure principle. Standard Edition, 18,* 7-64.

Freud, S. (1920). *A general introduction to psychoanalysis.* With a Preface by G. Stanley Hall. New York: Boni & Liveright. See also *Standard Edition, 15-16.*

Freud, S. (1925). An autobiographical study. *Standard Edition, 20,* 3-74.

Freud, S. (1932). The acquisition and control of fire. *Standard Edition, 22,* 185-193.

Freud, S. (1953-1974). *The standard edition of the complete psychological works of Sigmund Freud.* Translated and edited by J. Strachey, assisted by A. Strachey and A. Tyson. 24 vols. London: Hogarth Press. Cited as *Standard Edition.*

Freud, S. (1954). *The origins of psycho-analysis: Letters to Wilhelm Fliess, drafts and notes: 1887-1902.* M. Bonaparte, A. Freud and E. Kris (Eds.). Introduction by E. Kris. London: Imago. The original German edition of these letters was published by the same company, 1950. A later edition, translated and edited by J. M. Masson, was published by Harvard University Press (Cambridge), 1985. This edition has the complete letters, 1887-1902, but lacks the scholarly notes of the 1954 edition and Freud's "Project for a scientific psychology." The 1954 edition is cited in this book unless otherwise indicated.

Freud, S. (1961). *Letters of Sigmund Freud: 1873-1939.* E. L. Freud (Ed.). London: Hogarth.

Freud, S., & Abraham, K. (1965). *A psycho-analytic dialogue: The letters of Sigmund Freud and Karl Abraham, 1907-1926.* H. C. Abraham and E. L. Freud (Eds.). New York: Basic Books.

Freud, S., & Jung, C. G. (1974). *The Freud/Jung letters.* W. McGuire (Ed.). Princeton, NJ: Princeton University Press.

Freud, S., & Pfister, O. (1963). *Psychoanalysis and faith: The letters of Sigmund Freud & Oskar Pfister.* H. Meng & E. L. Freud (Eds.). New York: Basic Books.

Friedrich, M. (1883). Über die Apperceptionsdauer bei einfachen und zusammengesetzten Vorstellungen. *Philosophische Studien, 1,* 39-77.

Furumoto, L. (1979). Mary Whiton Calkins (1863-1930): Fourteenth President of the American Psychological Association. *Journal of the History of the Behavioral Sciences, 15,* 346-356.

Furumoto, L. (1989). The new history of psychology. *The G. Stanley Hall Lecture Series, 9,* 9-34.

Garcon, M., & Vinchon, J. (1929). *The devil: a historical and medical study.* London: Golancz.

Gay, P. (1988). *Freud: A life for our time.* New York: Doubleday.

Gifford, G. E. (1972). Freud and the porcupine. *Harvard Medical Alumni Bulletin,* March-April, 28-31.

Goethe, W. (1811). "Gross ist die Diana der Epheser." *Gedichte.* Zweiter Theil. Mit Einleitung und Anmerkungen von G. von Loeper. Bd. II, S. 162-163. Berlin: Gustav Hempel, 1883.

Goldman, E. (1931). *Living my life.* 2 vols. New York: Knopf.

Goldmark, J. (1934). An Adirondack friendship: Letters of William James. *Atlantic Monthly, 154,* September, 265-272; October, 440-447.

Goodwin, C. J. (1987). In Hall's shadow: Edmund Clark Sanford (1859-1924). *Journal of the History of the Behavioral Sciences, 23,* 153-168.

Gottlieb, R. M. (1989). Technique and countertransference in Freud's analysis of the Rat Man. *Psychoanalytic Quarterly, 58,* 29-62.

Graf, H. (1972). Biographical interview with Herbert Graf. *Opera News, 36,* 25-26.

Graf, M. (1942). Reminiscences of Professor Sigmund Freud. *Psychoanalytic Quarterly, 11,* 465-476.

Hale, N. G., Jr. (Ed.). (1971a). *James Jackson Putnam and psychoanalysis: Letters between Putnam and Sigmund Freud, Ernest Jones, William James, Sandor Ferenczi and Morton Prince, 1877-1917.* Cambridge, MA: Harvard University Press.

Hale, N. G., Jr. (1971b). *Freud and the Americans: The beginnings of psychoanalysis in the United States, 1876-1917.* New York: Oxford.

Hall, F. (1909). An ether "vision." *The Open Court, 23* (December), 736-737.

Hall, G. S. (1878). The muscular perception of space. *Mind, 3,* 433-450.

Hall, G. S. (1883). The contents of children's minds. *Princeton Review, 2,* 249-272. Reprinted in *Aspects of child life and education.* Boston: Ginn & Co., 1907, 1-52.

Hall, G. S. (1891). Review of *The principles of psychology* by William James. *American Journal of Psychology, 3,* 585-591.

Hall, G. S. (1893). Child-study: The basis of exact education. *Forum, 16,* 429-441.

Hall, G. S. (1895a). Editorial on experimental psychology in America. *American Journal of Psychology, 7,* 3-8.

Hall, G. S. (1895b). Psychical research (Review of current literature). *American Journal of Psychology, 7,* 135-142.

Hall, G. S. (1895c). Laboratory of the McLean Hospital, Somerville, Mass. *American Journal of Insanity, 51,* 358-364.

Hall, G. S. (1899). Note on early memories. *Pedagogical Seminary, 6,* 485-512 (December issue).

Hall, G. S. (1904a). *Adolescence.* 2 vols. New York: Appleton.

Hall, G. S. (1904b). The Jesus of history and of the Passion versus the Jesus of the Resurrection. *American Journal of Religious Psychology, 1,* 30-64.

Hall, G. S. (1904c). Mental science. *Science,* n.s. *20,* 481-490.

Hall, G. S. (1906a). The affiliation of psychology with philosophy and with the natural sciences. *Science,* n.s. *23,* 297-301.

Hall, G. S. (1906b). Tribute to President William R. Harper. *Biblical World, 27,* 233-234.

Hall, G. S., et al. (1907). *Aspects of child life and education,* edited by T. A. Smith. Boston: Ginn & Co.

Hall, G. S. (1908). Spooks and telepathy. *Appleton's Magazine, 12* (December), 677-683.

Hall, G. S. (1909a). Evolution and psychology. In *Fifty years of Darwinism: Modern aspects of evolution.* (Centennial addresses in honor of Charles Darwin before the American Association for the Advancement of Science. Baltimore, January 1, 1909.) New York: Holt, pp. 251-257.

Hall, G. S. (unsigned). (1909b). Twentieth anniversary of Clark University. *Nation, 89* (September 23), 284-285.

Hall, G. S. (1910a). Education in sexual hygiene. *Eugenics Review, 1,* 242-253.

Hall, G. S. (1910b). A children's institute. *Harper's Magazine, 120,* 620-624.

Hall, G. S. (1910c). The Children's Institute of Clark University, Worcester, Mass. (Prospectus of the Children's Institute, April 30, 1910.) Hall's Collected Papers, vol. 19. Worcester, MA: Clark University Archives.

Hall, G. S. (1910d). General outline of the new child study work at Clark University. *Pedagogical Seminary, 17,* 160-165.

Hall, G. S. (Ed.). (1910e). *Lectures and addresses delivered before the departments of psychology and pedagogy in celebration of the twentieth anniversary of the opening of Clark University, September 1909.* Worcester, MA: Clark University.

Hall, G. S. (1911). *Educational problems.* 2 vols. New York: Appleton.

Hall, G. S. (1912). *Founders of modern psychology.* New York: Appleton.

Hall, G. S. (1914a). The Freudian child (and ambivalence). *Psychological Bulletin, 11,* 29-30 (Abstract).

Hall, G. S. (1914b). A synthetic genetic study of fear. *American Journal of Psychology, 25,* 149-200, 321-392.

Hall, G. S. (1914c). *Die Begründer der modernen Psychologie.* Translated with Notes by Raymond Schmidt. With an Introductory Foreword by Dr. Max Brahn. Leipzig: Meiner.

Hall, G. S. (1914d). *Wilhelm Wundt, Begründer der modernen Psychologie.* Translated with Notes by Raymond Schmidt. With an Introductory Foreword by Dr. Max Brahn. Leipzig: Meiner.

Hall, G. S. (1915a). The Freudian methods applied to anger. *American Journal of Psychology, 26,* 438-443.

Hall, G. S. (1915b). Thanatophobia and immortality. *American Journal of Psychology, 26,* 550-613.

Hall, G. S. (1917a). *Jesus, the Christ, in the light of psychology.* 2 vols. Garden City, New York: Doubleday, Page. 2nd ed. (1923). New York: Appleton.

Hall, G. S. (1917b). A reminiscence. *American Journal of Psychology, 28,* 297-300.

Hall, G. S. (1918). A medium in the bud. *American Journal of Psychology, 29,* 144-158.

Hall, G. S. (1921a). The American Journal of psychology. *American Journal of Psychology, 32,* 1-30.

Hall, G. S. (1921b). In memory of Wilhelm Wundt. *Psychological Review, 28,* 154-155.

Hall, G. S. (1922). *Senescence.* New York: Appleton.

Hall, G. S. (1923). *Life and confessions of a psychologist.* New York: Appleton.

Hamilton, A. E. (1924). Stanley Hall: A memory. *American Mercury, 2,* 287-292.

Hamilton, S. W. (1945). Notes on the history of the American Psychopathological Association. *Journal of Nervous and Mental Disease, 102,* 30-53.

Harper, R. S. (1949). Tables of American doctorates in psychology. *American Journal of Psychology, 62,* 579-587.

Hawley, J. R. (1901). *The new animal cellular therapy.* Chicago: Clinic Publishing Co.

Haymond, R. (1982). On Carl Gustav Jung: Psycho-social basis of morality during the Nazi era. *Journal of Psychology & Judaism, 6,* 81-112.

Henri, V. (1895a). Enquête sue les premiers souvenirs de l'enfance. *Revue philosophique, 39* (February), 213-232.

Henri, V. (1895b). Enquête sur les premiers souvenirs de l'enfance. *Année psychologique, 1* (March), 534.

Henri, V. (1895c). On our earliest recollections of childhood. *Psychological Review, 2* (March), 215-216.

Henri, V. (1896). Our earliest memories. *American Journal of Psychology, 7* (January), 303-304 (with comment by G. S. Hall, Some constant sources of error in "recollection," 304-305.)

Henri, V., & Henri, C. (1897). Enquête sur les premiers souvenirs de l'enfance. *Année psychologique, 3,* 184-198.

Henri, V., & Henri, C. (1898). Earliest recollections. *Appletons' Popular Science Monthly, 53* (May), 108-115.

Hilgard, E. R. (1987). *Psychology in America: A historical survey.* New York: Harcourt Brace.

Hitler, A. (1925-1927). *Mein Kampf.* Translated by R. Manheim. Boston: Houghton Mifflin, 1943.

Jaffé, A. (1968). *From the life and work of C. G. Jung.* New York: Harper & Row.

Jaffé, A. (Ed.). (1979). *C. G. Jung: Word and image.* Princeton, NJ: Princeton University Press.

James, H., Sr. (1885). *The literary remains of the late Henry James.* Edited with an Introduction by W. James. Boston: Osgood & Co.

James, H. (1874). Professor Fargo. *Galaxy, 18,* 233-253.

James, H. (1894). The death of the lion. *Yellow Book, 1,* 7-52.

James, H. (1898). The turn of the screw. *Collier's Magazine,* February and April.

James, W. (1869). Review [unsigned] of *Planchette: or the despair of science* by E. Sargent. *Boston Daily Advertiser,* March 10.

James, W. (1875). Review [unsigned] of *The Unseen Universe. The Nation, 20,* 366-367.

James, W. (1890a). A record of observations of certain phenomena of trance. In *Essays in Psychical Research,* no. 12, 79-88. Cambridge, MA: Harvard University Press, 1986.

James, W. (1890b). *Principles of psychology.* 2 vols. New York: Holt.

James, W. (1895a). Reviews of current literature in psychical research. *Psychological Review, 2,* 65-73. In *Essays in Psychical Research.* Cambridge, MA: Harvard University Press, 1986.

James, W. (1895b). Is life worth living? *International Journal of Ethics, 6,* 1-24.

James, W. (1895c). Review of *Demon possession and allied themes* by J. Nevius. *Nation, 61* (August 22), 139.

James, W. (1896a). Address of the president before the Society for Psychical Research. In *Essays in Psychical Research,* no. 19, 127-137. Cambridge, MA: Harvard University Press, 1986.

James, W. (1896b). *Exceptional mental states: The 1896 Lowell lectures.* Reconstructed by E. Taylor. New York: Scribner, 1983.

James, W. (1896c). The will to believe. *New World, 5,* 327-347.

James, W. (1897a). *The will to believe and other essays in popular philosophy.* New York: Longmans.

James, W. (1897b). Demonical possession. Report of a lecture by James to the New York Neurological Society. *Boston Medical and Surgical Journal,* March 4, 210-212.

James, W. (1898). Philosophical conceptions and practical results. *University of California Chronicle,* pp. 24f. (Reprinted in *Collected essays and reviews.* New York, 1920, pp. 406-437.)

James, W. (1899). *Talks to teachers on psychology.* Cambridge, MA: Harvard University Press, 1983.

James, W. (1901). Frederic Myers's services to psychology. *Popular Science Monthly, 59,* 380-389.

James, W. (1902). *Varieties of religious experience: A study in human nature.* New York: Longmans, Green.

James, W. (1907). *Pragmatism: A new name for some old ways of thinking.* New York: Longmans, Green.

James, W. (1909a). The confidences of a "psychical researcher." *American Magazine,* October, 580-589. Reprinted in *Essays in psychical research,* no. 38, 361-375. Cambridge, MA: Harvard University Press, 1986.

James, W. (1909b). *A pluralistic universe.* New York: Longmans, Green.

James, W. (1909c). Report on Mrs. Piper's Hodgson control. *Proceedings of the American Society for Psychical Research,* vol. 3 (June). In *Essays in psychical research,* no. 37, 253-360. Cambridge, MA: Harvard University Press, 1986.

James, W. (1910a). A pluralistic mystic. *Hibbert Journal, 8,* 739-759.

James, W. (1910b). A suggestion about mysticism. *Journal of Philosophy, Psychology and Scientific Method,* 7 (no. 4, Feb. 17), 85-92. Reprinted in *Essays in Philosophy.* Cambridge, MA: Harvard University Press, 1978.

James, W. (1920). *The letters of William James,* 2 vols. Edited by his son Henry James. Boston: Little, Brown.

James, W. (1986). *William James: Selected unpublished correspondence 1885-1910,* edited by F. J. D. Scott. Columbus, OH: Ohio State University Press.

James, W., & Flournoy, T. (1966). *The letters of William James and Théodore Flournoy,* edited by R. C. LeClair. Madison, WI: University of Wisconsion Press.

Janet, P. (1907). *The major symptoms of hysteria.* New York: Macmillan.

Jastrow, J. (1890). Psychology in American colleges and universities. *American Journal of Psychology, 3,* 275-286.

Jenks, W. A. (1960). *Vienna and the young Hitler.* New York: Columbia University Press.

Jennings, H. S. (1906). *The behavior of the lower organisms.* New York: Columbia University Press.

Jennings, H. S. (1910). Divers ideals and divergent conclusions in the study of behavior in lower organisms. *American Journal of Psychology, 21,* 349-370.

Jerome, Saint. (389 A.D.). *Commentary on Ecclesiastes.* In *Corpus Christianorum,* 1959, *62.*

Jones, E. (1910). Freud's theory of dreams. *American Journal of Psychology, 21,* 283-308.

Jones, E. (1911). The psychopathology of everyday life. *American Journal of Psychology, 22,* 477-527.

Jones, E. (1953-1957). *The life and work of Sigmund Freud.* 3 vols. New York: Basic Books.

Jones, J. S. (1983). *Hitler in Vienna 1907-1913.* New York: Stein & Day.

Jung, C. G. (1906-1909). *Studies in word-association.* London: Heinemann, 1918.

Jung, C. G. (1906). *The psychology of dementia praecox.* Translated by F. Peterson and A. A. Brill. New York: Nervous and Mental Disease Publishing Co., 1910. Also in Jung's *Collected Works, 3.*

Jung, C. G. (1907). Association d'idées familiales. *Archives de Psychologie, 7,* 160-168.

Jung, C. G. (1910a). The association method. Translated by A. A. Brill. *American Journal of Psychology, 21,* 219-269.

Jung, C. G. (1910b). Lecture III. Experiences concerning the life of the child. *American Journal of Psychology, 21,* 251-269.

Jung, C. G. (1910c). Über Konflikte des kindlichen Seele. *Jahrbuch für psychoanalytische und psychopathologische Forschungen, 2,* 34-58 (2nd ed., 1916). An English translation of the 2nd ed. under the title, "Psychic conflicts in a child," is contained in *Collected Works, 17,* 1-35.

Jung, C. G. (1911-1912). *Transformations and symbols of the libido.* Translated as *Symbols of transformation* in *Collected Works, 5.*

Jung, C. G. (1921). *Psychological types.* New York: Harcourt, Brace. English translation, 1923.

Jung, C. G. (1933). Editorial. *Collected Works,* 1967, *10,* 533-534.

Jung, C. G. (1934a). A rejoinder to Dr. Bally. *Collected Works,* 1967, *10,* 535-544.

Jung, C. G. (1934b). The state of psychotherapy today. *Collected Works,* 1967, *10,* 157-176.

Jung, C. G. (1945). After the catastrophe. *Collected Works,* 1967, *10,* 194-217.

Jung, C. G. (1962). *Memories, dreams, reflections.* New York: Pantheon, 1963.

Jung, C. G. (1967). *Collected Works.* 19 vols. Princeton, NJ: Princeton University Press. Cited as *Collected Works.*

Jung, C. G. (1973-1975). *Letters.* 2 vols. Princeton, NJ: Princeton University Press.

Jung, E. (1957). *Animus and anima.* New York: Spring Publications, 1978.

Kaplan, M. A. (1979). *The Jewish feminist movement in Germany: The campaigns of the Jüdischer Frauenbund, 1904-1938.* Westport, CN: Greenwood Press.

Kempf, E. J. (1918). *The automatic functions of the personality.* New York: Nervous and Mental Disease Publishing Co.

Kempf, E. J. (1920). *Psychopathology.* St. Louis: Mosby.

Koch, S., & Leary, D. E. (1992). *A century of psychology as science.* 2nd ed. Washington, D.C.: American Psychological Association.

Koelsch, W. A. (1987). *Clark University, 1887-1987: a narrative history.* Worcester, MA: Clark University Press.

Kubizek, A. (1955). *The young Hitler I knew.* Translated from the German by E. V. Anderson. With an Introduction by H. R. Trevor-Roper. Boston: Houghton Mifflin.

Lee, N. (1980). Putnam Camp. *Adirondack Life,* Nov.-Dec., 42-46.

Lehmann, J. (1939). *Down river: A Danubian study.* London: Cresset Press.

Leys, R., & Evans, R. B. (Eds.). (1990). *Defining American psychology: The correspondence between Adolf Meyer and Edward Bradford Titchener.* Baltimore: Johns Hopkins University Press.

Lindner, S. (1879). Das Saugen an den Fingern, Lippen etc. bei den Kindern (Ludeln). *Jahrbuch für Kinderheilkunde, 14* (N.F.), 68-91.

Livingston, D. M. (1973). *The master of light: A biography of Albert A. Michelson.* New York: Scribner.

Ludwig, E. (1926). *Napoleon.* New York: Boni & Liveright.

Mahony, P. J. (1986). *Freud and the rat man.* New Haven: Yale University Press.

McGuire, W. (1982). *Bollingen. An adventure in collecting the past.* Princeton, NJ: Princeton University Press.

Melville, H. (1949). *Pierre or, the ambiguities.* With an Introduction and editorial notes by H. A. Murray. New York: Hendricks House (Farrar, Straus).

Meumann, E. (1903). *The psychology of learning: An experimental investigation of the economy and technique of memory.* Translated by J. W. Baird from the 3rd ed. New York: Appleton, 1913.

Meyer, A. (1910). The dynamic interpretation of dementia praecox. *American Journal of Psychology, 21,* 385-403.

Murphy, G., & Ballou, R. O. (1960). *William James on psychical research.* New York: Viking.

Murray, H. A., et al. (1938). *Explorations in personality.* New York: Oxford University Press.

Murray, H. A. (1951). *In Nomine Diaboli. New England Quarterly, 24,* 435-452.

Murray, H. A. (1962). The personality and career of Satan. *Journal of Social Issues, 18,* 36-54.

Myers, F. W. H. (1903). *Human personality and the survival of bodily death.* 2 vols. London: Longmans, Green.

Nearing, S. (1972). *The making of a radical: A political autobiography.* New York: Harper & Row.

Nunberg, H., & Federn, E. (Eds.). (1974). *Minutes of the Vienna Psychoanalytic Society: vol. 3, 1910-1911.* New York: International Universities Press.

Olmsted, J. M. D. (1946). *Charles-Édouard Brown-Séquard: A nineteenth century neurologist and endocrinologist.* Baltimore: Johns Hopkins Press.

Onuf, B. (1908). Über Psychotherapie. *New Yorker Medizinische Monatschrift, 19,* 291-301.

Onuf, B. (1909-1910). Dreams and their interpretation as diagnostic and therapeutic aids in psychopathology. *Journal of Abnormal Psychology, 4,* 339-350.

Onuf, B. (1924). Biographical sketch. In *Semi-centennial anniversary volume of the American Neurological Association,* pp. 217, 575-576. Albany, NY: American Neurological Association.

Ostwald, W. (1909). *Grosse Männer.* Leipzig: Academische Verlagsgesellschaft m. b. H. Chapter 11. Klassiker und Romantiker, pp. 371-388.

Partridge, G. E. (1912). *Genetic philosophy of education: An epitome of the published educational writings of President G. Stanley Hall of Clark University.* With an Introductory Note by President Hall. New York: Sturgis & Walton Co.

Peirce, C. S. (1878). How to make our ideas clear. *Popular Science Monthly, 12,* 286-302.

Peirce, C. S. (1891). Review of *Principles of psychology* by William James. *Nation, 53* (July 2 and 9), 15, 32-33.

Perry, R. B. (1935). *The thought and character of William James.* 2 vols. Boston: Little, Brown.

Piper, A. (1929). *Life and work of Mrs. Piper.* London: Kegan Paul.

Prince, M. (1905). *The dissociation of a personality: A biographical study in abnormal psychology.* New York: Longmans, Green.

Prince, M. (1910-1911). The mechanism and interpretation of dreams. *Journal of Abnormal Psychology, 5,* 139-195.

Pruette, L. (1926). *G. Stanley Hall: A biography of a mind.* New York: Appleton.

Putnam, J. J. (1895). Remarks on the psychical treatment of neuresthenia. *Boston Medical and Surgical Journal, 132,* No. 21, 505-511.

Putnam, J. J. (1906-1907). Recent experiences in the study and treatment of hysteria at the Massachusetts General Hospital, with remarks on Freud's method of treatment by "psycho-analysis." *Journal of Abnormal Psychology, 1,* 26-41.

Putnam, J. J. (1921). *Addresses on psycho-analysis.* With a Preface by Sigmund Freud. London: International Psycho-analytical Press.

Quen, J. M., & Carlson, E. T. (Eds). (1978). *American psychoanalysis: Origins and development.* New York: Brunner/Mazel.

Rank, O. (1907). *Art and artist.* New York: Knopf, 1932.

Rank, O. (1909). *The myth of the birth of the hero: A psychological interpretation of mythology.* English translation. New York: Robert Brunner, 1952. Pages 63-68 are an interpolation of a short essay by Freud later incorporated under the title "Family romances" in the *Standard Edition, 9,* 236-241.

Robinson, F. G. (1992). *Love's story told. A life of Henry A. Murray.* Cambridge, MA: Harvard University Press.

Roe, C. G. (1911). The great war on white slavery. Privately printed.

Rosenzweig, S. (1935). A test for types of reaction to frustration. *American Journal of Orthopsychiatry, 5,* 395-403.

Rosenzweig, S. (1938). The experimental measurement of types of reaction to frustration, pp. 585-599 in H. A. Murray, et al. *Explorations in personality.* New York: Oxford University Press.

Rosenweig, S. (1943). The ghost of Henry James. *Character and Personality, 12,* 79-100.

Rosenzweig, S. (1956). Unconscious self-defense in an uxoricide. *Journal of Criminal Law, Criminology and Police Science, 46,* 791-795.

Rosenzweig, S. (1958). The James's stream of consciousness. *Contemporary Psychology, 3,* 250-257.

Rosenzweig, S. (1970a). The day of Freud's death. *Journal of Psychology, 74,* 101-103.

Rosenzweig, S. (1970b). Erik Erikson on William James's dream: A note of correction. *Journal of the History of the Behavioral Sciences, 6,* 258-260.

Rosenzweig, S. (1985). Freud and experimental psychology: The emergence of idiodynamics. In S. Koch and D. E. Leary (Eds.), *A century of psychology as science* (pp. 135-207). New York: McGraw-Hill. 2nd rev. ed. St. Louis: Rana House and New York: McGraw-Hill, 1986.

Rosenzweig, S. (1986). Idiodynamics vis-à-vis psychology. *American Psychologist, 41,* 241-245.

Rosenzweig, S. (1987). Sally Beauchamp's career: A psychoarchaeological key to Morton Prince's classic case of multiple personality. *Genetic, Social and General Psychology Monographs, 113,* 5-60.

Ross, D. (1972). *G. Stanley Hall: The psychologist as prophet.* Chicago: University of Chicago Press.

Royce, J. (1980). *The philosophy of loyalty.* New York: Macmillan.

Sadger, J. (1910). Über Urethralerotik. *Jahrbuch für psychoanalytische Forschungen, 2,* 409-450.

Saltmarsh, J. A. (1991). *Scott Nearing: An intellectual biography.* Philadelphia: Temple University Press.

Samelson, F. (1974). History, origin myth, and ideology: "Discovery" of social psychology. *Journal for the Theory of Social Behaviour, 4,* 217-231.

Sanford, E. C. (1924). Granville Stanley Hall, 1845-1924. *American Journal of Psychology, 35,* 313-321.

Scarborough, E., & Furumoto, L. (1987). *Untold lives: The first generation of American women psychologists.* New York: Columbia University Press.

Schultz, D. (1990). *Intimate friends, dangerous rivals: The turbulent relationship between Freud and Jung.* Los Angeles: Jeremy Tarcher.

Shakow, D., & Rapaport, D. (1964). *The influence of Freud on American psychology. Psychological Issues, 4,* No. 1, Monograph 13. New York: International Universities Press.

Sidis, B. (1898). *The psychology of suggestion.* With an Introduction by William James. New York: Appleton.

Sidis, B. (1910-1911). Fundamental states in psychoneurosis. *Journal of Abnormal Psychology, 5,* 320-327.

Sinclair, U. (1922). *The goose step.* New York: Albert and Charles Boni.

Skinner, B. F. (1938). *The behavior of organisms.* New York: Appleton-Century.

Sokal, M. M. (1973). APA's First Publication: Proceedings of the American Psychological Association, 1892-1893. *American Psychologist, 28,* 277-292.

Sokal, M. M. (1990). G. Stanley Hall and the institutional character of psychology at Clark in 1889-1920. *Journal of the History of the Behavioral Sciences, 26,* 114-124.

Starbuck, E. C. (1925). G. Stanley Hall as a psychologist. *Psychological Review, 32,* 103-120.

Stekel, W. (1911). *Sex and dreams: The language of dreams.* Boston: Richard G. Badger, 1922.

Stern, P. J. (1976). *C. G. Jung: The haunted prophet.* New York: Braziller.

Stern, W. (1901). Review of Freud's *Traumdeutung. Zeitschrift für Psychologie und Physiologie der Sinnesorgane, 26,* 133.

Stern, W. (1910). Abstracts of lectures on the psychology of testimony and on the study of individuality. *American Journal of Psychology, 21,* 270-282.

Stern, W. (1913). Die Anwendung der Psychoanalyse auf Kindheit und Jugend. *Zeitschrift für angewandte Psychologie, 81,* 71-91.

Stoerring, G. (1923). Ernst Meumann 1862-1915. *American Journal of Psychology, 34,* 271-274.

Strouse, J. (1980). *Alice James: A biography.* Boston: Houghton, Mifflin.

Swift, F. H. (1946). Sleuthing for the birth date of G. Stanley Hall. *School and Society, 63,* 249-252.

Tanner, A. E. (1908). *History of Clark University through the interpretation of the will of the founder.* Worcester, MA: Clark University Archives. Unpublished manuscript.

Tanner, A. E. (1909). The Clark University Conference. *Psychological Bulletin, 6,* 326 (abstract).

Tanner, A. E. (1910). *Studies in spiritism.* With an Introduction by G. S. Hall. New York: Appleton.

Terman, L. M. (1932). Trails to psychology. In *A history of psychology in autobiography,* C. Murchison (Ed.), *2,* 297-331.

Thorndike, E. L. (1904). Review of *Adolescence* by G. S. Hall. *Science,* n.s. *20* (July), 143.

Thorndike, E. L. (1929). Biographical memoir of Granville Stanley Hall, 1846-1924. *National Academy of Sciences, 12,* 135-180.

Titchener, E. B. (1910). The past decade in experimental psychology. *American Journal of Psychology, 21,* 404-421.

Titchener, E. B. (1925). Edmund Clark Sanford 1859-1924. *American Journal of Psychology, 36,* 157-170.

Trautscholdt, M. (1883). Experimentelle Untersuchungen über die Association der Vorstellungen. *Philosophische Studien, 1,* 213-250.

Vande Kemp, H. (1992). G. Stanley Hall and the Clark school of religious psychology. *American Psychologist, 47,* 290-298.

van der Post, L. (1975). *Jung and the story of our time.* New York: Pantheon Books.

Veith, I. (1965). *Hysteria: The history of a disease.* Chicago: University of Chicago Press.

Waite, R. G. (1977). *The psychopathic god: Adolf Hitler.* New York: Basic Books.

Weaver, E. E. (1913). *Mind and health: with an examination of some systems of divine healing.* New York: Macmillan.

Wertheimer, M., & Klein, J. (1904). Psychologische Tatbestandsdiagnostik. *Archiv für Kriminal-Anthropologie und Kriminalistik, 15,* 72-113.

Westropp, H. M., & Walke, C. S. (1875). *Ancient symbol worship. Influence of the phallic idea in the religions of antiquity.* 2nd ed. New York: J. W. Bouton.

White, S. H. (1990). Child study at Clark University: 1894-1904. *Journal of the History of the Behavioral Sciences, 26,* 131-150.

Whiteside, A. (1975). *The socialism of fools.* Berkeley, CA: University of California Press.

Wickes, F. G. (1927). *The inner world of childhood.* New York: Appleton.

Wilson, L. N. (1914). *G. Stanley Hall: A sketch.* New York: G. E. Stechert.

Wilson, L. N. (1925a). *Granville Stanley Hall, Feb. 1, 1844-April 24, 1924. In memoriam. Publications of the Clark University Library,* vol. 7, no. 6. Worcester, MA: Clark University Library.

Wilson, L. N. (Ed.). (1925b). *Edmund Clark Sanford: In memoriam.* Worcester, MA: Clark University Press.

Wilson, L. R. (1960). *Harry Woodburn Chase.* Chapel Hill, NC: University of North Carolina Press.

Witmer, L. (1909). Mental healing and the Emmanuel movement. *Psychological Clinic, 2,* 212-223, 239-250, 282-300.

Wittels, F. (1924). *Sigmund Freud: His personality, his teaching, and his school.* London: Allen & Unwin.

Wolpe, J. (1958). *Psychotherapy by reciprocal inhibition.* Stanford, CA: Stanford University Press.

Wolpe, J., & Rachman, S. (1960). Psychoanalytic "evidence": A critique based on Freud's case of Little Hans. *Journal of Nervous and Mental Disease, 130,* 135-148.

Wright, T. (1970). *The big nail: The story of the Cook-Peary feud.* New York: John Day.

Wundt, W. (1874). *Grundzüge der physiologischen Psychologie.* Leipzig: Engelmann.

Wundt, W. (1879). Spiritualism as a scientific question. *Popular Science Monthly, 15* (September), 577-593.

Wundt, W. (1906). *Elements of folk psychology.* English translation, 1916. New York: Macmillan.

Wundt, W. (1909). Das Institut für Experimentelle Psychologie. In vol. 4, *Festschrift zur Feier des 500jährigen Bestehens der Universität Leipzig,* hrsg. von Rektor und Senat. Leipzig: S. Hirzel.

Wundt, W. (1910). Über reine und angewandte Psychologie. *Psychologische Studien, 5,* 1-47.

Wundt, W. (1915). Eine Berichtigung. *Literarisches Zentralblatt für Deutschland, 66,* 1079.

Wundt, W. (1916). Zur Erinnerung an Ernst Meumann. *Zeitschrift für pädagogische Psychologie, 16,* 211-214.

Wundt, W. (1920). Erlebtes und Erkanntes. Stuttgart: Alfred Kröner.

Frequently Cited Manuscript Sources

Abraham (Karl) Papers. Available from Abraham's son, Grant Allan.

Calkins (Mary W.) Papers. Wellesley College Archives, Wellesley, MA.

Freud's Travel Diary (1909). Library of Congress, Manuscript Division.

Freud/Hall Letters. Published here (for the first time) as Part Two.

Goldmark (Pauline) Papers. Bryn Mawr Archives, Bryn Mawr, PA.

Hall (G. S.) Papers. Clark University Archives, Worcester, MA.

James (William) Papers. Houghton Library, Harvard University, Cambridge, MA.

Jung (C. G.) Papers. Jung Institute Archives, Küsnacht, Switzerland.

Michelson (Albert A.) Papers. Nimitz Library, U.S. Naval Academy, Annapolis, MD.

Publisher Acknowledgements

For permission to quote from the following books thanks are extended to their publishers as follows:

Basic Books, New York, N.Y.
> Freud, S., & Abraham, K. *A psycho-analytic dialogue: The letters of Sigmund Freud and Karl Abraham, 1907-1926,* H. C. Abraham and E. L. Freud (Eds.), 1965.
> Jones, E. *The life and work of Sigmund Freud,* Volume I, 1953.

Harvard University Press, Cambridge, Mass.
> James, W. *Essays in psychical research,* 1986.
> James, W. *Essays in philosophy,* 1978.

Hogarth Press, London, England.
> Freud, S. *Standard edition of the complete psychological works of Sigmund Freud,* 1953-1974.

Houghton Mifflin, Boston, Mass.
> Strouse, J. *Alice James: A biography,* 1980.

Pantheon Books, A Division of Random House, New York, N.Y.
> Carotenuto, A. *A secret symmetry: Sabina Spielrein between Jung and Freud.* Translated by K. Winston, A. Pomerans, and J. Shepley, 1982.
> Jung, C. G. *Memories, dreams, reflections,* 1963.

Princeton University Press, Princeton, N.J.
> Freud, S., & Jung, C. G. *The Freud/Jung letters,* W. McGuire (Ed.), 1974.
> Jung, C. G. *Collected Works,* 1967.
> *C. G. Jung: Word and image,* A. Jaffé (Ed.), 1979.

Simon & Schuster, New York, N.Y.
> Bernays, E. L. *Biography of an idea: Memoirs of public relations counselor Edward L. Bernays,* 1965.

University of Wisconsin Press, Madison, WI.
  James, W., & Flournoy, T. *The letters of William James and Théodore Flournoy,* R. C. LeClair (Ed.), 1966.

*   *   *   *

Permission to reproduce the portrait of William James painted by Rand in 1910 was granted by Fogg Museum, Harvard University.

The illustration of the eight lecturers in the behavioral sciences (facing Chapter VI) is a reconstructed composite from existing photographs.

*   *   *   *

Other permissions are acknowledged in the introduction, "In the Beginning . . . ."

Index

Freud, Hall, James and Jung are indexed not by mention but by the specific topics connected with their names. Items in the Commentary, Part One, are indexed by page, not by note number.

About the Author

Saul Rosenzweig, born in Boston in 1907, received from Harvard University in 1929 the B.A. degree, *summa cum laude,* in philosophy and psychology; in 1930, the M.A., and in 1932, the Ph.D. in clinical psychology. At the newly established Harvard Psychological Clinic he worked as Research Associate from 1929-1934. There, using laboratory methods, he investigated the clinically derived concepts of psychoanalysis, e.g., repression. His first publication appeared in 1933 under the title "The experimental situation as a psychological problem." It anticipated the flurry of research in the 1950s on "experimenter bias" and related problems in experimental-social psychology.

In 1934 Rosenzweig joined the staff of the Research Service of the Worcester State Hospital, Worcester, Massachusetts, where, until 1943, he participated in a multidisciplinary investigation of schizophrenia, sponsored by the Rockefeller Foundation. He conducted psychotherapy with accessible schizophrenics and, in that context, developed concepts geared to the diverse problems and levels of behavior. The role of sex hormones in schizophrenia and other sexual phenomena were also examined.

From 1938-1943 Rosenzweig was Affiliate Professor of Psychology at Clark University in Worcester. During this period he developed the Rosenzweig Picture-Frustration (P-F) Study, based on a theory of aggression in relation to frustration. This psychological instrument is now used worldwide. The book *Aggressive Behavior and the Rosenzweig Picture-Frustration Study* appeared in 1978.

From 1943-1949 Rosenzweig was Chief Psychologist at the Western State Psychiatric Institute, Pittsburgh, and Lecturer at the University of Pittsburgh. *Psychodiagnosis: An Introduction to Tests in the Clinical Practice of Psychodynamics* was published in 1949.

Since 1949 Rosenzweig has been professor in the Departments of Psychology and Psychiatry at Washington University, St. Louis. In 1975 he was appointed Professor Emeritus. Significant events of this period are: appointment to the Study Panel of the History of the Life Sciences, National Institutes of Health; establishment of the International Society for Research on Aggression, of which Rosenzweig was the founder and first president; establishment of the Foundation for Idiodynamics and the Creative Process in 1972, of which he is the Managing Director.

In 1950 Rosenzweig introduced the approach of Idiodynamics which focuses on the dynamics of the life history by studying the blending of the biogenetic and cultural milieus in the matrix of the idioverse (the individual world of events), with stress on the creative process. From this orientation he has investigated the history of medical psychology.

In 1986 Rosenzweig published *Freud and Experimental Psychology: The Emergence of Idiodynamics,* and, in 1987, "Sally Beauchamp's Career: A Psychoarchaeological Key to Morton Prince's Classic Case of Multiple Personality." By idiodynamic methods the real-life identity of this patient was discovered, and the etiology and development of her mental disorder demonstrated. Rosenzweig is the author of 200 other scientific, historical and biographical articles.

The present volume applies the methods of idiodynamics to investigate the interactions of Freud, Jung, Hall and James in connection with the psychoanalytic expedition to America in 1909.